UNDERSTANDING

Islam

A GUIDE FOR THE JUDAEO-CHRISTIAN READER

First Edition
(1424AH/2003AC)

© Copyright 1424AH/2003AC
amana publications
10710 Tucker Street
Beltsville, Maryland 20705-2223 USA
Tel: (301) 595-5777 / Fax: (301) 595-5888
E-mail: amana@igprinting.com
Website: www.amana-publications.com

Library of Congress Cataloging-in-Publications Data

Dirks, Jerald.
  Understanding Islam : a guide for the Judaeo-Christian reader / Jerald
F. Dirks.
       p. cm.
Includes bibliographical references.
  ISBN 1-59008-021-1
  1. Islam. 2. Islam--Essence, genius, nature. I. Title.

  BP161.3.D57 2003
  297'.02'427--dc22

                                                    2003025598

2nd Printing 2007

Printed in the United States of America by
International Graphics
10710 Tucker Street
Beltsville, Maryland 20705-2223 USA
Tel: (301) 595-5999 Fax: (301) 595-5888
Website: igprinting.com
E-mail: ig@igprinting.com

UNDERSTANDING

Islam

A GUIDE FOR THE JUDAEO-CHRISTIAN READER

Jerald Dirks

amana publications

TABLE OF CONTENTS

Chapter 1

Introduction

A. PURPOSE

Over the last decade, Islam has been the fastest growing religion both in America and in Europe, despite the fact that Islam sponsors no official, systematic, and organized missionary effort to non-Muslims. At the present time, there are approximately seven million Muslims in the United States alone and over 1.2 billion Muslims worldwide. Mosques and Islamic schools dot the maps of most American and European cities. Needless to say, the size and growth of Islam have begun to foster a new interest in Islam within the ranks of non-Muslim Occidentals, many of whom have begun to look for reliable information about this religion in order to understand its mass appeal. Unfortunately, it is not always an easy task for the non-Muslim Occidental to find reliable and authentic information about Islam.

Moreoever, in the aftermath of September 11, 2001, any superficial perusal of the media, whether print or television, subjects the non-Muslim to an abundance of "insight" and "education" about Islam. The "talking heads" of television pontificate about a religion to which they do not belong and which they little understand. Ratings drive television coverage, and whatever increases ratings finds it way onto the silver screen, even if that necessitates hyperbole, quoting Islamic scriptures totally out of context, and frank distortion from an obvious (at least to a Muslim) anti-Islamic bias.

The authors of "instant books" on Islam appear to be no more objective than their television counterparts. Their primary concern is a quick publication date in order to harness a buying public's momentary arousal, and in order to avoid the anticipated decline in sales that would accompany a public loss of interest in the book's topic. As such, even the slightest delay on the way to public merchandising is anathema, even if such a delay were to result from serious research and thoughtful reflection. Given such a guiding philosophy, it is no wonder that such books often fall victim to reliance on erroneous stereotypes and caricatures, to misleading and fallacious sensationalism, and to what was termed "yellow journalism" in a by-gone era.

The present book is an attempt to offer a viable and factually correct alternative to understanding Islam. It is an introduction to Islam for the Western, and primarily Christian, reader, and its primary focus is on what is termed Sunni Islam, i.e., the Islam practiced by approximately 85-90% of the self-professed Muslims in the world. (The primary alternative to Sunni Islam is Shi'a Islam, which is practiced primarily in Iran and Iraq, but which has pockets of adherents throughout the world.)

In presenting Sunni Islam to the non-Muslim and Christian Occidental, the present book's uniqueness hinges on a combination of five factors. Firstly, it is written from inside Islam, as the author is a practicing Muslim. It is not written from the perspective of the non-Muslim who is attempting to look at the inside of a religion while standing outside that religion. Secondly, it is written by a natural-born American for other citizens of the Western world, and thus may avoid some of the cultural overlay that accompanies some books on Islam by other Muslim authors. Thirdly, it is written by an American who has practiced Islam both while living in America and while living in the Middle East, thus offering a somewhat broader perspective than would have otherwise been possible. Fourthly, as a convert from Christianity to Islam and as a former ordained minister within Christianity, the author has attempted to link and contrast Islam with Judaeo-Christian belief where possible, while still avoiding the temptation to distort Islam by interpreting Islam from within a Judaeo-Christian perspective. Fifthly, in introducing Islam to the reader, the author has relied almost exclusively on primary source material and has typically presented that primary source material in direct quotations to the reader. As such, the reader does not meet Islam through a barrage of "he-said", "she-said", "they- said" statements that were made after the fact of Islam by secondary sources. Nor is the reader primarily directed to subsequent scholars and theologians of a later date, regardless of their qualifications and expertise. Rather, the reader is introduced to Islam through the two primary sources of Islam, i.e., the *Qur'an* and the *Sunnah*, which are the only completely authoritative sources on Islam.

B. THE *QUR'AN* AND *SUNNAH*

As most non-Muslim readers probably already know, the *Qur'an* is the book of sacred scripture for Islam. Muslims believe that the *Qur'an* consists of the literal words of Allah (God) as given to Prophet Muhammad in the seventh century CE. As such, there can be no higher authority in Islam than the *Qur'an*.

In contrast to the *Qur'an*, the *Sunnah* may well be a new concept for most non-Muslims. Simply stated, the *Sunnah* is the religious teaching, practice, and behavioral example of Prophet Muhammad. It consists of his statements, his behavior, and his reactions to external events. For Sunni Muslims, the *Sunnah* of Prophet Muhammad is also religiously authoritative.

The non-Muslim reader may initially question how anyone can know exactly what Prophet Muhammad said and did. The answer is found in the *Ahadith*. *Ahadith* (singular=*Hadith*) are the narratives about and the sayings attributed to Prophet Muhammad. These *Ahadith* were collected, analyzed, and recorded in written form over the first few centuries after Prophet Muhammad and serve as a window through which to view the *Sunnah* of Prophet Muhammad. However, a distinction needs to be kept between *Sunnah* and *Ahadith*. The former is what Prophet Muhammad actually said and did, while the latter consists of attributions regarding what he said and did. Some of those attributions may be accurate, and some may not. Within Islamic studies as taught in an Islamic setting, an entire academic discipline exists that is devoted to sorting through the various *Ahadith* and to determining which ones are authentic and which ones are not.

3

The above discussion of the *Qur'an* and *Sunnah* is adequate for understanding the first three chapters of this book. Chapter IV presents a more in-depth discussion of the *Qur'an* and *Sunnah*, and serves as a preface to the remainder of the book, in which the Islamic articles of faith, the Islamic pillars of religious practice, and the concept of *Jihad* in Islam are presented.

C. VOCABULARY AND TERMS

C1. GENERAL CONSIDERATIONS

Many Occidentals and non-Muslims find their initial attempt to understand Islam hindered by the many Arabic words that are often part and parcel of any discussion of Islam. The Western media frequently mistranslates or obscures the actual meaning of many of these words, thus conveying an erroneous message, not only about the word in question, but also about Islam in general. The charitable explanation is that such errors are unintentional, and are secondary to the Western media's unfamiliarity with Islam and the Arabic language. However, the frequency with which such errors occur, the systematic nature of certain of those errors, and the negative image of Islam that is typically conveyed by such errors are more than enough to lead the cynically minded to the conclusion that such errors are intentional.

The most obvious example of mistranslation by the Western media is in terms of the word *Jihad*. Almost without exception, newspaper and magazine articles, television news and talk shows, and radio call-in shows systematically mistranslate *Jihad* as Holy War. Such a systematic mistranslation paints Islam as a warrior religion, a concept that is antithetical to Islam's true nature, which is one of peace and of submission to Allah (God). Unfortunately, the reprehensible behavior of certain, so-called "Muslim extremists" serves to reinforce the erroneous concept conveyed by this mistranslation. A discussion of the word *Jihad*, as well as its proper meaning and place in Islam, will be found in chapters VII- IX.

Other Arabic words frequently encountered in this introduction to Islam are defined as they occur in the text. In addition, a concise glossary of Arabic terms relevant to the current discussion can be found at the back of this book. However, before beginning a discussion of the religion of Islam, it is helpful to discuss two specific words of primary importance. These words are Allah and Islam.

C2. ALLAH

The use of the word Allah to refer to God frequently sounds rather strange, esoteric, and foreign to Western and Christian ears. After all, no English translation of the *Bible* includes the word Allah. However, a little instruction in linguistics may reduce that seeming strangeness and demonstrate that the word Allah fits quite comfortably into *Old Testament* tradition.

Allah is an Arabic word derived from the contraction of *Al* and *Ilahi*, meaning "the God", or by implication "the One God". Linguistically, Hebrew and Arabic are related Semitic languages, and the Arabic Allah or *Al-Ilahi* is related to the Hebrew words *El*, meaning God, and *El-Elohim*, meaning God of Gods or the God. When one reads the word God in an English translation of the *Old Testament*, the Hebrew words being translated as God are typically *El, Elohim*, and *El-Elohim*. Thus, one can see that the use of the word Allah is consistent not only with the *Qur'an* and with Islamic tradition, but with the oldest Biblical traditions as well.

This may be even more dramatically illustrated by contrasting the Arabic spelling of *Al-Ilahi* (Allah) with the Hebrew spelling of *El-Elohim*. As Arabic and Hebrew are related Semitic languages, it is not surprising that they share certain alphabetical features, including names of letters and an absence of vowels. Given the latter consideration, if one were to delete the vowel sounds introduced in the English transliteration of *Al-Ilahi* (Allah) and *El-Elohim*, one would be left with *Al-Ilh* and *El-Elhm*. Transforming these English transliterations into the names associated with each letter in the Arabic and Hebrew alphabets, *Al-Ilh* becomes *Alif-Lam-Alif-Lam-Ha* in Arabic letters, and *El-Elhm* becomes

5

Alif-Lam-Alif-Lam-Ha-Mim in Hebrew letters. In short, the only difference in spelling between the two words is the inclusion of the Hebrew letter *Mim* at the end of *El-Elhm*. The use of the Hebrew *Mim* merely introduces the plural of respect, which is a concept similar to the "royal we" as used by European monarchies. Given this understanding of the *Mim* of plural respect, it can be seen that the two terms are linguistically identical and that the word Allah is merely the Arabic version of the Hebrew words that are being typically translated as God in the *Old Testament*. The only alternative to accepting this linguistic identification is to reject the use of *Mim* as signifying the plural of respect, thus necessitating that *Elohim* be translated as gods, and thus introducing a virulent polytheism into the *Old Testament* teachings of the ancient Israelites. As it is quite doubtful that most Christians and Jews would want to accept a polytheistic strain running rampant throughout much of the *Old Testament*, intellectual consistency and fairness of thought demand that Allah and *Elohim* be treated as synonymous terms from two related Semitic languages, thus equating Allah with the God of the *Old Testament* canon. As such, throughout the remainder of this book, the term Allah will be utilized in place of the English word God.

C3. ISLAM

Islam is an Arabic word, which literally means submission, i.e., submission to the will and pleasure of Allah. However, this is not a mere lip service type of submission. Islam implies a total submission of the heart, mind, and body. This type of total submission still finds expression in the Jewish scriptures of the "received *Torah*".[1]

> You shall love the Lord your God with all your heart, and with all your soul, and with all your might. (*Deuteronomy* 6: 5)

The Christian scriptures (*Matthew* 22:37, *Mark* 12:30, and *Luke* 10:27) maintain that Jesus echoed the above verse, and thus also mandated a total submission to Allah. In addition, further expression of the need to submit to Allah can be found in the *New Testament*.

> Submit yourselves therefore to God...Draw near to God, and
> he will draw near to you." (*James* 4: 7-8)

However, the need to submit totally to Allah finds its clearest expression in the *Qur'an*. The English translation of a typical Qur'anic verse extolling the need to submit totally and wholly to Allah is quoted immediately below.

> So if they dispute with thee, say: "I have submitted my whole
> self to Allah, and so have those who follow me." (*Qur'an* 3: 20)

From the Islamic perspective, the majority of the children of Israel did not submit to Allah, initially resulting in the formation of Judaism and subsequently resulting in the formation of Christianity. With regard to the failure to submit that resulted in the development of Judaism, the *Bible* records that David spoke the following words of revelation from Allah.

> I am the Lord your God, who brought you up out of the
> land of Egypt. Open your mouth wide and I will fill it. But
> my people did not listen to my voice; Israel would not submit
> to me. (*Psalms* 81: 10-11)

With regard to the failure to submit to Allah that resulted in the sequential formation of both Judaism and Christianity, the *Qur'an* records the following words of Allah. (The phrase "people of the book", i.e., *Ahl Al-Kitab*, encountered in this and subsequently quoted verses of the *Qur'an* denotes Jews and Christians, i.e., those who had received earlier books of revelation, but who had not kept those books of revelation in their original and pristine state.)

> The religion before Allah is Islam (submission to His will):
> nor did the people of the book dissent therefrom except
> through envy of each other, after knowledge had come to
> them. But if any deny the signs of Allah, Allah is swift in
> calling to account. (*Qur'an* 3: 19)

The believer in and practitioner of Islam is known as a Muslim. The word Muslim derives from the same Arabic root word as does Islam, and Muslim literally means one who submits, i.e., one who wholly submits to Allah. While submission is the primary definition to be associated with the etymology of the word Islam, there is also a secondary definition, which is peace. The three-letter root word from which the word Islam is derived is *Seen-Lam-Mim*. This same three-letter root word is the foundation for the Arabic word *Salam*, which means peace and which is synonymous with the Hebrew word *Shalom*. Thus, the word Islam has the primary meaning of complete surrender to Allah, coupled with the secondary meaning of peace. It is only with full and complete submission to Allah that one begins to experience true, spiritual peace.

While most non-Muslims typically believe that Islam began in the seventh century CE with the advent of the preaching of Prophet Muhammad, Muslims adamantly reject that supposition. As documented in some detail in chapter II, Muslims believe that Islam began at the dawn of mankind, that Prophet Adam was the first person to practice Islam, and that Islam was the religion of Prophets Noah, Abraham, Moses, and Jesus.

We had already, beforehand, taken the covenant of Adam, but he forgot: and We found on his part no firm resolve. (*Qur'an* 20: 115)

The same religion has He established for you as that which He enjoined on Noah — that which We have sent by inspiration to thee — and that which We enjoined on Abraham, Moses, and Jesus... (*Qur'an* 42: 13a)

However, Muslims also believe that Islam has been given to mankind as a progressive revelation. While the core of that revelation, i.e., that there is no god but Allah, has never changed throughout the course of that progressive revelation, the revelation was only completed and finalized with the last revelation given to Prophet Muhammad, an important verse of which is quoted immediately below.

This day have I perfected your religion for you, completed my favor upon you, and have chosen for you Islam as your religion. (*Qur'an* 5: 3)

C4. *AHL AL-KITAB*

As noted previously, *Ahl Al-Kitab* (people of the book) is a term encountered in some of the passages of the *Qur'an* that are quoted in subsequent pages. The term refers to those people who have received books of divine revelation prior to the revelation of the *Qur'an*. Typically, the term is a synonym for Jews and Christians.

C5. THE USE OF CERTAIN PHRASES

It is customary in Islam to use the phrase "peace be upon him" after mentioning the name of one of the prophets recognized by Islam. Likewise, Muslims typically use the phrase "glorified and exalted is He" after referring to Allah. However, the repetitious use of these phrases is often a distraction to the reading ease of Occidentals and non-Muslims. As this book is written precisely for those two groups, and more specifically for Judaeo-Christian Occidentals, neither phrase has been utilized in the text of this book, although each phrase may at times be found within passages quoted from other sources.

C6. DATING

Muslims typically have objections to the Western practice of dating events as occurring either BC (before Christ) or AD (*anno domini*, i.e., in the year of our lord), as it is felt that such a practice implies the divinity of Jesus Christ, a concept rejected by Islam, which views Jesus as a steadfast prophet of Allah instead of as being divine. As such, in what follows, BCE (before the common era) is used in place of BC, and CE (the common era) is used in place of AD.

A further issue regarding dating has to do with the Islamic or *Hijri* calendar, the first year of which is marked by Prophet Muhammad's *Hijrah* (migration) from Makkah to Madinah in 622 CE. Reliable Islamic and Arab dating from before 622 CE is often problematic, as the *Hijri* calendar has no equivalent to the Western calendar's concept of before the common era (BCE). Two further complications also exist with regard to Islamic and Arab dating.

Firstly, the Islamic calendar, as well as the Arabic calendar that preceded it, was a lunar calendar consisting of 12 months that were defined by the sighting of the first crescent of the new moon. Since the beginning of any month was locally determined by the ability to sight the first crescent of the new moon, such issues as cloud cover etc. could often result in it being considered the 10th of the month in one locale, while it was considered to be the 11th of the month in another locale. Fortunately, it was seldom that any two locations differed by more than two days in tracking the day of the month.

Secondly, because it is a lunar calendar of 12 months, the Islamic calendar typically consists of only 354 days. As such, 34 years on the Islamic calendar equals 33 years on the Western or Gregorian calendar. Further, because each Islamic year is approximately 11 days shorter than each Gregorian year, the Islamic months rotate around the Gregorian calendar, with each Islamic month coming about 11 days sooner on the Gregorian calendar every subsequent Gregorian year. The 12 lunar months of the Islamic or *Hijri* calendar are presented below in Table 1.

Table 1

The 12 Lunar Months of the *Hijri* Calendar

1.	*Muharram*	7.	*Rajab*
2.	*Safar*	8.	*Sha'ban*
3.	*Rabi' Al-Awwal*	9.	*Ramadan*
4.	*Rabi' Al-Thani*	10.	*Shawwal*
5.	*Jumada Al-Awwal*	11.	*Dhu'l-Qa'da*
6.	*Jumada Al-Thani*	12.	*Dhu'l-Hijja*

As a further complication in transcribing from Arabic to Western dates, the pre-Islamic Arab calendar, while consisting of the same 12 lunar months as found in the Islamic or *Hijri* calendar, was highly inconsistent. At various times, certain Arab tribes would intercalate an additional 13th lunar month to bring the lunar calendar back into symmetry with the solar calendar. In doing so, these Arab tribes were following a procedure that had been long in use in the Jewish calendar. However, there was no universal agreement among the different Arab tribes as to when, or even if, an additional 13th month was to be intercalated into the calendar. Adding insult to injury, there was no agreed upon numbering system among the various Arab tribes for the pre-*Hijri* calendar years. Years were usually demarcated merely by reference to some special event that had occurred during that year. Both of these considerations raise special difficulties in understanding pre-*Hijri* dating from the Arab calendar.

For example, it is generally agreed that Prophet Muhammad received his prophetic call in 610 CE during the 40th year of his life and that he was born during the Year of the Elephant. However, without knowing when or if additional lunar months were intercalated, it is possible that he was born in either 570 or 571 CE. In dealing with pre-*Hijri* Arab dates, the author has generally proceeded cautiously and has often given an option of two different Gregorian years.

D. A PREVIEW OF THE FOLLOWING CHAPTERS

As noted above, while most Occidental and Christian readers assume that Islam began with the seventh-century preaching of Prophet Muhammad, this is an idea that is foreign to Islam. Muslims chart the beginning of Islam with Prophet Adam, the first of mankind, and see Prophet Muhammad as delivering the final revelations of Islam. Thus, it is with Prophet Muhammad that Islam was completed, not begun. This perspective is further advanced in chapter II, which offers a brief history of Islam prior to Prophet Muhammad.

However, it is with Prophet Muhammad that Islam reaches its full flowering, and it is with the final revelations given to Prophet Muhammad that Islam was completed and perfected. As such, no discussion of Islam can possibly be complete without examining the life and ministry of this last prophet and messenger of Allah. Drawing heavily upon the *Qur'an* and *Ahadith* literature, chapter III presents an introduction to the life of Prophet Muhammad. This introduction is necessarily brief and is not intended to serve as a substitute for a comprehensive biography.

As noted earlier, chapter IV provides a brief tour of the *Qur'an* and *Sunnah*. Included within this chapter is a discussion of the historical provenance of these two primary sources for Islam, as well as a discussion of their religious authority within Sunni Islam. Other issues covered are the distinction and overlap between the *Sunnah* and *Ahadith* and a brief presentation of some of the primary collections of *Ahadith*.

As a divinely completed and perfected religion, the skeletal structure of Islam can be summarized into six articles of faith and five pillars of practice. The six articles of faith are presented in chapter V, and the five pillars of practice are discussed in chapter VI.

As a result of the trajedy of September 11, 2001, considerable media coverage has focused the attention of non-Muslims on the concept and practice of *Jihad* within Islam. Unfortunately, the vast majority of this coverage has been markedly fallacious and highly distorted, resulting in a pop-cultural stereotype of Islam that does not even serve as a recognizable caricature of Islam. In an attempt to correct this wealth of misinformation about *Jihad* in Islam, chapter VII introduces the concept of *Jihad* in Islam, while chapters VIII and IX focus in on the one subtype of *Jihad* that the Western media attempts to make the whole of *Jihad*, i.e., *Jihad*- as-war.

Chapter X offers a brief closing statement and directs the reader to other resources on Islam. This closing chapter is followed by a small glossary of Arabic terms that one frequently encounters within Islam. Following this glossary, the reader will find a list of prominent Muslims named in the text of this book or in some of the quotations to be found within this book. A very brief biographical sketch informs the reader about the person in question and allows the reader to have at least some minimal understanding about many of the various narrators and recorders of the *Ahadith* quoted within the text. The book then closes with a list of reference notes and a bibliography.

Note

1. Islam acknowledges that a book of revelations, known as the *Torah*, was given by Allah to Moses. However, Islam maintains that the original *Torah* of Moses was adulterated by subsequent generations, and that the five books (*Genesis, Exodus, Leviticus, Numbers,* and *Deuteronomy*) presently known as the *Torah* are only a weak and frequently misleading echo of that original revelation. In contrast to the original *Torah*, what one currently has is merely the "received *Torah*". See "The books of revelation and scripture: A comparison of Judaism, Christianity, and Islam" in Dirks JF (2001).

Chapter 2
Islam Pre-Muhammad

A. INTRODUCTION

There are several different systems by which the different religions of the world may be classified. For example, the major, living religions of the world can be sorted according to such criteria as monotheistic vs. polytheistic godheads, prophetic vs. wisdom traditions, and Middle Eastern vs. Eastern origin. With regard to the first dichotomy, the so-called monotheistic religions are Judaism, Christianity, and Islam. Further, the prophetic religions are Judaism, Christianity, and Islam. Likewise, the religions of Middle Eastern origin are Judaism, Christianity, and Islam. Consistently, and without exception, these same three religions are repeatedly classified together.

The above classification systems, which are routinely utilized in the study of comparative religion, highlight the fact that Judaism, Christianity, and Islam share a common religious history and heritage. Beginning with the miraculous creation of the cosmos and continuing on through the life of the first man (Adam), through the pre-Israelite prophets (Enoch, Noah, Abraham, and Isaac), and to the Israelite prophets (Jacob, Joseph, Moses, Samuel, David, Solomon, Elijah, Elisha, and Jonah), the three religions of Judaism, Christianity, and Islam claim a common ground. However, the three religions, while sharing a common prophetic tradition, occasionally differ in their interpretation of specific historical and prophetic events. For example, Prophet Abraham's oldest son, Prophet Ismael, is recognized as a devout and obedient prophet in the *Qur'an*, but is presented in the *Bible* in a remarkably negative light, as seen in *Genesis* 16: 12 – "He shall be a wild ass of a man, with his hand against everyone, and everyone's hand against him; and he shall live at odds with all his kin." Additionally, each religion has some history and heritage that is not recognized by the other two.

Both Christianity and Islam recognize the unique roles of John the Baptist and Jesus Christ within their religious heritage, while disagreeing in their interpretation of the actual role of Jesus. For traditional Christians, Jesus is the son of God (simultaneously divine and human), is one of three persons of the same substance who comprise the trinity, and was crucified and resurrected. Muslims believe that Jesus was a prophet and messenger, was given a divine book of revelation, and was saved from crucifixion by Allah. Both the *Qur'an* and the *Bible* state that Jesus was miraculously born of a virgin and that he performed many miracles. In contrast, traditional Judaism claims that Jesus was crucified, but not resurrected, and it does not recognize Jesus as being divinely directed. In fact, scattered references to Prophet Jesus in the *Baraitha* and *Tosefta* (both of which are supplements to the *Mishnah*, which is part of the *Talmud*) state that he "practiced sorcery and enticed and led Israel astray" and was "Yeshu (Jesus) bin Pantera", the bastard son of an illicit union between Mary and a Roman soldier named Pantera[2]. Clearly, regarding the portrayal of Jesus, there is far more in common between Christianity and Islam, than there is between Judaism and Christianity.

However, Islam also claims some religious heritage that is acknowledged by neither Christianity nor Judaism. For example, the *Qur'an* repeatedly refers to several, specific prophets who were not Israelites and who are not directly named or acknowledged as prophets in the *Bible*. Among these non-Israelite prophets were Shu'ayb, Hud, Salih, and Muhammad.

How does one understand and value the commonalities of heritage that link Judaism, Christianity, and Islam without over-looking the differences among them in how they interpret that common heritage and without ignoring the occasional differences in what heritage is mutually acknowledged and what heritage is not? The answer may be found by using the simple analogy of a tree. Each of the three religions claims to be the one, true, vertical extension of a trunk of primary, prophetic revelation, with the other two religions being seen as lateral branches that deviate from the true verticality of the original trunk.

In what follows, the Islamic perspective of that trunk of primary, prophetic revelation is presented. Necessarily, this presentation is highly abridged, although references are frequently made to Biblical parallels to the Islamic perspective. Not every vertical inch of the trunk can be examined, and space does not permit the trunk to be cross-sectioned, with every ring of growth specifically documented. Nonetheless, the following does present an overview of Islam pre-Muhammad.

B. THE CREATION

The creation of the cosmos is mentioned in numerous passages of the *Qur'an*. Taken as a whole, these passages have excellent symmetry with the Biblical cosmogony. The following passages from the *Qur'an* were selected to highlight these similarities and to demonstrate some subtle differences from the Biblical account.

> Your Guardian-Lord is Allah, Who created the heavens and the earth in six days, then He established Himself on the throne (of authority): He draweth the night as a veil o'er the day, each seeking the other in rapid succession: He created the sun, the moon, and the stars, (all) governed by laws under His command. Is it not His to create and to govern? Blessed be Allah, the cherisher and sustainer of the worlds. (*Qur'an* 7: 54)

> It is He Who created the heavens and the earth in true (proportions): the day He saith, "Be." Behold! It is. (*Qur'an* 6: 73a)

> Do not the unbelievers see that the heavens and the earth were joined together (as one unit of creation), before We clove them asunder? We made from water every living thing. Will they not then believe? And We have set on the earth

mountains standing firm, lest it should shake with them, and We have made therein broad highways (between mountains) for them to pass through: that they may receive guidance. And We have made the heavens as a canopy well guarded: yet do they turn away from the signs which these things (point to)! It is He Who created the night and the day, and the sun and the moon: all (the celestial bodies) swim along, each in its rounded course. (*Qur'an* 21: 30-33)

Say: is it that ye deny Him Who created the earth in two days? And do ye join equals with Him? He is the Lord of (all) the worlds. He set on the (earth) mountains standing firm, high above it, and bestowed blessings on the earth, and measured therein all things to give them nourishment in due proportion, in four days, in accordance with (the needs of) those who seek (sustenance). Moreover, He comprehended in His design the sky, and it had been (as) smoke: He said to it and to the earth: "Come ye together, willingly or unwillingly." They said: "We do come (together) in willing obedience." So He completed them as seven firmaments in two days and He assigned to each heaven its duty and command. And We adorned the lower heaven with lights, and (provided it) with guard. Such is the decree of (Him) the exalted in might, full of knowledge. (*Qur'an* 41: 9-12)

The preceding quotations from the *Qur'an* speak for themselves. However, an overly cursory reading of these *Ayat* ("signs" or "verses"; singular=*Ayah*) may result in overlooking some important and interesting considerations. In what follows, each of the preceding quotations from the *Qur'an* is briefly examined.

(1) *Qur'an* 7:54 concisely summarizes the creation of the cosmos in one single *Ayah*. Yet, despite its remarkable brevity, this single *Ayah* parallels the creation story recounted in *Genesis* 1:1-2:4 by proclaiming that Allah accomplished the creation of the entire cosmos in just six days, with "days" being understood to be days as Allah reckons them[3]. However, the message of this

Qur'anic *Ayah* does not end with that single point, and three other issues need to be emphasized. Firstly, Allah not only created the cosmos, but He also created the natural laws that govern the cosmos, as illustrated by the phrase "governed by laws under His command". Thus, the *Qur'an* provides a theological basis for the scientific study of the universe by such fields of inquiry as physics, astronomy, chemistry, etc. Secondly, in referring to the many worlds that comprise the universe, *Qur'an* 1:2 refers to Allah as the "cherisher and sustainer of the worlds", implying an active and ongoing relationship between Allah and His creation, and leaving no room for such theologically impersonal constructs as that of *deus ex machina*. Thirdly, while Allah created the universe in six days by His reckoning, there is no mention in the above *Ayah* of Allah having on the seventh day "rested from all the work that he had done in creation", as is claimed in *Genesis* 2:3. While *Genesis* implies either that Allah needed to rest after working for six days or that Allah simply withdrew from His creation at that time, no such statement is to be found in the *Qur'an*. In fact, the *Qur'an* specifically rejects the concept that Allah needed to rest from His labors of creation.

> We created the heavens and the earth and all between them
> in six days, nor did any sense of weariness touch us.
> (*Qur'an* 50: 38)

(2) *Qur'an* 6:73a states that the creation of the cosmos was accomplished by nothing more than Allah's will and His subsequent statement of "Be". This concept is echoed in several other Qur'anic verses, as well as in the *Bible*.

> To Him is due the primal origin of the heavens and the
> earth: when He decreeth a matter, He saith to it: "Be." And
> it is. (*Qur'an* 2: 117)

> For to anything which We have willed, We but say the word,
> "Be", and it is. (*Qur'an* 16: 40)

Verily, when He intends a thing, His command is, "Be," and it is! (*Qur'an* 36: 82)

It is He Who gives life and death: and when He decides upon an affair, He says to it, "Be", and it is. (*Qur'an* 40: 68)

By the word of the Lord the heavens were made... (*Psalms* 33: 6a)

(3) *Qur'an* 21: 30-33 foreshadows later scientific theories and discoveries. Firstly, in stating, "We made from water every living thing", the *Qur'an* provides a theological grounding for scientific theorizing about the origin of life beginning in the oceans and did so well in excess of 1,200 years before modern science began to hypothesize in that direction. Secondly, in stating, "all (the celestial bodies) swim along, each in its rounded course", the *Qur'an* provides a theological basis for the scientific discoveries of the orbits of the various planets, stars, etc. Thirdly, in maintaining that "the heavens and the earth were joined together (as one unit of creation), before We clove them asunder", the *Qur'an* appears to be anticipating the Big Bang theory of creation some 1,350 years before 20th century physicists stumbled across that concept. (The Big Bang theory posits that all matter was originally one highly condensed unit of matter, which exploded outward into innumerable pieces of matter, thus creating the universe.)

(4) At first glance, it might appear that *Qur'an* 41: 9-12 is stating that the creation took place over eight days, i.e., two plus four plus two. However, a closer reading of the text reveals that the "four days" includes the previous "two days" and that the total number of days is thus six.

C. THE PRE-ISRAELITE PATRIARCHS

C1. INTRODUCTION

The fifth chapter of *Genesis* consists of genealogies, starting with Prophet Adam and continuing to Shem, the son of Prophet Noah. *Genesis* 11: 10-26 continues the ancestral theme, beginning with Shem and continuing to Prophet Abraham. Thereafter, scattered references inform the reader that Prophet Abraham was the father of Prophets Ismael (*Genesis* 16: 15) and Isaac (*Genesis* 21:5). According to *Genesis* 25: 19-26, Prophet Isaac was the father of Prophet Jacob, who was renamed Israel (*Genesis* 32: 22-32).

Given the above Biblical account, the origin of the Israelites begins only with Prophet Jacob, i.e., the original Israel. As such, the ancestors of Prophet Jacob can be referred to as being the pre-Israelite patriarchs. Among the pre-Israelite patriarchs of the *Bible*, several are either specifically mentioned in the *Qur'an* as being prophets of Allah or are referred to in a similar manner, including Adam, Abel, Enoch, Noah, Abraham, and Isaac. Table 2 is presented below, to help the reader orient to the reported relationship of these prophets with each other, and merges genealogical information recorded in *Genesis*, the *Qur'an*, Al-Tabari's 9th or 10th century, monumental history of the world, and the third or second century BCE Jewish book of *Jubilees*, the last two of which add the name of Qaynan between that of Arpachshad and Shelah.

Table 2:

The Pre-Israelite Patriarchs, with prophets in italics

Adam

Cain/Qabil   Seth   *Abel/Habil*

Enos

Cainan

Mahalaleel

Jared

Enoch/Idris

Methuselah

Lamech

Noah/Nuh

Shem

Arpachshad

Qaynan

Shelah

Eber

Peleg

Reu

Serug

Nahor

Terah/Azar

Abraham/Ibrahim

Isaac

C2. PROPHET ADAM

The Biblical story of the creation and fall of Prophet Adam is told in *Genesis* 2:4-3:24. According to this tradition, Allah created Prophet Adam from the dust of the ground and by blowing the breath of life into Adam. Thereafter, Prophet Adam was placed in the Garden of Eden, which *Genesis* locates at the headwaters of the Pishon, Gihon, Tigris, and Euphrates rivers. It was in Eden where Prophet Adam was asked to give names to every living creature and where Eve was formed from Adam's rib. Prophet Adam and his wife were given leave by Allah to eat the fruit from any of the trees of Eden, with one notable exception. Nonetheless, under the influence of Satan who was disguised as a serpent, the first two humans disobeyed Allah's command. They ate from the forbidden tree, resulting in their discovering the shame of their own nakedness, attempting to cover their nakedness by sewing together fig leaves, and being barred from further habitation in Eden. As seen by the following, the *Qur'an* offers a startlingly similar account.

> Behold! thy Lord said to the angels: "I am about to create man, from sounding clay from mud moulded into shape; when I have fashioned him (in due proportion) and breathed into him of My spirit, fall ye down in obeisance unto him." (*Qur'an* 15:28-29; see also *Qur'an* 32:7-9; 38:71-72; and 55:14)

> And He taught Adam the names of all things... (*Qur'an* 2: 31a)

> "O Adam! dwell thou and thy wife in the garden and enjoy (its good things) as ye wish: but approach not this tree, or ye run into harm and transgression." Then began Satan to whisper suggestions to them, in order to reveal to them their shame that was hidden from them (before): he said: "Your Lord only forbade you this tree lest ye should become angels or such beings as live forever." And he swore to them

both, that he was their sincere adviser. So by deceit he brought about their fall: when they tasted of the tree, their shame became manifest to them, and they began to sew together the leaves of the garden over their bodies. And their Lord called unto them: "Did I not forbid you that tree, and tell you that Satan was an avowed enemy unto you?" They said: "Our Lord! we have wronged our own souls: if Thou forgive us not and bestow not upon us Thy mercy, we shall certainly be lost." (Allah) said: "Get ye down, with enmity between yourselves. On earth will be your dwelling place and your means of livelihood — for a time." (*Qur'an* 7: 19-24)

Two subtle differences emerge from comparing the Biblical and Qur'anic accounts of the creation and fall of Prophet Adam. Firstly, *Genesis* has Adam naming all living creatures, while the *Qur'an* has Allah teaching Adam their names. Secondly, *Genesis* places the Garden of Eden on earth, while the statement of *Qur'an* 7:24, i.e., "...get ye down...on earth will be your dwelling place...", implies that the garden was not on earth.

In addition, a basic doctrinal difference between Islam and traditional Western Christianity should be noted at this time. Western Christian thought maintains the concept of original sin, i.e., that each child is born into a state of sin, secondary to the fall of Prophet Adam in eating the forbidden fruit. In essence, this concept of original sin represents an inheritance of sin from Prophet Adam, the ancestor of all humanity. While Islam recognizes the fall of Adam, the concept of an inheritance of original sin is totally foreign to Islam. Furthermore, *Qur'an* 2:37 states that Adam repented of his sin, i.e, "learnt...words of inspiration", and that he was forgiven. Thus, while the *Bible* and *Qur'an* contain similar narratives regarding the fall of Prophet Adam, Islam and Western Christianity draw very different theological constructs from these narratives.

C3. PROPHET ABEL (HABIL)

Genesis 4:1-16 details that Prophet Adam originally had two sons, Cain and Prophet Abel. As young men, both made sacrifices to Allah, but only Abel's sacrifice was accepted by Allah. Reacting to this, Cain was consumed by anger, murdered his younger brother, and was subsequently punished by Allah. Again, the *Qur'an* offers a strikingly similar narrative.

> Recite to them the truth of the story of the two sons of Adam. Behold! they each presented a sacrifice (to Allah): it was accepted from one, but not from the other. Said the latter: "Be sure I will slay thee." "Surely," said the former, "Allah doth accept of the sacrifice of those who are righteous. If thou dost stretch thy hand against me to slay me, it is not for me to stretch my hand against thee to slay thee: for I do fear Allah, the cherisher of the worlds. For me, I intend to let thee draw on thyself my sin as well as thine, for thou wilt be among the companions of the fire, and that is the reward of those who do wrong." The (selfish) soul of the other led him to the murder of his brother: he murdered him, and became (himself) one of the lost ones. Then Allah sent a raven, who scratched the ground, to show him how to hide the shame of his brother. "Woe is me!" said he; "Was I not even able to be as this raven, and to hide the shame of my brother?" Then he became full of regrets — (*Qur'an* 5: 27-31)

C4. PROPHET ENOCH (IDRIS)

The Biblical story of Enoch is briefly told in *Genesis* 5: 18-24, *Hebrews* 11:5, and *Jude* 1: 14. Within Islam, Enoch is typically identified with Prophet Idris, who is mentioned briefly in the *Qur'an*.

> Also mention in the book the case of Idris: he was a man of truth (and sincerity), (and) a prophet: and We raised him to a lofty station. (*Qur'an* 19: 56-57)

And (remember) Isma'il, Idris, and Dhu al Kifl, all (men) of constancy and Patience; We admitted them to Our mercy: for they were of the righteous ones. (*Qur'an* 21: 85-86)

C5. PROPHET NOAH (NUH)

The Biblical story of Prophet Noah is narrated in *Genesis* 6: 9-9: 28, where it is stated that humanity became exceedingly wicked and that Allah decided to destroy mankind in a worldwide flood. However, Prophet Noah found favor in Allah's sight and was directed by Allah to build an ark, in which he and his family (his wife, his three sons, and his three daughters-in-law) and representatives of each of the species would ride out the deluge until landing on the "mountains of Ararat". Once again, the *Qur'an* offers an excellent parallel to the *Genesis* account.

We sent Noah to his people (with a mission): "I have come to you with a clear warning: that ye serve none but Allah: verily I do fear for you the penalty of a grievous day." But the chiefs of the unbelievers among his people said: "We see (in) thee nothing but a man like ourselves: nor do we see that any follow thee but the meanest among us, in judgment immature: nor do we see in you (all) any merit above us: in fact we think ye are liars!" He said: "O my people! see ye if (it be that) I have a clear sign from my Lord, and that He hath sent mercy unto me from His own presence, but that the mercy hath been obscured from your sight? Shall we compel you to accept it when ye are averse to it? And O my people! I ask you for no wealth in return: my reward is from none but Allah: but I will not drive away (in contempt) those who believe: for verily they are to meet their Lord, and ye, I see, are the ignorant ones! And O my people! who would help me against Allah if I drove them away? Will ye not then take heed? I tell you not that with me are the treasures of Allah, nor do I know what is hidden, nor claim I to be an angel. Nor yet do I say, of those whom your eyes do despise that Allah will not grant them (all) that is good: Allah knoweth best what is in their souls: I should, if I did, indeed be a wrongdoer." They said: "O Noah! Thou hath disputed with us, and (much) hast thou prolonged the dispute with us: now bring upon us what thou threatenest us with, if thou speakest the truth!" He said: "Truly, Allah will bring it on you if He wills — and then, ye will not be able to frustrate it! Of no profit will be my counsel to you, much as I desire to give you (good) counsel, if it be that Allah willeth to leave you astray: He is your Lord! And to Him will ye return!"...It was revealed to Noah: "None of thy people will believe except those who have believed already! So grieve no longer over their (evil) deeds. But construct an ark under Our eyes and Our inspiration, and address Me no (further) on behalf of those who are in sin: for they are about to be overwhelmed (in the flood)." Forthwith he (starts) constructing the ark: every time that the chiefs of his people passed by him, they threw ridicule on him. He said: "If ye ridicule us now, we (in our turn) can look down on you with ridicule likewise! But soon will ye know who it is on whom will descend a penalty that will cover them with shame — on whom will be unloosed a penalty lasting:" at length, behold! there came Our command, and the fountains of the earth gushed forth! We said: "Embark therein, of each kind two, male and female, and your family — except those against whom the word has already gone forth — and the believers." But only a few believed with him. So he said: "Embark ye on the ark in the name of Allah, whether it move or be at rest! For my Lord is, be sure, oft-forgiving, most merciful!" So the ark floated with them on the waves (towering) like mountains, and Noah called out to his son, who had separated himself (from the rest): "O my son! embark with us, and be not with the unbelievers!" The son replied: "I will betake myself to some mountain: it will save me from the water." Noah said: "This day nothing can save, from the command of Allah, any but those on whom He hath mercy!" — and the waves came between them, and the son was among those overwhelmed in the flood. Then the word went forth: "O earth! swallow up thy water, and O sky! withhold (thy rain)!" And the water abated, and the matter was ended. The ark rested on Mount Judi, and the word went forth: "Away with those who do wrong!" And Noah called upon his Lord, and said: "O my Lord! surely my son is of my family! And Thy promise is true, and Thou art the justest of judges!" He said: "O Noah! he is not of thy family: for his conduct is unright-eous. So ask not of Me that of which thou hast no knowledge! I give thee counsel, lest thou act like the ignorant!" Noah said: "O my Lord! I do seek refuge with Thee, lest I ask Thee for that of what I have no knowledge. And unless Thou forgive me and have mercy on me, I should indeed be lost!" Then word came: "O Noah! come down (from the ark) with peace from Us, and blessing on thee and on some of the peoples (who will spring) from those with thee: but (there will be other) peoples to whom We shall grant their pleasures (for a time), but in the end will a grievous penalty reach them from Us." (*Qur'an* 11: 25-34, 36-48; see also *Qur'an* 23: 23-30; 26: 105-122; 37: 75-82; 54: 9-15; and 71: 1-28)

Several points need to be made in contrasting the narratives regarding Prophet Noah as found in *Genesis* and in the *Qur'an*. Firstly, unlike *Genesis*, the *Qur'an* does not list three specific sons of Prophet Noah as being on the ark, does not specifically confine the human inhabitants of the ark to being from Prophet Noah's immediate family, and does not specifically state that the flood was a worldwide phenomenon. Moeover, the directions given to Prophet Noah to "(e)mbark therein...your family...and the believers" would seem to imply that there may have been more people on the ark than just Prophet Noah's immediate family. However, in a *Hadith* narrated by Samurah ibn Jundub, Prophet Muhammad is quoted as saying that Shem, Ham, and Japheth were the three sons of Prophet Noah who survived the flood[4]. Further, the following passage in the *Qur'an* is often interpreted as implying that the offspring of Prophet Noah were the only humans to survive the flood, which would imply a worldwide flood.

> (In the days of old), Noah cried to Us, and We are the best
> to hear prayers. And We delivered him and his people from
> the great calamity, and made his progeny to endure (on this
> earth)... (*Qur'an* 37: 75-77)

Secondly, unlike *Genesis*, the *Qur'an* specifically states that one of Prophet Noah's sons was not on the ark. Arab tradition maintains that this son was Canaan, who was also known as Yam, and that Prophet Noah had a fifth son, Eber, who died before the flood[5]. With regard to the son who perished in the flood, *Qur'an* 11:42-47 states that members of Noah's true family were his fellow believers, not his biological offspring. Thirdly, while many Christians think that the ark landed on Mt. Ararat, *Genesis* 8: 4 states that "the ark came to rest on the mountains of Ararat", i.e., somewhere in the Ararat mountain range. The *Qur'an*'s Mt. Judi is in the Ararat range. Fourthly, while *Genesis* is basically silent about Prophet Noah's ministry to the pre-flood inhabitants of the earth, the *Qur'an* offers a rich narrative about the revealed message of Prophet Noah.

Finally, *Genesis* 9: 18-27 states that Prophet Noah became drunk on wine at some point after the flood and in his drunken sleep lay naked in his tent where he was seen by his son, Ham. As a result, Prophet Noah allegedly cursed Ham's son, Canaan.

> When Noah awoke from his wine and knew what his youngest
> son had done to him, he said, "Cursed be Canaan; lowest
> of slaves shall he be to his brothers." He also said, "Blessed by
> the Lord my God be Shem; and let Canaan be his slave.
> May God make space for Japheth, and let him live in the tents
> of Shem; and let Canaan be his slave." (*Genesis* 9: 24-27)

There are several disturbing aspects to this story from *Genesis*. (1) Prophet Noah is defamed as a drunkard. (2) Ham is blamed for viewing his father's nakedness, yet the responsibility appears to lie with the alleged drunkenness of his father. (3) Although Ham's son, Canaan, had nothing to do with the alleged event, Canaan is cursed, and he and his descendants are forever to be the slaves of Shem, Japheth, and their offspring, providing Biblical justification for the enslavement and attempted genocide of the Canaanites by the Israelites[6]. (4) Traditional Christian interpretation of Prophet Noah's alleged curse was that Ham or Canaan was given black skin and that the alleged curse provided Biblical justification for the abhorrent slave trade of the 16th through 19th centuries. Fortunately, this interpretation has long been rejected in Christian circles.

The Biblical accounts of the prophets of Allah frequently slander and defame these pious men, leading to the inevitable questioning of why these men were ever selected as prophets by Allah. Such is the case with the story of Prophet Noah's alleged drunkenness and cursing of Canaan. In marked contrast, no such account appears in the *Qur'an*, where the prophets of Allah are typically portrayed as men of virtue and marked spirituality. Still further, the now rejected, but formerly held, Judaeo-Christian association of "black-skinned" with "cursed" and "slave" can be contrasted with the Qur'anic view of racial and ethnic differences.

> O mankind! We created you from a single (pair) of a male and a female, and made you into nations and tribes, that ye may know each other (not that ye may despise each other). Verily the most honored of you in the sight of Allah is (he who is) the most righteous of you. And Allah has full knowledge and is well-acquainted (with all things). (*Qur'an* 49: 13)

C6. PROPHET ABRAHAM (IBRAHIM)

Both the *Qur'an* and *Àhadith* record numerous narratives regarding Prophet Abraham, many of which have no Biblical parallel. However, the sheer number of such narratives precludes being able to quote all of them in the space available. As such, the following represents only a highly selected overview of a few of the Islamic narratives about Prophet Abraham. Readers wishing a more thorough presentation are urged to consult the author's earlier book, *Abraham: The Friend of God*, which offers a synthesis of Islamic and Judaeo-Christian statements about this prophet of Allah.

In the following quotation from the *Qur'an*, the story is told of Prophet Abraham's reasoning to montheism via naturalistic observation of celestial objects, presumably when living in Ur at about 14 years of age. While there is no Biblical parallel to this narrative, a similar story appears in *Jewish Antiquities* by Josephus, the first century CE Jewish historian. As such, it appears that a parallel to the following Qur'anic story was part of the Jewish tradition by the time of Christ.

> So also did We show Abraham the power and the laws of the heavens and the earth, that he might (with understanding) have certitude. When the night covered him over, he saw a star: he said: "This is my lord." But when it set, he said: "I love not those that set." When he saw the moon rising in splendour, he said: "This is my lord." But when the moon set, he said: "Unless my Lord guide me, I shall surely be among those who go astray." When he saw the sun rising in splendour, he said: "This is my lord; this is the greatest (of all)." But when the sun set, he said: "O my people! I am indeed free from your (guilt) of giving partners to Allah. For me, I have set my face, firmly and truly, towards Him Who created the heavens and the earth, and never shall I give partners to Allah." (*Qur'an* 6: 75-79)

Having reasoned to a strict monotheism (*Tawheed*), the youthful Abraham began to preach to his family and to those around him, although few apparently accepted this message from the youthful prophet. With his monotheistic message basically falling on deaf ears, the *Qur'an* states that Prophet Abraham, presumably at about age 16, actually went so far as to destroy all but one of the temple idols at Ur, leaving the largest idol intact, so that Abraham could direct the people to ask this speechless idol who it was who had destroyed the other idols, thus illustrating the folly of idolatry. For his rebellion against state-sponsored polytheism, Prophet Abraham was sentenced to be burned to death, but Allah rescued him from the flames. This basic storyline is told in many different places within the *Qur'an*, and is briefly summarized in the following passage. Again, there is no Biblical parallel to this account from the *Qur'an*, although a similar story appears in the Jewish *Talmud*, with the setting being Abraham's father's workplace instead of the temple at Ur.

> We bestowed aforetime on Abraham his rectitude of conduct, and well were We acquainted with him. "Behold!" he said to his father and his people, "What are these images to which ye are (so assiduously) devoted?" They said, "We found our fathers worshipping them." He said, "Indeed ye have been in manifest error — ye and your fathers." They said, "Have you brought us the truth, or are you one of those who jest?" He said, "Nay your Lord is the Lord of the heavens and the earth, He Who created them (from nothing): and I am a witness to this (truth). And by Allah, I have a plan for your idols — after ye go away and turn your backs"...So he broke them to pieces, (all) but the biggest of them, that they might turn (and address themselves) to it. They said, "Who has done this to our gods? He must indeed be some man of impiety!" They said, "We heard a youth talk of them: he is called Abraham." They said, "Then bring him before the eyes of the people that they may bear witness." They said, "Art thou the one that did this with our gods, O Abraham?" He said, "Nay, this was done by — this is their biggest one! Ask them, if they can speak intelligently!" So they turned to themselves and said, "Surely ye are the ones in the wrong!" Then were they confounded with shame: (they said) "Thou knowest full well that these (idols) do not speak!" (Abraham) said, "Do ye then worship, besides Allah, things that can neither be of any good to you nor do you harm? Fie upon you, and upon the things that ye worship besides Allah! Have ye no sense?" ...They said, "Burn him and protect your gods, if ye do (anything at all)!" We said, "O fire! be thou cool, and (a means of) safety for Abraham!" Then they sought a stratagem against him, but We made them the ones

that lost most! But We delivered him and (his nephew) Lut, (and directed them) to the land which We have blessed for the nations. (*Qur'an* 21: 51-71)

Despite his near escape, the *Qur'an* states that Prophet Abraham continued to preach and witness to those around him, especially to his polytheistic father. Finally, his father threatened to kill Abraham if the latter did not stop preaching. At that point, Prophet Abraham sadly separated from his father, presumably moving with Sarah (his wife) and Prophet Lot (his nephew) from Haran to Palestine.

(The father) replied: "Dost thou hate my gods, O Abraham? If thou forbear not, I will indeed stone thee: now get away from me for a good long while!" Abraham said: "Peace be on thee: I will pray to my Lord for thy forgiveness: for He is to me most gracious. And I will turn away from you (all) and from those whom ye invoke besides Allah: I will call on my Lord: perhaps by my prayer to my Lord, I shall be not unblest!" (*Qur'an* 19: 46-48)

Genesis 12: 10-20 gives the Biblical account of Prophet Abraham's sojourn in Egypt and focuses on the abduction of Sarah, Prophet Abraham's wife, by the king. Similar accounts are preserved in the *Ahadith* or sayings of Prophet Muhammad, one of which is quoted immediately below.

Narrated Abu Huraira: "The Prophet said, 'The Prophet Abraham emigrated with Sarah and entered a village where there was a king or a tyrant. (The king) was told that Abraham had entered (the village) accompanied by a woman who was one of the most charming women. So, the king sent for Abraham and asked, 'O Abraham! Who is this lady accompanying you?' Abraham replied, 'She is my sister (i.e., in religion).' Then Abraham returned to her and said, 'Do not contradict my statement, for I have informed them that you are my sister. By Allah, there are no true believers on this land except you and I.' Then Abraham sent her to the king. When the king got to her, she got up and performed ablution, prayed and said, 'O Allah! If I have believed in You and Your apostle, and have saved my private parts from everybody except my husband, then please do not let this pagan overpower me.' On that the king fell in a mood of agitation and started moving his legs. Seeing the condition of the king, Sarah said, 'O Allah! if he should die, the people will say that I have killed him.' The king regained his power and proceeded towards her, but she got up again and performed ablution, prayed and said, 'O Allah! if I have believed in You and Your apostle and have kept my private parts safe from all except my husband, then please do not let this pagan overpower me.' The king again fell in a mood of agitation and started moving his legs. On seeing that state of the king, Sarah said, 'O Allah! if he should die, the people will say that I have killed him.' The king got either two or three attacks, and after recovering from the last attack he said, 'By Allah! You have sent a satan to me. Take her to Abraham and give her Ajar (Hagar).' So she came back to Abraham and said, 'Allah humiliated the pagan and gave us a slave girl for service.'" (*Al-Bukhari, Hadith* # 3: 420; see also *Al-Bukhari, Hadith* # 4: 578)

Genesis 21: 8-21 relates a story of Sarah demanding that Prophet Abraham banish Hagar (Abraham's second wife) and Prophet Ismael (Abraham and Hagar's son). By contrasting *Genesis* 16: 16, 21: 5, and 21: 8-10, it is clear that the *Genesis* account has Prophet Ismael being about 16 years old at the time of this story — Prophet Ismael was born 14 years before Prophet Isaac, and Prophet Isaac was being weaned at the time. Yet, the *Genesis* account has the improbable statements that Prophet Ismael was carried on Hagar's shoulder and that Hagar physically "cast the child under one of the bushes" (21: 14-15). This same story is recounted in several *Ahadith*, but with notable exceptions. Firstly, in the *Ahadith*, Prophet Ismael is still a nursing infant, which would be consistent with the statements made in *Genesis* 21: 14-15. Secondly, Prophet Abraham accompanies Hagar and the infant Ismael to Makkah, where he leaves them. Thirdly, Hagar and Ismael are saved, not by Hagar having her eyes opened to see an already existing well of water, but by the miraculous creation of a well of water.

> Narrated Ibn 'Abbas: "When Abraham had differences with his wife (Sarah), (because of her jealousy of Hagar, Ismael's mother), he took Ismael and his mother and went away. They had a water-skin with them containing some water. Ismael's mother used to drink water from the water-skin so that her milk would increase for her child. When Abraham reached Makkah, he made her sit under a tree and afterwards returned home. Ismael's mother followed him, and when they reached Kada', she called him from behind, 'O Abraham! to whom are you leaving us?' He replied, '(I am leaving you) to Allah's (care).' She said, 'I am satisfied to be with Allah.' She returned to her place and started drinking water from the water-skin, and her milk increased for her child. When the water had all been used up, she said to herself, 'I'd better go and look so that I may see somebody.' She ascended the Safa mountain and looked, hoping to see somebody, but in vain. When she came down to the valley, she ran till she reached the Marwa mountain. She ran to and fro (between the two mountains) many times. Then she said to herself, 'I'd better go and see the state of the child.' She went and found it in a state of one on the point of dying. She could not endure to watch it dying and said (to herself), 'If I go and look, I may find somebody.' She went and ascended the Safa mountain and looked for a long while but could not find anybody. Thus, she completed seven rounds (of running) between Safa and Marwa. Again she said (to herself), 'I'd better go back and see the state of the child.' But suddenly she heard a voice, and she said to that strange voice, 'Help us if you can offer any help.' Lo! it was Gabriel (who had made the voice). Gabriel hit the earth with his heel like this ... and so the water gushed out. Ismael's mother was astonished and started digging... (*Al-Bukhari, Hadith* #4:584; see also *Al-Bukhari, Hadith* # 4:583)

Genesis 22: 1-19 presents one version of the intended sacrifice of Prophet Abraham's son. This account variously identifies the sacrificial son as Prophet Isaac (by name) and as Prophet Ismael (by reference to Prophet Abraham's only son, a statement that could only apply to Prophet Ismael, as *Genesis* 16:16 and 21: 5 establish that Ismael was born 14 years prior to Isaac, and as *Genesis* 25: 8-9 indicates that both Ismael and Isaac were still alive at Abraham's death). The *Qur'an* also tells the story of the sacrifice, but suggests that Prophet Isaac was not even born until after the sacrificial event, thus indicating that the intended sacrificial victim was Prophet Ismael. Additionally, the narrative in *Genesis* 22: 1-10 suggests that Prophet Abraham tricked and duped his unknowing son with regard to the sacrifice and actually had to bind his son. In marked contrast, the following passage from the *Qur'an* illustrates that Prophet Abraham was open and honest with his son about what was to happen and that his son was a willing participant.

> He (Abraham) said: "I will go to my Lord! He will surely guide me! O my Lord! grant me a righteous (son!)" So We gave him the good news of a boy ready to suffer and forbear. Then, when (the son) reached (the age of serious) work with him, he said: "O my son! I see in vision that I offer thee in sacrifice: now see what is thy view!" (The son) said: "O my father! do as thou art commanded: thou wilt find me, if Allah so wills, one practicing patience and constancy!" So when they had both submitted their wills (to Allah), and he had laid him prostrate on his forehead (for sacrifice), We called out to him, "O Abraham! thou hast already fulfilled the vision!" — thus indeed do We reward those who do right. For this was obviously a trial — and We ransomed him with a momentous sacrifice. And We left (this blessing) for him among generations (to come) in later times: "Peace and salutation to Abraham!" Thus indeed do We reward those who do right for he was one of Our believing servants. And We gave him the good news of Isaac — a prophet — one of the righteous. (*Qur'an* 37: 99-112)

The *Qur'an* states that Prophet Abraham journeyed to Makkah, where he joined with Prophet Ismael in building the Ka'ba, i.e., the "house" of Allah, which serves a central function in the *Hajj* pilgrimage (see chapter VI). There is no known parallel to this story in the Judaeo-Christian tradition.

> Remember We made the house a place of assembly for men and a place of safety; and take ye the station of Abraham as a place of prayer; and We covenanted with Abraham and Isma'il, that they should sanctify My house for those who compass it round, or use it as a retreat, or bow, or prostrate themselves (therein in prayer). And remember Abraham said: "My Lord, make this a city of peace, and feed its people with fruits — such of them as believe in Allah and the last day." He said: "(Yea), and such as reject faith — for a while will I grant them their pleasure, but will soon drive them to the torments of fire — an evil destination (indeed)!" And remember Abraham and Isma'il raised the foundations of the house (with this prayer): "Our Lord! accept (this service) from us: for Thou art the all-hearing, the all-knowing. Our Lord! make of us Muslims, bowing to Thy (will), and of our progeny a people Muslim, bowing to Thy (will); and show us our places for the celebration of (due) rites; and turn unto us (in mercy); for Thou art the oft-returning, most merciful. Our Lord! send amongst them a messenger of their own, who shall rehearse Thy signs to them and instruct them in scripture and wisdom, and sanctify them:for Thou art the exalted in might, the wise."
> (*Qur'an* 2: 125-129; see also *Qur'an* 3:95-97 and 22:26-30)

In closing this brief overview of the Islamic perspective of Prophet Abraham, one final event is presented. *Qur'an* 22:78 states that Prophet Abraham was the person who coined the term "Muslim".

C7. PROPHET ISAAC

The Biblical story of Prophet Isaac is sporadically told throughout chapters 21-35 of *Genesis*. Prophet Isaac is mentioned briefly, but repeatedly, in the *Qur'an* as being given as a son to Prophet Abraham.

> We gave him Isaac and Jacob: all (three) we guided... (*Qur'an* 6: 84a)

> When he had turned away from them and from those whom they worshipped besides Allah, We bestowed on him Isaac and Jacob, and each one of them We made a prophet. (*Qur'an* 19: 49)

> And We bestowed on him Isaac and, as an additional gift, (a grandson) Jacob, and We made righteous men of every one (of them). (*Qur'an* 21: 72)

> And We gave him the good news of Isaac — a prophet — one of the righteous. We blessed him and Isaac: but of their progeny are (some) that do right, and (some) that obviously do wrong, to their own souls. (*Qur'an* 37: 112-113)

D. THE NON-ISRAELITE PROPHETS

D1. INTRODUCTION:

The *Qur'an* mentions several of Allah's prophets who were not ancestors or descendants of Prophet Jacob. Among these non-Israelite prophets are Hud, Salih, Lot, Ismael, Job, Dhu Al-Kifl, Shu'ayb, and Muhammad, the last of whom is discussed in chapter III. In order to gain some understanding of the reported relationship of these prophets to each other, to the pre-Israelite patriarchs, and to the Israelite prophets, Table 3 is presented below. The genealogical information contained therein is derived from *Genesis*, the *Qur'an*, *Jubilees*, and Al-Tabari.

Table 3

The Non-Israelite Prophets, with Prophets in italics

```
                              Shem
        ┌───────────────────────┴───────────────────────┐
      Aram                                          Arpachshad
        │                                                │
        │                                             Qaynan
 ┌──────┴──────────────┐                                 │
Gether              Auz/Uz                             Shelah
   │                   │                                 │
Thamud               'Ad                                Eber
   │                   │                                 │
 Iram              Al-Khalud                            Peleg
   │                   │                                 │
Thamud               Ribah                               Reu
   │                   │                                 │
Khadir            'Abd Allah                            Serug
   │                   │                                 │
'Abayd               Hud                               Nahor
   │                                                     │
Masikh                                              Terah/Azar
   │                          ┌──────────────────────────┤
 Asif                                                     
   │                        Haran                 Abraham /Ibrahim
'Abayd                        │                           │
   │                       Lot/Lut                        │
 Salih                ┌───────────┬──────────────────┐
                   Ismael       Isaac          Midian/Madyan
                      │           │                  │
                  Basemath      Esau              Thabit
                      └─────┬─────┘                  │
                                                   'Anqa
                   Reuel/Razih/Raghwil               │
                            │                      Sayfun
                   Zerah/Maws/Mawas                  │
                            │                      Shu'ayb
                      Job/Ayyub
                            │
                   Dhu Al-Kifl/Bishr
```

D2. PROPHET HUD

The lineage given for Prophet Hud in Figure #3 is based on Al-Tabari, and it is possible that some generations of descent between Aram and Hud may be missing, making it a precarious enterprise to attempt to date the precise time of Prophet Hud, although it appears to have been before the times of Prophet Salih and Prophet Shu'ayb. The *Qur'an* states that Allah sent Hud as a prophet to Hud's own people, the 'Ad. The 'Ad has been identified as a tribe that once lived in the southeastern part of the Arabian Peninsula and that centered around the ancient and lost city of Iram or Ubar. With regard to the association of the 'Ad with the city of Iram, the *Qur'an* states the following.

> Seest thou not how thy Lord dealt with the 'Ad (people) — of the (city of) Iram, with lofty pillars, the like of which were not produced in (all) the land? (*Qur'an* 89: 6-8)

Prophet Hud is discussed in four lengthy passages in the *Qur'an*, only one of which is quoted below. There are no Biblical references to this prophet of Allah.

> The 'Ad (people) rejected the messengers. Behold, their brother Hud said to them: "Will ye not fear (Allah)? I am to you a messenger worthy of all trust: so fear Allah and obey me. No reward do I ask of you for it: my reward is only from the Lord of the worlds. Do ye build a landmark on every high place to amuse yourselves? And do ye get for yourselves fine buildings in the hope of living therein (forever)? And when ye exert your strong hand do ye do it like men of absolute power? Now fear Allah and obey me. Yea, fear Him Who has bestowed on you freely all that ye know. Freely has He bestowed on you cattle and sons — and gardens and springs. Truly I fear for you the penalty of a great day." They said: "It is the same to us whether thou admonish us or be not among (our) admonishers! This is no other than a customary device of the ancients, and we are not the ones to receive pains and penalties!" So they rejected him, and We destroyed them. Verily in this is a

sign: but most of them do not believe. And verily thy Lord is He, the exalted in might, most merciful. (*Qur'an* 26: 123-140; see also *Qur'an* 7: 65-72, 11: 50-60, and 46: 21-26)

D3. PROPHET SALIH

The lineage given for Prophet Salih in Table 3 is based on Al-Tabari, and it is possible that this genealogy is incomplete. The *Qur'an* states that Prophet Salih was sent as a messenger to his own people, i.e., the Thamud tribe, which rose to prominence in the Arabian Peninsula at some time after the destruction of most of the 'Ad tribe during Prophet Hud's time, but before the destruction of the Midianite (Madyan) people during Prophet Shu'ayb's time. The story of Prophet Salih is told in four lengthy passages in the *Qur'an*, only one of which is quoted below. There is no Biblical account of Prophet Salih.

To the Thamud people (We sent) Salih, one of their own brethren: He said: "O my people! worship Allah; ye have no other god but Him. Now hath come unto you a clear (sign) from your Lord! This she-camel of Allah is a sign unto you: so leave her to graze in Allah's earth, and let her come to no harm, or ye shall be seized with a grievous punishment. And remember how He made you inheritors after the 'Ad people and gave you habitations in the land: ye build for yourselves palaces and castles in (open) plains, and carve out homes in the mountains; so bring to remembrance the benefits (ye have received) from Allah, and refrain from evil and mischief on the earth." The leaders of the arrogant party among his people said to those who were reckoned powerless — those among them who believed: "Know ye indeed that Salih is a messenger from his Lord?" They said: "We do indeed believe in the revelation which hath been sent through him." The arrogant party said: "For our part, we reject what ye believe in." Then they hamstrung the she-camel, and insolently defied the order of their Lord, saying: "O Salih! bring about thy threats, if thou art a messenger (of Allah)!" So the earthquake took them unawares, and they lay prostrate in their homes in the morning! So Salih left them, saying: "O my people! I did indeed convey to you the message for which I was sent by my Lord: I gave you good counsel, but ye love not good counselors!" (*Qur'an* 7: 73-79; see also *Qur'an* 11: 61-68, 26: 141-158, and 27: 45-53)

D4. PROPHET LOT (LUT)

Prophet Lot is mentioned in *Genesis* 11: 27-31 as being the nephew of Prophet Abraham and as having journeyed with Prophet Abraham from Ur to Haran. However, the Biblical account offers no other information about Lot's early life. In contrast, the *Qur'an* states that Prophet Lot was an early convert to Prophet Abraham's message of monotheism, presumably while both were living in Ur.

> So naught was the answer of (Abraham's) people except that they said: "Slay Him or burn him." But Allah did save him from the fire. Verily in this are signs for people who believe. And he said: "For you, ye have taken (for worship) idols besides Allah, out of mutual love and regard between your-selves in this life; but on the day of judgment ye shall disown each other and curse each other: and your abode will be the fire, and ye shall have none to help." But Lut had faith in him: he said: "I will leave home for the sake of my Lord: for He is exalted in might, and wise." (*Qur'an* 29: 24-26)

Genesis 13:1-13 states that Prophet Lot migrated with Prophet Abraham from Egypt back to Palestine, eventually separated from Abraham, and made his home in Sodom, whose people were "wicked, great sinners against the Lord". However, *Genesis* is basically silent about Prophet Lot's life in Sodom and offers no information about Lot's prophetic role and message. In contrast, several passages in the *Qur'an* address the mission and ministry of Prophet Lot.

The people of Lut rejected the messengers. Behold, their brother Lut said to them: "Will ye not fear (Allah)? I am to you a messenger worthy of all trust. So fear Allah and obey me. No reward do I ask of you for it: my reward is only from the Lord of the worlds. Of all the creatures in the world, will ye approach males, and leave those whom Allah has created for you to be your mates? Nay, ye are a people transgressing (all limits)!" They said. "If thou desist not, O Lut! thou wilt assuredly be cast out!" He said: "I do detest your doings: O my Lord! deliver me and my family from such things as they do!" (*Qur'an* 26:160-169; see also *Qur'an* 7: 80-81; 27: 54-56; and 29: 28-30)

The story of the angels' stay in Prophet Lot's home and of the eventual destruction of Sodom and Gomorrah is referred to or told in numerous passages in the *Qur'an*. However, the following represents one of the more complete narrations.

When our messengers came to Lut, he was grieved on their account and felt himself powerless (to protect) them. He said: "This is a distressful day." And his people came rushing towards him, and they had been long in the habit of practicing abominations. He said: "O my people! Here are my daughters: they are purer for you (if ye marry)! Now fear Allah, and cover me not with shame about my guests! Is there not among you a single right-minded man?" They said: "Well dost thou know we have no need of thy daughters: indeed thou knowest quite well what we want!" He said: "Would that I had power to suppress you or that I could betake myself to some powerful support." (The messengers) said: "O Lut! we are messengers from thy Lord! By no means shall they reach thee! Now travel with thy family while yet a part of the night remains, and let not any of you look back: but thy wife (will remain behind): to her will happen what happens to the people. Morning is their time appointed: is not the morning nigh?" When our decree issued, we turned (the cities) upside down, and rained down on them brimstones hard as baked clay, spread, layer on layer — marked as from thy Lord: nor are they ever far from those who do wrong! (*Qur'an* 11: 77-83; see also *Qur'an* 7: 80-84; 15: 57-77; 21: 74-75; 26: 160-175; 27: 54-58; 29: 28-35; 37: 133-138; 51: 31-37; and 54: 33-39)

In most respects, the account in *Genesis* 19: 4-16, 23-28 of the destruction of Sodom and Gomorrah parallels the Qur'anic passage quoted above. In both statements: (1) the men of Sodom gather around the house of Lot, demanding access to the strangers within it; (2) Lot begs the populace to leave his guests alone; (3) Lot offers his unmarried daughters as substitutes for his guests; and (4) Lot's offer of his daughters is rejected. Further, the *Qur'an* and *Genesis* agree that: (5) the men of Sodom are blinded and wander aimlessly around (*Qur'an* 15: 72 and *Genesis* 19:11); (6) Lot and his family flee the city of Sodom before morning or as dawn breaks (e.g., *Qur'an* 11: 81 and *Genesis* 19: 15-16); (7) Lot's wife is destroyed (e.g., *Qur'an* 7: 83 and *Genesis* 19: 26); and (8) the city of Sodom is destroyed by objects (variously described as being brimstone, sulfur, and fire) falling from the sky (e.g., *Qur'an* 7: 84 and *Genesis* 19: 24).

However, there is one glaring difference between *Genesis* and the *Qur'an*. *Genesis* 19: 30-38 continues the pattern of defaming the prophets of Allah by claiming that after the destruction of Sodom, Prophet Lot and his daughters initially settled in Zoar, and then moved to a cave where his two daughters succeeded in getting their father intoxicated and then had sexual relations with him, resulting in the births of the eponymous ancestors of the Moabites and 'Ammonites. *Genesis* claims that Prophet Lot's daughters seduced their father, because they believed there were no other men alive after the destruction of Sodom, a claim that is refuted by the narrative's earlier statement that Prophet Lot and his daughters went to Zoar after the destruction of Sodom, and in Zoar they would have encountered many men. No such scandalous situation is ever mentioned in the *Qur'an*, where Prophet Lot is portrayed as a man of piety, rectitude, and good conduct.

D5. PROPHET ISMAEL

The Biblical account of Prophet Ismael is found in *Genesis* 16: 1-16, 17: 18-27, 21: 8-21, 25: 8-18, and 28: 9. By and large, the Biblical story of Prophet Ismael is rather negative, with *Genesis* 17:18-21 maintaining that Prophet Ismael was denied a covenant with Allah and with an earlier passage in *Genesis* describing Prophet Ismael in a most unflattering manner.

> He shall be a wild ass of a man, with his hand against everyone, and everyone's hand against him; and he shall live at odds with all his kin. (*Genesis* 16: 12)

The Biblical portrayal of the prophets of Allah was written from an Israelite perspective, and this perspective often goes to great lengths to deny that any prophet of Allah could have been a non-Israelite or someone who was not a direct ancestor of Prophet Jacob (Israel). Thus, from an Islamic perspective, the Biblical narrative slanders Prophet Lot by accusing him of drunkenness and incest, defames Prophet Ismael by describing him as quoted above, seeks to hide the fact that Prophet Ismael was the intended victim of Prophet Abraham's trial of sacrifice, and falsely denies that Prophet Ismael was a co-heir with Prophet Isaac in inheriting the covenant Allah made with Prophet Abraham. Likewise, as noted later in this chapter, the Biblical narrative attempts to obscure the fact that Prophet Job was an Edomite, not an Israelite.

The Islamic portrayal of Prophet Ismael stands in stark contrast to the Biblical account. As noted previously in the discussion of Prophet Abraham, Islam views Prophet Ismael as having been the willing and steadfast sacrificial victim during Prophet Abraham's trial of sacrifice, and the *Qur'an* directly identifies Prophet Ismael as being the co-builder of the Ka'ba with Prophet Abraham. In the interest of brevity, these narratives are not repeated in full at this time. However, the following Qur'anic passages about Prophet Ismael are noted.

45

Remember We made the house a place of assembly for men and a place of safety; and take ye the station of Abraham as a place of prayer; and We covenanted with Abraham and Isma'il... (*Qur'an* 2:125a)

And Isma'il and Elisha, and Jonah, and Lot: and to all We gave favor above the nations... (*Qur'an* 6: 86)

Also mention in the book (the story of) Isma'il: he was (strictly) true to what he promised, and he was a messenger (and) a prophet. He used to enjoin on his people prayer and charity, and he was most acceptable in the sight of his Lord. (*Qur'an* 19: 54-55)

And (remember) Isma'il, Idris, and Dhu al Kifl, all (men) of constancy and patience; We admitted them to Our mercy: for they were of the righteous ones. (*Qur'an* 21: 85)

And commemorate Isma'il, Elisha, and Dhu al Kifl, each of them was of the company of the good. (*Qur'an* 38: 48)

D6. PROPHET SHU'AYB

The lineage given for Prophet Shu'ayb in Table 3 is based on Al-Tabari, and it is possible that this genealogy is incomplete. The *Qur'an* states that Prophet Shu'ayb was sent to his own people, i.e., the tribe of Midian (Madyan), which was centered in and around the northern Hijaz, i.e., the northwestern corner of contemporary Saudi Arabia. *Qur'an* 11: 89 states that Prophet Shu'ayb was sent some unknown length of time after Prophets Hud, Salih, and Lot. The story of Prophet Shu'ayb is primarily told in four passages in the *Qur'an*, only one of which is quoted below.

To the Madyan people we sent Shu'ayb, one of their own brethren: he said: "O my people! worship Allah; ye have no other god but Him. Now hath come unto you a clear (sign) from your Lord! Give just measure and weight, nor withhold from the people the things that are their due; and do no mischief on the earth after it has been set in order: that will be best for you, if ye have faith. And squat not on every road, breathing threats, hindering from the path of Allah those who believe in Him, and seeking in it something crooked; but remember how ye were little, and He gave you increase. And hold in your mind's eye what was the end of those who did mischief. And if there is a party among you who believes in the message with which I have been sent, and a party which does not believe, hold yourselves in patience until Allah doth decide between us: for He is the best to decide." The leaders, the arrogant party among his people, said: "O Shu'ayb! we shall certainly drive thee out of our city — (thee) and those who believe with thee; or else ye (thou and they) shall have to return to our ways and religion." He said: "What! even though we do detest (them)? We should indeed invent a lie against Allah, if we returned to your ways after Allah hath rescued us therefrom; nor could we by any manner of means return thereto unless it be as in the will and plan of Allah, our Lord. Our Lord can reach out to the utmost recesses of things by His knowledge. In Allah is our trust. Our Lord! decide Thou between us and our people in truth, for Thou art the best to decide." The leaders, the unbelievers among his people, said: "If ye follow Shu'ayb, be sure then ye are ruined!" But the earthquake took them unawares, and they lay prostrate in their homes before the morning! The men who rejected Shu'ayb became as if they had never been in the homes where they had flourished: the men who rejected Shu'ayb — it was they who were ruined! So Shu'ayb left them, saying, "O my people! I did indeed convey to you the messages for which I was sent by my Lord: I gave you good counsel, but how shall I lament over a people who refuse to believe!" (*Qur'an* 7: 85-93; see also *Qur'an* 11: 84-95, 26: 176-191, and 29: 36-37)

There is no Biblical account of Prophet Shu'ayb, although some Muslim commentators on the *Qur'an* have attempted to identify Prophet Shu'ayb with the Midianite father-in-law of Prophet Moses, who is variously identified in the *Bible* as having been: (1) Jethro, priest of Midian (*Exodus* 3: 1, 4:18, and 18: 1-12); (2) Reuel, priest of Midian (*Exodus* 2:15-21); (3) Hobab ibn Reuel, the Midianite (*Numbers* 10: 29); and (4) Hobab, the Kenite (*Judges* 1: 16 and 4: 11). While the *Qur'an* identifies Prophet Shu'ayb as having been a Midianite, and while the *Bible* usually identifies the father-in-law of Prophet Moses as having been a Midianite, this appears to be an extremely slender and flimsy reed, upon which to hang the identification of Prophet Shu'ayb with the father-in-law of Prophet Moses. In fact, the identification of Prophet Shu'ayb with the father-in-law of Prophet Moses appears to be based on nothing more than the fact that they were both Midianites. Further, a chronological consideration (500 years or so should separate Prophet Abraham from Prophet Moses) appears to conflict with the reported lineage of Prophet Shu'ayb, who supposedly was only five generations removed from Prophet Abraham. As such, at least in this author's view, the identification of Prophet Shu'ayb with the father-in-law of Prophet Moses should be rejected.

D7. PROPHET JOB (AYYUB)

The Biblical story of Prophet Job is primarily confined to its own book, which carries the same name as its hero. There are numerous reasons to identify Prophet Job with being an Edomite, rather than an Israelite, including: (1) the geographical names associated with the Biblical story of Prophet Job; (2) the Biblical name of Prophet Job and the names of most of his children and friends are non-Israelite names; (3) the *Bible* specifically identifies several of the friends of Prophet Job as being members of non-Israelite clans or tribes; and (4) the lineage of Prophet Job, as recorded by both Al-Tabari and the *Bible* (*Genesis* 36: 9-13, 34 and *I Chronicles* 1: 34-45, where Prophet Job appears to be listed as Jobab) clearly makes Prophet Job an Edomite, not an Israelite.

Four Qur'anic statements about Prophet Job are quoted immediately below, with the last two being concise parallels of the themes of loss, patient suffering, and eventual redemption that are associated with Prophet Job in the *Bible*.

> We have sent thee inspiration, as We sent it to Noah and the messengers after him: We sent inspiration to Abraham, Isma'il, Isaac, Jacob and the tribes, to Jesus, Job, Jonah, Aaron, and Solomon, and to David We gave the Psalms. (*Qur'an* 4: 163)

> We gave him Isaac and Jacob: all (three) We guided: and before him We guided Noah, and among his progeny, David, Solomon, Job, Joseph, Moses, and Aaron: thus do We reward those who do good... (*Qur'an* 6: 84)

> And (remember) Job, when he cried to his Lord, "Truly distress has seized me. But Thou art the most merciful of those that are merciful." So We listened to him: We removed the distress that was on him, and We restored his people to him, and doubled their number — as a grace from Ourselves, and a thing for commemoration, for all who serve Us. (*Qur'an* 21: 83-84)

> Commemorate Our servant Job. Behold he cried to his Lord: "The evil one has afflicted me with distress and suffering!" (The command was given:) "Strike with thy foot: here is (water) wherein to wash, cool and refreshing and (water) to drink." And We gave him (back) his people and doubled their number — as a grace from Ourselves, and a thing for commemoration, for all who have understanding. "And take in thy hand a little grass, and strike therewith: and break not (thy oath)." Truly, We found him full of patience and constancy, how excellent in Our service! Ever did he turn (to Us)! (*Qur'an* 38: 41-44)

D8. PROPHET DHU AL-KIFL (BISHR)

The identification of Prophet Dhu Al-Kifl, originally called Bishr, as being a son of Prophet Job is from Al-Tabari. He is not mentioned by name in the *Bible*, and only brief references are made to him in the *Qur'an*.

> And (remember) Isma'il, Idris, and Dhu al Kifl, all (men) of constancy and patience; We admitted them to Our mercy: for they were of the righteous ones. (*Qur'an* 21: 85)

> And commemorate Isma'il, Elisha, and Dhu al Kifl: each of them was of the company of the good. (*Qur'an* 38: 48)

E. THE PROPHETS OF BANI ISRAEL

E1. INTRODUCTION

The *Qur'an* mentions numerous prophets of Allah, either by name or by description, who were reportedly or presumably Israelites. Among these Israelite prophets are Jacob, Joseph, Moses, Aaron, Samuel, David, Solomon, Elijah, Elisha, and Jonah, all of whom are noted in the *Bible*. (Islam also considers John the Baptist, his father, Zechariah, and Jesus to be Israelite prophets, but they are discussed separately, as neither Christianity nor Judaism recognize all three of these as being prophets of Allah.)

Table 4

The Prophets of Bani Israel, with Prophets in italics

Abraham/Ibrahim

Isaac

Jacob/Israel/Y'aqub

Levi	*Joseph/Yusuf*	Judah
Kohath		Perez
Izhar		Hezron
		Aram

Korah	Amram/'Imran	Aminadab
Ebiasaph	*Aaron/Haroun* *Moses/Musa*	Nahson
Assir	Eleazar	Salmon
Tahath	Phineas	Boaz
Zephaniah	Yasin	Obed
Azariah	*Elijah/Elias*	Jesse
Joel		*David/Dawud*
Elkanah		*Solomon/Sulayman*
Amasai		
Zuph/Suph		
Tohu/Toah/Tahu		
Elihu/Eliel/Alihu		
Jeruham/Yarukham		
Elkanah/'Alqamah		
Bali		
Samuel		

Table 4 lists the reported relationship of the Israelite prophets to each other, to the pre-Israelite patriarchs, and to the non-Israelite prophets. The genealogies contained in Table 4 are derived from *Genesis, Exodus, I Samuel, I Chronicles*, the *Qur'an*, and Al-Tabari, but problems exist in several of these genealogies. (1) The sources occasionally disagree about the lineage of one or another of these prophets. Typically, such disagreements consist of one source omitting a person named in another source. For example, the Biblical lineage for Prophets Moses and Aaron lists Amram as being the son of Kohath, while Al-Tabari inserts the name of Izhar between Amram and Kohath. Likewise, the Biblical lineage for Prophet Samuel lists him as the son of Elkanah, while Al-Tabari inserts Bali between Elkanah and Prophet Samuel. (2) Another problem is that there does not appear to be enough generations to span the centuries that passed between key individuals in some of these lineages. For example, the three generations of descent between Prophets Aaron and Elijah, which is taken from Al-Tabari, is clearly insufficient to cover the 600 or so years that should separate these two prophets of Allah. Another problem can be illustrated by comparing the reported lineages of Prophet Samuel and Prophet David. Prophet Samuel anointed Saul (Talut) as King of Israel, and Saul was succeeded as king by Prophet David. However, the lineages list Prophet Samuel as being 19 generations removed from Prophet Jacob, while listing Prophet David as being only 11 generations removed from Prophet Jacob. Nonetheless, if not taken too literally and if one allows for the likelihood of missing generations of descent in some of the genealogical lines, Table 4 provides a framework for understanding the interrelationship of the various Israelite prophets with each other.

E2. PROPHET JACOB (Y'AQUB)

The Biblical story of Prophet Jacob is told sporadically and in some depth throughout chapters 25-49 of *Genesis*. In contrast, while acknowledging Jacob as a prophet of Allah, the *Qur'an* mentions Prophet Jacob mainly in passing.

And this was the legacy that Abraham left to his sons, and so did Jacob; "O my sons! Allah hath chosen the faith for you; then die not except in the state of submission (to Allah)." Were ye witnesses when death appeared before Jacob? Behold, he said to his sons: "What will ye worship after me?" They said: "We shall worship thy God and the God of thy fathers, of Abraham, Isma'il and Isaac — the One (True) God: to him we bow (in Islam)." (*Qur'an* 2:132-133)

We gave him Isaac and Jacob: all (three) We guided... (*Qur'an* 6:84a)

When he had turned away from them and from those whom they worshipped besides Allah, We bestowed on him Isaac and Jacob, and each one of them We made a prophet. (*Qur'an* 19:49)

And We bestowed on him Isaac and, as an additional gift, (a grandson) Jacob, and We made righteous men of every one (of them). (*Qur'an* 21:72)

E3. PROPHET JOSEPH (YUSUF)

The Biblical story of Prophet Joseph is told intermittently in chapters 30-50 of *Genesis*, while the Qur'anic account is narrated in a very long passage from the 12th *Surah* (chapter or step; plural is *Surat*) of the *Qur'an*. In what follows, this lengthy passage from the *Qur'an* is quoted verbatim, although it is frequently interrupted to draw parallels to the Biblical account.

Behold, Joseph said to his father: "O my father! I did see eleven stars and the sun and the moon: I saw them prostrate themselves to me!" Said (the father): "My (dear) little son! relate not thy vision to thy brothers, lest they concoct a plot against thee: for Satan is to man an avowed enemy! Thus will thy Lord choose thee and teach thee the interpretation of stories (and events) and perfect His favor to thee and to the posterity of Jacob — even as He perfected it to thy fathers Abraham and Isaac aforetime! For thy Lord is full of knowledge and wisdom." Verily in Joseph and his brethren are signs (or symbols) for seekers (after truth). (*Qur'an* 12:4-7)

The above is the beginning of the Qur'anic saga of Prophet Joseph. In it, one finds a direct parallel to *Genesis* 37: 9-11, including an identical account of Prophet Joseph's vision, which in *Genesis* is said to have been a dream. However, the one major difference between the two accounts is that in *Genesis* Prophet Jacob admonishes Prophet Joseph for daring to suggest that Joseph's parents (the sun and the moon) and brothers (the 11 stars) would bow down to him. In contrast, in the the Qur'anic account, Prophet Jacob asks Prophet Joseph to keep quiet about his vision, because he is worried about a possibly adverse reaction from his other sons, but immediately recognizes that Allah has bestowed His special favor upon Prophet Joseph.

> They said: "Truly Joseph and his brother are loved more by our father than we: but we are a goodly body! Really our father is obviously wandering (in his mind)! Slay ye Joseph or cast him out to some (unknown) land, that so the favor of your father may be given to you alone: (there will be time enough) for you to be righteous after that!" Said one of them: "Slay not Joseph, but if ye must do something, throw him down to the bottom of the well: he will be picked up by some caravan of travelers." (*Qur'an* 12: 8-10)

The above passage parallels the Biblical account of Prophet Joseph and his only full brother, Benjamin, being favored by their father and this favoritism causing jealousy and resentment among their brothers (*Genesis* 37:3-4). It also parallels the Biblical account of the brothers initially plotting to kill Prophet Joseph, but then being convinced by Reuben, Prophet Joseph's oldest half brother, to throw Prophet Joseph into a pit instead, allegedly so that Reuben could later rescue Prophet Joseph and restore him to their father (*Genesis* 37:18-24). Alternatively, *Genesis* 37: 26-27 says that it was Judah who persuaded his brothers not to kill Prophet Joseph, arguing that they should sell him into slavery, rather than kill him.

> They said: "O our father! why dost thou not trust us with Joseph—seeing we are indeed his sincere well-wishers? Send him with us tomorrow to enjoy himself and play, and we shall take every care of him." (Jacob) said: "Really it saddens me that ye should take him away: I fear lest the wolf should devour him while ye attend not to him." They said: "If the wolf were to devour him while we are (so large) a party, then should we indeed (first) have perished ourselves!" So they did take him away, and they all agreed to throw him down to the bottom of the well: and We put into his heart (this message): "Of a surety thou shalt (one day) tell them the truth of this their affair while they know (thee) not." Then they came to their father in the early part of the night, weeping. They said: "O our father! we went racing with one another, and left Joseph with our things; and the wolf devoured him...but thou wilt never believe us even though we tell the truth." They stained his shirt with false blood. He said: "Nay, but your minds have made up a tale (that may pass) with you. (For me) patience is most fitting: against that which ye assert, it is Allah (alone) Whose help can be sought"... (*Qur'an* 12:11-18)

The immediately preceding passage parallels *Genesis* 37:31-35. Both the Qur'anic and Biblical accounts include such details as the brothers staining Prophet Joseph's clothing with blood other than his own, and this clothing being then presented to Prophet Jacob as proof that Prophet Joseph had been devoured by some beast. However, there is one significant difference between the two accounts. In *Genesis*, Prophet Jacob is easily duped by the false story told to him by his sons and bewails the loss of his favorite son. In contrast, in the *Qur'an*, Prophet Jacob easily sees through the deception of his sons and patiently places his trust in Allah.

Then there came a caravan of travelers: they sent their water-carrier (for water), and he let down his bucket (into the well)...He said: "Ah there! Good news! Here is a (fine) young man!" So they concealed him as a treasure! But Allah knoweth well all that they do! The (brethren) sold him for a miserable price — for a few dirhams counted out: in such low estimation did they hold him! (*Qur'an* 12:19-20)

The above passage parallels *Genesis* 37:28, where it is stated that the caravan consisted of Midianites. However, surrounding verses in *Genesis* appear to have difficulty in keeping straight whether Prophet Joseph's captors were Midianites or Ismaelites.

The man in Egypt who bought him, said to his wife: "Make his stay (among us) honorable: maybe he will bring us much good, or we shall adopt him as a son." Thus did We establish Joseph in the land that We might teach him the interpretation of stories (and events). And Allah hath full power and control over His affairs; but most among mankind know it not. When Joseph attained his full manhood, We gave him power and knowledge: thus do We reward those who do right. But she in whose house he was sought to seduce him from his (true) self: she fastened the doors, and said: "Now come, thou (dear one)!" He said: "Allah forbid! Truly (thy husband) is my lord! He made my sojourn agreeable! Truly to no good come those who do wrong!" And (with passion) did she desire him, and he would have desired her, but that he saw the evidence of his lord: thus (did We order) that We might turn away from him (all) evil and shameful deeds: for he was one of Our servants, sincere and purified. So they both raced each other to the door, and she tore his shirt from the back: they both found her lord near the door. She said: "What is the (fitting) punishment for one who formed an evil design against thy wife, but prison or a grievous chastisement?" He said: "It was she that sought to seduce me — from my (true) self." And one of her household saw (this) and bore witness, (thus) — "If it be that his shirt is rent from the front, then is her tale true, and he is a liar! But if it be that his shirt is torn from the back, then is she the liar, and he is telling the truth!" So when he saw his shirt — that it was torn at the back — (her husband) said: "Behold! It is a snare of you women! Truly, mighty is your snare! O Joseph, pass this over! (O wife), ask forgiveness for thy sin, for truly thou hast been at fault!" (*Qur'an* 12: 21-29)

The above passage parallels *Genesis* 39:7-20. Both accounts state that Prophet Joseph's owner's wife tried to seduce him and that Joseph resisted these advances. However, the Qur'anic account states that the woman ripped the back of Prophet Joseph's shirt as he tried to flee, thus setting the stage for the proof of Joseph's innocence in the aborted affair and leading to the husband's demand that his wife apologize to Prophet Joseph. In contrast, the account in *Genesis* has Prophet Joseph slipping out of his garment in order to get away from her grasp, and thus leaving his garment in her hand as he fled, which allowed the wife to convince her husband to imprison Prophet Joseph for having attempted to assault her. In the Qur'anic narrative, Prophet Joseph is not imprisoned at this time, while he is immediately imprisoned in the parallel passage from *Genesis*.

Ladies said in the city: "The wife of the (great) 'Aziz is seeking to seduce her slave from his (true) self: truly hath he inspired her with violent love: we see she is evidently going astray." When she heard of their malicious talk, she sent for them and prepared a banquet for them: she gave each of them a knife: and she said (to Joseph), "Come out before them." When they saw him, they did extol him, and (in their amazement) cut their hands: they said, "Allah preserve us! No mortal is this! This is none other than a noble angel!" She said: "There before you is the man about whom ye did blame me! I did seek to seduce him from his (true) self but he did firmly save himself guiltless!... And now, if he doth not my bidding, he shall certainly be cast into prison, and (what is more) be of the company of the vilest!" He said: "O my Lord! the prison is more to my liking than that to which they invite me: unless

Thou turn away their snare from me, I should (in my youthful folly) feel inclined towards them and join the ranks of the ignorant." So his Lord hearkened to him (in his prayer) and turned away from him their snare: verily He heareth and knoweth (all things). Then it occurred to the men after they had seen the signs, (that it was best) to imprison him for a time. (*Qur'an* 12:30-35)

Unlike the Qur'anic account, *Genesis* 39: 7-20 had Prophet Joseph being unfairly judged guilty of attempting to assault his owner's wife in the affair of the garment, and thus being immediately imprisoned. As such, *Genesis* has no parallel to the main story of the immediately preceding passage from the *Qur'an*. However, a couple of minor points of comparison still need to be made. Firstly, *Genesis* 37: 36 and 39: 1 give Potiphar as being the name of Prophet Joseph's Egyptian owner. In contrast, the above passage from the *Qur'an* refers to the owner as being 'Aziz. 'Aziz means exalted in rank, and is probably a title, rather than a name. Secondly, *Genesis* 39: 6 refers to Prophet Joseph as being "handsome and good-looking", which compares favorably with Prophet Joseph's beauty, as stated in the above passage from the *Qur'an*. Thirdly, while *Genesis* 39: 7-20 has Prophet Joseph being unfairly judged guilty of assaulting his owner's wife, and thus being imprisoned, the *Qur'an* presents Prophet Joseph's imprisonment as being secondary to Allah answering Prophet Joseph's prayer to be imprisoned, rather than risk finally succumbing to attempts to seduce him. Thus, Prophet Joseph's imprisonment is seen as an illustration of his extreme piety and rectitude of conduct.

Now with him there came into the prison two young men. Said one of them: "I see myself (in a dream) pressing wine." Said the other: "I see myself (in a dream) carrying bread on my head, and birds are eating thereof." "Tell us" (they said) "the truth and meaning thereof: for we see thou art one that doth good (to all)." He said: "Before any food comes (in due course) to feed either of you, I will surely reveal to you the truth and meaning of this ere it befall you. That is part of the (duty) which my Lord hath taught me. I have (I assure you) abandoned the ways of a people that believe not in Allah and that (even) deny the hereafter. And I follow the ways of my fathers — Abraham, Isaac, and Jacob; and never could we attribute any partners whatever to Allah: that (comes) of the grace of Allah to us and to mankind: yet most men are not grateful. O my two companions of the prison! (I ask you): are many lords differing among themselves better, or Allah, the One, supreme and irresistible? If not Him, ye worship nothing but names which ye have named — ye and your fathers — for which Allah hath sent down no authority: the command is for none but Allah: He hath commanded that ye worship none but Him: that is the right religion, but most men understand not... O my two companions of the prison! as to one of you, he will pour out the wine for his lord to drink: as for the other, he will hang from the cross, and the birds will eat from off his head. (So) hath been decreed that matter whereof ye twain do enquire"... And of the two, to that one whom he considered about to be saved, he said: "Mention me to thy lord." But Satan made him forget to mention him to his lord: and (Joseph) lingered in prison a few (more) years. (*Qur'an* 12: 36-42)

The above passage offers many and striking parallels with the 40th chapter of *Genesis*. In both the *Qur'an* and *Genesis*, two men are imprisoned with Prophet Joseph, with *Genesis* stating that these men were formerly the chief cupbearer and the chief baker to the ruler of Egypt. In both the Qur'anic and Biblical versions, both of these men have dreams (one of pressing wine or grapes; the other of carrying bread or cakes on his head, and that these bread or cakes are then attacked by birds). In both versions, Prophet Joseph interprets the dreams of his prison comrades, but the *Qur'an* stresses that Prophet Joseph first witnessed to them about Allah, thus providing a more spiritual dimension to the story. In both versions, the dream interpretation reveals that the wine or grape presser will be restored to his former position, but that the other prisoner will be killed by being hung from a cross or pole. In both versions, Prophet Joseph requests that the to-be-freed prisoner mention Prophet Joseph's situation to his master, but that the prisoner forgets to do so. Clearly, one is here dealing with a common religious history and heritage!

> The king (of Egypt) said: "I do see (in a vision) seven fat kine, whom seven lean ones devour — and seven green ears of corn, and seven (others) withered. O ye chiefs! expound to me my vision, if it be that ye can interpret visions." They said: "A confused medley of dreams: and we are not skilled in the interpretation of dreams." But the man who had been released, one of the two (who had been in prison) and who now bethought him after (so long) a space of time, said: "I will tell you the truth of its interpretation: send ye me (therefore)." "O Joseph!" (he said). "O man of truth! expound to us (the dream) of seven fat kine whom seven lean ones devour, and of seven green ears of corn and (seven) others withered: that I may return to the people, and that they may understand." (Joseph) said: "For seven years shall ye diligently sow as is your wont: and the harvests that ye reap, ye shall leave them in the ear — except a little, of which ye shall eat. Then will come after that (period) seven dreadful (years), which will devour what ye shall have laid by in advance for them — (all) except a little which ye shall have (specially) guarded. Then will come after that (period) a year in which the people will have abundant water, and in which they will press (wine and oil)." (Qur'an 12: 43-49)

The Biblical parallel to the above Qur'anic passage is found in *Genesis* 41: 1-36. In both versions, the ruler of Egypt has the same two dreams, which his sages and counselors are unable to interpret. In both versions, Prophet Joseph's former prisonmate then belatedly remembers Prophet Joseph, who successfully interprets the dreams as indicating seven years of plenty to be followed by seven years of famine. However, there are two differences between the versions regarding certain details. (1) In

Genesis, Prophet Joseph is brought before the ruler to make his interpretation, while he relays his interpretation through his former prisonmate in the *Qur'an*. (2) In *Genesis*, only 20% of the harvest from the years of plenty is to be stored for the coming years of famine. In contrast, the *Qur'an* implies that most of the harvest during the years of plenty was to be stored. On a purely rational basis, the latter figure appears to be more realistic, as the stored grain had to be sufficient to sustain Egypt throughout seven full years of crop failure, and had to be sufficient to continue to allow for the export of grain and for the feeding of the masses that flocked to Egypt during the seven years of famine, including Prophet Joseph's brothers.

> So the king said: "Bring ye him unto me." But when the messenger came to him, (Joseph) said: "Go thou back to thy lord, and ask him, 'What is the state of mind of the ladies who cut their hands?' For my lord is certainly well aware of their snare." (The king) said (to the ladies): "What was your affair when ye did seek to seduce Joseph from his (true) self?" The ladies said: "Allah preserve us! No evil know we against him!" Said the 'Aziz's wife: "Now is the truth manifest (to all): it was I who sought to seduce him from his (true) self: he is indeed of those who are (ever) true (and virtuous). This (say I), in order that he may know that I have never been false to him in his absence, and that Allah will never guide the snare of the false ones. Nor do I absolve my own self (of blame): the (human) soul is certainly prone to evil, unless my Lord does bestow His mercy: but surely my Lord is oft- forgiving, most merciful." (*Qur'an* 12: 50-53)

The above passage illustrates that Prophet Joseph was reluctant to leave the prison until he was assured regarding the intentions of the women who had previously been infatuated with him. The wife of the 'Aziz again confessed her previous wrongs and appeared to be repentant. There is no Biblical parallel to this passage. However, the first of the two following passages appears to present a variant account to that of *Genesis* 41: 37-45.

So the king said: "Bring him unto me; I will take him specially to serve about my own person." Therefore when he had spoken to him, he said: "Be assured this day, thou art, before our own presence, with rank firmly established, and fidelity fully proved!" Joseph said: "Set me over the storehouses of the land: I will indeed guard them, as one that knows (their importance)." Thus did We give established power to Joseph in the land, to take possession therein as, when, or where he pleased. We bestow of our mercy on whom We please, and We suffer not, to be lost, the reward of those who do good. But verily the reward of the hereafter is the best, for those who believe, and are constant in righteousness. (*Qur'an* 12: 54-57)

Then came Joseph's brethren: they entered his presence, and he knew them, but they knew him not. And when he had furnished them forth with provisions (suitable) for them, he said: "Bring unto me a brother ye have, of the same father as yourselves, (but a different mother): see ye not that I pay out full measure, and that I do provide the best hospitality? Now if ye bring him not to me, ye shall have no measure (of corn) from me, nor shall ye (even) come near me." They said: "We shall certainly seek to get our wish about him from his father: indeed we shall do it." And (Joseph) told his servants to put their stock in trade (with which they had bartered) into their saddlebags, so they should know it only when they returned to their people, in order that they might come back. (*Qur'an* 12: 58-62)

The Biblical parallel to the second of the above passages is found in *Genesis* 42: 1-25. The two passages present similar, if not identical, information with regard to most details of the story. However, one noticeable difference exists between the two passages. Unlike the above passage from the *Qur'an*, *Genesis* states that Prophet Joseph accused his brothers of spying and threatened to imprison all but one of them, with the freed brother to go and fetch Prophet Joseph's 11th brother, Benjamin, who is identified as such in the *Qur'an* by implying that he was out of a different mother than Joseph's and Benjamin's 10 half brothers. Eventually, according to the account in *Genesis*, Prophet Joseph retains one brother, Simeon, as a bound and imprisoned hostage, and sends the other nine to fetch Benjamin.

Now when they returned to their father, they said: "O our father! no more measure of grain shall we get (unless we take our brother): so send our brother with us, that we may get our measure; and we will indeed take every care of him." He said: "Shall I trust you with him with any result other than when I trusted you with his brother aforetime? But Allah is the best to take care (of him), and He is the most merciful of those who show mercy!" Then when they opened their baggage, they found their stock in trade had been returned to them. They said: "O our father! what (more) can we desire? This, our stock in trade, has been returned to us: so we shall get (more) food for our family; we shall take care of our brother; and add (at the same time) a full camel's load (of grain to our provisions). This is but a small quantity." (Jacob) said: "Never will I send him with you until ye swear a solemn oath to me, in Allah's name, that ye will be sure to bring him back to me unless ye are yourselves hemmed in (and made powerless)." And when they had sworn their solemn oath, he said: "Over all that we say, be Allah the witness and guardian!" Further he said: "O my sons! enter not all by one gate: enter ye by different gates. Not that I can profit you aught against Allah (with my advice): none can command except Allah: on Him do I put my trust: and let all that trust put their trust on Him." (*Qur'an* 12: 63-67)

The Biblical parallel to the preceding passage from the *Qur'an* is found in *Genesis* 42: 26-43: 15. While there are differences in various details between the two passages, the main thrust of the story remains the same between them.

And when they entered in the manner their father had enjoined, it did not profit them in the least against (the plan of) Allah: it was but a necessity of Jacob's soul, which he discharged. For he was, by Our instruction, full of knowledge (and experience): but most men know not. Now when they came into Joseph's presence, he received his (full) brother to stay with him. He said (to him): "Behold! I am thy (own) brother; so grieve not at aught of their doings." At length when he had furnished them forth with provisions (suitable) for them, he put the drinking cup into his brother's saddlebag. Then shouted out a crier: "O ye (in) the caravan! behold! ye are thieves, without doubt!" They said, turning towards them: "What is it that ye miss?" They said: "We miss the great beaker of the king; for him who produces it, is (the reward of) a camel load; I will be bound by it." (The brothers) said: "By Allah! Well ye know that we came not to make mischief in the land, and we are no thieves!" (The Egyptians) said: "What then shall be the penalty of this, if ye are (proved) to have lied?" They said: "The penalty should be that he in whose saddlebag it is found, should be held (as bondman) to atone for the (crime). Thus it is we punish the wrongdoers!" So he began (the search) with their baggage, before (he came to) the baggage of his brother: at length he brought it out of his brother's baggage. Thus did We plan for Joseph. He could not take his brother by the law of the king except that Allah willed it (so). We raise to degrees (of wisdom) whom We please: but over all endued with knowledge is One, the all-knowing. They said: "If he steals, there was a brother of his who did steal before (him)." But these things did Joseph keep locked in his heart, revealing not the secrets to them. He (simply) said (to himself): "Ye are the worse situated; and Allah knoweth best the truth of what ye assert!" They said: "O exalted one! behold! he has a father, aged and venerable, (who will grieve for him); so take one of us in his place; for we see that thou art (gracious) in doing good." He said: "Allah forbid that we take other than him with whom we found our property:

indeed (if we did so), we should be acting wrongfully." (*Qur'an* 12: 68-79)

Although there are some differences in detail, e.g., the Biblical account talks about the brothers dining in Prophet Joseph's house, the above passage from the *Qur'an* is paralleled by *Genesis* 43: 16-44: 34. Both accounts tell the story of the cup being placed and found in Benjamin's bags, of the brothers being told that Benjamin would be held as a slave for his "crime", of the brothers asking that someone else be held in Benjamin's place, and of Prophet Joseph's refusal to replace Benjamin with another.

Now when they saw no hope of his (yielding), they held a conference in private. The leader among them said: "Know ye not that your father did take an oath from you in Allah's name, and how before this, ye did fail in your duty with Joseph? Therefore will I not leave this land until my father permits me, or Allah commands me; and He is the best to command. Turn ye back to your father, and say, 'O our father! behold! thy son committed theft! We bear witness only to what we know, and we could not well guard against the unseen! Ask at the town where we have been and the caravan in which we returned, and (you will find) we are indeed telling the truth.'" Jacob said: "Nay, but ye have yourselves contrived a story (good enough) for you. So patience is most fitting (for me). Maybe Allah will bring them (back) all to me (in the end). For He is indeed full of knowledge and wisdom." And he turned away from them, and said: "How great is my grief for Joseph!" And his eyes became white with sorrow, and he fell into silent melancholy. They said: "By Allah ! (never) wilt thou cease to remember Joseph until thou reach the last extremity of illness, or until thou die!" He said: "I only complain of my distraction and anguish to Allah, and I know from Allah that which ye know not... O my sons! go ye and enquire about Joseph and his brother, and never give up hope of Allah's soothing mercy: truly no one despairs of Allah's soothing mercy, except those who have no faith." (*Qur'an* 12: 80-87)

The above passage has no Biblical parallel. In *Genesis* 45: 1-3, Prophet Joseph identified himself to his brothers at the end of the story of the stolen cup. In contrast, the *Qur'an* has the preceding story separating the account of the stolen cup and the account of Prophet Joseph identifying himself to his remaining brothers.

Then, when they came (back) into (Joseph's) presence they said: "O exalted one! distress has seized us and our family: we have (now) brought but scanty capital: so pay us full measure, (we pray thee), and treat it as charity to us: for Allah doth reward the charitable." He said: "Know ye how ye dealt with Joseph and his brother, not knowing (what ye were doing)?" They said: "Art thou indeed Joseph?" He said, "I am Joseph, and this is my brother: Allah has indeed been gracious to us (all): behold, he that is righteous and patient — never will Allah suffer the reward to be lost, of those who do right." They said: "By Allah! indeed has Allah preferred thee above us, and we certainly have been guilty of sin!" He said: "This day let no reproach be (cast) on you: Allah will forgive you, and He is the most merciful of those who show mercy! Go with this my shirt, and cast it over the face of my father: he will come to see (clearly). Then come ye (here) to me together with all your family." When the caravan left (Egypt), their father said: "I do indeed scent the presence of Joseph: nay, think me not a dotard." They said: "By Allah! truly thou art in thine old wandering mind." Then when the bearer of the good news came, he cast (the shirt) over his face, and he forthwith regained clear sight. He said: "Did I not say to you, 'I know from Allah that which ye know not?'" They said: "O our father! ask for us forgiveness for our sins, for we were truly at fault." He said: "Soon will I ask my Lord for forgiveness for you: for He is indeed oft-forgiving, most merciful." Then when they entered the presence of Joseph, he provided a home for his parents with himself, and said: "Enter ye Egypt (all) in safety if it please Allah." And he raised his parents high on the throne (of dignity), and they fell down in prostration, (all) before him. He said: "O my father! this is the fulfillment of my vision of old! Allah hath made it come true! He was indeed good to me when He took me out of prison and brought you (all here) out of the desert, (even) after Satan had sown enmity between me and my brothers. Verily my Lord understandeth best the mysteries of all that he planneth to do. For verily He is full of knowledge and wisdom. O my Lord! Thou hast indeed bestowed on me some power, and taught me something of the interpretation of dreams and events – O Thou creator of the heavens and the earth! Thou art my protector in this world and in the hereafter. Take Thou my soul (at death) as one submitting to Thy will (as a Muslim), and unite me with the righteous." (*Qur'an* 12: 88-101)

The above passage concludes the Qur'anic account of the life of Prophet Joseph and parallels the main outlines of *Genesis* 45: 1-47: 12. However, there is one glaring inconsistency between the Qur'anic and Biblical accounts. *Qur'an* 12: 99 states that Prophet Joseph "provided a home for his parents", implying that his mother, Rachel, was still alive. In contrast, *Genesis* 35:16-21 states that Rachel died immediately after giving birth to Benjamin, necessitating that Rachel had been dead for many years before Prophet Jacob's family settled in Egypt. This discrepancy can be resolved by referring to *Genesis* 37: 9-10, which parallels *Qur'an* 12: 4-5 and which presents the Biblical version of Prophet Joseph's dream of the the sun, the moon, and the 11 stars bowing down to him.

He had another dream, and told it to his brothers, saying, "Look, I have had another dream: the sun, the moon, and eleven stars were bowing down to me." But when he told it to his father and to his brothers, his father rebuked him, and said to him, "What kind of dream is this that you have had? Shall we indeed come, I and your mother and your brothers, and bow to the ground before you?" (*Genesis* 37: 9-10)

The above Biblical passage certainly implies that Rachel was still alive at the time of the above dream, which would have been some time after her reported death in *Genesis* 35: 16-21. Further, given the interpretation of the dream as found in the above passage, the only way the dream could ever have been fulfilled would have been if Rachel were still alive at the time Prophet Jacob's family journeyed into Egypt to live. The Qur'anic account solves this problem by implying that Rachel was still alive at the time Prophet Jacob's family entered Egypt (*Qur'an* 12: 99), and by noting that at that time Prophet Joseph's parents and brothers prostrated before him (*Qur'an* 12: 100).

E4. PROPHETS MOSES (MUSA) AND AARON (HAROUN)

Prophet Moses' name is mentioned over 170 times in 'Ali's English translation of the meaning of the *Qur'an*. Frequently, these Qur'anic references to Prophet Moses are coupled with mention of his brother, Prophet Aaron. As can thus be seen, space does not permit a complete reporting of the passages in the *Qur'an* that deal with Prophets Moses and Aaron. As such, the author has selected only a few passages, picking those that recount stories that will be familiar to most students of the *Bible*.

> So We sent this inspiration to the mother of Moses: "Suckle (thy child), but when thou hast fears about him, cast him into the river, but fear not nor grieve: for We shall restore him to thee, and We shall make him one of Our messengers." Then the people of Pharaoh picked him up (from the river): (it was intended) that (Moses) should be to them an adversary and a cause of sorrow: for Pharaoh and Haman and (all) their hosts were men of sin. The wife of Pharaoh said: "(Here is) a joy of the eye, for me and for thee: slay him not. It may be that he will be of use to us, or we may adopt him as a son." And they perceived not (what they were doing)! But there came to be a void in the heart of the mother of Moses: she was going almost to disclose his (case), had We not strengthened her heart (with faith), so that she might remain a (firm)

believer. And she said to the sister of (Moses), "Follow him", so she (the sister) watched him in the character of a stranger, and they knew not. And We ordained that he refused to suck at first, until (his sister came up and) said: "Shall I point out to you the people of a house that will nourish and bring him up for you and be sincerely attached to him?"... Thus did We restore him to his mother that her eye might be comforted, that she might not grieve, and that she might know that the promise of Allah is true; but most of them do not understand. (*Qur'an* 28: 7-13; see also *Qur'an* 20: 37-40)

The Biblical parallel to the above passage from the *Qur'an* is found in *Exodus* 2: 1-10. In both accounts, the infant Moses is placed upon the river, his sister follows him from the river bank, and his sister arranges for Prophet Moses to be suckled by his own mother. However, in the Qur'anic account, Prophet Moses is rescued from the river by the wife of the pharaoh, while it is the daughter of the pharaoh who rescues him in the Biblical version. This discrepancy may be more illusory than real, as the pharaonic family of Egypt was known to marry within itself. As such, the rescuer of Prophet Moses may have been both daughter of one pharaoh and wife of another.

And he entered the city at a time when its people were not watching: and he found there two men fighting — one of his own people, and the other of his foes. Now the man of his own people appealed to him against his foe, and Moses struck him with his fist and made an end of him. He said: "This is a work of evil (Satan): for he is an enemy that manifestly misleads!" He prayed: "O my Lord! I have indeed wronged my soul! Do Thou then forgive me!" So (Allah) forgave him: for He is the oft-forgiving, most merciful. He said: "O my Lord! for that Thou hast bestowed Thy grace on me, never shall I be a help to those who sin!" So he saw the morning in the city, looking about in a state of fear, when behold, the man who had the day before sought his help called aloud for his help (again). Moses said to him: "Thou art truly, it is clear, a quarrelsome fellow!" Then, when he decided to lay hold of the man who was an enemy to both of them, that man said: "O Moses! is it thy intention to slay me as thou slewest a man yesterday? Thy intention is none other than to become a powerful violent man in the land, and not to be one who sets things right!" And there came a man, running, from the furthest end of the city. He said: "O Moses! the chiefs are taking counsel together about thee, to slay thee so get thee away, for I do give thee sincere advice." He therefore got away therefrom, looking about in a state of fear. He prayed: "O my Lord! save me from people given to wrong-doing." (*Qur'an* 28: 15-21)

The above passage from the *Qur'an* is a close parallel to the Biblical story found in *Exodus* 2: 11-15a. *Exodus* 2: 15b-22 continues the Biblical story by recounting how Prophet Moses fled to the land of the Midianites (Madyan), befriended the daughters of the priest of Midian at a shepherd's well as they were attempting to water their flock, and subsequently married one of them, i.e., Zipporah. The following passage from the *Qur'an* offers a close parallel to that account.

Then, when he turned his face towards (the land of) Madyan, he said: "I do hope that my Lord will show me the smooth and straight path." And when he arrived at the watering (place) in Madyan, he found there a group of men watering (their flocks), and besides them he found two women who were keeping back (their flocks). He said: "What is the matter with you?" They said: "We cannot water (our flocks) until the shepherds take back (their flocks); and our father is a very old man." So he watered (their flocks) for them; then he turned back to the shade, and said: "O my Lord! truly am I in (desperate) need of any good that Thou dost send me!"... Afterwards one of the (damsels) came (back) to him, walking bashfully. She said: "My father invites thee that he may reward thee for having watered (our flocks) for us." So when he came to him and narrated the story, he said: "Fear thou not: (well) hast thou escaped from unjust people." Said one of the (damsels): "O my (dear) father! engage him on wages: truly the best of men for thee to employ is the (man) who is strong and trusty"... He said: "I intend to wed one of these my daughters to thee, on condition that thou serve me for eight years; but if thou complete ten years, it will be (grace) from thee. But I intend not to place thee under a difficulty: thou wilt find me, indeed, if Allah wills, one of the righteous." He said: "Be that (the agreement) between me and thee: whichever of the two terms I fulfil, let there be no ill-will to me. Be Allah a witness to what we say." (*Qur'an* 28: 22-28)

According to *Exodus* 3:1-4:17, Prophet Moses received his prophetic call at the burning bush on Mt. Horeb at some point after marrying Zipporah. At that time, Prophet Moses was directed by Allah to return to Egypt to liberate the Israelites, was given miracles to perform (his rod would turn into a snake when cast upon the ground, and his hand would turn a leprous white when he removed it from his cloak), and was told that his brother, Prophet Aaron, who was more eloquent in speech than Prophet Moses, would assist him in confronting the pharaoh. This story is a close parallel to the following passage from the *Qur'an*.

Now when Moses had fulfilled the term, and was traveling with his family, he perceived a fire in the direction of Mount Tur. He said to his family: "Tarry ye; I perceive a fire; I hope to bring you from there some information, or a burning firebrand, that ye may warm yourselves." But when he came to the (fire), a voice was heard from the right bank of the valley, from a tree in hallowed ground: "O Moses! verily I am Allah, the Lord of the worlds... Now do thou throw thy rod!" But when he saw it moving (of its own accord) as if it had been a snake, he turned back in retreat, and retraced not his steps: "O Moses!" (it was said), "Draw near, and fear not:

for thou art of those who are secure. Move thy hand into thy bosom, and it will come forth white without stain (or harm), and draw thy hand close to thy side (to guard) against fear. Those are the two credentials from thy Lord to Pharaoh and his chiefs: for truly they are a people rebellious and wicked." He said: "O my Lord! I have slain a man among them, and I fear lest they slay me. And my brother Aaron — he is more eloquent in speech than I: so send him with me as a helper, to confirm (and strengthen) me: for I fear that they may accuse me of falsehood." He said: "We will certainly strengthen thy arm through thy brother, and invest you both with authority, so they shall not be able to touch you: with Our signs shall ye triumph — you two as well as those who follow you." (*Qur'an* 28: 29-35; see also *Qur'an* 19: 51-53, 20: 9-36, and 26: 10-17)

In the above passage, the mountain of the prophetic call is referred to as Mount Tur, and *Qur'an* 20:12 and 79: 15-16 identify this mountain as being next to a valley known as Tuwa. In contrast, *Exodus* 3: 1 identifies the mountain as being Horeb. However, it is not just the case that the *Qur'an* and *Exodus* disagree with each other on the name of this mountain. Within the second through fifth books of the *Bible*, there is significant disagreement as to whether this mountain was Horeb or Sinai. The former name is used in *Exodus* 3: 1, 17: 5-6, and 33: 6 and in *Deuteronomy* 1: 1-19, 4: 9-15, 5: 2, 9: 8, 18: 16, and 29: 1, while the latter name is found in *Exodus* 19: 11-23, 24: 16, 31: 18, and 34: 2-32, in *Leviticus* 7: 37-38, 25: 1, 26: 46, and 27: 34, and in *Numbers* 3: 1 and 28: 6.

Exodus 5:1-12: 32 gives the Biblical version of Prophets Moses and Aaron confronting the pharaoh of Egypt. According to this version, the two prophets initially confronted the pharaoh and demanded the release of the Israelites. The pharaoh responded with even harsher treatment to the Israelites, which caused the Israelites to complain to Prophets Moses and Aaron that the two prophets were creating hardships for them with the Egyptians (*Exodus* 5:19-21). The two prophets then approached the pharaoh a second time, and Prophet Aaron threw down his staff, and it became a snake that swallowed the snakes created by the magicians of Egypt from their rods (*Exodus* 7: 8-12). (Note: according to *Exodus* 4:1-5, this was the miracle that Allah had given to Prophet Moses, not to Prophet Aaron.) Nonetheless, the pharaoh would still not release the Israelites, and a succession of plagues fell upon the Egyptians as a result. The following passage from the *Qur'an* nicely parallels the above story as found in *Exodus*, clearly states that Prophet Moses was the one whose rod became a serpent, and adds a spiritual dimension by noting that the magicians of the pharaoh were converted by the signs and testimony of Prophets Moses and Aaron.

> Moses said: "O Pharaoh! I am a messenger from the Lord of the worlds — one for whom it is right to say nothing but truth about Allah. Now have I come unto you (people), from your Lord, with a clear (sign): so let the children of Israel depart along with me." (Pharaoh) said: "If indeed thou hast come with a sign, show it forth — if thou tellest the truth." Then (Moses) threw his rod, and behold! it was a serpent, plain (for all to see). And he drew out his hand, and behold! it was white to all beholders! Said the chiefs of the people of Pharaoh: "This is indeed a sorcerer well-versed. His plan is to get you out of your land: then what is it ye counsel?" They said: "Keep him and his brother in suspense (for awhile); and send to the cities men to collect — and bring up to thee all (our) socerers well-versed." So there came the sorcerers to Pharaoh: they said, "Of course we shall have a (suitable) reward if we win!" He said: "Yea, (and more) — for ye shall in that case be (raised to posts) nearest (to my person)." They said: "O Moses! wilt thou throw (first), or shall we have the (first) throw?" Said Moses: "Throw ye (first)." So when they threw, they bewitched the eyes of the people, and struck terror into them: for they showed a great (feat of) magic. We put it into Moses's mind by inspiration: "Throw (now) thy rod": and behold! it swallows up straightaway all the

falsehoods which they fake! Thus truth was confirmed. And all that they did was made of no effect. So the (great ones) were vanquished there and then, and were made to look small. But the sorcerers fell down prostrate in adoration. Saying: "We believe in the Lord of the worlds. The Lord of Moses and Aaron." Said Pharaoh: "Believe ye in Him before I give you permission? Surely this is a trick which ye have planned in the city to drive out its people: but soon shall ye know (the consequences). Be sure I will cut off your hands and your feet on opposite sides, and I will cause you all to die on the cross." They said:"For us, we are but sent back unto our Lord: but thou dost wreak thy vengeance on us simply because we believed in the signs of our Lord when they reached us! Our Lord! pour out on us patience and constancy, and take our souls unto Thee as Muslims (who bow to Thy will)!" Said the chiefs of Pharaoh's people: "Wilt thou leave Moses and his people, to spread mischief in the land, and to abandon thee and thy gods?" He said, "Their male children will we slay; (only) their females will we save alive; and we have over them (power) irresistible." Said Moses to his people: "Pray for help from Allah," and (wait) in patience and constancy: for the earth is Allah's to give as a heritage to such of His servants as He pleaseth; and the end is (best) for the righteous. They said: "We have had (nothing but) trouble, both before and after thou camest to us." He said: "It may be that your Lord will destroy your enemy and make you inheritors in the earth; that so He may try you by your deeds." We punished the people of Pharaoh with years (of drought) and shortness of crops; that they might receive admonition. But when good (times) came, they said, "This is due to us;" when gripped by calamity they ascribed it to evil omens connected with Moses and those with him! Behold! in truth the omens of evil are theirs in Allah's sight, but most of them do not understand! They said (to Moses): "Whatever be the signs thou bringest, to work therewith thy sorcery on us, we shall never believe in thee." So We sent (plagues) on them: wholesale death, locusts, lice, frogs, and blood: signs openly self-explained: but they were steeped in arrogance, a people given to sin. Every time the penalty fell on them, they said: "O Moses! on our behalf call on thy Lord in virtue of His promise to thee: if thou wilt remove the penalty from us, we shall truly believe in thee, and we shall send away the children of Israel with thee." But every time We removed the penalty from them according to a fixed term which they had to fulfil — behold! they broke their word! (*Qur'an* 7:104-135; see also *Qur'an* 10: 75-89, 11: 96-97, 17: 101-102, 20: 42-73, 23: 45-48, 26: 16-51, 28: 36-39, 43: 46-54, 51: 38-39, and 79: 15-24)

Exodus 12:33-14:31 presents the Biblical version of the Israelite exodus from Egypt, which ended with Prophet Moses parting the waters of what is variously held to be the Red Sea and the Sea of Reeds. With the waters parted, the Israelites crossed safely. When the Egyptians attempted to cross, the water closed in over them and drowned them. The following passage from the *Qur'an* provides an excellent parallel to this Biblical narrative.

By inspiration We told Moses: "Travel by night with My servants; for surely ye shall be pursued." Then Pharaoh sent heralds to (all) the cities, (saying): "These (Israelites) are but a small band, and they are raging furiously against us; but we are a multitude amply forewarned." ...So they pursued them at sunrise. And when the two bodies saw each other, the people of Moses said: "We are sure to be overtaken." (Moses) said: "By no means! My Lord is with Me! Soon will He guide me!" Then We told Moses by inspiration: "Strike the sea with thy rod." So it divided, and each separate part became like the huge, firm mass of a mountain. And We made the other party approach thither. We delivered Moses and all who were with him; but We drowned the others. (*Qur'an* 26:52-56 and 60-66; see also *Qur'an* 7:136, 10:90-92, 17:103, 20:77-78, 43:55-56, 51:40)

Having journeyed out of Egypt, the Israelites began the wanderings in the wilderness. *Exodus* 31: 18-32: 35 and *Deuteronomy* 9:8-29 report that it was during the sojourn in the wilderness that the following events took place. (1) Prophet Moses ascended Mt. Sinai and received the tablets of the covenant from Allah. (2) During Prophet Moses' absence, Prophet Aaron and the Israelites smelted gold to create a golden calf for idol worship. (3) Allah told Prophet Moses about the idolatry of the Israelites, and Prophet Moses descended from the mountain, carrying the tablets of the covenant. (4) When Prophet Moses approached the Israelite camp and saw the golden calf and the dancing of the Israelites, his "anger burned hot", he threw down and broke the tablets of the covenant, and he burned the golden calf, ground it to powder, mixed it with water, and made the Israelites drink it. (5) Thereafter, he upbraided Prophet Aaron, who had allegedly been a willing participant in the worship of the golden calf, and who had allegedly "let them (the Israelites) run wild". (6) Then, Prophet Moses had the Levites slaughter 3,000 of the Israelites and returned to the mountain to ask Allah's forgiveness for the Israelites. There are several Qur'anic parallels to this Biblical report, although all have some significant differences from the accounts of *Exodus* and *Deuteronomy*. The following passage from the *Qur'an* is one of the more complete narratives of this story.

> The people of Moses made in his absence, out of their ornaments, the image of a calf (for worship): it seemed to low: did they not see that it could neither speak to them, nor show them the way? They took it for worship and they did wrong. When they repented, and saw that they had erred, they said: "If our Lord have not mercy upon us and forgive us, we shall indeed be of those who perish." When Moses came back to his people, angry and grieved, he said: "Evil it is that ye have done in my place in my absence: did ye make haste to bring on the judgment of your Lord?" He put down the Tablets, seized his brother by (the hair of) his head, and

dragged him to him. Aaron said: "Son of my mother! the people did indeed reckon me as naught, and went near to slaying me! Make not the enemies rejoice over my misfortune, nor count thou me amongst the people of sin." Moses prayed: "O my Lord! forgive me and my brother! Admit us to Thy mercy! For Thou art the most merciful of those who show mercy!" Those who took the calf (for worship) will indeed be overwhelmed with wrath from their Lord, and with shame in this life: thus do We recompense those who invent (falsehoods). But those who do wrong but repent thereafter and (truly) believe — verily thy Lord is thereafter oft-forgiving, most merciful. When the anger of Moses was appeased, he took up the Tablets: in the writing thereon was guidance and mercy for such as fear their Lord. And Moses chose seventy of his people for Our place of meeting: when they were seized with violent quaking, he prayed: "O my Lord! if it had been Thy will Thou couldst have destroyed, long before, both them and me: wouldst Thou destroy us for the deeds of the foolish ones among us? This is no more than Thy trial: by it Thou causes whom Thou wilt to stray, and Thou leadest whom Thou wilt into the right path. Thou art our protector: so forgive us and give us Thy mercy; for Thou art the best of those who forgive. And ordain for us that which is good, in this life and in the hereafter: for we have turned unto Thee." He said: "With My punishment I visit whom I will; but My mercy extendeth to all things. That (mercy) I shall ordain for those who do right, and practise regular charity, and those who believe in Our signs —" (*Qur'an* 7: 148-156; see also *Qur'an* 2: 51-55 and 20: 86-98)

Several of the differences between the Qur'anic and Biblical accounts of the above events need to be emphasized. (1) While the *Bible* states that Prophet Moses threw down and broke the tablets of the covenant, the above passage from the *Qur'an* suggests that this event did not happen, for Prophet Moses "took up the Tablets", after having previously set them down. (2) The *Qur'an* includes

no parallel to the Biblical story of Prophet Moses allegedly ordering the Levites to slaughter 3,000 Israelites. (3) The *Bible* does
not mention Prophet Moses selecting 70 Israelites to accompany
him when he returned to the mountain to ask for forgiveness.
(4) While the *Bible* portrays Prophet Aaron as being a willing
participant, if not a ringleader, in the making and worshiping
of the golden calf, as well as in letting the Israelites "run wild",
the *Qur'an* does not debase this Prophet of Allah. Instead, the
above passage suggests that the Israelites refused to listen to
Prophet Aaron, i.e., "the people did indeed reckon me as naught,
and went near to slaying me". Prophet Aaron's objections to the
making and worshiping of the golden calf are made even more
clearly in the following passage of the *Qur'an*.

> Aaron had already, before this said to them, "O my people!
> ye are being tested in this: for verily your Lord is (Allah)
> most gracious: so follow me and obey my command." They
> had said: "We will not abandon this cult, but we will devote
> ourselves to it until Moses returns to us." (*Qur'an* 20: 90-91)

E5. PROPHET SAMUEL

The Biblical story of Prophet Samuel is primarily found in
I Samuel 1: 1-16: 13, 19: 18-24, and 28: 3-20. An abbreviated
story of Prophet Samuel is told in the *Qur'an*, in which he is
identified not by name, but by his role in having anointed Saul
(Talut in the *Qur'an*) as the first king of Israel. The parallel Biblical
story is found in *I Samuel* 8: 4-10: 8.

> Hast thou not turned thy vision to the chiefs of the children
> of Israel after (the time of) Moses? They said to a prophet
> (that was) among them: "Appoint for us a king, that we may
> fight in the cause of Allah." He said: "Is it not possible, if ye
> were commanded to fight, that ye will not fight?" They said:
> "How could we refuse to fight in the cause of Allah, seeing that
> we were turned out of our homes and our families?" But when
> they were commanded to fight, they turned back, except a

small band among them. But Allah has full knowledge of those who do wrong. Their prophet said to them: "Allah hath appointed Talut as king over you." They said: "How can he exercise authority over us when we are better fitted than he to exercise authority, and he is not even gifted, with wealth in abundance?" He said: "Allah hath chosen him above you, and hath gifted him abundantly with knowledge and bodily prowess: Allah granteth His authority to whom He pleaseth. Allah is all-embracing, and He knoweth all things." And (further) their prophet said to them: "A sign of his authority is that there shall come to you the Ark of the Covenant, with (an assurance) therein of security from your Lord, and the relics left by the family of Moses and the family of Aaron, carried by angels. In this is a symbol for you if ye indeed have faith." (*Qur'an* 2: 246-248)

The above passage from the *Qur'an* associates the return of the Ark of the Covenant with Saul becoming king of Israel. As stated in *I Samuel* 5: 1-7: 2, the Philistines had captured the Ark from the Israelites, and the Ark had remained with the Philistines for seven months, during which time the Philistines had experienced several plagues. Because of these plagues, the Philistines then decided to return the Ark to Israel, an event which *I Samuel* surrounds with stories of Prophet Samuel, suggesting that this event did take place during his time. *I Samuel* 14: 18-23 then specifically mentions King Saul taking the Ark into battle with the Israelites. Further, *I Samuel* 7: 1-2 suggests that the Ark, once returned to the Israelites by the Philistines, was housed at the home of Abinadab at Kiriathjearim for "some twenty years". This is most important, as *II Samuel* 6: 1-5 states that the Ark was housed at the home of Abinadab until Prophet David brought the Ark to Jerusalem, which could not have been before he had conquered Jerusalem, and which presumably happened shortly after Jerusalem fell to King David. A standard *Bible* chronology lists Saul being anointed king in 1020 BCE and David conquering Jerusalem in 1001 BCE, which is a difference of 19 years.

Assuming that Prophet David waited a year or two to get things settled in the newly conquered Jerusalem before moving the Ark from the home of Abinadab, and remembering that the Ark was in the home of Abinadab for about 20 years, one places the return of the Ark in 1020 BCE, which is the same year listed in the previously used *Bible* chronology for the anointing of King Saul. In short, the sequence of events listed in the above passage from the *Qur'an* lines up remarkably well with the chronological results obtained from some Biblical detective work.

Finally, it is noted that the non-Muslim reader may have some qualms about identifying Talut with Saul, as the two names do not appear to be similar. This concern is easily dismissed by examining the meaning of the Biblical name associated with the first king of Israel. Saul may be translated as "asked for", and given that the Israelites asked for a king (*I Samuel* 8: 4-5), it is quite possible that Saul was not the given name of the first king of Israel, but was merely a descriptor of him, i.e., he was asked for. Alternatively, but based on the same reasoning, Saul may have been a regnal name, instead of a given name.

E6. PROPHET DAVID (DAOUD)

In what follows, several passages from the *Qur'an* are quoted to illustrate the Islamic perspective of Prophet David. The first passage is paralleled by the 17th chapter of *I Samuel* and succinctly recounts Prophet David's victory over Goliath, the Philistine. The second passage associates Prophet David with the creation of psalms, a view consistent with traditional Judaeo-Christian teaching. The third and fourth passages reflect the Islamic view that Prophet David is to be associated with the creation of chain mail as a type of personal armor, a perspective that has no Biblical parallel. The fifth and final passage is discussed separately at the end of this section on Prophet David.

> By Allah's will, they routed them: and David slew Goliath: and Allah gave him power and wisdom and taught him whatever (else) He willed. (*Qur'an* 2: 251a)

And to David We gave the Psalms. (*Qur'an* 4: 163b; see also *Qur'an* 17: 55)

And remember David and Solomon, when they give judgment in the matter of the field into which the sheep of certain people had strayed by night: We did witness their judgment. To Solomon We inspired the (right) understanding of the matter: to each (of them) We gave judgment and knowledge; it was our power that made the hills and the birds celebrate Our praises. With David: it was We Who did (all these things). It was We Who taught him the making of coats of mail for your benefit, to guard you from each other's violence: will ye then be grateful? (*Qur'an* 21: 78-80)

We bestowed grace aforetime on David from Ourselves: "O ye mountains! sing ye back the praises of Allah with him! and ye birds (also)! And We made the iron soft for him" — (commanding), "Make thou coats of mail, balancing well the rings of chain armour, and work ye righteousness; for be sure I see (clearly) all that ye do." (*Qur'an* 34: 10-11)

Have patience at what they say, and remember Our servant David, the man of strength: for he ever turned (to Allah). It was We that made the hills declare, in unison with him, Our praises, at eventide and at break of day. And the birds gathered (in assemblies): all with him did turn (to Allah). We strengthened his kingdom, and gave him wisdom and sound judgment in speech and decision. Has the story of the disputants reached thee? Behold, they climbed over the wall of the private chamber; when they entered the presence of David, and he was terrified of them, they said: "Fear not: we are two disputants, one of whom has wronged the other: decide now between us with truth, and treat us not with injustice, but guide us to the even path. This man is my brother: he has nine and ninety ewes, and I have (but) one: yet he says, 'Commit her to my care,' and is (moreover) harsh to me in speech." (David) said: "He has undoubtedly wronged thee in demanding thy (single) ewe to be added to his (flock of) ewes; truly many are the partners (in business) who wrong each other: not so do those who believe and work deeds of righteousness, and how few are they?"... And David gathered that We had tried him: he asked forgiveness of his Lord, fell down, bowing (in prostration), and turned (to Allah in repentance). So We forgave him this (lapse): he enjoyed indeed a near approach to Us, and a beautiful place of (final) return. O David! We did indeed make thee a vicegerent on earth: so judge thou between men in truth (and justice): nor follow thou the lusts (of thy heart), for they will mislead thee from the path of Allah: for those who wander astray from the path of Allah is a penalty grievous, for that they forget the day of account. (*Qur'an* 38: 17-26)

The Muslim interpretation of the last quoted passage is usually that Prophet David erred in rushing to judgment before hearing the statement of the second disputant, and thus asked for forgiveness from Allah. However, it is noted that this passage from the *Qur'an* has certain affinities with *II Samuel* 12: 1-15, which describes Nathan presenting a hypothetical issue to Prophet David, one involving a rich man who took the only ewe of a poor man. When Prophet David decried this hypothetical act, Nathan reportedly identified the rich man as being Prophet David himself, who had allegedly committed adultery with Bathsheba, the only wife of Uriah, and who had allegedly arranged for Uriah to be placed in a very high-risk, military venture, which resulted in his death in battle. On the face of it, this story appears to be a continuation of the Biblical proclivity for defaming the prophets of Allah. However, it must be noted that Al-Tabari records several traditions that pertain to the same situation involving Bathsheba and Uriah and that are associated with the above Qur'anic passage[7]. In these traditions, the two disputants are said to have actually been angels, who were used to convey a message similar to that conveyed by Nathan. As to the correct interpretation of *Qur'an* 38: 17-26, as in all things, Allah knows best.

E7. PROPHET SOLOMON (SULAYMAN)

The Biblical story of Prophet Solomon, the son of Prophet David and the third king of Israel, is scattered across parts of *II Samuel, I Kings, II Kings, I Chronicles*, and *II Chronicles*. Of the various Biblical stories regarding Prophet Solomon, one finds particular expression in the *Qur'an*. This is the story of the visit of the Queen of Sheba (an area in modern Yemen), which is narrated in *I Kings* 10:1-13 and then retold in *II Chronicles* 9: 1-12. According to the Biblical narratives, the Queen of Sheba came to test Prophet Solomon "with hard questions", presumably in order to assess the veracity of the claims of Prophet Solomon's wisdom. She brought gifts to him and received gifts from him. Given the Biblical portrayal of this visit, it would appear that the purpose of the visit was to establish trade and diplomatic relations, and this interpretation is bolstered by both Biblical accounts interrupting the story of the Queen of Sheba's visit by mentioning other trade established by Prophet Solomon with other countries in the south of the Arabian Peninsula.

The parallel story from the *Qur'an*, which is quoted immediately below, differs in many respects from that presented in the *Bible*. (1) Unlike the Biblical account that makes hardly any mention of religion and worship, the *Qur'an* emphasizes that the visit was a response from the Queen of Saba (Sheba), known as Bilqis in the Islamic tradition, to Prophet Solomon's invitation that she submit to Allah. In the more spiritually oriented narrative of the *Qur'an*, trade and diplomacy were secondary considerations to the primary importance of Prophet Solomon's helping to convert Queen Bilqis to the worship of the Oneness of Allah, an attempt which proved successful as attested by the final words of Queen Bilqis in the following quotation from the *Qur'an*. (2) In the *Bible*, it is Bilqis who tests Prophet Solomon "with hard questions". In contrast, in the *Qur'an*, it is Prophet Solomon who tests Bilqis and her spiritual character by assessing her ability to recognize her own throne, which had been transported to Prophet Solomon in advance of Bilqis' arrival. (3) The Qur'anic account also adds that Prophet Solomon was served by the jinn (see chapter V, sections E1-E3 for a discussion of the jinn), a fact not mentioned in the Biblical narrative.

> (The queen) said: "Ye chiefs! here is — delivered to me — a letter worthy of respect. It is from Solomon, and is (as follows): 'In the name of Allah, most gracious, most merciful: be ye not arrogant against me, but come to me in submission (to the true religion)'." She said: "Ye chiefs! advise me in (this) my affair: no affair have I decided except in your presence." They said: "We are endued with strength, and given to vehement war: but the command is with thee; so consider what thou wilt command." She said: "Kings, when they enter a country, despoil it, and make the noblest of its people its meanest thus do they behave. But I am going to send him a present, and (wait) to see with what (answer) return (my) ambassadors." Now when (the embassy) came to Solomon, he said: "Will ye give me abundance in wealth? But that which Allah has given me is better than that which He has given you! Nay it is ye who rejoice in your gift! Go back to them, and be sure we shall come to them with such hosts as they will never be able to meet: we shall expel them from there in disgrace, and they will feel humbled (indeed)." He said (to his own men): "Ye chiefs! which of you can bring me her throne before they come to me in submission?" Said an 'ifrit, of the jinns: "I will bring it to thee before thou rise from thy council: indeed I have full strength for the purpose, and may be trusted." Said one who had knowledge of the book: "I will bring it to thee within the twinkling of any eye!" Then when (Solomon) saw it placed firmly before him, he said: "This is by the grace of my Lord! — to test me whether I am grateful or ungrateful! And if any is grateful, truly his gratitude is (a gain) for his own soul; but if any is ungrateful, truly my Lord is free of all needs, supreme in honor!" He said: "Transform her throne out of all recognition by her: let us see whether she is guided (to the truth) or is one of those who receive no guidance." So when

she arrived, she was asked, "Is this thy throne?" She said, "It was just like this; and knowledge was bestowed on us in advance of this, and we have submitted to Allah (in Islam)." And he diverted her from the worship of others besides Allah: for she was (sprung) of a people that had no faith. She was asked to enter the lofty palace: but when she saw it, she thought it was a lake of water, and she (tucked up her skirts), uncovering her legs. He said: "This is but a palace paved smooth with slabs of glass." She said: "O my Lord! I have indeed wronged my soul: I do (now) submit (in Islam), with Solomon, to the Lord of the worlds." (*Qur'an* 27: 29-44)

E8. PROPHET ELIJAH (ELIAS)

The Biblical story of Prophet Elijah is told in chapters 17-19 and 21 of *I Kings* and in chapters 1-2 of *II Kings*. Prophet Elijah is also mentioned briefly in the *Qur'an*.

And Zakariyya and John, and Jesus and Elias: all in the ranks of the righteous... (*Qur'an* 6: 85)

So also was Elias among those sent (by Us). Behold, he said to his people, "Will ye not fear (Allah)? Will ye call upon Ba'l and forsake the best of creators — Allah, your Lord and Cherisher of your fathers of old?" But they rejected him, and they will certainly be called up (for punishment) — except the sincere and devoted servants of Allah (among them). And We left (this blessing) for him among generations (to come) in later times: "Peace and salutation to such as Elias!" Thus indeed do We reward those who do right. For he was one of Our believing servants. (*Qur'an* 37: 123-132)

E9. PROPHET ELISHA

The story of Prophet Elisha finds its Biblical expression in the 19th chapter of *I Kings* and in chapters 2-9 and 13 of *II Kings*. He is also mentioned briefly in the *Qur'an*.

And Isma'il and Elisha, and Jonah, and Lot: and to all We gave favor above the nations... (*Qur'an* 6: 86)

And commemorate Isma'il, Elisha, and Dhu al Kifl: each of them was of the company of the good. (*Qur'an* 38: 48)

E10. PROPHET JONAH (YUNUS)

The book of *Jonah* tells the Biblical story of Prophet Jonah, the son of Amittai and a prophet to the Assyrian city of Nineveh. Because he reportedly did not want the inhabitants of Nineveh to be saved, Prophet Jonah disobeyed Allah's command for him to go to Nineveh and preach to its inhabitants. Instead, he fled to Joppa, where he boarded a ship sailing for Tarshish. Once the ship had set sail, Allah created a great storm, which threatened to sink the ship. In response, the crew cast lots to see on whose account the storm had been created, and "the lot fell on Jonah". After hearing Prophet Jonah's story, the crew continued to try to row to safety, but the storm continued unabated. Finally, the crew threw Prophet Jonah overboard as a sacrifice in hopes that this sacrifice would result in a calming of the storm. Jonah was swallowed by a large fish, and he remained in its belly for three days and three nights. Therein, Jonah prayed to Allah for forgiveness, and the fish then spat Jonah out on dry land. Having been freed from the belly of the fish, Jonah went to Nineveh and preached to its inhabitants. Over 120,000 people responded to Jonah's preaching by praying to Allah for His forgiveness. Thereafter, Jonah retired outside the city, angry that Nineveh had been saved. As he sat there lamenting, Allah caused a "bush" to grow up over Jonah and offer a comforting shade to him. The next day, Allah reportedly caused the bush to wither.

The above story is very eloquently related in the following passage from the *Qur'an*, wherein one has most of the details from the Biblical book of *Jonah*. The similarities between the two descriptions are truly impressive.

So also was Jonah among those sent (by Us). When he ran away (like a slave from captivity) to the ship (fully) laden, he (agreed to) cast lots, and he was condemned: then the big fish did swallow him, and he had done acts worthy of blame.

Had it not been that he (repented and) glorified Allah, he would certainly have remained inside the fish till the Day of Resurrection. But We cast him forth on the naked shore in a state of sickness, and We caused to grow, over him, a spreading plant of the gourd kind, and We sent him (on a mission) to a hundred thousand (men) or more. And they believed; so We permitted them to enjoy (their life) for a while. (*Qur'an* 37: 139-148)

F. PROPHETS ZECHARIAH (ZAKARIYA) AND JOHN (YAHYA) THE BAPTIST

The Biblical story of Prophets Zechariah and John the Baptist is primarily confined to *Luke* 1:5-80, which recounts the events preceding the birth of Prophet John through the start of his ministry, although scattered references to prophet John are found throughout the *New Testament* gospels. Focusing on the story of the birth of Prophet John, *Luke* reports that Prophet Zechariah and his wife, Elizabeth, were an aged couple who had never had children — Elizabeth being barren. Once, when Prophet Zechariah was praying in the sanctuary, the angel Gabriel appeared and announced to Zechariah that his prayer had been heard and accepted by Allah. Prophet Zechariah and Elizabeth would soon have a son who would be named John and would be a prophet to his people. Prophet Zechariah then asked for a sign to confirm this message. According to the account of *Luke*, the sign was that Prophet Zechariah was made mute, and allegedly remained mute throughout the conception, gestation, birth, and first eight days of life of Prophet John. Only upon confirming his wife's choice of the name John for their son did Prophet Zechariah regain his speech. Bearing in mind that "Yahya" is merely the Arabic for "John", the following passage from the *Qur'an* offers an impressive parallel to the account of *Luke*. The only significant discrepancy concerns the length of time that Prophet Zechariah remained mute, which the *Qur'an* limits to three days and three nights.

(This is) a recital of the mercy of thy Lord to His servant Zakariya. Behold! he cried to his Lord in secret, praying: "O my Lord! infirm indeed are my bones, and the hair of my head doth glisten with grey: but never am I unblest, O my Lord, in my prayer to Thee! Now I fear (what) my relatives (and colleagues will do) after me: but my wife is barren: so give me an heir as from Thyself — (one that) will (truly) represent me, and represent the posterity of Jacob; and make him, O my Lord! one with whom Thou art well-pleased." (His prayer was answered): "O Zakariya We give thee good news of a son: his name shall be Yahya: on none by that name have We conferred distinction before." He said: "O my Lord! how shall I have a son, when my wife is barren and I have grown quite decrepit from old age?" He said: "So (it will be): thy Lord saith, 'That is easy for Me: I did indeed create thee before when thou hadst been nothing!'" (Zakariya) said: "O my Lord! give me a sign." "Thy sign," was the answer, "shall be that thou shalt speak to no man for three nights, although thou art not dumb." So Zakariya came out to his people from his chamber: he told them by signs to celebrate Allah's praises in the morning and in the evening. (To his son came the command): "O Yahya! take hold of the book with might": and We gave him wisdom even as a youth. And pity (for all creatures) as from Us, and purity: he was devout, and kind to his parents, and he was not overbearing or rebellious. So peace on him the day he was born, the day that he dies, and the day that he will be raised up to life (again)! (*Qur'an* 19: 2-15; see also *Qur'an* 3: 37-41 and 21: 89-90)

The *Qur'an* also refers to Prophet Zechariah as being a care-giver to the Virigin Mary, a statement that parallels the report in *Luke* 1: 39-56 that Mary remained in the care of Prophet Zechariah and his wife, Elizabeth, for about three months.

Right graciously did her Lord accept her: He made her grow in purity and beauty; to the care of Zakariya was she assigned. Every time that he entered (her) chamber to see her, he found her supplied with sustenance. He said: "O Mary! whence (comes) this to you?" She said: "From Allah: for Allah provides sustenance to whom He pleases, without measure." (*Qur'an* 3: 37)

G. PROPHET JESUS (ISA) CHRIST

The *Qur'an* contains two lengthy passages (3: 35-59 and 19:16-40) about Prophet Jesus, as well as numerous other references to him. In what follows, various passages from the *Qur'an* are presented in something approaching a chronological history of Prophet Jesus and his mother. Where appropriate, parallels from the *Bible* and from the *New Testament* apocrypha are presented.

> Behold! a woman of 'Imran said: "O my Lord! I do dedicate unto Thee what is in my womb for Thy special service: so accept this of me: for Thou hearest and knowest all things." When she was delivered, she said: "O my Lord! behold! I am delivered of a female child!" — And Allah knew best what she brought forth — "And no wise is the male like the female. I have named her Mary, and I commend her and her offspring to Thy protection from the evil one, the rejected." Right graciously did her Lord accept her: He made her grow in purity and beauty; to the care of Zakariya was she assigned. Every time that he entered (her) chamber to see her, he found her supplied with sustenance. He said: "O Mary! whence (comes) this to you?" She said: "From Allah: for Allah provides sustenance to whom He pleases, without measure." (*Qur'an* 3: 35-37)

The above quotation raises four issues that warrant further discussion. (1) The reference to "a woman of 'Imran" implies that Mary's mother traced to the Biblical Amram, the father of Prophet Moses and a member of the Levite tribe of Israel (see Table 4). As the Israelites frequently married within their own tribe, the *Qur'an* seems to indicate that Mary was a Levite, a proposition that is paralleled in early Christian writing in a variant, but no longer extant, version of *The Gospel of the Birth of Mary*, the relevant passage from which is preserved in a reference given by Faustus, the Bishop of Riez in Provence. (2) *Qur'an* 3: 35 also states that Mary was dedicated to Allah's "special service" while still in the womb, a statement that has some affinities with *The Gospel of the Birth of Mary*, which states that Mary's parents devoted her "to the service of the Lord" even before she was conceived (1: 6), and then rededicated her to that service after she reached puberty (5: 6). (3) The above quotation from the *Qur'an* further states that Mary was miraculously "supplied with sustenance" from Allah. This statement is paralleled in the early Christian apocrypha by the *Protevangelion of James* 8: 2, which states that an angel fed Mary during her stay in the temple in Jerusalem. (4) As previously noted, *Luke* 1: 39-56 parallels the Qur'anic statement that Mary was in the care of Prophet Zechariah, which finds additional support in the *New Testament* apocrypha (*Protevangelion of James* 8: 3-4), which states that Prophet Zechariah petitioned the Jewish high priest about Mary[8].

The Biblical account of the angelic announcement to Mary of the coming birth of Jesus is related in *Luke* 1: 26-38. Skipping over the later theologizing to be found in this passage from *Luke*, the basic outline is that the angel Gabriel informed Mary that she had found favor in the sight of Allah and that she would soon give birth to a son who would be named Jesus. Mary then asked how she could possibly give birth when she was still a virgin, to which Gabriel reportedly answered that: "The Holy Spirit will come upon you, and the power of the Most High will overshadow you; therefore the child to be born will be holy; he will be called Son of God". The words attributed to Gabriel in the above quoted passage call to mind the polytheistic Greek myths of the gods descending from Mount Olympus to rape and impregnate mortal women. In contrast to this polytheistic residual as found in *Luke*, the *Qur'an*, while paralleling the account from *Luke* in most other respects, presents the virgin birth of Jesus as an act of miraculous creation, not as an act of impregnation.

Behold! The angels said: "O Mary! Allah hath chosen thee and purified thee — chosen thee above the women of all nations. O Mary! Worship thy Lord devoutly: prostrate thyself, and bow down (in prayer) with those who bow down." This is part of the tidings of the things unseen, which We reveal unto thee (O Prophet!) by inspiration: thou wast not with them when they cast lots with arrows, as to which of them should be charged with the care of Mary: nor wast thou with them when they disputed (the point). Behold! The angels said: "O Mary! Allah giveth thee glad tidings of a word from Him: his name will be Christ Jesus. The son of Mary, held in honor in this world and the hereafter and of (the company of) those nearest to Allah; he shall speak to the people in childhood and in maturity. And he shall be (of the company) of the righteous." She said: "O my Lord! How shall I have a son when no man hath touched me?" He said: "Even so: Allah createth what He willeth: when He hath decreed a plan, He but saith to it, 'Be,' and it is!" (*Qur'an* 3: 42-47)

The above passage from the *Qur'an* states that "they cast lots with arrows, as to which of them should be charged with the care of Mary". While there is no Biblical parallel to this statement, there is a similar event recorded in the *New Testament* apocrypha (*Gospel of the Birth of Mary* 5: 4-6: 7 and *Protevangelion of James* 8:6-16), where it is stated that Joseph was chosen by a similar method to succeed Prophet Zechariah in caring for Mary.

Relate in the book (the story of) Mary, when she withdrew from her family to a place in the east. She placed a screen (to screen herself) from them; then We sent to her our angel, and he appeared before her as a man in all respects. She said: "I seek refuge from thee to (Allah) most gracious: (come not near) if thou dost fear Allah." He said: "Nay, I am only a messenger from thy Lord, (to announce) to thee the gift of a holy son." She said: "How shall I have a son, seeing that no man has touched me, and I am not unchaste?" He said: "So (it will be): thy Lord saith, 'That is easy for Me: and (We wish) to appoint him as a sign unto men and a mercy from Us': it is a matter (so) decreed." So she conceived him, and she retired with him to a remote place. And the pains of childbirth drove her to the trunk of a palm tree: she cried (in her anguish): "Ah! would that I had died before this! Would that I had been a thing forgotten and out of sight!" But (a voice) cried to her from beneath the (palm tree): "Grieve not! for thy Lord hath provided a rivulet beneath thee; and shake towards thyself the trunk of the palm tree; it will let fall fresh ripe dates upon thee. So eat and drink and cool (thine) eye. And if thou dost see any man, say, 'I have vowed a fast to (Allah) most gracious, and this day will I enter into no talk with any human being'." At length she brought the (babe) to her people, carrying him (in her arms). They said: "O Mary! truly an amazing thing hast thou brought! O sister of Aaron! thy father was not a man of evil, nor thy mother a woman unchaste!" But she pointed to the babe. They said: "How can we talk to one who is a child in the cradle?" He said: "I am indeed a servant of Allah: He hath given me revelation and made me a prophet; and He hath made me blessed wheresoever I be, and hath enjoined on me prayer and charity as long as I live: (He) hath made me kind to my mother, and not overbearing or miserable; so peace is on me the day I was born, the day that I die, and the day that I shall be raised up to life (again)!" Such (was) Jesus the son of Mary: (it is) a statement of truth, about which they (vainly) dispute. (*Qur'an* 19: 16-34)

Four points need to be highlighted from the above passage. (1) The prior quotation from *Qur'an* 3: 35-37 indicated that Mary had previously been under the care of Prophet Zechariah, presumably in Jerusalem. However, *Qur'an* 19: 16 states that Mary now "withdrew from her family to a place in the east", presumably east of Jerusalem. *Qur'an* 19: 22 states that she then retired "to a remote place", where, according to *Qur'an* 19: 23-25, date palms were growing. It was there that she gave birth to Prophet Jesus. These points are important in that *Matthew* 2: 1 and *Luke* 2: 4-7 maintain that Prophet Jesus was born in Bethlehem. However, Bethlehem is not east of Jerusalem, would not be considered a "remote place", and does not support the growing of date palms. The Qur'anic descriptions of the site of Prophet Jesus' birth would be more consistent with the area surrounding Jericho than with Bethlehem. Of note, the *Protevangelion of James* 12: 10-13: 1 states that Prophet Jesus was not born in Bethlehem, but in a desert cave that his mother past on the way to Bethlehem. While this apocryphal gospel places the desert cave within the region surrounding Bethlehem, the desert does not encroach near Bethlehem, but would be found at its nearest point to the east of Bethlehem and Jerusalem. Further, *The First Gospel of the Infancy of Jesus Christ* 1:6 also maintains that Jesus was born in a cave that was on the way to, but not in, Bethlehem. (2) The reference to Mary being a "sister of Aaron" in *Qur'an* 19: 28, presumably meaning of the lineage of Prophet Aaron, again suggests that Mary was of the Israelite tribe of Levi, an issue that has been previously discussed. (3) In *Qur'an* 19: 29-33, Prophet Jesus speaks as a neonate in order to defend his mother's reputation against the indirect accusations of promiscuity leveled against Mary by her people (*Qur'an* 19: 27-28). There is no corresponding Biblical story, but *The First Gospel of the Infancy of Jesus Christ* 1: 2 parallels the *Qur'an* in reporting that Prophet Jesus miraculously spoke during his infancy. That there was a need to defend the honor of Mary can be illustrated by the fact that various commentaries on the Jewish *Mishnah*, the first part of the *Talmud*, refer to Prophet Jesus as being Jesus bin Pantera, the bastard son of an illicit union between Mary and a Roman soldier[9]. (4) Finally, it should be stressed that the reference in *Qur'an* 19:33 to "the day that I die, and the day that I shall be raised up to life (again)" does not relate to any alleged crucifixion and resurrection after three days, both of which are concepts rejected by Islam, but to the death of Prophet Jesus after his return to earth during the end times (see chapter V, section F2) and to his resurrection on the final Day of

Judgment as part of the general resurrection of all of humanity.

Returning to the theme of the nature of the birth of Prophet Jesus, both Islam and Christianity proclaim the virgin birth of Prophet Jesus. However, there is a fundamental difference between the two religions in terms of how the virgin birth is typically conceptualized. Contemporary Christianity portrays the virgin birth of Prophet Jesus in terms of his being the "begotten" son of Allah. For example, *Matthew* 1:18 states that Mary was "with child from the Holy Spirit", and *Luke* 1: 35 has an angel telling Mary that the "Holy Spirit will come upon you". While these Biblical verses may be seen as rather ambiguous by some, the Nicene Creed of Christianity allows for no such ambiguity when it states: "We believe in one Lord, Jesus Christ, the only Son of God, eternally begotten of the Father, God from God, Light from Light, true God from true God, begotten, not made, one in Being with the Father." Further, the so-called Apostles' Creed holds that: "I believe in God the Father Almighty; maker of heaven and earth; and in Jesus Christ his only Son, our Lord; who was conceived by the Holy Ghost..." In contrast, Islam's portrayal of the virgin birth is that of a miraculous creation, not that of divine begetting. In that regard, the following two verses from the *Qur'an* are especially relevant.

> She said: "O my Lord! How shall I have a son when no man hath touched me?" He said: "Even so: Allah createth what He willeth: when He hath decreed a plan, He but saith to it 'Be', and it is!"...The similitude of Jesus before Allah is as that of Adam; He created him from dust, then said to him: "Be": and he was. (*Qur'an* 3: 47, 59)

The *Qur'an* refers to Jesus fashioning a clay bird, and then, by Allah's leave, making it come alive. This story of Jesus causing, by the leave of Allah, a clay bird to come to life is not found in the contemporary *New Testament*. However, once again, a story mentioned in the *Qur'an* can be found in the *New Testament* apocrypha (*The First Gospel of the Infancy of Jesus Christ* 15: 6

and *Thomas' Gospel of the Infancy of Jesus Christ* 1: 4-10), where a similar event is reported to have occurred during the childhood of Prophet Jesus.

> She said: "O my Lord! How shall I have a son when no man hath touched me?" He said: "Even so: Allah createth what He willeth: when He hath decreed a plan, He but saith to it, 'Be", and it is! And Allah will teach him the book and wisdom, the law and the gospel, and (appoint him) a messenger to the children of Israel, (with this message): 'I have come to you, with a sign from your Lord, in that I make for you out of clay, as it were, the figure of a bird, and breathe into it, and it becomes a bird by Allah's leave: and I heal those born blind, and the lepers, and I quicken the dead, by Allah's leave; and I declare to you what ye eat, and what ye store in your houses. Surely, therein is a sign for you if ye did believe;...'"
> (*Qur'an* 3: 47-49; see also *Qur'an* 5: 110)

While many passages in the *Qur'an* deal with the mission, ministry, and miracles of Prophet Jesus, the following two passages provide a succinct encapsulation of these themes.

> And (appoint him (Jesus)) a messenger to the children of Israel, (with this message): "I have come to you, with a sign from your Lord, in that I make for you out of clay, as it were, the figure of a bird, and breathe into it, and it becomes a bird by Allah's leave. And I heal those born blind, and the lepers, and I quicken the dead, by Allah's leave; and I declare to you what ye eat, and what ye store in your houses. Surely therein is a sign for you if ye did believe; (I have come to you), to attest the law which was before me. And to make lawful to you part of what was (before) forbidden to you; I have come to you with a sign from your Lord. So fear Allah and obey me."
> (*Qur'an* 3: 49-50)

And in their footsteps We sent Jesus the son of Mary, confirming the law that had come before him: We sent him the gospel: therein was guidance and light, and confirmation of the law that had come before him: a guidance and an admonition to those who fear Allah. (*Qur'an* 5: 46)

Several points of comparison with the Christian tradition can be illustrated by considering the above verses of the *Qur'an*. (1) While Christianity likes to maintain that Jesus' ministry and mission were to the world at large, there are several passages in the canonical gospel that appear to agree with the Islamic position that he was sent only to the "children of Israel", e.g., *Matthew* 10: 5-6; 15: 21-28. (2) The comparison between Christianity and Islam regarding the story of the clay birds and of Jesus speaking in infancy have been previously discussed. (3) The list of miracles given in *Qur'an* 3: 49 appears to overlap quite comfortably with the list given in *Luke* 7: 22 and *Matthew* 11: 4-5. (4) Finally, there are certain affinities between the *Qur'an*'s statement regarding "confirmation of the law that had come before him" and *Matthew* 5: 17, where Prophet Jesus is reported to have said that he did not come to abolish the law, but to fulfill it.

The following passage from the *Qur'an* recounts an event from the ministry of Prophet Jesus after he had accumulated disciples. This narrative has no direct *New Testament* parallel, but is reminiscent of the *New Testament* accounts of Prophet Jesus miraculously feeding either 5,000 (*Matthew* 14: 13-21, *Luke* 9: 10-17, and *John* 6: 1-14) or 4,000 individuals (*Mark* 8: 1-9).

Behold! the disciples said: "O Jesus the son of Mary! can thy Lord send down to us a table set (with viands) from heaven?" Said Jesus: "Fear Allah, if ye have faith." They said: "We only wish to eat thereof and satisfy our hearts, and to know that thou hast indeed told us the truth; and that we ourselves may be witnesses to the miracle." Said Jesus the son of Mary: "O Allah our Lord! send us from heaven a table set (with viands) that there may be for us — for the first and the last of us — a solemn festival and a sign from Thee; and provide for our sustenance, for Thou art the best sustainer (of our needs)." Allah said: "I will send it down unto you; but if any of you after that resisteth faith, I will punish him with a penalty such as I have not inflicted on anyone among all the peoples." (Qur'an 5: 112-115)

Unlike traditional Christianity, Islam denies both the alleged crucifixion and resurrection of Prophet Jesus. However, like Christianity, Islam acknowledges the ascension of Prophet Jesus.

That they said (in boast), "We killed Christ Jesus the son of Mary, the messenger of Allah" — but they killed him not, nor crucified him, but so it was made to appear to them, and those who differ therein are full of doubts, with no (certain) knowledge, but only conjecture to follow, for of a surety they killed him not. Nay, Allah raised him up unto Himself; and Allah is exalted in power, wise — (Qur'an 4: 157-158)

The alleged crucifixion and resurrection of Prophet Jesus is a cornerstone of traditional Christianity. However, the early Christian communities were apparently quite unsure as to who was actually crucified. Various alternative candidates for the crucifixion are repeatedly encountered in early Christian writings, including Judas Iscariot, a similacrum of Prophet Jesus, Simon the Cyrene, Barabbas, etc. For an in-depth discussion of this issue, the reader is referred elsewhere.[10]

Further, at least one Biblical passage has Jesus Christ stating that his earthly work and ministry had been completed before there was any alleged crucifixion event. Regardless of the identity of the crucified victim, this verse maintains that being crucified was not part of Christ's mission.

And this is eternal life, that they may know you, the only true God, and Jesus Christ whom you have sent. I glorified you on earth by finishing the work that you gave me to do. (John 17: 3)

In summary, Islam recognizes Jesus Christ as a prophet of Allah. While contemporary Christianity typically does not refer to Jesus as being a prophet, there are several Biblical passages that do support the concept of Jesus as a prophet, as opposed to being divine.

> When he entered Jerusalem, the whole city was in turmoil, asking, "Who is this?" The crowds were saying, "This is the prophet Jesus from Nazareth in Galilee." (*Matthew* 21: 10)

Of note, there is no indication anywhere in the verses surrounding the above passage that Jesus ever denied the accolades from the crowds that he was a prophet. The same lack of denial that he was a prophet is true of the following passages, the first of which recounts the reaction of the people after Prophet Jesus resurrected the widow's son at Nain, the second of which narrates an encounter between Prophet Jesus and a Samaritan woman, and the third of which records the statement of a blind man whom Jesus had healed.

> Fear seized all of them; and they glorified God, saying, "A great prophet has risen among us!" and "God has looked favorably on his people!" (*Luke* 7: 16)

> The woman said to him, "Sir, I see that you are a prophet." (*John* 4:19)

> So they said again to the blind man, "What do you say about him? It was your eyes he opened." He said, "He is a prophet." (*John* 9: 17)

Further, there are Biblical passages, allegedly the words of Jesus Christ, in which he portrays himself as being a prophet.

> And he said, "Truly I tell you, no prophet is accepted in the prophet's hometown." (*Luke* 4: 24; see also *John* 4: 43)

Yet today, tomorrow, and the next day I must be on my way, because it is impossible for a prophet to be killed outside of Jerusalem. (*Luke* 13: 33)

H. SUMMARY

The history of Islam prior to Prophet Muhammad substantially overlaps with the religious and historical heritage claimed by both Judaism and Christianity. All three religions claim to be monotheistic, and all three proclaim a final Day of Judgment. Nonetheless, significant differences exist among the three religions in certain areas, including those of history, doctrine, and dogma. From an Islamic perspective, those differences reflect distortions of the true religion of Islam. The earlier distortions were codified into Judaism, and the subsequent and later distortions were codified into Christianity. The differences between Islam, on the one hand, and Judaism and Christianity, on the other hand, were to become even greater with the progressive and final revelations given to Prophet Muhammad—revelations that have yet to be fully accepted by the adherents of Christianity and Judaism.

Notes

2. Wilson I (1985), pages 54-56.

3. *Qur'an* 22:47 compares a day in the sight of Allah to 1,000 years in human reckoning, and *Qur'an* 70:4 compares Allah's day to 50,000 years in human time, suggesting that a day in the sight of Allah is an indeterminable and lengthy period of time.

4. *Al-Tabari* (1989), page 369.

5. *Al-Tabari* (1989), pages 360 and 368.

6. See, for example, the account in *Joshua* of the conquest of Canaan/Palestine by the Israelites.

7. *Al-Tabari* (1991), pages 144-149. Only one of these traditions appears to claim a provenance back to Prophet Muhammad. While this particular *Hadith* was reportedly narrated by Anas ibn Malik, a reliable narrator of *Ahadith*, to whom over 2,000 *Ahadith* are credited in *Al-Bukhari* and *Muslim*, two of the individuals in the *Isnad* going back to Anas ibn Malik in this particular *Hadith* are often judged to be weak transmitters. As such, these traditions are often discounted by Muslim scholars.

8. All references to and passages from the *New Testament* apocrypha in this and in the following paragraphs of this section may be found in Platt RH, Brett JA (---).

9. Wilson I (1985), pages 54-56.

10. Dirks JF (2001), chapter 5.

Chapter 3

Muhammad, Messenger of Allah

A. INTRODUCTION

Islam was finalized and perfected as a religion with the final revelations given to Prophet Muhammad. These revelations constitute the *Qur'an*, the book of sacred scripture of Islam, which is believed by Muslims to contain the verbatim words of Allah as relayed to Prophet Muhammad through the mediation of the angel Gabriel (Jibril). As such, no presentation of Islam can be complete without considering the life and person of Prophet Muhammad. Unfortunately, the present chapter can but serve as a brief synopsis of and introduction to the life and teaching of this final prophet of Allah. Readers wishing more detailed information about Prophet Muhammad are urged to consult the bibliography at the end of this book, where several excellent biographies of Prophet Muhammad are listed.

In attempting to present the following information on the life of Prophet Muhammad, one is immediately confronted with several, although fortunately minor, chronological problems. These chronological problems were previously discussed in chapter I, section C4, and are not reiterated at this time. However, the reader is urged to remember that dating by the Gregorian calendar for significant events in the life of Prophet Muhammad can sometimes be less than certain.

B. SETTING THE STAGE

B1. THE *JAHILIYA*

Life in Arabia in the years before the rise of Islam has been referred to as the *Jahiliya*, i.e., the age of ignorance. The Ka'ba, originally built by Prophets Abraham and Ismael in Makkah as a house of worship dedicated to the Oneness of Allah (*Tawheed*), had degenerated into a cult center of polytheistic idolatry, to which the pagan Arabs made pilgrimage to worship their particular tribal idols and to circumambulate the Ka'ba while in the nude. Fearing economic duress caused by "unproductive" members of their society, the Arabs of Makkah and of the surrounding area frequently buried their newborn daughters while still alive. Women were little more than chattel, and any man could have an unlimited number of wives. Alcohol abuse was rampant. Intertribal raiding of flocks and herds was part and parcel of economic maintenance and stability in the harsh environment of Arabia. Blood feuds could last for decades, with retaliation being taken against the aggressor's kinfolk if the aggressor was not available. In turn, this retaliation could then lead to a cycle of counter-retaliation *ad infinitum ad nauseum*. Intertribal warfare could spring up over a matter of honor, over the control of grazing land, over the control of desert wells, etc. One famous war, the War of Dahis and Al-Ghabra, was even started over a disputed horse race. This last noted war between the related tribes of the Dhubyan and 'Abs was intermittently fought across several decades in the latter half of the sixth and the early part of the seventh centuries CE.

It was into this environment that Prophet Muhammad was born in Makkah in 570 or 571 CE.

B2. MAKKAH AS THE SITE OF BIRTH

Makkah as Prophet Muhammad's site of birth is especially noteworthy, not only because Makkah was the site of the Ka'ba, but also because Makkah was where Prophet Ismael lived and raised his family after he and his mother were left there by Prophet Abraham (see chapter II, section C5, as well as *Al-Bukhari, Ahadith* 4:583-584). With regard to where Prophet Ismael lived, it is instructive to note that *Genesis* 21:21 places Prophet Ismael's home within "the wilderness of Paran". Moving from Hebrew to Arabic, "Paran" becomes "Faran", which may be translated as "two who migrated", thus sealing the identification of Paran with Prophet Ismael and indicating that Makkah was within the confines of Paran. While Paran is typically equated with the Sinai Peninsula in most Biblical atlases, the *Bible* clearly differentiates between the wilderness of Sinai and the wilderness of Paran.[11]

> Then the Israelites set out by stages from the wilderness of Sinai, and the cloud settled down in the wilderness of Paran. (*Numbers* 10: 12)

In short, the wilderness of Paran encompassed an area extending from northeastern Arabia down to and including Makkah, and Mt. Paran can be located in the Sirat Mountains that surround Makkah. Given these identifications, the following Biblical verse becomes relevant, especially when one considers that the word "Muhammad" may be translated as "praised one".

> God came from Teman, the Holy One from Mount Paran. Selah. His glory covered the heavens, and the earth was full of his praise. (*Habakkuk* 3: 3)

B3. THE LINEAGE OF PROPHET MUHAMMAD

The parents of Prophet Muhammad were 'Abd Allah ibn Al-Muttalib ibn Hashim and Aminah bint Wahb ibn 'Abd Munaf ibn Zuhrah. Both were members of the Quraysh tribe of Makkah, and, as such, both could trace their lineage back through their respective ancestors to 'Adnan, the eponymous ancestor of the 'Adnani Arabs, from whom descended such famous Arab tribes as the Quraysh, the various tribes of the 'Anezah confederation, the Bani Saleem, the various tribes of the Bani Ghatafan, the Bani Hawazin, etc. Given the Arab preoccupation with genealogy at that time, it was seen as an illustrious lineage, with 'Abd Allah tracing to Fahr (aka Quraysh, the eponymous ancestor of the Quraysh tribe of Makkah) within 10 generations, and with Aminah tracing to him within nine generations. In what follows, Table 5 presents the male-line lineage from 'Adnan to Prophet Muhammad through both his paternal and maternal lineage.

Table 5
From 'Adnan to Prophet Muhammad

'Adnan
|
Ma'ad
|
Nizar
|
Mudar
|
Elias
|
Mudrikah/'Amir
|
Khuzaiman
|
Kinana
|
Al-Nadr/Qais
|
Malik
|
Fahr/Quraysh
|
Ghalib
|
Lo'i
|
Ka'b
|
Murra
|
Kilab
|

Zuhrah	Qusai/Zaid
|	|
'Abd Munaf	'Abd Munaf/Al-Mugheera
|	|
Wahb	Hashim
|	|
Aminah	'Abd Al-Muttalib/Shaiba
|	|
Prophet Muhammad	'Abd Allah
	|
	Prophet Muhammad

All reliable sources are in agreement regarding the information contained in Table 5. Somewhat more problematic is the exact ancestry of 'Adnan[12], although all reliable sources agree that he was a descendant of Qaydar (the Biblical Kedar), the second son of Prophet Ismael.

> These are the descendants of Ishmael, Abraham's son, whom Hagar the Egyptian, Sarah's slave-girl, bore to Abraham. These are the names of the sons of Ishmael, named in the order of their birth: Nebaioth, the firstborn of Ishmael; and Kedar, Adbeel, Mibsam, Mishma, Dumah, Massa, Hadad, Tema, Jetur, Naphish, and Kedemah. These are the sons of Ishmael and these are their names, by their villages and by their encampments, twelve princes according to their tribes. (*Genesis* 25:12-16)

B4. THE PROPHET YET TO COME

During the sixth century CE, the Jews of the Middle East were awaiting a great prophet whom they expected to come in the near future. Earlier echoes of this belief among the Jews can be found in the Biblical report of the questioning of Prophet John the Baptist.

> This is the testimony given by John when the Jews sent priests and Levites from Jerusalem to ask him, "Who are you?" He confessed and did not deny it, but confessed, "I am not the Messiah." And they asked him, "What then? Are you Elijah?" He said, "I am not." "Are you the prophet?" He answered, "No." Then they said to him, "Who are you? Let us have an answer for those who sent us. What do you say about yourself?" He said, "I am the voice of one crying out in the wilderness, 'make straight the way of the Lord'," as the prophet Isaiah said. Now they had been sent from the Pharisees. They asked him, "Why then are you baptizing if you are neither the Messiah, nor Elijah, nor the prophet?" (*John* 1: 19-25)

The above passage, in clearly contrasting the coming messiah, i.e., Jesus Christ, with "the prophet", illustrates that the Jews of Prophet Jesus' day were expecting both a messiah and "the prophet" yet to come. Further, Prophet John the Baptist, while clearly a prophet of Allah, specifically denied that he was "the prophet" about whom the Jews were inquiring. The contrast between the messiah and "the prophet" yet to come is further illustrated in a second Biblical passage in which the listening crowd responds to the words of Prophet Jesus.

> When they heard these words, some in the crowd said, "This is really the prophet." Others said, "This is the Messiah." (*John* 7:40-41b)

Who was "the prophet" yet to come? The Jews of the sixth century believed he would be born in Paran in Arabia, a belief consistent with the previously quoted passage from *Habakkuk* 3: 3. As such, many of them immigrated to Yathrib, which began to host a thriving Jewish community among its pagan Arabs. More specifically, based upon various *Old Testament* passages, many of these Jews believed the prophet would be born among the Arabs, i.e., the "riders on camels", would be an Arab descending from Qaydar/Kedar, would gather all the people (flocks) of Qaydar/Kedar to monotheistic worship, would glorify the "glorious house" (the Ka'ba), and would sing "a new song" of revelation.

> For thus the Lord said to me: "Go, post a lookout, let him announce what he sees. When he sees riders, horsemen in pairs, riders on donkeys, riders on camels, let him listen diligently, very diligently." (*Isaiah* 21: 6-7)

> Woe is me, that I am an alien in Meshech, that I must live among the tents of Kedar. (*Psalms* 120: 5)

> All the flocks of Kedar shall be gathered to you, the rams of Nebaioth shall minister to you; they shall be acceptable on my altar, and I will glorify my glorious house. (*Isaiah* 60: 7)

Sing to the Lord a new song, his praise from the end of the earth! Let the sea roar and all that fills it, the coastlands and their inhabitants. Let the desert and its towns lift up their voice, the villages that Kedar inhabits; let the inhabitants of Sela sing for joy, let them shout from the tops of the mountains. (*Isaiah* 42: 10-11)

As previously seen, Prophet Muhammad was born in Makkah in the Paran and was an Arab descendant of Qaydar.

C. BIRTH AND YOUTH

C1. CIRCUMSTANCES OF BIRTH

Shortly after Prophet Muhammad's conception, his father, 'Abd Allah, joined one of the regular trading caravans that journeyed from Makkah to Syria and Palestine. On the return journey from the north, 'Abd Allah stopped to visit relatives in Madinah, where he fell ill and died. Back in Makkah, only a few weeks after word finally reached Makkah of the death of 'Abd Allah, Aminah gave birth to Prophet Muhammad, who was born with a slightly raised oval mark on his upper back. Thus, while Prophet Muhammad was born into an illustrious lineage, he was also born an orphan with little financial means and substance. His mother was poor, and his father had died too young to have acquired much in the way of worldly goods, leaving his orphaned son an inheritance consisting only of five camels, a small flock of sheep and goats, and one slave girl, who was variously known as Barakah and as Um Ayman.

C2. HIS WET NURSES

Shortly after his birth, Prophet Muhammad was briefly placed in the care of a wet nurse, Thuwaybah, who was the slave of his uncle, Abu Lahab. Although he nursed from Thuwaybah for only a few days, Prophet Muhammad would later always act as a loving and caring son to her.

Prophet Muhammad's short stay with Thuwaybah was occasioned by the arrival of the Bani Sa'd in Makkah. The Bani Sa'd ibn Bakr was a branch of the Hawazin tribe of Bedouins, and it was the custom of the people of Makkah to send their infant children to be nursed by and raised with the Bedouins, with the children sometimes remaining with the Bedouins for as long as eight to ten years. This was done in order that the children might learn a refined Arabic language and might renew the original familial bond with the desert that was the heritage of all of the city-dwelling families of Makkah. As a matter of honor, the families of the Bani Sa'd performed this duty free of charge, although their long-term goal was to form beneficial and powerful alliances with the families of the Makkan children they raised.

In such a system, the raising of an orphan offered little advantage to the families of the Bani Sa'd, as the orphan had no father from whom future benefits might flow. As such, Aminah's efforts to place her infant son with the Bani Sa'd met with repeated rejection. Finally, after much searching among the potential wet nurses of the Bani Sa'd, Aminah found one woman, Halimah bint Abu Du'ayb, whose family was so wretchedly poor and hungry that she had been consistently rejected by the families of Makkah as a potential wet nurse. With no other prospects in sight for nursing a Makkan child, Halimah finally decided to accept the infant Muhammad into her care. The rejected had found a home with the rejected.

However, returning from Makkah to the desert with the infant Muhammad, Halimah's family began to experience a repeated sequence of good fortune. Their grazing animals began to find forage in the desert terrain and unexpectedly began to put on weight. Their dairy livestock suddenly increased their supply of milk, and their beasts of burden found new strength and vitality. However Halimah's family might have originally interpreted their change of fortune, they apparently believed that it was somehow tied to the presence of the Makkan child in their midst. As such, when Muhammad was weaned at age two, Halimah and her family returned to Makkah and begged Aminah to allow

Muhammad to remain with them for an additional while. Although wanting her only child with her, Aminah reluctantly agreed to Halimah's request, and Muhammad returned to the desert with Halimah and her family.

After additional tempering among the Bedouin of the desert, Muhammad was finally returned to the care of his mother in Makkah. Sources differ as to how old Muhammad was when he was returned to his mother's care in Makkah, with some sources suggesting that he was as young as three and with other sources suggesting that he was as old as five.

C3. REPEATED LOSSES

When Muhammad was six years old, Aminah took Muhammad and a slave girl, Barakah, with her on a caravan journey to Madinah to visit her uncles among the Bani Al-Najjar tribe. After a month's visit in Madinah and while on the way back to Makkah, Aminah became ill, and the three of them were forced to drop out of their caravan at Abwa. Aminah subsequently died and was buried at Abwa, leaving Muhammad a double orphan, having neither mother nor father. Fortunately, Barakah, who was also known as Um Ayman, was true to her trust, cared for the grieving Muhammad, and arranged for travel back to Makkah for the two of them. Arriving back in Makkah, the six-year-old Muhammad now fell under the care and guardianship of his paternal grandfather, 'Abd Al-Muttalib, who was about 78 years old at the time.

By all accounts, 'Abd Al-Muttalib was especially fond of his orphaned grandson and was closer to him than to his own children, the youngest of whom were around Muhammad's own age. Day in and day out, 'Abd Al-Muttalib and the young Muhammad were inseparable, with the former even taking the latter with him when he went to attend the meetings of the Makkan Assembly. Not only was Muhammad the only child present on the august occasions of these Assembly meetings, but 'Abd Al-Muttalib would even interrupt Assembly discussions to ask the opinion of his young grandson on the issues being discussed.

Unfortunately, this bond between grandfather and grandson was short-lived, as 'Abd Al-Muttalib died when Muhammad was about eight years old.

Upon his death, 'Abd Al-Muttalib had entrusted his orphaned grandson to the guardianship and protection of Abu Talib, who was a full brother to Muhammad's deceased father, 'Abd Allah. While Abu Talib and his wife, Fatimah, clearly loved their orphaned nephew, Abu Talib's economic resources were limited. As such, in order to help relieve the financial burden on his uncle's family, Muhammad began the often solitary and independent work of a shepherd at the tender age of eight, pasturing sheep and goats in the mountains and valleys surrounding Makkah.

It is perhaps not out of line at this point to note the pattern of traumatic losses that marked Muhammad's first eight years of life. His father had died before Muhammad was even born, and Muhammad had been an orphan from birth. While still in infancy, Muhammad was assigned to the care of Halimah, and thus experienced the second great loss of his early childhood by being separated from his mother for the better part of the first three to five years of his life. While this latter event was typical for Makkan children at that time, it was still another traumatic loss for the future prophet of Allah. Somewhere between his third and fifth year of life, Muhammad experienced his third major loss when he was returned to Aminah in Makkah and was thus separated from Halimah, the only mother whom he had consistently known up until then. Muhammad's fourth major loss occurred with the death of his mother when he was only six years old. About two years after that, Muhammad suffered the fifth major loss of his childhood when his loving grandfather, 'Abd Al-Muttalib, died. Finally, beginning with his work as a shepherd at age eight, Muhammad lost the normal play of childhood. Such a pattern of traumatic losses occurring across the first eight years of life would have left deep psychological scars and a pathological sense of interpersonal impermanence in a lesser individual. However, in Muhammad's case, the repetitious pattern of traumatic loss may have actually contributed to a heightened sensitivity to and caring for others. In any case, Muhammad's ability to rise above these traumatic losses revealed Allah's benevolence to Muhammad.

> Did He not find thee an orphan and give thee shelter (and care)? And He found thee wandering, and He gave thee guidance. And He found thee in need, and made thee independent. Therefore treat not the orphan with harshness, nor repulse the petitioner (unheard); but the bounty of thy Lord—rehearse and proclaim. (*Qur'an* 93: 6-11)

D. FROM CHILD TO ADULT

D1. ACQUISITION OF A NICKNAME

Even as a youth, Muhammad demonstrated unusually admirable qualities of character. In particular, his honesty, trustworthiness, reliability, and loyalty were much appreciated by those around him, both children and adults. As such, the people of Makkah began to refer to him as Al-Amin, i.e., the trustworthy or the faithful.

D2. ENCOUNTER WITH BAHIRA

When he was either nine or 12 years old, Muhammad's life as a shepherd was interrupted for several months. Abu Talib was preparing to travel with a merchant caravan to Syria in order to engage in trade, and he decided to take his nephew with him. As the caravan approached Busra (Bostra), their arrival was eagerly awaited by Bahira, a Christian monk. Bahira lived a solitary life in a cave that had reportedly been occupied generation after generation by one or another Christian monk. There, Bahira studied his books of religious instruction that had been handed down to him by his predecessors. Given his study of these books, and perhaps partially based upon the Biblical verses quoted earlier in this chapter, Bahira believed that a prophet was to arise from within the Arab people, and he eagerly awaited his arrival.

As the caravan approached ever closer to his cave, it seemed to Bahira that a low-lying cloud was keeping pace with the caravan and constantly shading some members of that caravan. Was this the sign for which Bahira had been waiting? His eager anticipation was further heightened when the caravan stopped at a tree. It seemed to the monk that the cloud stopped its movement when the caravan halted and that a tree was somehow lowering its branches to provide further shade to someone within the caravan. Could this be a second sign?

Wasting no time, Bahira invited all the members of the caravan to a meal at which he carefully examined those in front of him. Not finding that for which he was looking, he inquired if all of the members of the caravan had come to his repast. He was told that they had left the youthful Muhammad to tend to their camels, and Bahira then immediately insisted that Muhammad also join them. Arriving at the monk's cave, Bahira examined Muhammad and found certain features about Muhammad that corresponded with the features of the coming prophet that were mentioned in Bahira's books. Included in those features was the slightly raised oval mark that Muhammad had carried between his shoulder blades since birth and that signified a mark of prophethood to Bahira. Examination completed, Bahira announced to Abu Talib that his young nephew was destined to be a prophet and that Abu Talib should take special care to protect his nephew from those who would wish him harm.

D3. THE WAR OF *FIJAR*

It happened during Muhammad's teenage years that Al-Barrad ibn Qays of the Kinanah tribe of Bedouins murdered 'Urwah Al-Rahhal ibn 'Utbah of the 'Amr clan of the Hawazin tribe of Bedouins. Compounding the crime was the fact that the murder occurred during one of the Arabs' sacred months in which all forms of warfare were prohibited. Given the Bedouin law of retaliation, the Hawazin demanded the life of the perpetrator of this crime, who had taken refuge in the fortress of Khaybar, from which the Hawazin were unable to dislodge him.

As a brief digression, it should be noted that the Bedouin law of retaliation was in many ways consistent with the *Lex Talionis* (law of retaliation in kind) found in the so-called Mosaic Law of *Exodus*.

> If any harm follows, then you shall give life for life, eye for eye, tooth for tooth, hand for hand, foot for foot, burn for burn, wound for wound, stripe for stripe. (*Exodus* 21: 23-25)

Consistent with the Bedouin practice of the law of retaliation, the Hawazin, having failed to exact their blood vengeance on the actual perpetrator of the crime, next sought their life-for-a-life from among the Kinanah, the tribe to which the perpetrator belonged. The end result was a desert war, which has gone down in the pages of history as the War of *Fijar* (the immoral war), so named because it began in the sacred months when all warfare was prohibited. Ironically, while the war lasted for three or four years, until honor and debt were satisfied, there were only about five days of actual combat across the entirety of the war.

Because of its longstanding alliance with the Kinanah, the Quraysh tribe of Makkah was rather reluctantly involved in the War of *Fijar*. As a result, Muhammad was present on at least two occasions during the five days of combat that transpired. On the first occasion, he was judged to be too young to be involved in the actual combat, but was delegated to gather the arrows shot by the Hawazin that had missed their marks and hand these arrows over to the men of Quraysh, so that they could be shot back at the Hawazin. On the second occasion, Muhammad was involved in the combat as an archer and received accolades for his courage under fire.

E. EARLY ADULTHOOD

E1. THE ALLIANCE OF *FUDUL*

In the Arabian Peninsula of the late sixth century, one's ability to demand justice was regrettably tied to the strength of the clan or tribe with which one was affiliated. If one were a stranger without clan or tribal representation, one basically had no standing before the "court" of justice. Thus it was that a merchant from Zabid in Yemen sold some merchandise to a person of the Makkan clan of Sahm, who promptly refused to pay for the merchandise, reasoning that the seller was bereft of any Makkan affiliations that would necessitate the buyer having to make payment. Realizing his predicament, the Yemeni merchant publicly appealed to the Quraysh as a whole. In response, several clans of the Quraysh came together to form a league to represent those distressed individuals who had no clan or tribal identification that could protect them in the environs of Makkah. This chivalrous enterprise was known as *Hilful Fudul* (Alliance for Charity).

It is a testament to Muhammad's early commitment to justice and to the plight of the weak and oppressed that, although he was only 20 or 21 years old at the time of the formation of *Hilful Fudul*, he was a charter member of this league.

E2. LIFE AS A CARAVAN TRADER

In about 594 CE, a wealthy widow of the Bani Asad clan of the Quraysh was preparing to send a caravan to trade in Syria and had let it be known that she was looking for a reliable man to lead her caravan and act as her business manager on this trip. The widow was Khadijah bint Khuwaylid ibn Asad ibn 'Abd Al-'Uzza ibn Qusai (Zaid), and thus was Muhammad's fourth cousin once removed. Khadijah had several times previously sent trading caravans to Syria and had typically paid two camels as wages to the man who had acted as her business manager. Hearing of this proposed caravan, Muhammad's uncle, Abu Talib, intervened with Khadijah on Muhammad's behalf. Muhammad's reputation for honesty and trustworthiness were such that Khadijah quickly agreed with Abu Talib's request that the caravan be entrusted to Muhammad's care. After all, where else could she find someone to manage her affairs who had already earned the nickname of Al-Amin, i.e., the trustworthy or the faithful. To secure Muhammad as her business manager, she even went so far as to double the proposed salary to four camels.

Few details have survived about the business side of this

caravan journey. However, two facts have been recorded. Firstly, Muhammad's honesty and kindness throughout the journey greatly impressed Khadijah's slave, Maysarah, who had been sent along with Muhammad and the caravan. Secondly, through Muhammad's astute, although scrupulously fair, business dealings, Khadijah almost doubled the wealth that she had originally assigned to this caravan. However, the business side of the caravan trip was far less remarkable than an event that happened during the journey in the vicinity of Busra (Bostra) and that called to mind the earlier meeting between Muhammad and Bahira.

E3. ENCOUNTER WITH NESTOR

Approximately 12 to 15 years previously, Muhammad had arrived at Busra (Bostra) with his uncle, Abu Talib, and had been identified by a Christian monk, Bahira, as the prophet who was yet to come. Now, as he sat under the shade of a tree, a different Christian monk, Nestor, came out of his monastic cell and inquired of Maysarah, Khadijah's young slave, who it was who was sitting under the tree. Maysarah answered that it was a man of the tribe of Quraysh, to which Nestor replied that this man was a prophet. Maysarah had already been impressed with the character and virtue of Muhammad, and he probably now began to observe Muhammad even more closely than he had before. As such, it was not too much later that Maysarah caught a brief vision of two angels shading Muhammad from the oppressive heat of the sun.

To briefly digress, attention should be paid to this monk's name, Nestor. The name, Nestor, might well suggest that this Christian monk was from that branch of early Christianity known as Nestorians. Certainly, Nestorian Christianity was centered in and around the Middle East, with its primary strongholds being in Greece, Turkey, and Syria. Given that Nestor was probably a Nestorian Christian and given the geographical association between Nestor and Bahira, it is possible that Bahira was also a Nestorian Christian.

At the risk of oversimplifying, Nestorian Christianity strongly objected to the title "*theotokos*" (literally, "God bearer", but often translated as "mother of God") being applied to the Virgin Mary and was one of the many branches of early Christianity that held to the adoptionist view of the relationship between Prophet Jesus and Allah. Expressed in various forms across the first several centuries of Christianity, the adoptionist position basically maintained that Prophet Jesus stood in relation to Allah as an adopted son to his adoptive father, not as a begotten son to his begetting father. As such, the Nestorians insisted on the full humanity of Prophet Jesus, although recognizing that the "Word of God" descended upon him at his baptism. The Nestorians drew their inspiration from Nestorius, a bishop of Constantinople in the first half of the fifth century, whose adoptionist views were condemned at the Council of Ephesus in 431 and at the Council of Chalcedon in 451. Besides Nestorius, other early Christian adoptionists of note included: (1) the Ebionites, who apparently arose as early as the first century, upheld most aspects of the so-called Mosaic Law of the *Old Testament*, rejected animal sacrifice, practiced ritual ablution by washing, and continued in existence until the fourth century; (2) Theodotus the Tanner, a late second century adoptionist and the founder of Dynamic Monarchianism or the Theodotian branch of early Christianity, which lasted as a force within early Christianity into the fourth century; (3) Paul of Samosata, a third century bishop of Antioch, who espoused a form of Dynamic Monarchianism; (4) Eusebius of Nicomedia, an early fourth century bishop of Berytus, Nicomedia, and Constantinople, who refused to recognize Christ as being of the same substance as the "Father", who thus rejected the usual trinitarian position, and who was the founder of the Eusebian branch of early Christianity; and (5) Arius, an early fourth century priest and presbyter at Alexandria, who was condemned at the Council of Nicaea in 325 CE, and who founded the Arian movement within Christianity, a movement which lasted into the seventh century among some Germanic tribes, may have been the dominant and majority movement within Christianity during parts of the fourth century, maintained that Jesus Christ was not truly divine but was created, and insisted on the uniqueness and unity of God. All of the above adoptionist movements shared some important Christological features with Islam.

E4. MARRIAGE TO KHADIJAH

Returning to Makkah from the long and arduous journey to Syria, Muhammad immediately reported to Khadijah on his successful trading in her behalf. Khadijah was impressed. Clearly, here was an able, skilled, and talented young man of surprising acumen and unimpeachable character. Could he not be something more than just her business agent? At the time, Muhammad was only 25 years old, while Khadijah was 40 and had been twice widowed. Further, Khadijah was quite wealthy, belonging to the mercantile aristocracy of Makkah, while Muhammad was poor and had few economic prospects. Despite the disparities between them, Khadijah thoughts turned to marriage. She consulted a female friend, Nufaysah, who offered to raise the issue of marriage with Muhammad on Khadijah's behalf. To this Khadijah, assented.

Not long after Khadijah's conversation with Nufaysah, Khadijah received a glowing report on Muhammad from Maysarah, the slave of Khadijah who had accompanied Muhammad to Syria. Included in his report were the declaration of Nestor and that brief vision of two angels shading Muhammad. What was Khadijah to make of this? She wasn't sure, and so decided to consult her first cousin, Waraqah, who happened to be one of the very few Christians in Makkah. After listening to Khadijah's concern about the unusual report she had received from Maysarah, Waraqah immediately pronounced that Muhammad was the prophet yet to come, the long awaited prophet to the Arab people.

Meanwhile, Nufaysah was broaching the issue of marriage in a general and non-specific way with Muhammad, who responded that he did not yet have the economic self-sufficiency to marry. Undeterred, Nufaysah wondered aloud whether that problem would still hold if Muhammad's bride were a woman of great wealth and nobility. At that point, Muhammad inquired as to the identity of this proposed bride. When told it was Khadijah, Muhammad immediately assented to the proposed wedding. Arrangements were then made between the two families, Muhammad paid a dowry of 20 female camels, and the formalities of the wedding were conducted. To celebrate his marriage, Muhammad manumitted Barakah, the loyal slave whom he had inherited from his father. Barakah would later marry, become the mother of Ayman, and become known as Um Ayman.

By all historical accounts, the marriage between Muhammad and Khadijah was one of great happiness, contentment, and companionship. The two were devoted to each other throughout their 24 years of marriage, with each being a pillar of support for the other. Despite Khadijah's age at the onset of their marriage, she bore six children to Muhammad, two sons (Qasim and 'Abd Allah[13]) who died in childhood and four daughters (Zaynab, Ruqayyah, Um Kulthum, and Fatimah) who lived into adulthood. In addition, there were two other members of the household. Firstly, at the time of their marriage, Khadijah had given Muhammad a teenage slave, Zayd, who was immediately manumitted and adopted by Muhammad, and who was thereafter raised by Muhammad and Khadijah as a member of their family. Secondly, to ease the financial burden on Abu Talib's large family during a time of famine, Muhammad and Khadijah invited 'Ali ibn Abu Talib into their home and raised him from around the age of five. 'Ali would later marry Fatimah bint Muhammad and become the fourth caliph of Islam.

E5. THE REBUILDING OF THE KA'BA

When Muhammad was about 35 years old, the Quraysh of Makkah decided that the structural integrity of the Ka'ba had deteriorated to the point that it needed to be rebuilt. With more than a little trepidation, they began dismantling the sacred edifice and worked their way down to the original foundation stones. Having reached the foundation stones laid by Prophets Abraham and Ismael, they began to gather additional stones to add to those they had removed, in order that their rebuilding of the Ka'ba would result in a much taller building. However, as they were engaged in the rebuilding of the Ka'ba, a fierce inter-clan dispute arose over which of the clans would have the honor of placing *Hajr Al-Aswad* (the Black Stone of Makkah) into the wall of the Ka'ba. (See chapter VI, section F2, for details regarding this special stone).

After several days of quarreling over which clan would place the *Hajr Al-Aswad* into its appropriate place in the wall of the Ka'ba, a solution was finally proposed. It was suggested and agreed to that the next man to enter the precincts of the Ka'ba would be given binding arbitration power to settle the inter-clan dispute. The various clans of the Quraysh had no sooner ratified this solution to the impasse, when Muhammad walked into the Ka'ba area. The problem was placed before him, and Muhammad quickly proposed a fitting solution worthy of the best traditions of Solomonic wisdom. Muhammad called for a cloak which he then spread on the ground. Placing the *Hajr Al-Aswad* onto the cloak, Muhammad then requested representatives from each clan to grab hold of the border of the cloak and to lift the rock-bearing cloak to the site in the wall where the *Hajr Al-Aswad* was to be placed. When this was done, Muhammad lifted the rock from the cloak and placed it in the wall. The honor of all of the clans had been satisfied, a major inter-clan dispute had been resolved, and Muhammad's reputation as the trustworthy and faithful Al-Amin had been enhanced.

F. THE PROPHETIC CALL

F1. THE FIRST REVELATION

Having settled into married life and with immediate economic concerns now behind him, Muhammad began to cultivate a life of intense spiritual contemplation. Such issues as personal piety, social justice, and universal and absolute truth became an ever-increasing focus in his already admirable lifestyle. In addition, he began to experience dreams of an intensely spiritual nature. As such, he began to withdraw into periods of isolated and solitary contemplation. He would pack provisions for himself, leave the comfort of his home and family, and spend increasing periods of time in a cave on Mt. Hira, one of the mountains surrounding the valley of Makkah. There, his spiritual retreats were marked by long periods of prayer and fasting.

> Narrated 'Aisha, the wife of the Prophet: "The commencement (of the Divine Inspiration) to Allah's Apostle was in the form of true dreams in his sleep, for he never had a dream but it turned out to be true and clear as the bright daylight. Then he began to like seclusions, so he used to go in seclusion in the cave of Hira where he used to worship Allah continuously for many nights before going back to his family to take the necessary provision (of food) for the stay." (*Al-Bukhari, Hadith # 6:478*; see also *Al-Bukhari, Ahadith# 1: 3 and 9: 111*)

Finally, in one of the odd numbered days of the last 10 days of the month of *Ramadan* in 610 CE, Muhammad's spiritual quest began to be fulfilled. He was visited by the angel Gabriel (Jibril) and received his first revelation as a prophet of Allah.

> Narrated 'Aisha, the wife of the Prophet..."He would come back to (his wife) Khadijah again to take his provision (of food) likewise, till one day he received the guidance while he was in the cave of Hira. An angel came to him and asked him to read. Allah's Apostle replied, 'I do not know how to read.' The Prophet added, 'Then the angel held me (forcibly) and pressed me so hard that I felt distressed. Then he released me and again asked me to read, and I replied, 'I do not know how to read.' Thereupon he held me again and pressed me for the second time till I felt distressed. He then released me and asked me to read, but again I replied, 'I do not know how to read.' Thereupon he held me for the third time and pressed me till I got distressed, and then he released me and said...'" (*Al-Bukhari, Hadith # 6: 478*; see also *Al-Bukhari, Ahadith # 1: 3 and 9: 111*)

Before proceeding to the actual wording of this first revelation to Prophet Muhammad, it is worth pausing briefly to note the remarkable similarity between the above *Hadith* and the following Biblical passage. The latter reports an *Old Testament* vision of a sealed document of revelation being first presented to a literate, but unidentified, prophet. This prophet is told to read the document of revelation, but correctly replies that the revelation is still sealed, thus implying that this revelation must await the coming of a later prophet. Subsequently, the document is presented to another prophet, who is told to read the revelation, but replies that he cannot read.

> The vision of all this has become for you like the words of a sealed document. If it is given to those who can read, with the command, "Read this," they say, "We cannot, for it is sealed." And if it is given to those who cannot read, saying, "Read this," they say, "We cannot read." (*Isaiah* 29: 11-12)

The first revelation to Prophet Muhammad was delivered by the angel Gabriel. After squeezing and releasing Prophet Muhammad for the third time, Gabriel pronounced the first words of this new revelation. Of note, the first word of this revelation, i.e., *Iqra'*, can be translated into English as "proclaim", "recite", or "read", and has the same Arabic root as the word *Qur'an*, i.e., "recitation" or "reading".

> Proclaim! (or read!) in the name of thy Lord and cherisher, Who created — created man, out of a (mere) clot of congealed blood: proclaim! And thy Lord is most bountiful — He Who taught (the use of) the pen — taught man that which he knew not. (*Qur'an* 96:1-5)

As shown in the following *Hadith*, Prophet Muhammad's initial encounter with the angel Gabriel was immensely frightening. What was this miraculous event that he had encountered? Was he being pursued and tormented by an evil spirit or jinn? Had the event been real, or was he losing his mind? Above all,

what was happening to him? Greatly distressed, Prophet
Muhammad struggled home to Khadijah and begged her to
cover him. Khadijah responded with all the comfort and support
of a loving wife who sometimes knows her husband better than
he knows himself. After calming her husband and perhaps
remembering the earlier pronouncement by her cousin, Waraqah,
that Muhammad was the prophet yet to come, Khadijah took
Muhammad to consult with Waraqah.

> Narrated 'Aisha:..."Then Allah's Apostle returned with the
> inspiration and with his heart beating severely. Then he went
> to Khadijah bint Khuwaylid and said, 'Cover me, cover me!'
> They covered him till his fear was over, and after that he
> told her everything that had happened and said, 'I fear that
> something may happen to me.' Khadijah replied, 'Never! By
> Allah, Allah will never disgrace you. You keep good relations
> with your kith and kin, help the poor and the destitute, serve
> your guests generously and assist the deserving calamity-
> afflicted ones.' Khadijah then accompanied him to her cousin,
> Waraqah ibn Naufal ibn Assad ibn 'Abdul 'Uzza, who during
> the pre-Islamic period became a Christian, and used to write
> the writing with Hebrew letters. He would write from the
> gospel in Hebrew as much as Allah wished him to write. He
> was an old man, and had lost his eyesight. Khadijah said to
> Waraqah, 'Listen to the story of your nephew, O my cousin!'
> Waraqah asked, 'O my nephew! what have you seen?' Allah's
> Apostle described whatever he had seen. Waraqah said, 'This
> is the same one who keeps the secrets (angel Gabriel) whom
> Allah had sent to Moses. I wish I were young and could live
> up to the time when your people would turn you out.' Allah's
> Apostle asked, 'Will they drive me out?' Waraqah replied
> in the affirmative and said, 'Anyone (man) who came with
> something similar to what you have brought was treated with
> hostility, and if I should remain alive till the day when you
> will be turned out, then I would support you strongly.' But
> after a few days Waraqah died, and the divine inspiration

was also paused for a while." (*Al-Bukhari, Hadith* # 1: 3; see also *Al-Bukhari, Ahadith* # 6: 478 and 9: 111)

F2. THE SECOND REVELATION

No exact dating is possible for the second revelation given to Prophet Muhammad. Likewise, the details of where and how Prophet Muhammad received this revelation have not been recorded. This second revelation began with a single Arabic letter, i.e., "*Nun*", the exact meaning of which is unclear. (See chapter IV, section B4, for more on the "detached letters" within the *Qur'an*.) Immediately thereafter, there was a divine message of personal reassurance to Prophet Muhammad. The nature of this divine revelation suggests that Prophet Muhammad, despite the reassurances of Khadijah and Waraqah, was still most concerned about his earlier encounter with Gabriel and continued to have some lingering doubts about his own sanity.

Nun. By the pen and by the (record) which (men) write — thou art not, by the grace of thy Lord, mad or possessed. Nay, verily for thee is a reward unfailing: and thou (standest) on an exalted standard of character. (*Qur'an* 68: 1-4)

F3. THE *FATRAH* AND THE THIRD REVELATION

Following the first two revelations, the revelations ceased for a period of time. This period is known as the *Fatrah* or "gap". The exact length of the *Fatrah* is unknown, but scholars have generally believed that it lasted from several days to as long as three years. Two different traditions survive as to what was the third revelation, each of which is presented below.

In the first tradition, the *Fatrah* lasted sufficiently long that Prophet Muhammad was mortally concerned that he had somehow incurred the displeasure of Allah and that the revelations had permanently ceased. Reportedly, he may even have been plagued by some suicidal ideation during this time. The ever-faithful Khadijah continually reassured her husband that Allah had not abandoned him and that Allah was not displeased with him. Finally, the third revelation was delivered. It directly addressed Prophet Muhammad's concern that he had somehow inadvertently displeased Allah, i.e., "thy Guardian-Lord hath not forsaken thee, nor is He displeased", and promised further revelations would be forthcoming, i.e., "and soon will thy Guardian-Lord give thee (that wherewith) thou shalt be well-pleased". Further, in this revelation's initial contrast between the "glorious morning light" and "the night when it is still", it offered an explanation of the *Fatrah*. Just as the activity of a man's day necessitated a period of nighttime stillness in which one could regain one's strength, so too the initial intensity of receiving divine revelation required a period of rest and tranquility in which a new prophet could regain his psychic equilibrium. Later, as Prophet Muhammad became accustomed to receiving revelation, such pauses in revelation would no longer be necessary.

> By the glorious morning light, and by the night when it is still — thy Guardian-Lord hath not forsaken thee, nor is He displeased. And verily the hereafter will be better for thee than the present. And soon will thy Guardian-Lord give thee (that wherewith) thou shalt be well-pleased. Did He not find thee an orphan and give thee shelter (and care)? And He found thee wandering, and He gave thee guidance. And He found thee in need, and made thee independent. Therefore treat not the orphan with harshness, nor repulse the petitioner (unheard); but the bounty of thy Lord – rehearse and proclaim. (*Qur'an* 93: 1-11)

The following *Hadith*, representing the second of the two traditions regarding the third revelation, offers a brief synopsis of the *Fatrah* and of the revelation that ended the *Fatrah*.

> Jabir ibn 'Abdullah Al-Ansari narrated while talking about the period of pause in revelation, reporting the speech of the Prophet: "While I was walking, all of a sudden I heard a voice from the sky. I looked up and saw the same angel who

had visited me at the cave of Hira sitting on a chair between the sky and the earth. I got afraid of him, and came back home, and said, 'Wrap me (in blankets).' And then Allah revealed the following holy verses (of Qur'an)..." (*Al-Bukhari, Hadith # 1: 3; see also Al-Bukhari, Ahadith #4:* 461 and 6: 478)

O thou wrapped up (in a mantle)! arise and deliver thy warning! And thy Lord do thou magnify! And thy garments keep free from stain! And all abominations shun! (*Qur'an* 74: 1-5)

Regardless of which Qur'anic passage was the third revelation, Prophet Muhammad had been given clear instructions, i.e., "rehearse and proclaim" or "arise and deliver thy warning". It was now time for the ministry of the last prophet of Allah to begin. Consistent with the Biblical and Qur'anic portrayals of those prophets who had preceded him, he was directed to deliver a warning.

G. THE PROPHET IN MAKKAH

G1. THE PRIVATE MINISTRY

Initially, the ministry of Prophet Muhammad was a private affair, and he delivered the message obtained from his early revelations only to his immediate family and to selected friends. Included in that message was a strict monotheism, the need for the proper worship of and manner of praying to the One God, the need for social justice to one's fellow man, the intense mercy of Allah, and the inevitability of death, resurrection and a coming Day of Judgment. The first to convert to this revival of the true monotheism was the Prophet's wife, Khadijah. Other early converts followed in rapid succession, and included, but were not limited to: (1) 'Ali ibn Abu Talib, the Prophet's nephew and ward; (2) Zayd ibn Harithah, the Prophet's adopted son and former slave; (3) Abu Bakr ibn Abu Quhafah Al-Taymi, who would later become the first caliph of Islam; (4) 'Abd 'Amr ibn 'Awf, later renamed by the Prophet as 'Abd Al-Rahman ibn 'Awf; (5) Abu

'Ubaydah ibn Al-Jarrah of the Bani Al-Harith; (6) Khalid ibn Sa'id ibn Al-'Aws, who had been warned by Allah in a dream to seek out Prophet Muhammad and to accept the message that he preached; (7) 'Uthman ibn 'Affan Al-Umawi, who also had received a divine warning in a dream, and who would later become the third caliph of Islam; (8) Talhah ibn 'Ubaid Allah Al-Taymi, whose conversion had been prompted by his having been returning to Makkah from Syria when he had been approached at Busra (Bostra) by a Christian monk, most probably Nestor, who inquired if Muhammad had yet revealed himself as a prophet of Allah; (9) Al-Zuhri ibn 'Ubaid Allah Al-Taymi; (10) 'Abd Allah ibn Mas'ud, who was at the time a young shepherd; (11) Asma bint Abu Bakr; (12) Arqam ibn Abu Arqam; (13) 'Amr ibn Nufail and his wife, Fatimah bint Al-Khattab; and (14) several cousins of the Prophet, including Ja'far ibn Abu Talib, Zubayr, 'Abd Allah ibn Jahsh, 'Ubayd Allah ibn Jahsh, Abu Salamah, Sa'd ibn Abu Waqqas, and 'Umayr ibn Abu Waqqas.

The conversions continued, the early community of Muslims gradually expanded and quickly numbered over 40 individuals, the divine revelations were eagerly memorized, and the revival of the true and correct worship of Allah was lovingly embraced. Further, the divine revelations continued to flow, among the earliest of which were the following.

O thou wrapped up (in a mantle)! arise and deliver thy warning! And thy Lord do thou magnify! And thy garments keep free from stain! And all abomination shun! Nor expect, in giving, any increase (for thyself)! But, for thy Lord's (cause) be patient and constant! Finally, when the trumpet is sounded, that will be — that day — a day of distress — far from easy for those without faith. (*Qur'an* 74: 1-10)

O thou folded in garments! stand (to prayer) by night, but not all night — half of it — or a little less, or a little more; and recite the Qur'an in slow, measured rhythmic tones. Soon shall We send down to thee a weighty message. Truly the rising by night is most potent for governing (the soul), and most suitable for (framing) the word (of prayer and praise). True, there is for thee by day prolonged occupation with ordinary duties: but keep in remembrance the name of thy Lord and devote thyself to Him wholeheartedly. (He is) Lord of the East and the West: there is no god but He: take Him therefore for (thy) disposer of affairs. (*Qur'an* 73: 1-9)

Patiently, then, persevere: for the promise of Allah is true: and ask forgiveness for thy fault, and celebrate the praises of thy Lord in the evening and in the morning. (*Qur'an* 40: 55)

The Muslim *Ummah* or community was growing, and regular prayer was now being practiced twice a day. However, these early Muslims were still cautious and fearful of persecution from their pagan neighbors and family members. As such, they practiced their religion quietly and away from public view, gathering on the outskirts of Makkah to receive instruction and to worship Allah. However, rumors inevitably began to circulate among the Quraysh of Makkah that Prophet Muhammad and his followers were covertly practicing a new religion.

G2. THE PUBLIC MINISTRY

The public ministry of Prophet Muhammad began circa 613 CE, approximately three years after the start of his prophethood, took two forms — one to his extended family and one to all the Quraysh of Makkah, and was prompted by the following revelations.

And admonish thy nearest kinsmen, and lower thy wing to the believers who follow thee. Then if they disobey thee, say: "I am free (of responsibility) for what ye do!" (*Qur'an* 26: 214-216)

Therefore expound openly what thou art commanded, and turn away from those who join false gods with Allah.

For sufficient are We unto thee against those who scoff —
those who adopt, with Allah, another god: but soon will they
come to know. (*Qur'an* 15: 94-96)

In reaching out to his extended family, Prophet Muhammad
had meals prepared for his relatives on two successive nights.
After his extended family had partaken of the first evening's
meal, Prophet Muhammad attempted to address his relatives
about his revelations and about the message that he had
been commanded to preach. However, Abu Lahab, the Prophet's
paternal uncle, immediately interrupted his nephew, announced
that a spell had been cast upon the assemblage, and managed
to get the extended family to disperse before the Prophet could
address them. After the second evening's meal, the Prophet was
successful in addressing his kinsmen, but only a few responded to
the Prophet's clarion call, and most of his relatives dismissed
him with ridicule and laughter.

The story of Prophet Muhammad beginning his public
ministry to the Quraysh as a whole is told in several *Ahadith*, one
of which is quoted below.

> Narrated Ibn Abbas: "When the verse: 'And warn your tribe
> of near-kindred,' was revealed, the Prophet ascended the
> Safa (mountain) and started calling, 'O Bani Fihr! O Bani
> 'Adi!', addressing various tribes of Quraysh till they were
> assembled. Those who could not come themselves, sent their
> messengers to see what was there. Abu Lahab and other
> people from Quraysh came, and the Prophet then said,
> 'Suppose I told you that there is an (enemy) cavalry in the
> valley intending to attack you, would you believe me?' They
> said, 'Yes, for we have not found you telling anything other
> than the truth.' He then said, 'I am a warner to you in face
> of a terrific punishment.' Abu Lahab said (to the Prophet),
> 'May your hands perish all this day. Is it for this purpose
> you have gathered us?' ..." (*Al-Bukhari, Hadith* #6:293;
> see also *Al-Bukhari, Ahadith* # 4: 16, 4: 728, 6:294, 6: 325,
> and 6: 495-497, as well as *Muslim, Ahadith* # 399-407)

The above *Hadith* then goes on to inform that Abu Lahab's ridicule of Prophet Muhammad was the precipitating event for yet another revelation. This revelation mentioned Abu Lahab by name (Abu Lahab may be translated as "father of flame) and prophesied his own destruction.

> Perish the hands of the Father of Flame! Perish he! No profit to him from all his wealth, and all his gains! Burnt soon will he be in a fire of blazing flame! His wife shall carry the (crackling) wood — as fuel! — a twisted rope of palm leaf fibre round her (own) neck! (*Qur'an* 111:1-5)

G3. REJECTION, RIDICULE, AND PERSECUTION

The message of Islam had now been publicly proclaimed. While some, especially from the more economically disadvantaged classes of Makkah, responded favorably and accepted Islam, most of the Quraysh rejected the message and ministry of Prophet Muhammad, heaped ridicule upon him, and actively persecuted those Muslims who were not fortunate enough to be protected by a clan or family willing to stand up for them. While Prophet Muhammad continued to enjoy the physical protection of his clan, which was then headed by his loving uncle, Abu Talib, the Prophet was not protected from the endless string of verbal abuse and ridicule that was directed at him. Some measure of the content and frequency of this ridicule and of the charges leveled at Prophet Muhammad can be gleaned from multiple passages in the *Qur'an*. While the following quoted passages of the *Qur'an* are quite numerous, it is only by reading through all of them that one begins to appreciate the extent and repetitious nature of the ridicule that was constantly being heaped upon the Prophet.

> If We had sent unto thee a written (message) on parchment, so that they could touch it with their hands, the unbelievers would have been sure to say: "This is nothing but obvious magic!" They say: "Why is not an angel (that we can see) sent down to him?" If We did send down an angel (that

they could see), the matter would be settled at once, and no respite would be granted them. If We had made it an angel, We should have sent him as a man, and We should certainly have caused them confusion in a matter which they have already covered with confusion. Mocked were (many) messengers before thee; but their scoffers were hemmed in by the thing that they mocked. (*Qur'an* 6: 7-10)

We know indeed the grief which their words do cause thee: it is not thee they reject: it is the signs of Allah, which the wicked condemn. (*Qur'an* 6: 33)

Do they not reflect? Their companion is not seized with madness: he is but a perspicuous warner. (*Qur'an* 7: 184)

But when Our clear signs are rehearsed unto them, those who rest not their hope on their meeting with Us, say: "Bring us a reading other than this, or change this." Say: "It is not for me, of my own accord, to change it: I follow naught but what is revealed unto me: if I were to disobey my Lord, I should myself fear the penalty of a great day (to come)." (*Qur'an* 10: 15)

The unbelievers say: "No messenger art thou." Say: "Enough for a witness between me and you is Allah, and such as have knowledge of the book." (*Qur'an* 13: 43)

They say: "O thou to whom the message is being revealed! truly thou art mad (or possessed)! Why bringest thou not angels to us if it be that thou hast the truth?"...We did send messengers before thee amongst the religious sects of old: but never came a messenger to them but they mocked him. (*Qur'an* 15: 6-7, 10-11)

We know indeed that they say, "It is a man that teaches him." The tongue of him they wickedly point to is notably foreign, while this is Arabic, pure and clear. (*Qur'an* 16: 103)

Never comes (aught) to them of a renewed message from their Lord, but they listen to it as in jest — their hearts toying as with trifles. The wrongdoers conceal their private counsels, (saying), "Is this (one) more than a man like yourselves? Will ye go to witchcraft with your eyes open?" Say: "My Lord knoweth (every) word (spoken) in the heavens and on earth: He is the One that heareth and knoweth (all things)." "Nay," they say, "(these are) medleys of dreams! — Nay, he forged it! — Nay, he is (but) a poet! Let him then bring us a sign like the ones that were sent to (prophets) of old!" (*Qur'an* 21: 2-5)

When the unbelievers see thee, they treat thee not except with ridicule. "Is this," (they say), "the one who talks of your gods?" And they blaspheme at the mention of (Allah) most gracious! (*Qur'an* 21: 36)

When Our clear signs are rehearsed to them, thou wilt notice a denial on the faces of the unbelievers! They nearly attack with violence those who rehearse Our signs to them. Say, "Shall I tell you of something (far) worse than these signs? It is the fire (of hell)! Allah has promised it to the unbelievers! And evil is that destination!" (*Qur'an* 22: 72)

Or do they not recognize their messenger, that they deny him? Or do they say, "He is possessed"? Nay, he has brought them the truth, but most of them hate the truth. (*Qur'an* 23: 69-70)

They say: "What! When we die and become dust and bones, could we really be raised up again? Such things have been promised to us and to our fathers before! They are nothing but tales of the ancients!" (*Qur'an* 23: 82-83)

But the misbelievers say: "Naught is this but a lie which he has forged, and others have helped him at it." In truth, it is they who have put forward an iniquity and a falsehood. And they say: "Tales of the ancients, which he has caused to be written: and they are dictated before him morning and evening." Say: "The (Qur'an) was sent down by Him Who knows the mystery (that is) in the heavens and the earth: verily He is oft-forgiving, most merciful. And they say: "What sort of a messenger is this, who eats food, and walks through the streets? Why has not an angel (that we can see) been sent down to him to give admonition with him? Or (why) has not a treasure been bestowed on him, or why has he (not) a garden for enjoyment?" The wicked say: "Ye follow none other than a man bewitched." See what kinds of companions they make for thee! But they have gone astray, and never a way will they be able to find! (*Qur'an* 25: 4-9)

When they see thee, they treat thee not otherwise than in mockery: "Is this the one whom Allah has sent as a messenger? He indeed would well nigh have misled us from our gods, had it not been that we were constant to them!" — Soon will they know, when they see the penalty, who it is that is most misled in path! (*Qur'an* 25: 41-42)

But there are, among men, those who purchase idle tales, without knowledge (or meaning), to mislead (men) from the path of Allah and throw ridicule (on the path): for such there will be a humiliating penalty. When Our signs are rehearsed to such a one, he turns away in arrogance, as if he heard them not, as if there were deafness in both his ears: announce to him a grievous penalty. (*Qur'an* 31: 6-7)

(This is) the revelation of the book in which there is no doubt — from the Lord of the worlds. Or do they say, "He has forged it"? Nay, it is the truth from thy Lord, that thou mayest admonish a people to whom no warner has come before thee: in order that they may receive guidance. (*Qur'an* 32: 2-3)

The unbelievers say (in ridicule): "Shall we point out to you a man that will tell you, when ye are all scattered to pieces in disintegration, that ye shall (then be raised) in a new creation? Has he invented a falsehood against Allah, or has a spirit (seized) him?"— Nay, it is those who believe not in the hereafter, that are in (real) penalty, and in farthest error. (*Qur'an* 34: -8)

When our clear signs are rehearsed to them, they say, "This is only a man who wishes to hinder you from the (worship) which your fathers practiced." And they say, "This is only a falsehood invented!" And the unbelievers say of the truth when it comes to them, "This is nothing but evident magic!" (*Qur'an* 34: 43)

For they, when they were told that there is no god except Allah, would puff themselves up with pride, and say: "What! Shall we give up our gods for the sake of a poet possessed?" Nay! He has come with the (very) truth, and he confirms (the message of) the messengers (before him). (*Qur'an* 37: 35-37)

So they wonder that a warner has come to them from among themselves! And the unbelievers say, "This is a sorcerer telling lies! Has he made the gods (all) into one God? Truly this is a wonderful thing!" And the leaders among them go away (impatiently, saying), "Walk ye away, and remain constant to your gods! For this is truly a thing designed (against you)! We never heard (the like) of this among the people of these latter days: this is nothing but a made-up tale! What! Has the message been sent to him — (of all persons) among us?" But they are in doubt concerning My (Own) message! Nay, they have not yet tasted My punishment!" (*Qur'an* 38: 4-8)

What! Do they say, "He has forged a falsehood against Allah"? But if Allah willed, He could seal up thy heart. And Allah blots out vanity, and proves the truth by His words. For He knows well the secrets of all hearts. (*Qur'an* 42: 24)

When Our clear signs are rehearsed to them, the unbelievers say, of the truth when it comes to them: "This is evident sorcery!" Or do they say, "He has forged it"? Say: "Had I forged it, then can ye obtain no single (blessing) for me from Allah. He knows best of that whereof ye talk (so glibly)! Enough is He for a witness between me and you! And He is oft-forgiving, most merciful." (*Qur'an* 46: 7-8)

Therefore proclaim thou the praises (of thy Lord): for by the grace of thy Lord, thou art no (vulgar) soothsayer, nor art thou one possessed. Or do they say — "A poet! We await for him some calamity (hatched) by time!" Say thou: "Await ye! — I too will wait along with you!" Is it that their faculties of understanding urge them to this, or are they but a people transgressing beyond bounds? Or do they say, "He fabricated the (message)"? Nay, they have no faith! Let them then produce a recital like unto it — if (it be) they speak the truth! (*Qur'an* 52: 29-34)

...this is verily the word of an honored messenger; it is not the word of a poet: little it is ye believe! Nor is it the word of a soothsayer: little admonition it is ye receive. (This is) a message sent down from the Lord of the worlds. (*Qur'an* 69: 40-43)

And (O people)! your companion is not one possessed; and without doubt he saw him (angel Gabriel) in the clear horizon. Neither doth he withhold grudgingly a knowledge of the unseen. Nor is it the word of an evil spirit accursed. (*Qur'an* 81: 22-25)

A careful reading of many of the above passages reveals the biting sarcasm that was leveled against Prophet Muhammad by his contemporaries. One must marvel at the psychological fortitude and spiritual stamina of any individual who can withstand such constant humiliation and rejection. By publicly proclaiming his ministry, Prophet Muhammad had gone from being the universally recognized and accepted Al-Amin, i.e., the faithful or the trustworthy, to being considered by most of his fellow Quraysh as no more than a sorcerer or magician, an insane madman, a liar and fabricator of myths, a spinner of dreams, a man possessed by a jinn or demon, an object of mockery and ridicule, the tool or puppet of a foreigner, a man bewitched, an ungrateful rejecter of clan and tribal heritage, a deranged poet, or a vulgar soothsayer. Is it any wonder that so many of the Qur'anic passages dealing with this verbal abuse and ridicule are bracketed by statements of reassurance from Allah to His prophet? Surely, such reassurances were a welcome relief to the Prophet, and a loving mercy from Allah, most gracious and most merciful.

As noted earlier, so long as Abu Talib lived and was leader of Prophet Muhammad's clan, the Prophet enjoyed all the physical protection that his clan could afford him, although this could not stop all physical assaults. For example, dirt was thrown at him, and garbage and filth were scattered in his path and on his doorstep. Once while Prophet Muhammad was praying, 'Uqbah ibn Abu Mu'ayt wrapped a twisted sheet around the Prophet's neck and began to choke him. The Prophet merely and calmly continued his prayer to Allah. On another occasion when Prophet Muhammad was praying, 'Uqbah ibn Abu Mu'ayt physically humiliated the Prophet in the following manner.

Narrated 'Abdullah ibn Masud: "Once the Prophet was offering prayers at the Ka'ba. Abu Jahl was sitting with some of his companions. One of them said to the others, 'Who amongst you will bring the abdominal contents (intestines, etc.) of a camel of Bani so and so and put it on the back of Muhammad, when he prostrates?' The most unfortunate of them got up and brought it. He waited till the Prophet prostrated, and then placed it on his back between his shoulders. I was watching but could not do anything. I wish I had some people with me to hold out against them. They started laughing and falling on one another. Allah's Apostle was in prostration, and he did not lift his head up till Fatimah (the Prophet's daughter) came and threw that (camel's abdominal contents) away from his back." (*Al-Bukhari Hadith* # 1: 241; see also *Al-Bukhari, Ahadith* # 1: 499, 4: 185, 4: 409, and 5: 193)

However, many of the early Muslims were not as "fortunate" as the Prophet. Some were slaves, e.g., Bilal and 'Amr ibn Fuhayrah, who had no clan protecting them. Some were simply rejected by their clans or had clans too weak to protect them, and were thus left to their own devices for their self-protection. Many were the tales of persecution and torture that were handed down through the generations within the Muslim *Ummah*. For example, in unsuccessful efforts to get Bilal to recant his Islamic faith, a rope was placed around his neck, and he was drug through the streets of Makkah and over the hillsides surrounding Makkah. At times, he was starved and deprived of all water. At other times, he was bound, made to lie in the burning sands, and had heavy rocks placed upon his body, which came near to crushing him. Nonetheless, Bilal remained true to his faith, and he did not recant. Likewise, 'Ammar ibn Yasir, who was not a slave, but who received no clan protection, was several times beaten into unconsciousness and was even tossed onto burning embers. He, also, refused to recant. Many of these early Muslims carried the physical scars of their torture with them the rest of their lives.

G4. THE FIRST AND SECOND *HIJRAH* TO ABYSSINIA

Because of the persecution being leveled against some of his followers, Prophet Muhammad authorized a small group of Muslims to leave Makkah in order to search for religious freedom in the Christian kingdom of Abyssinia (roughly corresponding to modern Ethiopia and Eritrea). As such, in 615 CE, 14 or 16 Muslims (either 11 men and five women, or 10 men and four women) emigrated from Makkah to Abyssinia. This constituted the first *Hijrah* (migration) to Abyssinia.

However, the Quraysh of Makkah were not to be put off so easily, and sent envoys to Abyssinia to demand the extradition of these early Muslims. The matter quickly came to the attention of the Negus or ruler of Abyssinia.

In presenting their claims against the Muslim immigrants to Abyssinia, the envoys of the Quraysh made two claims: (1) that the Muslims had rejected the prevailing religious tradition in Makkah; and (2) that the Muslims blasphemed Prophet Jesus by denying him divine status. The Negus then asked the Muslims what their religion taught. Ja'far ibn Abu Talib then stood in the court and recited the opening verses of the 19th *Surah* of the *Qur'an*, which deal with the births of Prophets John the Baptist and Jesus. It is reported that the Negus and his bishops were moved to tears and that the Negus pronounced that these verses obviously came from the same source of revelation as had the words of Jesus Christ. The Quraysh then insisted on pushing their second point, i.e., that the Muslims denied divine status to Prophet Jesus. To this charge, Ja'far correctly and honestly stated that Prophet Muhammad taught that Jesus Christ was the slave and messenger of Allah and that he was born of the Virgin Mary.

The Negus had heard enough, publicly acknowledged that the view of Prophet Jesus held by these Muslims from Makkah was no different than his own view, and stated that Prophet Jesus was no more than what Ja'far had stated. (This statement would suggest that the Negus had been a member of an adoptionist branch of early Christianity.) The Muslims were granted their request for political and religious asylum, and the Negus shortly thereafter converted to Islam.

About a year later, circa 616 CE, these early Muslim immigrants to Abyssinia began to hear rumors that the persecution of the Muslims in Makkah had ceased. As such, they packed up and began to journey back to Makkah, only to find out that the rumors had been overly optimistic. The persecution of the Muslims in Makkah was continuing. Discovering the truth, they retraced their steps back to Abyssinia. However, this time, many more Muslims who were fleeing persecution accompanied them. As such, about 80 Muslims made the second *Hijrah* to Abyssinia.

Some of these early Muslim immigrants returned to Makkah after the lifting of the boycott against the clan of Hashim in 619 CE (see below). However, others remained in Abyssinia until after the Prophet's *Hijrah* to Madinah in 622 CE.

G5. THE YEARS OF BOYCOTT

As previously noted, Prophet Muhammad had been spared most forms of actual physical persecution, because he enjoyed the protection of his Hashimite clan. However, in 617 CE, the Quraysh of Makkah began a broad social and economic boycott of Prophet Muhammad's clan of Hashim, because the Hashimite clan was still protecting the Prophet. The Hashimites were informed that the boycott would not be lifted until the Hashimites renounced their protection of Prophet Muhammad. By and large, with the exception of the Prophet's uncle, Abu Lahab, the Hashimites held firm to their clan honor and refused to renounce their protection of the Prophet. Further, the clan of Muttalib stood firmly with their Hashimite cousins and thus were included in the boycott.

For the next two years, the clans of Hashim and Muttalib were isolated in a hollow on the outskirts of Makkah. As no one would trade with them or have any economic commerce with them, it was a time of great privation, hunger, and suffering. Nonetheless, the boycott was not foolproof, and the non-Hashimite Muslims of Makkah bravely depleted their financial resources in order to buy and send contraband food and supplies to support the boycotted clans of Hashim and Muttalib. Finally, in 619 CE, having failed to achieve the desired effect of Hashimite renunciation of Prophet Muhammad, the boycott was finally lifted.

G6. THE YEAR OF SORROW

With the lifting of the boycott, 619 CE should have been a year of celebration. However, two events transpired later that year, which would forever characterize 619 CE as the year of sorrow. In rapid succession, the Prophet's uncle and guardian, Abu Talib, and the Prophet's wife, Khadijah, both died, with the former dying during either *Rajab* or *Ramadan* of 619 and with the latter dying during *Ramadan* of 619 CE. While he never publicly converted to Islam, Abu Talib had been a stalwart friend and guardian to his nephew, and his death marked the end of Hashimite protection of the Prophet. Although it would be tempting to say that, having lost the protection of his Hashimite clan, the Prophet now stood alone against the persecution of the Quraysh of Makkah, such a statement would be false, as indicated by the following verses of the *Qur'an*.

> Allah is the protector of those who have faith: from the depths of darkness He will lead them forth into light. (*Qur'an* 2: 257a)

> Nay, Allah is your protector, and He is the best of helpers. (*Qur'an* 3: 150)

> ...and hold fast to Allah! He is your protector — the best to protect and the best to help! (*Qur'an* 22: 78b)

The above verses from the *Qur'an* should not minimize or detract from the loss of Abu Talib's support to the Prophet. However, by far the greater loss had to be that of the Prophet's wife. Khadijah had carried the Prophet's six children, had been the first of the Prophet's converts to Islam, and had never wavered in her support of her husband and in her faith in the divine message revealed to him. She had been a bulwark of strength in the Prophet's personal life and to the early Muslim *Ummah*.

G7. JOURNEY TO TA'IF

In 620 CE, having lost the protection of his Hashimite clan and with his personal safety deteriorating at a rapid rate, Prophet Muhammad journeyed to Ta'if, a town some 40 odd miles east southeast of Makkah. There, he preached the divine revelation, sought converts to Islam, and labored to attract some clan of Ta'if to offer him protection. It was all to no avail, and the Prophet found neither converts nor clan protection. He was jeered at in the streets, pelted with rocks, and was finally driven out of town with blood running down his body. The mob did not cease hounding him until he was some two or three miles out of town.

When the enraged crowd finally let him go, the battered Prophet found temporary shelter and a place to rest in an orchard along the way. There, he encountered 'Addas, a Christian slave from Nineveh, who fed him grapes, listened respectfully to the Prophet's message, and acknowledged him as a true prophet of Allah.

> And nearest among them in love to the believers wilt thou find those who say, "We are Christians": Because amongst these are men devoted to learning and men who have renounced the world, and they are not arrogant. (*Qur'an* 5: 82b)

Leaving the outskirts of Ta'if, the Prophet traveled on until stopping for the night at the valley of Nakhlah, which was about the halfway point between Ta'if and Makkah. There, he performed his nightly prayer and recited from those parts of the *Qur'an* that had so far been revealed to him. While he was thus reciting the *Qur'an*, seven jinn from Nasibin passed by, lingered to hear the divine words of Allah that were being recited by Prophet Muhammad, and converted to Islam. This event was later referenced in two different Qur'anic revelations.

> Say: It has been revealed to me that a company of jinns listened (to the Qur'an). They said, "We have really heard a

wonderful recital! It gives guidance to the right, and we have believed therein: we shall not join (in worship) any (gods) with our Lord." (*Qur'an* 72: 1-2)

Behold, We turned towards thee a company of jinns (quietly) listening to the Qur'an: when they stood in the presence thereof, they said, "Listen in silence!" When the (reading) was finished, they returned to their people, to warn (them of their sins). They said, "O our people! we have heard a book revealed after Moses, confirming what came before it: it guides (men) to the truth and to a straight path. O our people, hearken to the one who invites (you) to Allah, and believe in him: He will forgive you your faults, and deliver you from a penalty grievous. If any does not hearken to the one who invites (us) to Allah, he cannot frustrate (Allah's plan) on earth, and no protectors can he have besides Allah: such men (wander) in manifest error." (*Qur'an* 46: 29-32)

Yet that night and again on the next day, fearing to enter Makkah without clan protection, Prophet Muhammad sent emissaries into Makkah, hoping to enlist some clan of the Quraysh to offer him their protection. After receiving several rejections of his request for clan protection, the Prophet detoured to Mount Hira, the site of his original revelation. From Mount Hira, Prophet Muhammad sent an emissary requesting protection from Mut'im, the head of the clan of Nawfal. Mut'im, who had been one of the leaders of the Quraysh who had helped to end the boycott of the Hashimite clan the year before, agreed to the Prophet's request and sent back word to him that he had been granted the protection of the Nawfal. The next morning, Mut'im, his sons, and his nephews armed themselves and escorted the Prophet into Makkah and to the Ka'ba. At least for the moment, Prophet Muhammad's life was safe.

G8. *AL-ISRA'* (THE NIGHT JOURNEY)
AND *AL-MI'RAJ* (THE ASCENSION)

Al-Isra' and *Al-Mi'raj* are closely linked in most traditional biographies of Prophet Muhammad, which typically have the Prophet making the night journey from Makkah to Jerusalem, then ascending into heaven from the site of what would later become the Dome of the Rock Mosque in Jerusalem before descending back to earth, and then being returned to Makkah. While the traditions regarding *Al-Isra'* and *Al-Mi'raj* are well known to almost every Muslim, there are several questions that remain about them. (1) Are these two events to be joined, or were they separate events occurring at different times? As noted previously, almost all the biographies that deal with *Al-'Isra* and *Al-Mi'raj* place them together as one basic event. However, the *Qur'an* refers to the night journey without directly linking it to the ascension. Further, the relevant *Ahadith* that specifically describe the place from which Prophet Muhammad ascended into heaven in *Al-Bukhari* (e.g., # 1: 345, 4:429, 4: 770, 5: 227, and 9: 608) locate the ascension as having taken place from Makkah, not from Jerusalem, and make no mention of the night journey. (2) When did the night journey and the ascension take place? Assuming that they were joined or linked events, most biographies place them as happening somewhere between late in 620 CE and early in 622 CE, with 621 CE being the most probable date. (3) Were the night journey and the ascension made bodily, spiritually, or in a dream state? There is some debate among Muslims on this question, although all Muslims agree that Allah has the power to have accomplished this event in any of the three modalities and that the events in question contained divine inspiration and direction. As such, the debate is largely superfluous.

Having listed the three primary questions that are debated about *Al-'Isra* and *Al-Mi'raj*, the author must now acknowledge that he has no intention of attempting to answer these questions within the current context of a single chapter on the life of Prophet Muhammad. The issues are simply too complex for a simple analysis and solution to be presented within the confines of the present limitations in space. Nonetheless, the reader has been informed that the questions do exist and is now informed that the author will follow traditional custom in linking these two events within the framework of a single night.

With regard to *Al-'Isra* or the night journey, it is usually maintained that Prophet Muhammad was spending the night at the Ka'ba, i.e., the Sacred Mosque, when he was transported on Al-Buraq (a winged, horse-like, heavenly animal) to the Farthest Mosque, i.e., the site of what would later become the Al-Aqsa Mosque in Jerusalem. There, Prophet Muhammad led the prior prophets of Allah in prayer. Al-'Isra is mentioned briefly in the *Qur'an*.

> Glory to (Allah) Who did take His servant for a journey by night from the Sacred Mosque to the Farthest Mosque, whose precincts We did bless — in order that We might show him some of Our signs: for He is the One Who heareth and seeth (all things). (*Qur'an* 17: 1)

> ...We granted the vision which We showed thee, but as a trial for men — as also the cursed tree (mentioned) in the *Qur'an*: We put terror (and warning) into them, but it only increases their inordinate transgression! (*Qur'an* 17:60b; see also *Al-Bukhari, Ahadith* # 5: 228, 6: 240, and 8: 610)

Al-Mi'raj is described in some detail in various *Ahadith*, one of which is quoted below. It should be noted that while the following *Hadith* reports *Al-Mi'raj* as though this were a spiritual journey undertaken during sleep or in a dream state, not all *Ahadith* on this subject convey this same idea.

> Narrated Anas ibn Malik: "The night Allah's Apostle was taken for a journey from the Sacred Mosque, Al-Ka'ba, three persons came to him (in a dream) while he was sleeping in the Sacred Mosque, before the divine inspiration was revealed to him. One of them said, 'Which of them is he?' The middle (second)

angel said, 'He is the best of them.' The last (third) angle said, 'Take the best of them.' Only that much happened on that night, and he did not see them till they came on another night, i.e., after the divine inspiration was revealed to him, and he saw them. His eyes were asleep but his heart was not — and so is the case with the prophets: their eyes sleep while their hearts do not sleep. So those angels did not talk to him till they carried him, and placed him beside the well of Zam-Zam. From among them, Gabriel took charge of him. Gabriel cut open (the part of his body) between his throat and the middle of his chest (heart), and took all the material out of his chest and abdomen, and then washed it with Zam-Zam water with his own hands, till he cleansed the inside of his body, and then a gold tray containing a gold bowl full of belief and wisdom was brought, and then Gabriel stuffed his chest and throat blood vessels with it, and then closed it (the chest). He then ascended with him to the heaven of the world, and knocked on one of its doors.

"The dwellers of the heaven asked, 'Who is it?' He said, 'Gabriel.' They said, 'Who is accompanying you?' He said, 'Muhammad.' They said, 'Has he been called?' He said, 'Yes.' They said, 'He is welcomed.' So the dwellers of the heaven became pleased with his arrival, and they did not know what Allah would do to the Prophet on earth unless Allah informed them. The Prophet met Adam over the nearest heaven. Gabriel said to the Prophet, 'He is your father; greet him.' The Prophet greeted him, and Adam returned his greeting and said, 'Welcome, O my son! O what a good son you are!' Behold, he saw two flowing rivers, while he was in the nearest sky...Then Gabriel ascended (with him) to the second heaven, and the angels asked the same questions as those on the first heaven...Then he (Gabriel) ascended with the Prophet to the third heaven, and the angels said the same as the angels of the first and the second heavens had said.

"Then he ascended with him to the fourth heaven and they said the same; and then he ascended with him to the fifth heaven and they said the same; and then he ascended with him to the sixth heaven and they said the same; then he ascended with him to the seventh heaven and they said the same. On each heaven there were prophets whose names he had mentioned, and of whom I remember Idris on the second heaven, Aaron on the fourth heaven, another prophet whose name I don't remember on the fifth heaven, Abraham on the sixth heaven, and Moses on the seventh heaven because of his privilege of talking to Allah directly. Moses said (to Allah), 'O Lord! I thought that none would be raised up above me.'

"But Gabriel ascended with him (the Prophet) for a distance above that ... Among the things that Allah revealed to him (the Prophet), was: fifty prayers were enjoined on his followers in a day and a night. Then the Prophet descended till he met Moses, and then Moses stopped him and asked, 'O Muhammad! What did your Lord enjoin upon you?' The Prophet replied, 'He enjoined upon me to perform fifty prayers in a day and a night.' Moses said, 'Your followers cannot do that; go back, so that your Lord may reduce it for you and for them.' So the Prophet turned to Gabriel, as if he wanted to consult him about that issue. Gabriel told him of his opinion, saying, 'Yes, if you wish.' So, Gabriel ascended with him to the Irresistible, and (Prophet Muhammad) said while he was in his place, 'O Lord, please lighten our burden as my followers cannot do that.' So, Allah deducted for him ten prayers, whereupon he returned to Moses, who stopped him again, and kept on sending him back to his Lord till the enjoined prayers were reduced to only five prayers.

"Then Moses stopped him when the prayers had been reduced to five, and said, 'O Muhammad! by Allah, I tried to persuade my nation, Bani Israel, to do less than this, but they could not do it and gave it up. However, your followers are weaker in body, heart, sight, and hearing, so return to your Lord so that He may lighten your burden.'

"The Prophet turned towards Gabriel for advice and Gabriel did not disapprove of that. So, he ascended with him for the fifth time. The Prophet said, 'O Lord, my followers are weak in their bodies, hearts, hearing and constitution, so lighten our burden.' On that, the Irresistible said, 'O Muhammad!' The Prophet replied, 'Labbayk and Sa'dayk' (here I am at Your service). Allah said, 'The word that comes from Me does not change, so it will be as I enjoined on you in the Mother of the Book.' Allah added, 'Every good deed will be rewarded as ten times, so it is fifty (prayers) in the Mother of the Book (in reward), but you are to perform only five (in practice).'

"The Prophet returned to Moses, who asked, 'What have you done?' He said, 'He has lightened our burden: He has given us for every good deed a tenfold reward.' Moses said, 'By Allah! I tried to make Bani Israel observe less than that, but they gave it up. So go back to your Lord that He may lighten your burden further.' Allah's Apostle said, 'O Moses! by Allah, I feel shy of returning too many times to my Lord.' On that, Gabriel said, 'Descend in Allah's name.' The Prophet then woke while he was in the Sacred Mosque (at Makkah)." (*Al-Bukhari, Hadith* # 9: 608; see also *Al-Bukhari, Ahadith* # 1: 345, 4: 429, 4: 462, 4: 607-608, 4: 640, 4: 647-648, 4: 770, 5: 227, 6: 232, 7: 482, 7: 508, and 8: 583, as well as *Al-Tirmidhi, Hadith* # 1445)

A few addenda can be added to the above accounts of *Al-'Isra* and *Al-Mi'raj*. Firstly, either in Jerusalem or during the ascension, Prophet Muhammad was given a choice of liquid refreshments.

Narrated Abu Huraira...The Prophet further said, "(That night) I was given two cups; one full of milk, and the other full of wine. I was asked to take either of them which I liked, and I took the milk and drank it. On that it was said to me, 'You have taken the right path (religion). If you had taken the wine, your (Muslim) nation would have gone astray.'" (*Al-Bukhari, Hadith # 4: 647; see also Al-Bukhari, Ahadith # 4: 607, 5: 227, 6: 232, 7: 482, and 7: 508*)

Secondly, despite the opportunity it provided for the Quraysh to ridicule him, Prophet Muhammad immediately proclaimed his overnight journey to Jerusalem and back, and offered proof of the veracity of his report by describing the various caravans that he saw moving from Jerusalem to Makkah (reports that were later verified when the caravans reached Makkah) and by describing Jerusalem and what was happening there.

> Narrated Jabir ibn 'Abdullah that he heard Allah's Apostle saying, "When the people of Quraysh did not believe me (i.e., the story of my night journey), I stood up in Al-Hijr (a semi-circular area adjoining the Ka'ba) and Allah displayed Jerusalem in front of me, and I began describing it to them while I was looking at it." (*Al-Bukhari, Hadith # 5: 226*)

Thirdly, during the ascension and at the farthest point of heaven into which Prophet Muhammad traveled, he encountered the Lote Tree, beyond which he was not allowed to go. This phase of the ascension, as well as the Quraysh's doubts about the Prophet's story, are referenced in the following passage from the Qur'an.

> For indeed he (Prophet Muhammad) saw him (Gabriel) at a second descent, near the Lote-tree beyond which none may pass: near it is the garden of abode. Behold, the Lote-tree was shrouded (in mystery unspeakable!) (His) sight never swerved, nor did it go wrong! For truly did he see of the signs of his Lord, the greatest! (*Qur'an 53: 13-18*)

G9. AN INVITATION FROM YATHRIB:

The city of Yathrib, which was located about 200 miles due north of Makkah, had been experiencing intertribal conflict for a number of years. Two tribes of Arabs, the Aws and the Khazraj, were engaged in a blood feud that was sucking more and more clans of the two tribes into its disastrous destructiveness. Three pitched battles had already been fought, and the fourth, the Battle of Bu'ath, was on the immediate horizon. Complicating the situation, the Jewish tribes of Yathrib were using their various alliances with the two Arab tribes to exploit the situation for their personal gain. As such, the men of Yathrib were desperately looking for a unifying arbiter and leader who could end the ceaseless round of bloodshed and destruction. They were shortly to find their man in Prophet Muhammad.

In 620 CE, while making the *Hajj* at Makkah, six men of Khazraj had listened attentively to the Prophet's message and had converted to Islam. The following *Hajj* season, in 621 CE, five of the six converts returned from Yathrib to Makkah and brought seven others with them, two of whom were members of the Aws tribe. These seven also embraced Islam, and the 12 converts from Yathrib had then taken the First Pledge of 'Aqabah. The pledge was a simple affair in which the 12 converts from Yathrib pledged their allegiance to Prophet Muhammad, testified that there was no god but Allah and that they would associate nothing in the way of partners with Him, and promised that they would not steal, fornicate, slay their unwanted female offspring, commit slander against another, and fail to obey the Prophet. When the 12 converts left Makkah for Yathrib, Prophet Muhammad sent Mus'ab of 'Abd Al-Dar back with them to lead the Muslim converts of Yathrib in their five daily prayers, to recite the *Qur'an* to them, to instruct them in Islam, and to seek additional converts to Islam in Yathrib.

By the grace of Allah, Mus'ab was quite successful in his missionary efforts, and many members of Yathrib embraced Islam during the following year. As such, during the *Hajj* season of 622 CE, some 73 Muslim men (62 from the Khazraj and 11 from the Aws) and two Muslim women (both from the Khazraj) journeyed from Yathrib to Makkah to meet the Prophet. At 'Aqabah, they met with Prophet Muhammad and his uncle, Al-'Abbas. While

Al-'Abbas was not a Muslim, he insisted on being present in order to safeguard the personal interests and safety of his nephew. A total of 12 men (nine from Khazraj and three from Aws) were selected to represent the entire Muslim community at Yathrib. These 12 then took the Second Pledge of 'Aqabah, which was like the first, but which included the additional pledge to protect Prophet Muhammad with force if necessary. In return, Prophet Muhammad pledged to move with the Muslim community of Makkah to Yathrib, where he would serve as chief arbiter of all disputes.

> Narrated 'Aisha: "...At that time, Allah's Apostle was still in Makkah, and he said to his companions, 'Your place of emigration has been shown to me. I have seen salty land, planted with date palms and situated between two mountains, which are the two Harras.' So, when the Prophet told it, some of the companions migrated to Madinah, and some of those who had migrated to Ethiopia (Abyssinia) returned to Madinah." (*Al-Bukhari, Hadith* # 3: 494; see also *Al-Bukhari, Hadith* # 5: 245)

Immediately after the end of the *Hajj* season in 622 CE, Prophet Muhammad began to send the Muslims of Makkah in small groups to Yathrib, where they were taken in and cared for by their fellow Muslims. Although the Quraysh of Makkah tried strenuously to stop this emigration of manpower and wealth from Makkah to Yathrib, the emigrations continued until there were very few Muslims left in Makkah excepting Prophet Muhammad, Abu Bakr, and 'Ali ibn Abu Talib.

G10. THE *HIJRAH* OF THE PROPHET

After his disappointing journey to Ta'if, Prophet Muhammad had been allowed to enter Makkah through the protection of Mut'im, the head of the clan of Nawfal. While Mut'im lived, this protection held. However, around 622 CE, Mut'im died, and Prophet Muhammad was again left without significant clan protection. As such, the Quraysh now came up with a plan designed to rid themselves of the Prophet once and for all.

The plan was simple in its design, but satisfied the desire of the various clans of Quraysh to avoid being drawn into blood feuds following the proposed assassination of the Prophet. Each clan was to select a representative from within its midst. These clan representatives would then meet and jointly assassinate the Prophet with simultaneous thrusts of their swords. In this way, blood retribution could be sought only by someone willing to go to war with all of the clans of the Quraysh — a most unlikely prospect. This plan of the Quraysh to assassinate Prophet Muhammad is mentioned briefly in the following passage from the *Qur'an*.

> Remember how the unbelievers plotted against thee, to keep thee in bonds, or slay thee, or get thee out (of thy home). They plot and plan, and Allah too plans, but the best of planners is Allah. (*Qur'an* 8: 30)

The Quraysh had planned their assassination of the Prophet with meticulous care, but "Allah too plans, but the best of planners is Allah". The Prophet was warned of the plan against him, and immediately began his own preparations to leave Makkah for Yathrib.

> Narrated 'Aisha: "...One day while we were sitting in our house at midday, someone said to Abu Bakr, 'Here is Allah's Apostle, coming with his head and a part of his face covered with a cloth covering at an hour he never used to come to us.' Abu Bakr said, 'Let my father and mother be sacrificed for you, (O Prophet)! An urgent matter must have brought you here at this hour.' The Prophet came and asked permission to enter, and he was allowed. The Prophet entered, and said to Abu Bakr, 'Let those who are with you go out.' Abu Bakr replied, '(There is no stranger); they are your family. Let my father be sacrificed for you, O Allah's Apostle!' The Prophet said, 'I have been allowed to leave (Makkah).' Abu Bakr said, 'Shall I

accompany you, O Allah's Apostle? Let my father be sacrificed for you!' The Prophet said, 'Yes.' Abu Bakr said, 'O Allah's Apostle! let my father be sacrificed for you! Take one of these two she-camels of mine.' The Prophet said, 'I will take it only after paying its price.' So we prepared their baggage and put their journey food in a leather bag." (*Al-Bukhari, Hadith # 7: 698; see also Al-Bukhari, Ahadith # 5: 245, 5: 419*)

That night as the assassins gathered around the Prophet's house to carry out their murderous plan, Prophet Muhammad made his final preparations to leave. Despite his ostracism and persecution by the Quraysh, he was still Al-Amin (the trustworthy and the faithful), on account of which many people had left some of their property and wealth with him for safekeeping. Prophet Muhammad instructed his nephew and ward, 'Ali ibn Abu Talib, regarding the return of this property. Then, the Prophet requested that 'Ali cover himself in the Prophet's robe and lie in the Prophet's bed. In this manner, the assassins would think that the Prophet was still at home and would delay their assassination attempt until the Prophet exited his home first thing in the morning. Having made these preparations, the Prophet then began to recite the first nine verses of the 36th chapter of the *Qur'an*.

Ya Sin. By the Qur'an, full of wisdom — thou art indeed one of the messengers on a straight way. It is a revelation sent down by (Him), the exalted in might, most merciful, in order that thou mayest admonish a people, whose fathers had received no admonition, and who therefore remained heedless (of the signs of Allah). The word is proved true against the greatest part of them; for they do not believe. We have put yokes round their necks right up to their chins, so that their heads are forced up (and they cannot see). And We have put a bar in front of them and a bar behind them, and further, We have covered them up; so that they cannot see. (*Qur'an* 36: 1-9)

When the Prophet reached the key phrase, "they cannot see", he exited his house, unobserved by any of the assassins who were waiting to pounce upon him. He rendezvoused with Abu Bakr, and the two of them journeyed south, in the direction opposite of Yathrib, to the cave of Thaur.

> Narrated 'Aisha: "...Then Allah's Apostle and Abu Bakr reached a cave on the mountain of Thaur, and stayed there for three nights. 'Abdullah ibn Abu Bakr, who was intelligent and a sagacious youth, used to stay (with them) overnight. He used to leave them before daybreak, so that in the morning he would be with Quraysh as if he had spent the night in Makkah. He would keep in mind any plot made against them, and when it became dark, he would (go and) inform them of it. 'Amir ibn Fuhaira, the freed slave of Abu Bakr, used to bring the milch sheep (of his master, Abu Bakr) to them a little while after nightfall, in order to rest the sheep there. So, they always had fresh milk at night, the milk of their sheep, and the milk which they warmed by throwing heated stones in it. 'Amir ibn Fuhaira would then call the herd away when it was still dark (before daybreak). He did the same in each of those three nights." (*Al-Bukhari, Hadith* # 5: 245; see also *Al-Bukhari, Ahadith* # 5: 419 and 7: 698)

The morning after the Prophet's departure from Makkah, the assassins soon discovered that 'Ali ibn Abu Talib had been masquerading as the Prophet. The word quickly spread among the Quraysh that the Prophet was gone. A reward was posted for his capture, and search parties headed out in the direction of Yathrib, hoping to overtake Prophet Muhammad. Meanwhile, the Prophet and Abu Bakr remained safely hidden in the cave of Thaur to the south of Makkah, although there was one close call for the Prophet and his companion. At some point during their three days in the cave, a search party from Makkah did approach the cave and would have entered to search it, except for what they encountered at the mouth of the cave. They found a spider's web covering part of the mouth of the cave, a pigeon sitting on her nest at the mouth of the cave, and the branches of a tree partially blocking entrance into the cave. These three signs convinced them that no one could possibly be in the cave, and they left without inspecting it. This instance of divine intervention is mentioned in the following verse from the *Qur'an*.

> If ye help not (your leader, it is no matter): for Allah did indeed help him, when the unbelievers drove him out: he had no more than one companion: the two were in the cave, and he said to his companion, "Have no fear for Allah is with us": then Allah sent down His peace upon him, and strengthened him with forces which ye saw not, and humbled to the depths the word of the unbelievers, but the word of Allah is exalted to the heights: for Allah is exalted in might, wise. (*Qur'an* 9: 40; see also *Al-Bukhari, Ahadith* # 5: 5, 5: 259, and 6: 185)

Having hidden in the cave for three days, having received Allah's protection, and having waited until the Quraysh's frantic searching for them had died down somewhat, the Prophet and Abu Bakr were now ready to leave for Yathrib.

> Narrated 'Aisha: "...Allah's Apostle and Abu Bakr had hired a man from the tribe of Bani Al-Dail from the family of Bani 'Abd ibn 'Adi as an expert guide... The Prophet and Abu Bakr trusted him, and gave him their two she-camels, and took his promise to bring their two she-camels to the cave of the mountain of Thaur in the morning after three nights later. And (when they set out), 'Amir ibn Fuhaira and the guide went along with them, and the guide led them along the seashore." (*Al-Bukhari, Hadith* # 5: 245; see also *Al-Bukhari, Ahadith* # 3: 464-465)

Traveling surreptitiously, Prophet Muhammad's journey north to Yathrib was slow and cautious. Nonetheless, there was still one more obstacle that had to be encountered.

The nephew of Suraqa ibn Ju'sham said that his father informed him that he heard Suraqa ibn Ju'sham saying, "The messengers of the heathens of Quraysh came to us declaring that they had assigned for the persons who would kill or arrest Allah's Apostle and Abu Bakr, a reward equal to their blood money. While I was sitting in one of the gatherings of my tribe, Bani Mudlij, a man from them came to us and stood up while we were sitting, and said, 'O Suraqa! no doubt, I have just seen some people far away on the seashore, and I think they are Muhammad and his companions'." Suraqa added, "I too realized that it must have been they. But, I said, 'No, it is not they, but you have seen so-and-so, and so-and-so whom we saw set out.' I stayed in the gathering for a while, and then got up and left for my home, and ordered my slave girl to get my horse, which was behind a hillock, and keep it ready for me. Then, I took my spear, and left by the back door of my house, dragging the lower end of the spear on the ground, and keeping it low. Then, I reached my horse, mounted it, and made it gallop. When I approached them (Prophet Muhammad and his companions), my horse stumbled, and I fell down from it. Then, I stood up, got hold of my quiver, and took out the divining arrows, and drew lots as to whether I should harm them or not, and the lot which I disliked came out. But, I remounted my horse and let it gallop, giving no importance to the divining arrows. When I heard the recitation of the Qur'an by Allah's Apostle, who did not look hither and thither, while Abu Bakr was doing it often, suddenly the forelegs of my horse sank into the ground up to the knees, and I fell down from it. Then, I rebuked it, and it got up, but could hardly take out its forelegs from the ground. And when it stood up straight again, its forelegs caused dust to rise up in the sky like smoke. Then again, I drew lots with the divining arrows, and the lot which I disliked came out. So, I called upon them to feel secure. They stopped, and I remounted my horse and went to them. When I saw how I had been hampered from harming them, it came to my mind that the cause of Allah's Apostle will become victorious. So, ι said to him, 'Your people have assigned a reward equal to the blood money for your head.' Then, I told them all the plans the people of Makkah had made concerning them. Then, I offered them some journey food and goods, but they refused to take anything, and did not ask for anything, but the Prophet said, 'Do not tell others about us.' Then, I requested him to write for me a statement of security and peace. He ordered 'Amr ibn Fuhaira who wrote it for me on a parchment, and then Allah's Apostle proceeded on his way." (*Al-Bukhari, Hadith # 5: 245*)

In the meantime, word had reached Yathrib that the Prophet had left Makkah, and worry and anticipation quickly began to build in equal measure among the Muslims who were awaiting him. The outlying village of Yathrib closest to Makkah was known as Al-Quba, and, as soon as word reached Yathrib that the Prophet was on his way, the residents of Al-Quba would daily go out beyond the cultivated orchards and gardens of Al-Quba to the lava flows, where they would spend the mornings awaiting any sign of the Prophet's appearance. On the 12th day after the Prophet left the cave of Thaur, the residents of Al-Quba had again made their daily morning watch. However, as the heat of the day became unbearable, they had retreated back to the shade of Al-Quba. That afternoon, a Jew of Al-Quba, who happened to be standing on the roof of his house, saw camel riders dressed in white and approaching from the direction of Makkah. He immediately began a public cry that was quickly echoed throughout all of Al-Quba: "Sons of Qaylah, he is come, he is come!" The date of Prophet Muhammad's arrival at Al-Quba was the 8th of *Rabi' Al-Awwal* in the first *Hijri* year (Monday, September 23, 622 CE).

G11. YATHRIB BECOMES MADINAH

The Prophet spent three full days in Al-Quba. During this time, he stayed at the home of the elderly Kulthum, recuperated from his travel, helped lay the foundation of a mosque, and was finally joined by 'Ali ibn Abu Talib, who had made his own successful escape from Makkah after returning all of the property that had been entrusted to the Prophet's care. Then, on the following Friday, the 12th of *Rabi' Al-Awwal* (September 27, 622 CE), the Prophet entered Yathrib, which would forever after be known as Al-Madinah, i.e., "the city (of the Prophet)".

> Call to mind when ye were a small (band), despised through the land, and afraid that men might despoil and kidnap you; but He provided a safe asylum for you, strengthened you with His aid, and gave you good things for sustenance: that ye might be grateful. (*Qur'an* 8: 26)

H. THE PROPHET IN MADINAH

H1. ESTABLISHING A HOME AND MOSQUE

When Prophet Muhammad entered Madinah, he was immediately faced with the task of securing a residence. Many people wanted the honor of hosting the Prophet and giving him land and a house. While this was gratifying on the one hand, it also raised the danger that those whose offers were declined would feel personally rejected and might feel jealous of the person whose hospitality had been accepted. Prophet Muhammad handled this potential pitfall with tact and adroit diplomacy by announcing that he would stay where his camel, Qaswa', stopped of her own accord. After all, who could feel slighted or rejected by a camel's whim?

The Prophet gave free reign to Qaswa', and she walked through the streets of Madinah until stopping and kneeling at a courtyard. She then arose, began to walk away, and then returned to where she had knelt before. Once again, she knelt and settled down at the same place she had previously. The Prophet inquired as to who owned the courtyard, and was informed that it belonged to two orphans, Sahl and Suhayl, who were under the guardianship of As'ad. The two orphans immediately offered their courtyard to the Prophet as a gift, but Prophet Muhammad insisted that the transaction must be a purchase agreement. An equitable price was determined by negotiations with As'ad, and the transaction was completed.

Prophet Muhammad and the Muslims immediately began building a mosque at the courtyard, to which was attached the apartments of the Prophet's small dwelling. Construction took seven months, and during the interim, Prophet Muhammad lodged with Abu Ayyub Khalid ibn Zayd. The construction process was relatively simple. The walls were made of mud bricks, palm tree trunks were used as the support pillars for the roof, and the roof was constructed from palm leaves and twigs. Needless to say, when it rained, the roof leaked. When completed, the mosque was in the shape of a square, with each wall being approximately 50 yards in length.

One might pause for a moment to consider the new home of Prophet Muhammad. Although he was the equivalent of being a king in Madinah, his own home was a small and simple affair, which was made of mud bricks, had a leaky roof, and used camel-hair blankets as doors. Such was the humility of this last prophet of Allah, to whom wordly wealth and comfort meant so very little.

Having established his personal home in 623 CE, Prophet Muhammad now moved his household into it. Among them were: (1) Sawdah bint Zama'ah ibn Qays, the Prophet's wife, whom he had married circa 620 CE about a year after the death of his beloved Khadijah, who was an elderly widow with an orphaned son, and who died in the 22nd year of *Hijri* (642-643 CE); (2) his unmarried daughters, Fatimah and Um Kulthum; and (3) 'Aisha, the daughter of Abu Bakr. 'Aisha had been betrothed to Prophet Muhammad around the time of the Prophet's marriage to Sawdah, but the marriage to 'Aisha was not finalized until 623-625 CE in Madinah, by which time 'Aisha had passed through puberty and was of an age to give her own informed consent to the marriage. 'Aisha would later become one of the first female scholars of Islam, would narrate about 2,210 *Ahadith*, and would die on the 17th of *Ramadan* in the 58th year of *Hijri* (Monday, July 15, 678 CE).

H2. THE BEGINNINGS OF AN ISLAMIC STATE

When Prophet Muhammad entered Madinah, it was the beginning of the first Islamic nation-state. Prophet Muhammad had become the temporal ruler of Madinah, as well as being the prophet and messenger of Allah. For the first time, he had to assume the responsibilities of providing guidance and government in temporal and secular affairs. In accepting those responsibilities, he was faced with two immediate issues.

Firstly, many of the *Muhajirah* ("emigrants", i.e., those Muslims who had emigrated from Makkah to Madinah) had been forced by circumstances to leave their wealth and possessions behind in Makkah. All of the *Muhajirah* were now homeless, and many of them were destitute. In response to this need, Prophet Muhammad instituted the Pact of Brotherhood whereby the *Muhajirah* were paired with the *Ansar* ("helpers", i.e., the Muslims of Madinah). Each emigrant from Makkah was paired with a helper from Madinah in a pact of brotherhood, which specified that the latter should help sustain the former until he could again stand on his own financial feet.

Secondly, the Prophet recognized the need for some formal agreement that would serve as the basis of government in Madinah and that would bind the disparate populace of Madinah into one community. This latter need should not be minimized, as Madinah now consisted of two tribes of indigenous Arabs (the Khazraj and the Aws), three tribes of Jews (the Bani Nadir, the Bani Qurayzah, and the Bani Qaynuqa'), and the *Muhajirah* from Makkah. In response, Prophet Muhammad issued the Covenant of Madinah, which may well have been the first formal constitution enacted by any state government, as well as being an example of the ideal Islamic state. The Covenant of Madinah began with the words: "In the name of Allah, most gracious, most merciful. This is a covenant given by Muhammad, the messenger of Allah..."; and guaranteed religious freedom and basic human and civil rights some 1,100 years before similar principles were embedded into the United States Constitution. Some of the key principles enunciated in the Covenant of Madinah are listed in Table 6 immediately below.

Table 6
The Key Provisions of the Covenant of Madinah

A. Provisions pertaining to the Muslims and Arabs

1. The *Muhajirah* and the *Ansar* form one *Ummah* (community) to the exclusion of all others.
2. Each tribe and clan is responsible for its own blood money, retribution fees, and ransom payments.
3. The believers shall not leave anyone destitute by refusing to pay blood money, retribution fees, or ransom payments.
4. All believers shall unite against anyone who is rebellious or who seeks to spread enmity and sedition, regardless of family or tribal ties.
5. No believer may kill another believer, nor support an unbeliever against a believer.
6. The protection of Allah is extended to all believers, regardless of class or tribal background.
7. The believers are to support each other.
8. No believer may support a criminal or give him refuge.

B. Provisions pertaining to the Jews

1. The Jews are one community with the believers.
2. The Jews may continue to profess their own religion, and are guaranteed the freedom of their own religious practices.
3. Any Jew who adheres to this covenant shall have the aide and succor of the believers, and shall be entitled to all the rights pertaining to a believer.
4. Each tribe and clan of Jews is responsible for its own blood money, retribution fees, and ransom payments.

C. Provisions pertaining to both Jews and Arabs.

1. The Jews and Arabs of Madinah enter into a mutual defense pact with each group sustaining its own costs entailed by honoring that pact.
2. The Jews and Arabs of Madinah will hold counsel with each other, and mutual relations shall be founded on righteousness, while sin is prohibited.

3. Neither the Jews or the Arabs shall commit sins to the prejudice of the other group.

4. If the Jews wrong the Arabs, or if the Arabs wrong the Jews, the wronged party shall be aided.

5. Madinah shall remain sacred and inviolate for all that join this covenant, except for those who perpetrate an injustice or commit a crime.

6. All parties to this covenant are to boycott the non-Muslim Quraysh of Makkah.

7. All parties to this covenant will defend Madinah from any foreign attack.

8. No provision of this covenant shall prohibit any party from seeking lawful retribution.

9. No party to this covenant may initiate war without the permission of the Prophet.

D. Whenever a dispute arises between any two parties to this agreement, the dispute shall be submitted to Allah and His messenger for arbitration.

As can be seen by perusing Table 6, the Jews of Madinah were seen to be one commuity with the Muslims, were entitled to all the civil and legal rights held by a Muslim, and were still granted the freedom to practice their religious beliefs in their own way. In establishing one civil law for both Muslims and Jews, the Covenant of Madinah was in essential agreement with the so-called Mosaic Law, which established that there would be only one law for both the Israelites and the aliens in their midst.

You shall have one law for the alien and for the citizen: for I am the Lord your God. (*Leviticus* 24: 22)

With the establishment of an Islamic state, the nature of the revelations received by Prophet Muhammad began to change. While the Prophet had been in Makkah, the revelations had primarily focused on the basic religious truths that were to become the core of Islam. In Madinah, the divine revelations more frequently focused on legal issues that would inevitably confront an Islamic state. Issues such as inheritance, crime and punishment, and marriage and divorce all began to be specified and resolved by the continuing revelations. This change in the type of revelatory message received by Prophet Muhammad would later be useful to scholars in helping to classify the revelations of the *Qur'an* into early (Makkah) revelations vs. later (Madinah) revelations.

H3. THE CONTINUING EVOLUTION OF ISLAM

During the first few years in Madinah, the basic practices of Islam continued to evolve as a direct result of the Prophet's continuing revelations. Foremost among those early Madinah revelations concerning religious practice and worship were those that enjoined *Sawm* (fasting during the Islamic month of *Ramadan*) and *Zakat* (obligatory charity from those who have an economic surplus). (These two pillars of Islamic practice are presented in some detail in chapter VI, sections D and E.) In addition, revelation was received that changed the *Qiblah* (the direction one faces to pray) from Jerusalem to Makkah.

> The fools among the people will say: "What hath turned them from the Qiblah to which they were used?" Say: "To Allah belong east and west: He guideth whom He will to a way that is straight". Thus have We made of you an Ummah justly balanced, that ye might be witnesses over the nations, and the messenger a witness over yourselves; and We appointed the Qiblah to which thou wast used, only to test those who followed the messenger from those who would turn on their heels (from the faith). Indeed, it was (a change) momentous, except to those guided by Allah. And never would Allah make your faith of no effect. For Allah is to all people most surely full of kindness, most merciful. We see the turning of thy face (for guidance) to the heavens: now shall We turn thee to a Qiblah that shall please thee. Turn then thy face in the direction of the Sacred Mosque: wherever ye are, turn your

faces in that direction. The people of the book know well that that is the truth from their Lord, nor is Allah unmindful of what they do. (*Qur'an* 2: 142-144)

Finally, it should be noted that it was in the early years in Madinah that the *Adhan* (the call to prayer) was developed.

H4. THE HYPOCRITES

The persecutions that had earlier plagued the Muslims in Makkah had insured that those who embraced Islam were true believers. A radically different situation was present in Madinah. An Islamic state had now been formed, and Prophet Muhammad was the temporal ruler of Madinah, as well as being the spiritual leader of the Muslims. Given this situation, there were those who found it politically expedient to declare themselves Muslims publicly, while continuing their private disbelief and engaging in secret plots against the Prophet and the true believers in Islam. The *Qur'an* repeatedly refers to these individuals as *Munafiqun* (hypocrites), and discusses them and their machinations in several passages.

> Of the people, there are some who say: "We believe in Allah and the last day;" but they do not (really) believe. Fain would they deceive Allah and those who believe, but they only deceive themselves, and realize (it) not! In their hearts is a disease; and Allah has increased their disease: and grievous is the penalty they (incur), because they are false (to themselves). When it is said to them: "Make not mischief on the earth," they say: "Why, we only want to make peace!" Of a surety, they are the ones who make mischief, but they realize (it) not. When it i said to them: "Believe as the others believe:" they say: "Shall we believe as the fools believe?"— nay, of a surety they are the fools, but they do not know. When they meet those who believe, they say: "We believe;" but when they are alone with their evil ones, they say: "We are really with you, we (were) only jesting." (*Qur'an* 2: 8-14)

Indeed, they had plotted sedition before, and upset matters for thee — until the truth arrived, and the decree of Allah became manifest, much to their disgust. Among them is (many) a man who says: "Grant me exemption and draw me not into trial." Have they not fallen into trial already? And indeed hell surrounds the unbelievers (on all sides). If good befalls thee, it grieves them; but if a misfortune befalls thee, they say, "We took indeed our precautions beforehand." And they turn away rejoicing. (*Qur'an* 9: 48-50)

They swear by Allah that they are indeed of you; but they are not of you: yet they are afraid (to appear in their true colors). If they could find a place to flee to, or caves, or a place of concealment, they would turn straightway thereto, with an obstinate rush. And among them are men who slander thee in the matter of (the distribution of) the alms. If they are given part thereof, they are pleased, but if not, behold! they are indignant! (*Qur'an* 9: 56-58)

The hypocrites, men and women, (have an understanding) with each other: they enjoin evil, and forbid what is just, and are close with their hands. They have forgotten Allah; so He hath forgotten them. Verily the hypocrites are rebellious and perverse. Allah hath promised the hypocrites, men and women, and the rejecters of faith, the fire of hell: therein shall they dwell: sufficient is it for them: for them is the curse of Allah, and an enduring punishment— (*Qur'an* 9: 67-68)

Certain of the desert Arabs round about you are hypocrites, as well as (desert Arabs) among the Madinah folk: they are obstinate in hypocrisy: thou knowest them not: We know them: twice shall We punish them: and in addition shall they be sent to a grievous penalty. (*Qur'an* 9: 101)

And there are those who put up a mosque by way of mischief and infidelity — to disunite the believers — and in preparation for one who warred against Allah and His messenger aforetime. They will indeed swear that their intention is nothing but good; but Allah doth declare that they are certainly liars. (*Qur'an* 9: 107)

We know best why it is they listen, when they listen to thee; and when they meet in private conference, behold, the wicked say, "Ye follow none other than a man bewitched!" See what similes they strike for thee; but they have gone astray, and never can they find a way. (*Qur'an* 17: 47-48)

They say, "We believe in Allah and in the messenger, and we obey": but even after that, some of them turn away: they are not (really) believers. When they are summoned to Allah and His messenger, in order that he may judge between them, behold, some of them decline (to come). But if the right is on their side, they come to him with all submission. Is it that there is a disease in their hearts? Or do they doubt, or are they in fear, that Allah and His messenger will deal unjustly with them? Nay, it is they themselves who do wrong. (*Qur'an* 24: 47-50)

Truly, if the hypocrites, and those in whose hearts is a disease, and those who stir up sedition in the city, desist not, We shall certainly stir thee up against them: then will they not be able to stay in it as thy neighbours for any length of time... (*Qur'an* 33: 60)

When the hypocrites come to thee, they say, "We bear witness that thou art indeed the messenger of Allah." Yea, Allah knoweth that thou art indeed His messenger, and Allah beareth witness that the hypocrites are indeed liars. They have made their oaths a screen (for their misdeeds): thus they obstruct (men) from the path of Allah: truly evil are their deeds. That is because they believed, then they rejected faith: so a seal was set on their hearts: therefore they understand not. When thou lookest at them, their exteriors please thee; and when they speak, thou listenest to their words. They are as (worthless as hollow) pieces of timber propped up, (unable to stand on their own). They think that every cry is against them. They are the enemies; so beware of them. The curse of Allah be on them! How are they deluded (away from the truth)! And when it is said to them, "Come, the messenger of Allah will pray for your forgiveness", they turn aside their heads, and thou wouldst see them turning away their faces in arrogance. It is equal to them whether thou pray for their forgiveness or not. Allah will not forgive them. Truly, Allah guides not rebellious transgressors. They are the ones who say, "Spend nothing on those who are with Allah's messenger, to the end that they may disperse (and quit Madinah)." But to Allah belong the treasures of the heavens and the earth; but the hypocrites understand not. They say,"If we return to Madinah, surely the more honorable (element) will expel therefrom the meaner". But honor belongs to Allah and His messenger, and to the believers, but the hypocrites know not. (*Qur'an* 63: 1-8)

It should be emphasized that the trouble and discord initiated by the hypocrites were not confined to Prophet Muhammad's early years in Madinah, but continued throughout the remainder of his life. As late as 631 CE, when the Prophet was returning from his expedition to Tabuk, the hypocrites were still active, and even formulated an unsuccessful plot to assassinate the Prophet. This incident is preserved in the following passage from the *Qur'an*.

O Prophet! strive hard against the unbelievers and the hypocrites, and be firm against them. Their abode is hell — an evil refuge indeed. They swear by Allah that they said nothing (evil), but indeed they uttered blasphemy, and they did it after accepting Islam; and they meditated a plot which they were unable to carry out; this revenge of theirs was (their) only return for the bounty with which Allah and His messenger had enriched them! If they repent, it will be best for them; but if they turn back (to their evil ways), Allah will punish them with a grievous penalty in this life and in the hereafter: they shall have none on earth to protect or help them. Amongst them are men who made a covenant with Allah, that if He bestowed on them of His bounty, they would give (largely) in charity, and be truly amongst those who are righteous. But when He did bestow of His bounty, they became covetous, and turned back (from their covenant), averse (from its fulfillment). So He hath put as a consequence hypocrisy into their hearts, (to last) till the day whereon they shall meet Him: because they broke their covenant with Allah, and because they lied (again and again). Know they not that Allah doth know their secret (thoughts) and their secret counsels, and that Allah knoweth well all things unseen? Those who slander such of the believers as give themselves freely to (deeds of) charity, as well as such as can find nothing to give except the fruits of their labor — and throw ridicule on them — Allah will throw back their ridicule on them: and they shall have a grievous penalty. Whether thou ask for their forgiveness or not, (their sin is unforgivable): if thou ask seventy times for their forgiveness, Allah will not forgive them: because they have rejected Allah and His messenger; and Allah guideth not those who are perversely rebellious. (*Qur'an* 9: 73-80)

H5. CONTINUED CONVERSIONS TO ISLAM

While some hypocrites remained among those who claimed to be Muslims, most of the former polytheists of Madinah who converted to Islam became sincere and devout Muslims. In the first few years of the Prophet's stay in Madinah, the overwhelming majority of the former polytheists of Madinah had become Muslims in more than just name. However, conversion to Islam was not limited to the former polytheists. Despite being guaranteed freedom of religion and of religious practice, at least some Jews (e.g., Husayn ibn Sallam, the chief rabbi of the Bani Qaynuqa, who was later known as 'Abd Allah ibn Sallam, and his immediate family) and Christians (e.g., Salman, a Christian from Persia, who had migrated to Madinah in search of the prophet yet to come) also converted to Islam.

H6. THE BATTLE OF BADR

With the establishment of an Islamic state at Madinah, a state of war existed between Makkah and Madinah, and the first significant military confrontation between the two cities came in *Ramadan* (March) of 624 CE. A richly-loaded caravan was returning to Makkah from Syria, and the Quraysh of Makkah decided to send a substantial army into the field to escort the caravan past Madinah and on into Makkah. At the same time, Prophet Muhammad led a small army of Muslims out of Madinah.

The small Muslim army hoped that it would be able to confront and capture the caravan, while avoiding the sizable army of Makkah, even though the Makkan army had been presented to the Prophet in a dream as being much smaller than it actually was. However, this hope to capture the caravan while avoiding the Makkan army was soon dashed. By divine decree, the two armies were headed for military confrontation near the wells of Badr (located 90 some miles south of Madinah), and the caravan would later reach Makkah without difficulty.

> Behold! Allah promised you one of the two (enemy) parties (the caravan or the army), that it should be yours: ye wished that the one unarmed (the caravan) should be yours, but Allah willed to justify the truth according to His words, and to cut off the roots of the unbelievers — that He might justify truth and prove falsehood false, distasteful though it be to those in guilt. (*Qur'an* 8: 7-8)

> Remember ye were on the hither side of the valley, and they on the farther side, and the caravan on lower ground than ye. Even if ye had made a mutual appointment to meet, ye would certainly have failed in the appointment: but (thus ye met),

that Allah might accomplish a matter already enacted; that those who died might die after a clear sign (had been given), and those who lived might live after a clear sign (had been given). And verily Allah is He Who heareth and knoweth (all things). Remember in thy dream Allah showed them to thee as few: if He had shown them to thee as many, ye would surely have been discouraged, and ye would surely have disputed in (your decision): but Allah saved (you) for He knoweth well the (secrets) of (all) hearts. And remember when ye met, He showed them to you as few in your eyes, and He made you appear as contemptible in their eyes: that Allah might accomplish a matter already enacted. For to Allah do all questions go back (for decision). (*Qur'an* 8: 42-44)

The small Muslim army of Madinah traveled rapidly, and was able to secure the wells of Badr before the arrival of the Makkan army, thus gaining the logistical advantage of a secure supply of fresh water. The night before the two armies met, a gentle rain fell as a gift from Allah, and this rain rested and refreshed the small Muslim army of Madinah, as well as serving as an ablution that spiritually purified the Muslims.

Remember He covered you with a sort of drowsiness, to give you calm as from Himself, and He caused rain to descend on you from heaven, to clean you therewith, to remove from you the stain of Satan, to strengthen your hearts, and to plant your feet firmly therewith. (*Qur'an* 8: 9-11)

On the 17th of *Ramadan* in the 2nd year of *Hijri* (Tuesday, March 16, 624 CE), the two armies confronted each other on the battlefield at Badr. There was a huge disparity between the two armies as they met on the battlefield. The army of Makkah fielded 900 to 1,000 fully armed men, many of whom were in chain mail. Their cavalry consisted of 600 to 700 camels, as well as about 100 horses. In dramatic contrast, the greatly outnumbered army of Madinah consisted of only about 305 men, 70 camels, and two or three horses. Through Satan's deception, the Makkan army believed it was invincible.

> And be not like those who started from their homes insolently and to be seen of men, and to hinder (men) from the paths of Allah: for Allah compasseth round about all that they do. Remember Satan made their (sinful) acts seem alluring to them, and said: "No one among men can overcome you this day, while I am near to you": but when the two forces came in sight of each other, he turned on his heels, and said: "Lo! I am clear of you; lo! I see what ye see not; lo! I fear Allah; for Allah is strict in punishment." (*Qur'an* 8: 47-48)

As was the custom at that place and time, the actual battle was preceded by bouts of individual combat among the champions of the two armies. Three men from each side stepped forward to fight, three against three. Representing the Muslims of Madinah were an uncle (Hamzah ibn 'Abd Al-Muttalib) and two cousins ('Ubaydah ibn Al-Harith and 'Ali ibn Abu Talib) of the Prophet. 'Ubaydah received a mortal wound when his leg was severed and became an early martyr for Islam, but all three of the Makkan champions were killed. Preliminaries having been satisfied, the two armies rapidly engaged each other at odds of three to one in favor of the polytheists of Makkah.

As the actual battle commenced, Prophet Muhammad threw a handful of dust at the attacking army of Makkah, and the angels of Allah swept down onto the battlefield to aid the outnumbered Muslim army, which was perceived by the soldiers of Makkah to be much larger than it actually was.

> It is not ye who slew them; it was Allah: when thou threwest (a handful of dust), it was not thy act, but Allah's: in order that He might test the believers by a gracious trial from Himself: for Allah is He Who heareth and knoweth (all things). (*Qur'an* 8: 17)

Remember ye implored the assistance of your Lord, and He answered you: "I will assist you with a thousand of the angels, ranks on ranks." Allah made it but a message of hope, and an assurance to your hearts: (in any case) there is no help except from Allah: and Allah is exalted in power, wise...Remember thy Lord inspired the angels (with the message): "I am with you: give firmness to the believers: I will instill terror into the hearts of the unbelievers: smite ye above their necks and smite all their finger tips off them." (*Qur'an* 8: 9-10, 12)

There has already been for you a sign in the two armies that met (in combat): one was fighting in the cause of Allah, the other resisting Allah; these saw with their own eyes twice their number. But Allah doth support with His aid whom He pleaseth. In this is a warning for such as have eyes to see. (*Qur'an* 3: 13)

What had appeared to be a sure victory for the polytheists of Makkah turned into their being routed at the hands of their numerically inferior, but spiritually superior, foes. When the dust of battle had cleared, the army of Makkah had lost 49 soldiers killed in combat, and a similar number had been taken captive. In contrast, the Muslim army of Madinah had lost only 14 men in combat. This totally unexpected and lopsided victory had been a powerful sign from Allah, and it invigorated the Muslim *Ummah* of Madinah and led to additional conversions to Islam.

Of the approximately 50 Makkan soldiers who were captured, two were executed for the crimes against humanity that they had previously and consistently perpetrated when they had persecuted and tortured unarmed Muslims prior to the *Hijrah* to Madinah. The remaining prisoners were treated justly and humanely.

The haughty and arrogant Quraysh of Makkah, the direct descendants of Qaydar (Kedar) ibn Ismael had previously made the Muslim *Ummah* flee from their swords and bows. Yet, only 18 months later, a small and greatly outnumbered Muslim army had defeated the Makkan army of Quraysh and had thereby "ended the glory of Kedar". Well over 1,000 years earlier, a remarkably similar event had been prophesized, but had not been fulfilled until the Battle of Badr.

> The oracle concerning the desert plain. In the scrub of the desert plain you will lodge, O caravans of Dedanites. Bring water to the thirsty, meet the fugitive with bread, O inhabitants of the land of Tema. For they have fled from the swords, from the drawn sword, from the bent bow, and from the stress of battle. For thus the Lord said to me: Within a year, according to the years of a hired worker, all the glory of Kedar will come to an end; and the remaining bows of Kedar's warriors will be few; for the Lord, the God of Israel, has spoken. (*Isaiah* 21: 13-17)

H7. ANOTHER LOSS

Prophet Muhammad's second daughter and third child was Ruqayyah. Ruqayyah had married 'Uthman ibn 'Affan, who would later become the third caliph of Islam, prior to the *Hijrah* to Abyssinia. 'Uthman and Ruqayyah had immigrated to Abyssinia in 615 CE, had returned to Makkah prior to 622 CE, and had moved to Madinah early in 622 CE. Ruqayyah had fallen seriously ill before the Battle of Badr and died before the Prophet's return to Madinah. Upon returning from Badr, one of the Prophet's first tasks was to visit the grave of Ruqayyah. In this graveside moment, the Prophet was accompanied by his youngest daughter, Fatimah.

H8. MARRIAGES

It was not long after the death of Ruqayyah that the Prophet's fourth daughter, Fatimah, married 'Ali ibn Abu Talib. Approximately one year later in *Ramadan* (February or March of 625 CE), Fatimah gave birth to Al-Hasan, the first of her two sons. The following year, in 626 CE, she would give birth to her second son, Al-Husayn. The marriage of Fatimah was followed by the marriage of the Prophet's third daughter, Um Kulthum, to 'Uthman ibn 'Affan, the widower of Ruqayyah.

Sometime following the marriage of Um Kulthum, in *Sha'ban* of the third *Hijri* year (January or February of 625 CE), Prophet Muhammad married Hafsah bint 'Umar ibn Al-Khattab. Hafsah's prior husband, Khunays, had died in the year following the Battle of Badr from the wounds that he had received in that combat, leaving her a widow at age 18 or 19.

In *Ramadan* of the third *Hijri* year (February or March of 625 CE), Prophet Muhammad married another widow of a martyr of the Battle of Badr. She was Zaynab bint Khuzaymah ibn Harith, who was known as Um Al-Masakin (mother of the poor), because of her longstanding generosity to the poor and those in need. While she was only about 30 years old at the time of her marriage to the Prophet, Um Al-Masakin died within the next eight months, passing away in *Rabi Al-Awwal* (August or September of 625 CE).

In 626 CE, Prophet Muhammad married another widow. She was Um Salamah Hind bint Abu Umayyah ibn Al-Mughirah, whose husband had died in late 625 CE, secondary to wounds he had received eight months previously at the Battle of Uhud. He left Um Salamah a widow with four orphan children. Um Salamah would later die in *Shawwal* of the 63rd *Hijri* year (June or July of 683 CE).

Following the Battle of the Trench in 627 CE, Prophet Muhammad married Juwayriyah (Barrah) bint Harith ibn Abu Darir of the Bani Mustaliq. In doing so, Prophet Muhammad once again demonstrated his care and concern by marrying a widow who had no independent means of support. Juwayriyah died in the 50th *Hijri* year (670 CE).

Shortly thereafter, apparently also in 627 CE, Prophet Muhammad married Um Al-Hakim Zaynab bint Jahsh. At the time of their marriage, Zaynab was about 38 years old and had been divorced, leaving her in a precarious financial position. Zaynab died in the 20th *Hijri* year (641 CE).

Circa 629 CE, Prophet Muhammad married Um Habibah bint Abu Sufyan. Um Habibah had been an early convert to Islam and had migrated to Abyssinia with her husband. She had remained in Abyssinia when the other Muslims returned to Arabia, and it was in Abyssinia that she had been left a widow with an orphan daughter. Hearing of her plight, Prophet Muhammad offered marriage, and resettled her in Madinah. She died in the 44th *Hijri* year (664-665 CE).

At some point after his marriage to Um Habibah, but also circa 629 CE, Prophet Muhammad married Zaynab (Safiyyah) bint Huyayy ibn Akhtab of the Bani Nadir tribe of the Jews. This was her third marriage, as her first husband had divorced her, and her second husband had been killed in combat at the Battle of Khaybar. Upon being taken captive by the Muslim army, Propht Muhammad gave her a choice between being released outright and remaining a Jew, or converting to Islam and becoming the Prophet's wife. Despite the fact that she had always been a Jew, she had long believed in the Prophet's divine call, having several years before overheard her father resentfully admit that Muhammad was the Prophet of Allah. Despite her father's admission, her father refused to convert to Islam because he could not stand the thought of a prophet arising from any lineage other than that of Prophet Jacob. Upon being liberated from her Jewish family, Zaynab immediately converted to Islam and married the Prophet shortly thereafter. She died in *Ramadan* of the 50th *Hijri* year (September or October of 670 CE).

After his marriage to Zaynab bint Huyayy, but also circa 629 CE, Prophet Muhammad married Maymunah bint Harith of the Hawazin tribe. This was her third marriage, having been previously divorced from her first husband and having been widowed by her second husband. She was about 51 years old at the time of the marriage and had no independent means of support. She died in the 61st year of *Hijri* (680-681 CE).

Prophet Muhammad's last wife was Maryam bint Shim'un, whom he married circa 629-630 CE. Maryam had been raised as a Christian in Egypt, where she had been a slave. At some point, she came into the possession of Muqawqas (Cyrus [14]), the Christian patriarch and bishop of Alexandria, who sent her to Prophet Muhammad as a gift. She then converted to Islam, received her freedom, and married Prophet Muhammad. Of note, she was the only wife of the Prophet, besides Khadijah, who ever bore any children of the Prophet, giving birth to a son, Ibrahim, who died in infancy. Maryam died circa 637 CE.

Given the sensitivities of most Occidentals to the issue of polygamy, it is helpful to put the Prophet's multiple marriages in perspective, as well as to offer a brief word about polygamy within Islam. With regard to that task, several points need to be noted.

Firstly, the *Qur'an* limits to four the number of wives a man may have simultaneously, although this limitation did not apply to the Prophet.

> If ye fear that ye shall not be able to deal justly with the orphans, marry women of your choice, two, or three, or four; but if ye fear that ye shall not be able to deal justly (with them), then only one, or (a captive) that your right hands possess. That will be more suitable to prevent you from doing injustice...Ye are never able to be fair and just as between women, even if it is your ardent desire: but turn not away (from a woman) altogether, so as to leave her (as it were) hanging (in the air). If ye come to a friendly understanding, and practise self-restraint, Allah is oft-forgiving, most merciful. (*Qur'an* 4: 3, 129)

As can be seen from the above verses, a man's right to multiple wives is a conditional right, not an absolute right. Only if the man can be scrupulously fair to all of his wives is he allowed to have more than one wife. Further, prior to this revelation, a man was allowed to have as many wives as he desired. Thus, Islam actually limited and constricted the number of simultaneous wives a man is allowed.

Secondly, the institution of polygamy is well established in the *Bible*. Cain's descendant, Lamech, had two wives (*Genesis* 4: 19). Prophet Abraham was simultaneously married to Sarah and to Hagar (*Genesis* 16:1-4). Prophet Jacob was simultaneously married to Rachel and Leah and used their two female slaves as concubines (*Genesis* 29:21-30:22). Esau, the brother of Prophet

Jacob was polygamous (*Genesis* 28:6-9). Ashur, a descendant of Judah, had two wives (*I Chronicles* 4:5). Shaharaim, a descendant of Benjamin, had two wives simultaneously (*I Chronicles* 8: 8). The so-called Mosaic Law of Judaism recognized polygamy (*Deuteronomy* 21:15). Gideon, one of the judges of pre-monarchial Israel had multiple wives and at least one concubine (*Judges* 8:30-31). Elkanah, the *Bible*'s father of Prophet Samuel, had two wives (*I Samuel* 1:1-2). Prophet David had multiple wives (*I Samuel* 25:39-44, *II Samuel* 5:13, *I Chronicles* 14: 3). Prophet Solomon reportedly had at least 700 wives and 300 concubines (*I Kings* 11: 1-3). Rehoboam, the son of Prophet Solomon and a king of Judah, had 18 wives and 60 concubines (*II Chronicles* 11:21). Abijah, king of Judah, had 14 wives (*II Chronicles* 13: 21). Jehoram, king of Judah, had multiple wives simultaneously (*II Chronicles* 21:16-17). Joash, king of Judah, had two wives simultaneously (*II Chronicles* 24: 1-3). Jehoiachin, king of Judah, had multiple wives (*II Kings* 24: 15). Further, there is no record in the *Bible* of Prophet Jesus or any other of the prophets of Allah forbidding the practice of polygamy.

Thirdly, Judaism did not abrogate the right of a man to have multiple wives simultaneously until the famous ruling of Rabbi Gershom b. Judah in the 11th century. Even then, some Jews continued to practice polygamy. Within the early Christian churches, polygamy continued to be practiced for several centuries after Prophet Jesus. With regard to this last point, one only needs to note that Muqawqas, the Christian bishop and patriarch of Alexandria, actually sent Maryam bint Shim'un to Prophet Muhammad as a slave and concubine. Further, the Protestant Reformation brought new instances of church-sanctioned polygamy into Christianity. As one example, one can point to the Anabaptist rule in Munster, Germany, in 1534 CE. As a second example, one notes the preaching of Bernardino Ochino in 16th century Poland. As yet a third example, Martin Luther acknowledged that he could find no scriptural prohibition against polygamy. In 19th century America, polygamy was practiced by the Joseph Smith and his followers and continues to be practiced to the current time by certain splinter groups from this movement. Even today, at least two Christian denominations in Africa recognize polygamy, including the Legion of Mary Church and the African Orthodox Autonomous Church South of the Sahara.

Thirdly, when one examines the 12 wives of Prophet Muhammad, not all of whom were his wives simultaneously, one discovers a very definite pattern. Nine of the 12 wives were widows at the time of marrying Prophet Muhammad, and at least four of them had orphaned children. Of the remaining three wives, one was divorced at the time of marriage to the Prophet, and one had been a slave. Clearly, the Prophet's multiple marriages were acts of mercy and compassion, not acts of lust.

Fourthly, despite the conditional permission for Muslim men to practice a limited polygamy, very few of them do. Despite occasional estimates that up to 02% of Muslim men have multiple wives, the author, who has been a practicing Muslim for over ten years and who has lived in both America and in the Middle East, has personally known only two Muslim brothers who have more than one wife. In addition, it might be noted that the author has maintained monogamy throughout his 34-year marriage, and has no intention of changing his monogamous state.

H9. CONFLICT WITH THE JEWS

While the victory at Badr had led to many additional converts to Islam in Madinah, and had caused many Arab tribes in the vicinity to seek alliances with the Prophet, many of the Jews of Madinah were dismayed at Prophet Muhammad's continuing successes. Many of them began to agitate against the Prophet, attempting to reinvigorate their old tactic of divide-and-conquer that they had used so successfully against the Arabs of Madinah in the past. Against this backdrop of intrigue and political treason, the Prophet began to be warned by divine revelation. The following passages from the *Qur'an* illustrate these warnings, as well as what was transpiring among some of the Jews in Madinah.

The religion before Allah is Islam (submission to His will): nor did the people of the book dissent therefrom except through envy of each other, after knowledge had come to them. But if any deny the signs of Allah, Allah is swift in calling to account. So if they dispute with thee, say: "I have submitted my whole self to Allah and so have those who follow me." And say to the people of the book and to those who are unlearned: "Do ye (also) submit yourselves?" If they do, they are in right guidance, but if they turn back, thy duty is to convey the message; and in Allah's sight are (all) His servants. (*Qur'an* 3: 19-20)

Say: "O people of the book! why reject ye the signs of Allah, when Allah is Himself witness to all ye do?" Say: "O ye people of the book! why obstruct ye those who believe, from the path of Allah, seeking to make it crooked, while ye were yourselves witnesses (to Allah's covenant)? But Allah is not unmindful of all that ye do." O ye who believe! if ye listen to a faction among the people of the book, they would (indeed) render you apostates after ye have believed! (*Qur'an* 3: 98-100)

O ye who believe! take not into your intimacy those outside your ranks: they will not fail to corrupt you. They only desire your ruin: rank hatred has already appeared from their mouths: what their hearts conceal is far worse. We have made plain to you the signs, if ye have wisdom. Ah! ye are those who love them, but they love you not — though ye believe in the whole of the book, when they meet you, they say, "We believe": but when they are alone, they bite off the very tips of their fingers at you in their rage. Say: "Perish in your rage: Allah knoweth well all the secrets of the heart." If aught that is good befalls you, it grieves them; but if some misfortune overtakes you, they rejoice at it. But if ye are constant and do right, not the least harm will their cunning do to you; for Allah compasseth round about all that they do. (*Qur'an* 3: 118-120)

O messenger! let not those grieve thee, who race each other into unbelief; (whether it be) among those (the hypocrites) who say "We believe" with their lips but whose hearts have no faith; or it be among the Jews — men who will listen to any lie — will listen even to others who have never so much as come to thee, they change the words from their (right) times and places: they say, "If ye are given this, take it, but if not, beware!" If anyone's trial is intended by Allah, thou hast no authority in the least for him against Allah. For such — it is not Allah's will to purify their hearts. For them there is disgrace in this world, and in the hereafter a heavy punishment. (They are fond of) listening to falsehood, of devouring anything forbidden. If they do come to thee, either judge between them, or decline to interfere. If thou decline, they cannot hurt thee in the least. If thou judge, judge in equity between them. For Allah loveth those who judge in equity. But why do they come to thee for decision, when they have (their own) law before them? — Therein is the (plain) – command of Allah; yet even after that, they would turn away. For they are not (really) people of faith. (*Qur'an* 5: 41-43)

Of the Jews there are those who displace words from their (right) places and say: "We hear and we disobey"; and "Hear, may you not hear;" and "Ra'ina"; with a twist of their tongues and a slander to faith.[15] If only they had said: "We hear and we obey"; and "Do hear"; and "Do look at us": it would have been better for them, and more proper; but Allah hath cursed them for their unbelief; and but few of them will believe. (*Qur'an* 4: 46)

The Jews say: "Allah's hand is tied up." Be their hands tied up and be they accursed for the (blasphemy) they utter. Nay, both His hands are widely outstretched: He giveth and spendeth (of His bounty) as He pleaseth. But the revelation that cometh to thee from Allah increaseth in most of them their obstinate rebellion and blasphemy. Amongst them We have placed enmity and hatred till the Day of Judgment. Every time they kindle the fire of war, Allah doth extinguish it; but they (ever) strive to do mischief on earth. And Allah loveth not those who do mischief...Say: "O people of the book! ye have no ground to stand upon unless ye stand fast by the law, the gospel, and all the revelation that has come to you from your Lord." It is the revelation that cometh to thee from thy Lord, that increaseth in most of them their obstinate rebellion and blasphemy. But sorrow thou not over (these) people without faith. (*Qur'an* 5 :64, 68)

They (also) said: "Allah took our promise not to believe in a messenger unless he showed us a sacrifice consumed by fire (from heaven)." Say: "There came to you messengers before me with clear signs and even with what ye ask for: why then did ye slay them, if ye speak the truth?" (*Qur'an* 3: 183)

Some commentators on the last quoted verse from the *Qur'an* have assumed that the reference to fire from heaven consuming a sacrificial offering refers to the following Biblical event involving Prophets Moses and Aaron.

Aaron lifted his hands toward the people and blessed them; and he came down after sacrificing the sin offering, the burnt offering, and the offering of well-being. Moses and Aaron entered the tent of meeting, and then came out and blessed the people; and the glory of the Lord appeared to all the people. Fire came out from the Lord and consumed the burnt offering and the fat on the altar; and when all the people saw it, they shouted and fell on their faces. (*Leviticus* 9: 22-24)

However, given that fire from heaven is being used as a test of whether or not a person is a prophet, it appears far more likely that the reference is to another Biblical event, one involving a contest between Prophet Elijah and the false prophets of Baal.

So Ahab sent to all the Israelites, and assembled the prophets at Mount Carmel. Elijah then came near to all the people, and said, "How long will you go limping with two different opinions? If the Lord is God, follow him; but if Baal, then follow him." The people did not answer him a word. Then Elijah said to the people, "I, even I only, am left a prophet of the Lord; but Baal's prophets number four hundred fifty. Let two bulls be given to us; let them choose one bull for themselves, cut it in pieces, and lay it on the wood, but put no fire to it; I will prepare the other bull and lay it on the wood, but put no fire to it. Then you call on the name of your god and I will call on the name of the Lord; the god who answers by fire is indeed God." All the people answered, "Well spoken!" Then Elijah said to the prophets of Baal, "Choose for yourselves one bull and prepare it first for you are many; then call on the name of your god, but put no fire to it." So they took the bull that was given them, prepared it, and called on the name of Baal from morning until noon, crying, "O Baal, answer us!" But there was no voice, and no answer. They limped about the altar that they had made. At noon Elijah mocked them, saying, "Cry aloud! Surely he is a god; either he is meditating, or he has wandered away, or he is on a journey, or perhaps he is asleep and must be awakened." Then they cried aloud and, as was their custom, they cut themselves with swords and lances until the blood gushed out over them. As midday passed, they raved on until the time of the offering of the oblation, but there was no voice, no answer, and no response. Then Elijah said to all the people, "Come closer to me"; and all the people came closer to him. First he repaired the altar of the Lord that had been thrown down; Elijah took twelve stones, according to the number of the tribes of the sons of Jacob, to whom the word of the Lord came, saying, "Israel shall be your name"; with the stones he built an altar in the name of the Lord. Then he made a trench around the altar, large enough to contain two measures of seed. Next he put the wood in order, cut the bull in pieces, and laid it on the wood. He said, "Fill four jars with water and pour it on the burnt offering and on the wood." Then he said, "Do it a second time"; and they did it a second time. Again he said, "Do it a third time"; and they did it a third time, so that the water ran all around the altar, and filled the trench also with water. At the time of the offering of the oblation, the prophet Elijah came near and said, "O Lord, God of Abraham, Isaac, and Israel, let it be known this day that you are God in Israel, that I am your servant, and that I have done all these things at your bidding. Answer me, O Lord, answer me, so that this people may know that you, O Lord, are God, and that you have turned their hearts back." Then the fire of the Lord fell and consumed the burnt offering, the wood, the stones, and the dust, and even licked up the water that was in the trench. When all the people saw it, they fell on their faces and said, "The Lord indeed is God; the Lord indeed is God." Elijah said to them, "Seize the prophets of Baal; do not let one of them escape." Then they seized them; and Elijah brought them down to the Wadi Kishon, and killed them there. (*I Kings* 18: 20-40)

Lest any reader gain the misimpression that Islam offers nothing but condemnation of the Jews, the following should be noted. Firstly, as will be seen in section H10 of this chapter, one Jewish rabbi (Mukhayriq of the Tha'labah clan) died fighting at the Battle of Uhud while honoring the mutual self-defense clause of the Covenant of Madinah, and thus kept his commitments to Prophet Muhammad, whom he had named as the beneficiary to his estate. Rabbi Mukhayriq was an excellent example of the honorable and trustworthy Jews of Madinah, even though he apparently never actually converted to Islam. Secondly, several Jews did convert to Islam, including 'Abd Allah ibn Sallam and his immediate family, Al-Najashi, 'Amr ibn Su'da, Rifa'ah ibn Samaw'al, Rayhanah bint Zayd, Salman Al-Farsi, and Zaynab (Safiyyah) bint Huyayy ibn Akhtab, who would later become a wife of the Prophet. Thirdly, it should be noted that several of the above-quoted passages from the *Qur'an* specifically state that it is only some part or faction of the Jews of Madinah who were accused of bad conduct, and the early biographies of the Prophet occasionally mention one or another Jew who argued fiercely with his own clan and tribe in trying to get them to honor their commitments to Prophet Muhammad. Fourthly, the words of Allah specifically state that there are some Jews who are "on the right course".

There is from among them a party on the right course: but many of them follow a course that is evil. (Qur'an 5: 66b)

Those who believe (in the Qur'an), those who follow the Jewish (scriptures), and the Sabians and the Christians — any who believe in Allah and the last day, and work righteousness — on them shall be no fear, nor shall they grieve (Qur'an 5: 69; see also Qur'an 2: 62)

Not all of them are alike: of the people of the book are a portion that stand (for the right); they rehearse the signs of Allah all night long, and they prostrate themselves in adoration. They believe in Allah and the last day; they enjoin what is right, and forbid what is wrong; and they hasten (in emulation) in (all) good works: they are in the ranks of the righteous. Of the good that they do, nothing will be rejected of them; for Allah knoweth well those that do right. (Qur'an 3: 113-115)

Finally, Prophet Muhammad's own disposition to the Jews was one of loving kindness, interpersonal respect, and compassion. This is well illustrated in the following Hadith.

'Abd Al-Rahman ibn Abu Laila narrated that Sahl ibn Hunaif and Qais ibn Sad were sitting in the city of Al-Qadisiya. A funeral procession passed in front of them, and they stood up (in respect). They were told that the funeral procession was of one of the inhabitants of the land, i.e., of a non- believer, under the protection of Muslims. They said: "A funeral procession passed in front of the Prophet, and he stood up. When he was told that it was the coffin of a Jew, he said, 'Is it not a living being (soul)?'" (*Al-Bukhari, Hadith # 2: 399*)

Nonetheless, despite Prophet Muhammad's respect and compassion for them, despite his fairness to them, and despite his guarantee of their religious freedom, it appears that a majority of the Jews of Madinah were actively plotting against the Prophet and were seeking to undermine his authority. Some even entered into a treasonous alliance with the polytheists of the Quraysh of Makkah. Because of such activities, the Jews of the Bani Qaynuqa' tribe were exiled from Madinah late in 624 CE. Skipping ahead in time and across events that will be covered later, it is noted that the Jews of the Bani Nadir tribe were exiled in 625 CE. Further, in *Shawwal* of the fifth *Hijri* year (February and March of 627 CE), following their treason in allying with the Quraysh of Makkah while Madinah was under direct attack during the Battle of the Trench, most adult male Jews of the Bani Qurayzah were executed for treason against the state, and the women and children were made captives.

H10. THE BATTLE OF UHUD

Although the Quraysh of Makkah had been defeated at the Battle of Badr in *Ramadan* (March) of 624 CE, they were far from being done in their attempts to rid the world of Prophet Muhammad and the Muslim *Ummah* of Madinah. Thus, it was in *Ramadan* of 625 CE, only a few days after the birth of the Prophet's grandson, Al-Hasan, that a letter arrived by messenger from the Prophet's uncle, Al-'Abbas, back in Makkah. The letter warned that the Quraysh of Makkah were planning to attack the Muslim *Ummah* at Madina, and had mobilized a large army consisting of 3,000 men, 700 of whom were shielded with chain mail. Accompanying the army would be several wives of the soldiers, 100 men from the Thaqif and an unknown number of men from the Kinanah and other tribes allied with the Quraysh, 3,000 riding camels, an unknown number of transport camels, and 200 horses with which to mount cavalry charges. All in all, it was a decidedly formidable force for that time and place.

The advance warning from Al-'Abbas allowed the Prophet a week or two to decide upon his response. During that time, all the inhabitants and livestock from the villages and farms surrounding Madinah were brought inside the walls of Madinah for protection, requiring a major expenditure of time and effort in finding appropriate housing for the people and stabling for the livestock. Also, there was the issue of making Madinah ready for a possible siege, entailing a massive amount of food provisions and fodder to be placed in stock within the city.

In *Shawwal* of 625 CE, the army of Makkah arrived about five miles west of Madinah, having taken the Red Sea route between the two cities. After a brief halt, they circled around to the north of Madinah, where they made camp in the vicinity of Uhud. At that point, Prophet Muhammad called a conference of the men of Madinah to discuss strategy. Should they remain within the walls of Madinah, and attempt to withstand a siege? Should they march out of the city and engage the enemy at Uhud in a desperate act of self-defense? After much discussion, the latter course of action prevailed.

On Friday evening, the 14th of *Shawwal* (April 1, 625 CE), the Prophet led his small army out of Madinah. It numbered about 1,000 foot soldiers, with the only horse present, Sakb, being the Prophet's personal mount, which he had acquired from the Bani Fazara for 10 *Awaqi* of silver at some point between 622 and 625 CE. Of the approximately 1,000 men who accompanied the Prophet, eight were boys and teenagers. Discovering their presence among his army, the Prophet sent the six youngest and least physically developed back to Madinah, instructing them that they were too young to fight, regardless of how dire the situation was. He allowed the other two to stay with the army only after they had personally demonstrated that they were physically capable of engaging in combat. In contrast to these brave lads, there were many who were looking for an excuse to escape the coming combat. Before sunrise the next morning, about 300

hypocrites deserted the army of Madinah prior to the commence-
ment of hostilities, preposterously claiming that they left
because they thought that no battle would actually transpire and
leaving the 700-man army of Madinah at a decided disadvantage
in confronting the 3,000 and some combatants arrayed against
them.

> And the hypocrites also. These were told: "Come, fight in
> the way of Allah, or (at least) drive (the foe from your city)."
> They said, "Had we known there would be a fight, we should
> certainly have followed you." They were that day nearer to
> unbelief than to faith, saying with their lips what was not in
> their hearts. But Allah hath full knowledge of all they conceal.
> (They are) the ones that say, (of their brethren slain),
> while they themselves sit (at ease): "If only they had listened
> to us, they would not have been slain." Say: "Avert death from
> your own selves if ye speak the truth." Think not of those who
> are slain in Allah's way as dead. Nay, they live, finding their
> sustenance in the presence of their Lord. (*Qur'an* 3: 167-169)

As can be imagined, the decision to engage the Makkan army
at Uhud had not pleased the hypocrites and most of the Jews
of Madinah. In general, they were loathe to risk their lives in
the Prophet's behalf, regardless of the prior pledges they had
made. However, there was one noticeable exception. Mukhayriq, a
rabbi of the Ta'labah clan, gathered his fellow Jews together and
passionately pleaded with them to honor the Covenant of Madinah
and to support the Prophet and his army in the upcoming battle.
His plea was met with strong opposition, as many of his fellow
Jews protested that it was the Jewish Sabbath, which precluded
their fighting. Mukhayriq was not impressed with their use of the
Sabbath as a justification for not honoring their prior agreements
with Prophet Muhammad and reportedly replied that his fellow
Jews were not truly honoring the Sabbath. He then publicly
announced that he would join the Muslim army at Uhud and
that if he were to be killed in battle, the sole beneficiary of his

estate would be Prophet Muhammad. Arming for battle, he then joined the Muslim army at Uhud, where he was later killed.

On Saturday morning, the 15th of *Shawwal* (April 2, 625 CE), the Prophet and the army of Madinah advanced to Uhud, where they staked out the high ground while it was still dark. The army was arrayed into combat lines, the *Adhan* (call to prayer) was sung, and the Prophet led the army in the *Fajr* prayer. Worship completed, the prophet selected 50 of the best archers in the army, and directed them to take the highest ground in the vicinity, from where they could guard the rear of the Muslim army from any flanking charge of the Makkan cavalry. These archers were instructed to hold their ground, neither advancing nor retreating, no matter what the apparent outcome of the battle was. Their sole purpose was to guard the rear of the army of Madinah from any flanking action by the enemy cavalry.

As the sun rose, the army of Makkah formed into battle lines and began to advance. As the Prophet had surmised, the Makkan army arrayed 100 cavalry on each of its flanks, hoping to flank and encircle the Muslim army. When the Makkan army had advanced to within range of the Muslims, the customs of the times again necessitated the preliminary action of individual combat between the champions of each side. As had been the case at the Battle of Badr, these bouts were decisively won by the Muslim combatants. Preliminaries having been satisfied, the actual battle began.

Despite their numerical superiority of over four to one, the army of Makkah was having to fight uphill. As such, against all expectations, the army of Madinah began to drive the Makkan army back step by step. Meanwhile, the cavalry of Makkah was neutralized by the 50 archers of Madinah, who were successfully keeping the horses and riders of Makkah isolated on the far ends of the battlefield. The Muslim advance continued unabated until the center of the Makkan line finally collapsed. The battle was turning into a rout, and the Makkan army was beginning to flee.

At that point in the battle, 40 of the 50 archers who were guarding the Muslim rear from a cavalry charge fell to disputing about the Prophet's order to hold their position. These 40 decided that they could now safely desert their position and begin to scavenge for booty. With the rearguard of Madinah reduced to only 10 archers, Khalid ibn Al-Walid, the leader of the right wing of Makkan cavalry, led his horse soldiers in a charge that obliterated the last 10 archers and exposed the Muslim rear to a devastating cavalry charge from both wings of the Makkan cavalry. As 200 cavalry charged into the Muslim rear, the retreating Makkan army quit fleeing and returned to the attack. The Muslim army was now encircled and in dire straits. Fighting furiously, most of the Muslims were able to claw their way back to the high ground from which they had begun the day's battle or to surrounding hills and mountains.

> Allah did indeed fulfill His promise to you when ye with His permission were about to annihilate your enemy — until ye flinched and fell to disputing about the order, and disobeyed it after He brought you in sight (of the booty) which ye covet. Among you are some that hanker after this world and some that desire the hereafter. Then did He divert you from your foes in order to test you: for Allah is full of grace to those who believe. Behold! ye were climbing up the high ground, without even casting a side glance at anyone, and the Messenger in your rear was calling you back. There did Allah give you one distress after another by way of requital, to teach you not to grieve for (the booty) that had escaped you and for (the ill) that had befallen you. For Allah is well aware of all that ye do... Those of you who turned back on the day the two hosts met — it was Satan who caused them to fail, because of some (evil) they had done. But Allah has blotted out (their faults) for Allah is oft-forgiving, most forbearing. (*Qur'an* 3: 152-153, 155)

Some of the Muslims rallied around the Prophet and were able to hold the high ground on which they stood. However, Prophet Muhammad was twice wounded. The first time, he was struck by a stone that smashed into his mouth and broke off one tooth. The second time, he was struck by a sword on his helmeted head and on the chain mail protecting his right shoulder. As a result, he temporarily lost the use of his right arm and was knocked to the ground unconscious. Seeing Prophet Muhammad fall, the army of Makkah erroneously assumed that they had killed the Prophet. Growing weary of the fray and assuming that the Prophet was dead, the army of Makkah finally ceased fighting and began to withdraw, leaving the surviving Muslims to bury their dead, say the funeral prayer for each of their fallen comrades, and return to Madinah. In the act of burying their dead, the Muslims discovered how horribly the Makkan army had mutilated the corpses of the fallen Muslims. The body of Hamza ibn 'Abd Al-Muttalib, the Prophet's uncle, had been particularly mutilated. His nose, ears, liver, and other parts of his flesh had been cut away, and Hind bint 'Utbah, one of the women who had accompanied the army of Makkah, celebrated Hamza's death by partially eating his liver.

Upon seeing the mutilated body of his beloved uncle, Prophet Muhammad reportedly vowed that he would seek retribution by mutilating the bodies of 30 of the Quraysh, if he ever had the chance. However, this anguished vow was soon abrogated by divine revelation.

> And if ye do catch them out, catch them out no worse than they catch you out: but if ye show patience, that is indeed the best (course) for those who are patient. (*Qur'an* 16: 126)

It is a testimony to the Prophet's faith in and obedience to Allah that he immediately absolved himself of his prior vow. Moreover, he responded by prohibiting Muslims from ever mutilating a corpse.

Despite the fury of the battle, only 22 men of the Makkan army had been killed, although a number had sustained wounds. In contrast, the army of Madinah had 72 members killed in battle, including Hamza ibn 'Abd Al-Muttalib, the Prophet's uncle. In addition, almost all of the survivors had sustained one or another wound, with many having sustained severe wounds. Within the next few days, at least a couple of these wounded veterans of Uhud would die.

Following the Battle of Uhud, there were those in the Muslim *Ummah* who wanted to put the hypocrites, especially those who had deserted before the battle began, to death. However, despite the perfidy and lack of faith demonstrated by the hypocrites, Prophet Muhammad followed Allah's decree and dealt gently with them, showing them every mercy.

> O ye who believe! be not like the unbelievers, who say of their brethren, when they are traveling through the earth or engaged in fighting: "If they had stayed with us, they would not have died, or been slain." This that Allah may make it a cause of sighs and regrets in their hearts. It is Allah that gives life and death, and Allah sees well all that ye do. And if ye are slain, or die, in the way of Allah, forgiveness and mercy from Allah are better than all they could amass. And if ye die, or are slain, lo! it is unto Allah that ye are brought together. It is part of the mercy of Allah that thou dost deal gently with them. Wert thou severe or harsh-hearted, they would have broken away from about thee: so pass over (their faults), and ask for (Allah's) forgiveness for them; and consult them in affairs (of moment). Then, when thou hast taken a decision, put thy trust in Allah. For Allah loves those who put their trust (in Him). If Allah helps you, none can overcome you: if He forsakes you, who is there, after that, that can help you? In Allah, then, let believers put their trust. (*Qur'an* 3: 156-160)

As the Muslim *Ummah* reflected back on its defeat at the Battle of Uhud, revelation came that put the situation in a broader context.

> If a wound hath touched you, be sure a similar wound hath touched the others. Such days (of varying fortunes) We give to men and men by turns: that Allah may know those that believe and that He may take to Himself from your ranks

martyr – witnesses (to truth). And Allah loveth not those that do wrong. Allah's object also is to purge those that are true in faith and to deprive of blessing those that resist faith. (*Qur'an* 3: 140-141)

H11. THE BATTLE OF THE TRENCH

The third, final, and most ambitious assault on Madinah by the polytheistic Quraysh of Makkah occurred in 627 CE during the Battle of the Trench. The Quraysh of Makkah were determined to rid themselves once and for all of Prophet Muhammad and the Muslim *Ummah* of Madinah. To this end, Makkah allied itself with numerous confederates, for which reason the Battle of the Trench is also referred to as the Battle of the Confederates.

The saying is that politics make for strange bedfellows, and this was never more evident than in the alliances formed by the confederates who marched against Madinah in 627 CE. The two mastermind groups behind the proposed attack on Madinah were the polytheistic Quraysh of Makkah and the Jews of the Bani Nadir tribe. For their part, the Quraysh promised to march against Madinah from the south with their allied tribes from the vicinity of Makkah. In turn, the Jews of the Bani Nadir promised to provide an army from the ranks of the Arab tribes with whom they had alliances in the vicinity of Madinah. This second army was to march against Madinah from the east.

The Bani Nadir had been previously exiled from Madinah to Khaybar, following their plotting to assassinate Prophet Muhammad after the Battle of Uhud in 625 CE. Their present motive was simple. They sought to recover their holdings in Madinah, and thus eagerly joined the pagan polytheists from Makkah. In doing so, the Bani Nadir let perceived personal self-interest dominate over natural religious affiliation, and went so far as to assure the Quraysh of Makkah that the polytheistic practices and pagan rituals of Makkah were closer to their own religious beliefs than were the *Qur'an* and the monotheistic and ethical teachings of Prophet Muhammad.

As the march to Madinah began, the southern army, under the leadership of the Quraysh, consisted of 4,000 men and 300 horses from the Quraysh and their closest allies, as well as additional men from some of their more distant allies. The eastern army consisted of those Arab Bedouin tribes that the Bani Nadir had managed to persuade or bribe to join the endeavor. Comprising the eastern army were the Bani Asad tribe of Bedouin Arabs, 700 men of the Bani Sulaym tribe, and around 2,000 men and 300 horses from the Fazara, Murrah, and Ashja' clans of the Bani Ghatafan Bedouins, who entered the fracas when the Jews of the Bani Nadir offered them half of the date harvest of Khaybar as a bribe. All together, the combined strength of the two armies was more than three times the strength that the Quraysh of Makkah had brought to bear at the Battle of Uhud, consisting of about 10,000 men and 1,000 horses.

Once again, Prophet Muhammad received advance word that an attack against Madinah was imminent. Again, he called for a conference to discuss the matter. How was Madinah to withstand the assault of two armies numbering 10,000 men and 1,000 cavalry? At that meeting, Salman Al-Farsi, whose name meant Salman the Persian, proposed an intriguing defense that had until then never been utilized in Arabia. Salman proposed that Madinah follow the custom of the Persians and dig a large, defensive trench around Madinah. Such a trench would prevent any horse cavalry from reaching the city, and would greatly impede the movement and progress of any attacking foot soldiers. At any given place along the trench, a handful of defenders on the city side of the trench could successfully repel a much larger group of attackers who would be trying to cross the trench.

Salman's proposed plan was quickly adopted. With only a week remaining before the anticipated arrival of the two armies, every devout and able-bodied Muslim male began digging the trench, including Prophet Muhammad, and the work schedule extended from sunrise to sunset. Fortunately, the natural topography of Madinah was such that the trench did not have to be dug continuously around the entire city. Here and there, the trench merely had to run from one impassable rock outcropping to another, or from one fortress to another. Nonetheless, it was backbreaking work and was performed under dire time constraints. Further, as had been the case at the Battle of Uhud, the people and livestock surrounding Madinah had to be brought into the city for their own protection, resulting in additional logistic difficulties. Additionally, all of the crops in the vicinity of Madinah had to be harvested, in order that the attackers would not have a ready source of food and fodder.

After six days of frantic digging, the trench was completed just as word arrived that the southern army of the Quraysh and the eastern army of the allied Bedouin tribes had been spotted in the vicinity. It was *Shawwal* of the fifth *Hijri* year (February and March of 627 CE). Prophet Muhammad and his Muslim army of 3,000 men, camped on the city side of the trench and awaited the coming confrontation. Of note, the Jews of the Bani Qurayzah, the last Jewish tribe remaining in Madinah, refused to honor their mutual defense pact with the Prophet, and immediately entered into negotiations with the attacking confederates to help the confederates breach the city's defenses. Hearing of this treachery and treason, Prophet Muhammad was forced to deplete his defensive forces even further by sending 300 Muslim cavalry to patrol the streets of Madinah, in order to insure against an uprising from within the city.

The arrival of the 10,000 men and 1,000 horses of the confederated forces brought forth two different reactions among the people of Madinah. For the true believers in Allah and in His prophet, the arrival of the confederates was nothing more than a confirmation of what they had been told to expect. As such, despite the formidable enemy looming around them, they were strengthened in faith and spirit.

> When the believers saw the confederate forces they said, "This is what Allah and His messenger had promised us, and Allah and His messenger told us what was true." And it only added to their faith and their zeal in obedience. (*Qur'an* 33: 22)

However, for the hypocrites and for those weak of faith, the enemy presence exacerbated their lack of faith and brought on a rush of fear. Some of them tried to make vain excuses as to why they should be allowed to return to their homes. Had the armies of the confederates managed to breach the trench around Madinah, some of them would have immediately switched sides, betraying their fellows with treasonous insult. Compelled to man the trench, their efforts were only halfhearted, they fought but little, and in their panic looked desperately to the Prophet to save them, although they had previously maligned and would subsequently speak out against Prophet Muhammad. When the Muslim forces finally prevailed through the intervention of Allah, they still doubted the outcome, and wanted to absent themselves from any future such confrontation with the enemy.

> Behold! they came on you from above you and from below you, and behold, the eyes became dim and the hearts gaped up to the throats, and ye imagined various (vain) thoughts about Allah! In that situation were the believers tried: they were shaken as by a tremendous shaking. And behold! the hypocrites and those in whose hearts is a disease (even) say: "Allah and His messenger promised us nothing but delusions!" Behold! a party among them said: "Ye men of Yathrib! ye cannot stand (the attack)! Therefore go back!" And a band of them ask for leave of the Prophet saying, "Truly our houses are bare and exposed," though they were not exposed: they intended nothing but to run away. And if an entry had been effected to them from the sides of the (city), and they had been incited to sedition, they would certainly have brought it to pass, with none but a brief delay! And yet they had already covenanted with Allah not to turn their backs, and a covenant with Allah must (surely) be answered for. Say: "Running away will not profit you if ye are running away from death or slaughter: and even if (ye do escape), no more than a brief (respite) will ye be allowed to enjoy!" Say: "Who is it that can screen you from Allah if it be His wish to give

you punishment or to give you mercy?" Nor will they find for themselves, besides Allah, any protector or helper. Verily Allah knows those among you who keep back (men) and those who say to their brethren, "Come along to us", but come not to the fight except for just a little while, covetous over you. Then when fear comes thou wilt see them looking to thee, their eyes revolving, like (those of) one over whom hovers death: but when the fear is past, they will smite you with sharp tongues, covetous of goods. Such men have no faith, and so Allah has made their deeds of none effect: and that is easy for Allah. They think that the confederates have not withdrawn; and if the confederates should come (again), they would wish they were in the deserts (wandering) among the Bedouins, and seeking news about you (from a safe distance); and if they were in your midst, they would fight but little. (*Qur'an* 33: 10-20)

For day after day, the confederate armies besieged Madinah, but the Muslim defenders stood firm, and actual combat was reduced to the archers' exchanges of arrows from one side of the trench to the other. Occasionally, the confederates would attempt an ill-fated cavalry charge to breach the trench, but all of these were successfully repelled. As time dragged on, the food and fodder of the confederates began to run out. Frustration and mutual recriminations mounted within the camp of the confederates. Finally, the seige was broken, not by armed men in sweating combat, but by the divine intervention of Allah. A hurricane blew in from the west one night, with winds destroying the tents and camp of the confederates. Their horses and camels were scattered by the wind-driven and icy deluge, and the cold reduced the movements of their soldiers to a slow motion stiffness. In contrast, the Muslim camp of Prophet Muhammad's army was protected by a rock outcropping, and they were spared the brunt of the storm. With food and fodder having been previously exhausted, the hurricane was the final blow against the confederates. Amidst mutual recriminations and blame, they broke camp and disbanded.

> O ye who believe! remember the grace of Allah, (bestowed) on
> you, when there came down on you hosts (to overwhelm you):
> but We sent against them a hurricane and forces that ye
> saw not: but Allah sees (clearly) all that ye do. (Qur'an 33: 9)

In the immediate aftermath of the surprising Muslim victory
at the Battle of the Trench, the Prophet reluctantly turned his
attention to the treasonous behavior of the Jewish tribe of Bani
Qurayzah. They had not only refused to honor their mutual
self-defense pact with the Prophet, but they had actually negotiated with the enemy to throw open the city to the invading forces.
Intentional and active treason is a capital offense in almost
every nation. Previously, following their plotting to assassinate
the Prophet after the Battle of Uhud, the Jews of the Bani Nadir
tribe had merely been exiled to Khaybar. At Khaybar, they had
regrouped and had entered into an alliance with the Quraysh
of Makkah that had resulted in the Battle of the Trench. Given that
history and context, the Prophet had to restrain his own natural
mercy and leniency, and most of the men of the Bani Qurayzah
were executed for treason, while most of the women and children
of the Bani Qurayzah were held captive for their participation in
the treason.

> And Allah turned back the unbelievers for (all) their fury: no
> advantage did they gain: and enough is Allah for the believers
> in their fight. And Allah is full of strength, able to enforce
> His will. And those of the people of the book who aided
> them — Allah did take them down from their strongholds and
> cast terror into their hearts (so that) some ye slew and some
> ye made prisoners. And He made you heirs of their lands,
> their houses, and their goods, and of a land which ye had not
> frequented (before). And Allah has power over all things.
> (Qur'an 33: 25-27)

Dealing with the Bani Nadir in their fortresses at Khaybar would have to wait for a year, until after the Truce of Hudaybiyah freed the southern flank of Madinah from possible attack from Makkah. Following this truce, a small Muslim army of 1,600 men marched against Khaybar. One by one, the fortresses of the Bani Nadir fell to the Muslims, until the Bani Nadir surrendered and accepted exile from Arabia. Of note, the Bani Nadir had not committed active treason against the fledgling Muslim state at Madinah, because at the time of the Battle of the Trench they were not citizens of Madinah. As such, they were not executed. Prophet Muhammad's mercy and tenderheartedness shone through as usual, and he allowed the Bani Nadir to go into distant exile.

H12. THE TRUCE OF HUDAYBIYAH

In *Dhu'l-Qa'da* of the sixth *Hijri* year (March and April of 628 CE), Prophet Muhammad had a vision of him performing the *'Umrah* (the lesser pilgrimage to Makkah, as compared to *Hajj*— see chapter VI, section F), and invited the Muslims of Madinah to join him in fulfilling that vision. Traditionally, *Dhu'l-Qa'da* had been considered by the Arabs to be a sacred month in which no fighting was permitted, and the Prophet had decided to use this opportunity to perform one of the rites of Islam. Nonetheless, in order to insure peace, the Prophet sent an envoy ahead of him to Makkah to warn the Quraysh of his peaceful intentions and to minimize any possibility of armed conflict.

Many of the Prophet's companions in Madinah immediately joined the pilgrimage, as did some representatives from some of the Bedouin tribes in the vicinity of Madinah. However, these Bedouins tended to lag behind the Muslims from Madinah, as though hoping to avoid any misfortune or conflict that might befall those traveling in the immediate company of Prophet Muhammad.

The desert Arabs who lagged behind will say to thee: "We were engaged in (looking after) our flocks and herds, and our families: do thou then ask forgiveness for us," they say with their tongues what is not in their hearts. Say: "Who then has any power at all (to intervene) on your behalf with Allah, if His will is to give you some loss or to give you some profit? But Allah is well acquainted with all that ye do. Nay, ye thought that the messenger and the believers would never return to their families; this seemed pleasing in your hearts, and ye conceived an evil thought, for ye are a people lost (in wickedness)." (Qur'an 48: 11-12)

News of the proposed pilgrimage by Prophet Muhammad and the Muslim *Ummah* immediately threw the Quraysh into a dither. They were caught between a rock and a hard place. Either they could break the longstanding convention of maintaining the peace during *Dhu'l-Qa'da*, thus earning the contempt of most Arab tribes, or they could let the Muslim pilgrims complete *'Umrah* in Makkah, thus legitimizing Islam in the eyes of many non-Muslims and emphasizing the relative powerlessness of the Makkans to stand against the Muslim *Ummah*. Neither choice was satisfactory to them. Thus, after much bluffing and blustering, they decided to try to reach a compromise solution with the Prophet.

While the Quraysh were debating their options, the Prophet and his companions had almost completed the journey from Madinah to Makkah, and had reached Hudaybiyah on the outskirts of the sacred territory surrounding Makkah. There, in preparation for the trial that was about to come, the companions of Prophet Muhammad formally pledged their allegiance to him while he sat under an acacia tree.

Shortly thereafter, three men of Makkah arrived at the Muslim camp to negotiate a settlement to the current predicament facing the pagan polytheists of Makkah. After much discussion, and especially after much nitpicking by the men of Makkah as to the exact wording of the truce that had been negotiated, a compromise was reached. The provisions of the truce were as shown in Table 7.

Table 7
Provisions of the Truce of Hudaybiyah

1. For 10 years, a state of peace would exist between Makkah and its allies, on the one hand, and Madinah and its allies, on the other hand.

2. The group from Madinah would withdraw back to Madinah and not perform *'Umrah* this year, but would do so the following year.

3. When the Muslims performed *'Umrah* on the following year, the Quraysh of Makkah would withdraw from Makkah for three days, to allow the Muslims to perform their rites by themselves.

4. Should any man of Makkah attempt hereafter to leave Makkah and join the Muslims at Madinah without permission of his guardian or family, the Muslims were bound to return the refugee to the representatives of Makkah upon request.

5. Should any man of Madinah attempt to leave Madinah and join the polytheists of Makkah, there would be no return of the refugee.

Despite what appeared to be a gross disparity in terms favorable to the pagan polytheists of Makkah, the treaty was signed by Prophet Muhammad and by additional representatives from all relevant parties. This apparent disparity concerned many of Prophet Muhammad's companions, especially when a chained Muslim managed to escape from Makkah and to arrive at the Prophet's camp just after the treaty was signed. True to his word and maintaining his absolute integrity, in spite of his personal distress at returning this Muslim refugee, the Prophet scrupulously upheld the treaty and had the unfortunate man returned to the Makkan envoys. While some of Prophet Muhammad's companions complained about the treaty, Allah saw things differently. The divine word stated that the Truce of Hudaybiyah was a "manifest", "clear", and "speedy victory" that would result in "many gains" and that it had prevented a needless bloodbath from taking place.

Verily We have granted thee a manifest victory...(*Qur'an* 48:1)

Allah's good pleasure was on the believers when they swore fealty to thee under the tree: He knew what was in their hearts, and He sent down tranquility to them; and He rewarded them with a speedy victory; and many gains will they acquire (besides): and Allah is exalted in power, full of wisdom. Allah has promised you many gains that ye shall acquire, and He has given you these beforehand; and He has restrained the hands of men from you; that it may be a sign for the believers, and that He may guide you to a straight path; and other gains (there are), which are not within your power, but which Allah has compassed: and Allah has power over all things. If the unbelievers should fight you, they would certainly turn their backs; then would they find neither protector nor helper. (Such has been) the practice (approved) of Allah already in the past: no change wilt thou find in the practice (approved) of Allah. And it is He Who has restrained their hands from you and your hands from them in the midst of Makkah, after that He gave you the victory over them. And Allah sees well all that ye do. They are the ones who denied revelation and hindered you from the Sacred Mosque and the sacrificial animals, detained from reaching their place of sac- rifice. Had there not been believing men and believing women whom ye did not know that ye were trampling down and on whose account a crime would have accrued to you without (your) knowledge, (Allah would have allowed you to force your way, but He held back your hands) that He may admit to His mercy whom He will. If they had been apart, We should certainly have punished the unbelievers among them with a grievous punishment. While the unbelievers got up in their hearts heat and cant — the heat and cant of ignorance — Allah sent down His tranquility to His messenger and to the believers, and made them stick close to the command of self-restraint; and well were they entitled to it and worthy of it. And Allah has full knowledge of all things. Truly did Allah fulfill the vision for His messenger: ye shall enter the Sacred Mosque, if Allah wills, with minds secure, heads shaved, hair cut short, and without fear. For He knew what ye knew not, and He granted besides this, a speedy victory. (*Qur'an* 48: 18-27)

As always, the perspective of Allah was unerring, as the following post Hudaybiyah events affirm. (1) Muslim men who escaped from Makkah quickly learned to congregate away from Madinah, so that the treaty would have no force upon them. (2) Muslim women were free to escape to Madinah, because the treaty was specific to men, not to women refugees. (3) The Muslim *Ummah* of Madinah was now free to deal with the threat from the Jews of the Bani Nadir tribe at Khaybar who, despite their vicarious participation in the Battle of the Trench, were not actual allies of the Quraysh of Makkah, and were not signatories to the treaty. (4) In *Dhu'l-Qa'da* of the following year (March and April of 629 CE), the Muslim *Ummah* of Madinah performed the *'Umrah* in peace and safety, during which time the pagan polytheists of Makkah withdrew from their city. (5) Additionally, and most importantly, with no reason to fear for their personal safety, the Muslims were free to spread the message of Islam throughout the area, and the size of the Muslim *Ummah* quickly grew to more than twice its pre-Hudaybiyah size as new converts quickly joined the fold of Islam.

H13. CONQUEST OF MAKKAH

The Truce of Hudaybirah had resulted in a temporary peace. However, early in *Sha'ban* of the eighth *Hijri* year (late November or early December of 629 CE), the truce was flagrantly broken. A group from the Bani Bakr tribe, co-signatories of the treaty and with the Quraysh of Makkah, attacked and massacred a contingent of the Bani Kuza'ah, co-signatories with and allies of the Muslim

Ummah of Madinah. Making matters still worse, Makkah had supplied the Bani Bakr with weapons, and one or two of the Makkan Quraysh had even joined the Bani Bakr in the attack. Adding insult to injury, the survivors of the initial attack had been hunted down by the Bani Bakr within the precincts of Makkah. The Bani Kuza'ah responded by appealing to their allies in Madinah.

Somewhat belatedly, the Quraysh of Makkah sent an envoy, Abu Sufyan ibn Harb of the Umayyad clan of the Quraysh, to Madinah. At first glance, the selection of Abu Sufyan appeared to be a stroke of inspiration. Not only was he one of the leading men of Makkah, he was also the father of the Prophet's wife, Um Habibah. However, Abu Sufyan had been a bitter foe of Islam, and he came to Madinah offering nothing but a proposal to strengthen and lengthen the duration of the Truce of Hudaybirah. There was not a word about reparations or about punishing the perpetrators of the attack on the Bani Kuza'ah. The Prophet remained non-committal. When Abu Sufyan later tried to get his daughter, Um Habibah, to intercede for him, she refused, and Abu Sufyan returned to Makkah without having accomplished his goal.

Still in *Sha'ban* (December of 629 CE), Prophet Muhammad issued a call for the Bedouin tribes allied with Madinah to gather in Madinah by early in *Ramadan* (late December of 629 CE or early January of 630 CE). The tribes gathered, and an army was formed, although the Prophet refused to disclose the purpose to which this force was to be directed, thus maintaining the advantage provided by tactical surprise. While everyone knew that Makkah might be the object of attack, there were other possibilities as well.

On the 10th of *Ramadan* in the eighth *Hijri* year (Tuesday, January 5, 630 CE), the combined army marched out of Madinah under the leadership of Prophet Muhammad. It consisted of 10,000 men, at least as many camels, and over 800 horses. (Of note, one wing of the army was under the command of Khalid ibn Al-Walid, who had been the leader of the cavalry charge that had defeated the Muslims at the Battle of Uhud. This most dangerous of all the military leaders of the Quraysh had finally converted to Islam, and now rode under the command of Prophet Muhammad. (Later, he would distinguish himself as the greatest of the Muslim generals during the so-called period of Islamic Conquest.) The army headed to the south out of Madinah in the direction of Makkah. But even then, the object of the coming attack could not be defined with certainty.

At one point along the way, Prophet Muhammad noticed a dog lying alongside the road. The dog had just given birth to a litter of puppies, and was nursing her litter as the army began to pass by. Symptomatic of his care and concern for all living things, the Prophet immediately ordered a soldier to stand guard over the dog and her puppies, in order to make sure that no harm came to them by the passing of the large army. Even in the midst of the march to war, Prophet Muhammad's tenderheartedness and mercy were evident.

As the army neared Makkah, it became increasingly difficult to maintain the element of surprise. Indeed, the citizens of Makkah were well aware of what was about to befall them. Those Muslims and Muslim sympathizers that still lived in Makkah, e.g., the Prophet's paternal uncle, Al-'Abbas ibn 'Abd Al-Muttalib, hastened out to meet and join the advancing army. Also among those who came out to meet the army was Abu Sufyan ibn Harb. He had finally had enough. After meeting with Prophet Muhammad and spending a night thinking about it, he converted to Islam.

Even though he had just converted to Islam, Abu Sufyan ibn Harb was then sent as an envoy to the Quraysh of Makkah. He carried with him a most astounding declaration from Prophet Muhammad. He was instructed to announce to all those within Makkah that everyone who sought asylum in the house of Abu Sufyan, everyone who remained in their own homes behind locked doors, and everyone who sought asylum at the Ka'ba would be granted full clemency. Never before and never since has the world witnessed such an act of mercy and magnanimity by a conquering army.

On the 17th of *Ramadan* (Tuesday, January 12, 630 CE), the army of Prophet Muhammad entered Makkah. With the exception of one small band of Quraysh that tried to mount an attack, not one drop of blood was spilled. Makkah had fallen to Prophet Muhammad, and it had been a bloodless conquest. The various idols in and around the Ka'ba were destroyed, and Makkah was once again a center of monotheistic worship of Allah. The last of the Quraysh hurried forth to renounce their former paganistic polytheism and to convert to Islam. Among them was Hind bint 'Utbah, the wife of Abu Sufyan, who had celebrated the pagan victory at the Battle of Uhud by mutilating the body of the Prophet's paternal uncle, Hamza ibn 'Abd Al-Muttalib, and by eating part of Hamza's liver. The Prophet's mercy and clemency extended even to her.

H14. THE FAREWELL PILGRIMAGE

Following the conquest and cleansing of Makkah, Prophet Muhammad returned to Madinah. During the subsequent months, the fold of Islam grew rapidly, as more and more people flooded into the Muslim *Ummah* via conversion. Prophet Muhammad and Islam were now a force to be reckoned with across most of the Arabian Peninsula. Nonetheless, the Prophet continued his humble lifestyle. In many ways, he was a king in all but title, but he continued to live no differently than the humblest of the subjects of the realm. Whatever wealth flowed to him was quickly distributed to the poor and needy. He could have been the king, but he was far more — he was the prophet and messenger of Allah.

Beginning on the eighth of *Dhu'l-Hijja* of the 10th *Hijri* year (Saturday, March 10, 632 CE), having previously traveled from Madinah to Makkah, the Prophet began the performance of *Hajj* during his Farewell Pilgrimage. His manner and practice in performing this *Hajj* set the standard and example for all subsequent *Hajj* pilgrimages to Makkah. Even today, over two million Muslims every year faithfully follow the example of the Prophet's Farewell Pilgrimage.

H15. THE DEATH OF THE PROPHET

Returning to Madinah following the Farewell Pilgrimage, the Prophet's health grew steadily weaker. Finally, on the 12th of *Rabi' Al-Awwal* in the 11th *Hijri* year (Monday, June 11, 632 CE), Prophet Muhammad died. At first, the Muslim *Ummah* was beside itself. Blatant denial alternated with uncomprehending anxiety and grief. It was left to Abu Bakr, the Prophet's longtime companion, to put the death of the Prophet in perspective.

Narrated 'Aisha: "...Abu Bakr praised and glorified Allah, and said: 'No doubt! Whoever worshipped Muhammad, then Muhammad is dead, but whoever worshipped Allah, then Allah is alive and shall never die.'" (*Al-Bukhari, Hadith* #5:19)

Abu Bakr then went on two quote the following two verses from the *Qur'an*.

Truly, thou (Muhammad) will die (one day), and truly they (too) will die (one day). (*Qur'an* 39: 30)

Muhammad is no more than a messenger: many were the messengers that passed away before him. If he died or were slain, will ye then turn back on your heels? If any did turn back on his heels, not the least harm will he do to Allah; but Allah (on the other hand) will swiftly reward those who (serve him) with gratitude. (*Qur'an* 3: 144)

I. POSTSCRIPT

In concluding this chapter, the author must acknowledge once again that there is no way in which a single chapter in any book can begin to present an adequate and complete picture of Prophet Muhammad. In the present instance, the author has merely provided a series of snapshots of some of the significant events in the life of Allah's last prophet. Such an approach necessarily lends itself to a skeletal portrayal of historical facts, while omitting the flesh and blood portrayal of the impeccable character, personal integrity, and deep-seated love, affection, mercy, and tender heartedness that comprised the more personal aspects of the Prophet's life. As such, the interested reader is urged to consult one of the biographies of Prophet Muhammad that are listed in the bibliography.

Notes

11. With regard to the location of Paran, it is also instructive to note that many Biblical scholars reject the identification of Mt. Horeb or Mt. Sinai as being within the Sinai Peninsula, and insist that it must have been in northeastern Arabia, which further suggests that Paran was located in eastern Arabia. For more on this, see Noth (1960), pages 130-132.

12. The issue of the lineage between 'Adnan and Prophet Ismael is complicated by the fact that many of the individuals in the lineage were known by more than one name, and by the tendency to skip generations at times. By merging two different genealogies found in Al-Tabari (1988) with the one found in Al-Mubarakpuri (1996), the following lineage can be constructed: 'Adnan, the son of Add / Udad, the son of Hamaysa / Umayn / Salman, the son of Shajab / Hamayta/Hamayda, the son of Salaman / Nabit/Munjir Nabit Salaman, the son of 'Aws / Tha'labah, the son of Buz/Bura / 'Atr Al-'Ata'ir, the son of Shuha / Sa'd Rajab, the son of Qamwal / Ya'mana / Yarbah Al-Nasib, the son of 'Abai / Kasdana / Muhallam Dhu Al-'Ayn, the son of Al 'Awwam / Hazana, the son of Nashid, the son of Haza, the son of Bildasa / Al-Muhtamil, the son of Badlana / Yidlaf / Ra'imah, the son of Tabikh / Tahba / Tahab / Al-'Ayqan, the son of Jahma / Jaham / 'Allah, the son of Nahish / Mahsha / Tahash / Al-Shahdud, the son of Ma'jala / Makha/ Al-Zarib Khatim Al-Nar, the son of Aid, the son of 'Abqar, the son of 'Aqara / 'Aqir / Ibrahim Jami' Al-Shaml, the son of Banda'a / Al-Da'a / Ismael Dhu Al-Matabikh, the son of Abda'i / 'Ubayd / Yazan Al-Ta'an, the son of Al-Da'a, the son of Hamada / Hamdan / Ismael Dhu Al-A'waj, the son of Sanbir / Bashmani / Yasbin/Al-Mut'im Fi Al-Mahl, the son of Yathrabi / Bathrani / Bathram / Al-Tamh, the son of

Bahrani / Yahzan / Al-Qasur, the son of Yalhani / Yalhan / Al-'Anud, the son of Ar'awi / Ra'wa / Al-Da'da, the son of Aid/Mahmud / 'Aqara / 'Azir, the son of Deshan / Dasan / Al-Za'id, the son of 'Asar / 'Asir / Al-Naydawan Dhu Al-Andiyah, the son of Afnad / Atamah /Ayyamah/ Qanadi / Qanar, the son of Aiham / Thamar / Bahami / Daws Al-'Itq, the son of Hisn, the son of Muqsir / Maqasiri / Nahath / Al-Nizal, the son of Nahith, the son of Zarih / Al-Qumayr, the son of Sammi / Samma / Al-Mujashshir, the son of Mazzi / Mu'damir / Marza / Marhar, the son of 'Awda / Sanfa / Al-Samr / Al-Safi, the son of 'Uram / Al-Nabit, the son of Qaydar / Kedar, the son of Prophet Ismael.

13. Some sources add Tayyib and Tahir to the list of sons born to Prophet Muhammad and Khadijah, but it appears likely that one or both of these names are merely alternative names for 'Abd Allah.

14. Cyrus, bishop of Phasis, in the Caucasus, was appointed patriarch and governor of Alexandria by Heraclius. Given that he came from the Caucasus, he was known in Arab circles as Muqawqas. See Kennedy H (1988), page 6.

15. When pronounced correctly, *Ra'ina* means "please attend to us". However, by slightly altering the word, they were able to imply "O thou that takes us to pasture" or "our bad one".

Chapter 4
Qur'an and *Sunnah*

A. INTRODUCTION

With the death of Prophet Muhammad in 632 CE, the Muslim *Ummah* lost both its spiritual guide and its temporal ruler. On any spiritual and religious scale, the former loss was of far more weight and consequence than was the latter. No longer was the Prophet there to instruct the *Ummah* with his verbal teaching and with his behavioral example of conduct and religious practice. No longer was there a person to whom to turn for completely authoritative answers to spiritual doubts and religious questions. However, all was not lost. Prophet Muhammad had bequethed two crucial legacies that would serve the *Ummah* in the following centuries. The first was the *Qur'an*, and the second was his *Sunnah* (customary religious practice).

> (Prophet Muhammad said:) Verily, I have left amongst you the Book of Allah and the Sunnah of His Apostle, which if you hold fast, you shall never go astray.[16]

> Some companions of Mu'adh ibn Jabal said: "When the Apostle of Allah (peace be upon him) intended to send Mu'adh ibn Jabal to the Yemen, he asked: 'How will you judge when the occasion of deciding a case arises?' He replied: 'I shall judge in accordance with Allah's Book'. He asked: '(What will you do) if you do not find any guidance in Allah's Book?' He replied: '(I shall act) in accordance with the Sunnah of the Apostle of Allah (peace be upon him)'. He asked: '(What will you do) if you do not find any guidance in the Sunnah of the Apostle of Allah (peace be upon him) and in Allah's Book?' He replied: 'I shall do my best to form an opinion, and I shall spare no effort'. The Apostle of Allah (peace be upon him) then patted him on the breast and said: 'Praise be to Allah Who has helped the messenger of the

207

Apostle of Allah to find something which pleases the Apostle of Allah'." (*Abu Dawud, Hadith* # 3585)

B. THE *QUR'AN*

B1. INTRODUCTION

The Arabic word *Qur'an* (recitation or reading) derives from the Arabic verb *Qara'a* (to recite or to read). As such, the *Qur'an* is the recitation of divine revelation as recited by Gabriel, upon the command of Allah, to Prophet Muhammad. In turn, the *Qur'an* is the recitation of that divine revelation as passed on by Prophet Muhammad to the *Sahabah* (companions of Prophet Muhammad) and to the world at large.

B2. PROVENANCE

Prophet Muhammad had received his first revelation in *Ramadan* of 610 CE, while engaging in a spiritual retreat outside Makkah in a cave on Mt. Hira. At that time and place and at Allah's direction, the angel Gabriel had visited Prophet Muhammad and had recited to him the first revelation that was to form part of the earthly *Qur'an*.

> Proclaim! (or read!) in the name of thy Lord and cherisher, Who created — created man, out of a (mere) clot of congealed blood: proclaim! And thy Lord is most bountiful — He Who taught (the use of) the pen — taught man that which he knew not. (*Qur'an* 96:1-5)

Over the course of the next 22 years, Gabriel brought revelation after revelation in an episodic manner, with each revelation contributing to the formation of the earthly *Qur'an* as Muslims now read it. By revealing the *Qur'an* in easy stages, Allah allowed time for spiritual strengthening of the human heart, for the early Muslim *Ummah* to evolve as a religious community, and for the questions of early Muslims to be answered through divine revelation to the Prophet.

Those who reject faith say: "Why is not the Qur'an revealed to him all at once?" Thus (is it revealed), that We may strengthen thy heart thereby, and We have rehearsed it to thee in slow, well-arranged stages, gradually. And no question do they bring to thee but We reveal to thee the truth and the best explanation (thereof). (*Qur'an* 25: 32-33)

Not only did Gabriel serve as the messenger angel who brought continuing revelation to Prophet Muhammad, but, at Allah's command, he also guided the Prophet in other ways. On a yearly basis, Gabriel would instruct and rehearse Prophet Muhammad in the recitation of the whole of the *Qur'an* to the extent that it had then been revealed up through that year. The sole exception was the Prophet's last year of life, in which Gabriel reviewed the entirety of the *Qur'an* twice with Prophet Muhammad.

Gabriel had rehearsed Prophet Muhammad in the memorization and recital of the *Qur'an*, and Prophet Muhammad had instructed his companions in turn. As such, by the time of the Prophet's death, there were many *Hafiz* (those who had memorized the entirety of the *Qur'an*) among the Muslim *Ummah*. However, the preservation of the *Qur'an* was not solely dependent upon the prodigious memorization skills of the various *Hafiz*. Not only did various *Sahabah* memorize as much of the *Qur'an* as was individually possible, they also wrote down Qur'anic passages on stones, palm leaves, animal skins, bones, what paper was available, and whatever other writing surface they could acquire.

In 633 CE, only about one year after the death of Prophet Muhammad and following the death of many *Hafiz* at the Battle of Yamamah, Abu Bakr, the first *Khalifah Rasul Allah* (caliph, i.e., successor to the messenger of Allah) of Islam, commissioned Zayd ibn Thabit to produce in written form a single book containing all of the revelations given to Prophet Muhammad. The choice of Zayd ibn Thabit for the task was propitious. Besides being a *Hafiz* in his own right, Zayd was highly literate and had served as one of the principal secretaries to Prophet Muhammad. Zayd was most thorough and conscientious, and thus did not rely exclusively on his own memorization of the Qur'anic revelations. Rather, he consulted with other *Hafiz* and made extensive use of the numerous written fragments of the Qur'anic revelation. Finally, after about a year's worth of diligent work, Zayd produced a complete copy of the *Qur'an* in written form, which was entrusted to the care of Abu Bakr.

Abu Bakr maintained personal possession of this one and only written copy of the complete *Qur'an* until his death in 634 CE. Thereafter, possession of the written *Qur'an* was in the care of 'Umar ibn Al-Khattab, the second *Khalifah Rasul Allah* of the Muslim *Ummah*, who entrusted this single copy of the *Qur'an* to his daughter, Hafsah, who was one of the widows of Prophet Muhammad. The *Qur'an* thus remained in the custody of Hafsah until after the death of her father in 644 CE.

Following the death of 'Umar ibn Al-Khattab, 'Uthman ibn 'Affan became the third *Khalifah Rasul Allah*. Apparently being concerned about minor differences in Qur'anic recitation that were secondary to differences among the various Arabic dialects, 'Uthman retrieved the written *Qur'an* from Hafsah and commissioned Zayd ibn Thabit, the original compiler of the written *Qur'an*, to utilize this single copy of the written *Qur'an* to produce a final recension of the *Qur'an*, in order to standardize any dialectical differences. There has never been another recension of the *Qur'an*. The *Qur'an* of today is the same as that found in the 'Uthman recension, being different from the original recension of Abu Bakr only in the standardization of Arabic dialects.

As can be seen from the above, the provenance of the *Qur'an* is quite different from that of the Christian *Bible*. This can be illustrated in reference to at least three issues confronting the provenance of the *Bible*, two of which are noted at this time. (1) The historical provenance of the *Bible* is plagued by a bewildering array of ancient manuscripts and recensions, many of which are quite different from each other in certain key particulars having to do with such foundational issues as basic law, doctrine, and dogma. In contrast, the *Qur'an* of today is the same as the *Qur'an* of the seventh century, and there has been no changes in it during the 13 centuries since the *Qur'an* was first gathered into written form. (2) Furthermore, regarding the contents of the *Qur'an*, there have been no additions or deletions since the first recension of Abu Bakr. In contrast, the Christian *Bible* underwent centuries of formulation and reformulation before a standard canon of Biblical books was even delineated. The writings of the so-called Apostlic Fathers illustrate that these early church leaders were in substantial disagreement as to which books should and should not comprise the *New Testament* canon. It was not until 367 CE, over three centuries after the earthly life of Prophet Jesus, that Athanasius, the bishop of Alexandria, circulated his Easter Letter, which is famous for being the first listing of *New Testament* books that conforms entirely to the contemporary *New Testament*. However, various other lists continued to circulate, and such books as the *Shepherd of Hermas*, the *Epistle of Barnabas*, the *Epistles of Clement,* etc. occasionally continued to find their way onto various lists of *New Testament* books and into various *New Testament* manuscripts for well over another 100 years.

B3. LANGUAGE

The language of the *Qur'an* is classical Arabic. Indeed, the *Qur'an* serves as the foundation for the basic vocabulary and grammar of the entire Arabic language. Numerous passages within the *Qur'an* refer to the fact that the *Qur'an* was revealed in Arabic, and several provide explicit justification for that fact.

> Alif Lam Ra.[17] These are the symbols (or verses) of the perspicuous book. We have sent it down as an Arabic Qur'an, in order that ye may learn wisdom. (*Qur'an* 12:1-2)

> Those to whom We have given the book rejoice at what hath been revealed unto thee: but there are among the clans those who reject a part thereof. Say: "I am commanded to worship Allah, and not to join partners with Him. Unto Him do I call, and unto Him is my return." Thus have We revealed it to be a judgment of authority in Arabic. Wert thou to follow

their (vain) desires after the knowledge which hath reached thee, then wouldst thou find neither protector nor defender against Allah. (*Qur'an* 13:36-37)

Say, the Holy Spirit has brought the revelation from thy Lord in truth, in order to strengthen those who believe, and as a guide and glad tidings to Muslims. We know indeed that they say, "It is a man that teaches him." The tongue of him they wickedly point to is notably foreign, while this is Arabic, pure and clear. (*Qur'an* 16:102-103)

Thus have We sent this down—an Arabic Qur'an—and explained therein in detail some of the warnings, in order that they may fear Allah, or that it may cause their remembrance (of Him). (*Qur'an* 20:113)

Verily this is a revelation from the Lord of the worlds: with it came down the Spirit of Faith and Truth — to thy heart and mind, that thou mayest admonish in the perspicuous Arabic tongue. (*Qur'an* 26:192-195)

We have put forth for men, in this Qur'an every kind of parable, in order that they may receive admonition. (It is) a Qur'an in Arabic, without any crookedness (therein): in order that they may guard against evil. (*Qur'an* 39:27-28)

A revelation from (Allah), most gracious, most merciful—a book, whereof the verses are explained in detail—a Qur'an in Arabic, for people who understand—giving good news and admonition: yet most of them turn away, and so they hear not. (*Qur'an* 41:2-4)

Had We sent this as a Qur'an (in a language) other than Arabic, they would have said: "Why are not its verses explained in detail? What! (a book) not in Arabic? And (a messenger) an Arab?" Say: "It is a guide and a healing to those who believe; and for those who believe not, there is a deafness in their ears, and it is blindness in their (eyes): they are (as it were) being called from a place far distant!" (*Qur'an* 41: 44)

Thus have We sent by inspiration to thee an Arabic Qur'an: that thou mayest warn the mother of cities and all around her — and warn (them) of the day of assembly, of which there is no doubt: (when) some will be in the garden, and some in the blazing fire. (*Qur'an* 42: 7)

By the book that makes things clear — We have made it a Qur'an in Arabic, that ye may be able to understand (and learn wisdom). And verily, it is in the mother of the book in Our presence, high (in dignity), full of wisdom. (*Qur'an* 43: 2-4)

And before this, was the book of Moses as a guide and a mercy: and this book confirms in the Arabic tongue; to admonish the unjust, and as glad tidings to those who do right. (*Qur'an* 46: 12)

As above passages indicate, the *Qur'an* was revealed in Arabic because it was the language of Prophet Muhammad and because its initial audience was the Arabic-speaking community of Makkah. Just as the revelation given to Prophet David and Prophet Solomon would have been in Hebrew, and just as the revelation given to Prophet Jesus would have been in either Hebrew or Aramaic, the revelation given to Prophet Muhammad was given in his native tongue, which was Arabic. Thus, despite the pride of language demonstrated by some Arabic-speaking Muslims, there is no special or intrinsic worth inherent in the Arabic language.

With regard to the last point, this author cannot help but remember a story from his childhood in a predominantly German-speaking community in rural Kansas. An elderly member of the community, who was a devout Christian of the Mennonite persuasion, adamantly maintained that German was the language of God. As "proof", the elderly gentleman pointed with obvious pride to a passage in his German *Bible* from *Genesis* 3:9. The passage in question concerned Adam and Eve having hidden in the Garden of Eden after eating the forbidden fruit, and God calling out to Prophet Adam, *"Adam, Adam, wo bist du, Adam?"*, i.e., Adam, Adam, where are you, Adam. Clearly, the elderly gentleman's German translation of the *Bible* had God speaking in German, but what would one expect!

Just because Allah's words in the *Qur'an* are in Arabic is no reason for anyone to conclude that Arabic is the language of Allah. Such an assessment would be nothing less than attempting to limit the illimitable and to circumscribe Him Who is beyond any circumscription. After all, *Qur'an* 10:47 and 16:36 specifically state that Allah sent a messenger to every people, and it is only logical to assume that the revelation given to each such messenger would have been in his own language, suggesting that Allah has spoken to mankind in a myriad of different languages. Further, this very point was explicitly stated in the *Qur'an*.

> We sent not a messenger except (to teach) in the language
> of his (own) people, in order to make (things) clear to them.
> (*Qur'an* 14:4a)

Nonetheless, it remains an historical fact that the *Qur'an* was revealed in Arabic and that those words of Allah that comprise the *Qur'an* were spoken in Arabic. As such, any translation of the *Qur'an* from Arabic to any other language no longer constitutes the literal words of Allah as found in the *Qur'an*. For this reason, Muslims typically refer to a translation "of the meaning of the *Qur'an*", rather than to a translation of the *Qur'an* per se. While this distinction has little practical meaning in the day-to-day lives of Muslims, it does serve to preserve an important, if subtle, theological position.

The above distinction also provides a suitable jumping off

point for considering another important comparison between the *Bible* and the *Qur'an*. The *Qur'an* per se is the original Arabic revelation, and the preserved Arabic *Qur'an* is the only final and authoritative recording of that original Arabic revelation. In contrast, students of the *Bible* are confronted by a maze of ancient manuscripts across a wide spectrum of languages. With regard to a particular *New Testament* passage, is the Greek, the Latin, the Coptic, or the Syriac passage to be considered authoritative? No such dilemma confronts the Muslim, as the original Arabic *Qur'an* is the pristine *Qur'an*.

B4. FORM AND STRUCTURE

The individual revelations comprising the *Qur'an* constitute 30 *Ajza* (portions; singular = *Juz*) of approximately equal length. This division allows for the easy reading of 1/30th of the *Qur'an* each day during the Islamic month of *Ramadan* (see chapter VI, heading D). However, the more commonly used division of the *Qur'an* is into *Surat* (steps or chapters; singular = *Surah*). There are a total of 114 *Surat* of greatly varying length in the *Qur'an*. The second *Surah* of the *Qur'an*, i.e., *Surah Al-Baqarah*, is the longest, and consists of 286 *Ayat* (signs or verses; singular = *Ayah*). In contrast, the 108th *Surah*, i.e., *Surah Al-Kawthar*, consists of only three *Ayat*. All but one of the *Surat* of the *Qur'an* begin with *Bismillah Al-Rahman Al-Rahim* (in the name of Allah, most gracious, most merciful). The sole exception is the ninth *Surah*, i.e., *Surah Al-Tawbah*. Following this opening phrase, 29 *Surat* of the *Qur'an* immediately follow with *Fawatih*, the so-called detached letters.

The *Fawatih*, also known as *Al-Muqatta'at* ("the abbreviated letters"), consist of a varied sequence of letters from the Arabic alphabet. Each *Fawatih* consists of between one and five letters. In total, 14 different letters from the Arabic alphabet are used in comprising the various *Fawatih*. While a variety of theories have been proposed to explain the meaning of the *Fawatih*, none of these theories has ever attracted any consensus of support from the Muslim *Ummah*.

215

Although there are noticeable exceptions to the general rule, the 114 *Surat* of the *Qur'an* are typically arranged according to length, with the various *Surat* progressing from longest to shortest. This arrangement generally conforms to a reverse chronological ordering of the revelations, as the longer *Surat* were typically revealed to Prophet Muhammad in Madinah, while the shorter *Surat* were usually revealed during the Prophet's life in Makkah. As the Muslim *Ummah* did not coalesce into a nation-state until the migration to Madinah, the lengthy *Surat* revealed at Madinah typically focus on statecraft and the law codes of the Muslim *Ummah*, while the shorter Makkan *Surat* generally deal with basic theological issues and proclamations.

As the preceding would imply, one can separate the *Qur'an* with some degree of accuracy into earlier revelations and later revelations, into revelations received at Makkah and revelations received at Madinah, and into content areas such as sacred history, community rules and laws, and basic doctrine. In turn, the doctrinal sections of the *Qur'an* can be grouped into categories conforming to doctrines regarding: (1) instruction in the proper belief in and worship of Allah; (2) the universe (cosmology and cosmogony); (3) the creation, nature, and purpose of mankind; (4) Satan, sin, and repentance; (5) prophecy and the role and history of the prophets; (6) eschatology (the end times, resurrection, and final judgment); and (7) social service and one's duties to one's fellow man. Nonetheless, despite various schema of categorization, the *Qur'an* remains a single, unitary book of revelation, i.e., a verbatim recording of Prophet Muhammad's recitation of the revelations he received.

In length, the *Qur'an* is much shorter than the Christian *Bible*, and is about the same size as the Christian *New Testament*.

B5. THE STATUS OF THE *QUR'AN* IN ISLAM

For Muslims, there can be no higher religious authority than the *Qur'an*. The *Qur'an* is seen as standing uniquely alone as the only book of revelation preserved in its original and pristine purity. (See chapter V, heading D2 for a fuller presentation of the inviolate nature of the *Qur'an*.) For over 1.2 billion Muslims the world over, the *Qur'an* is the immaculate recording of the verbatim words of Allah as revealed by Gabriel to Prophet Muhammad. These are not the words of Prophet Muhammad as inspired by Allah, but the actual words of revelation sent by Allah to His messenger.

C. THE *SUNNAH*

C1. THE AUTHORITY OF THE *SUNNAH*

The Arabic word "*Sunnah*" can be literally translated as a "well-trodden path", and may be understood to mean the customary practice of a person or group. Within an Islamic context, the *Sunnah* refers to the religious teaching and customary religious practice of Prophet Muhammad. With regard to the *Sunnah*, the *Qur'an* repeatedly proclaims that Muslims are to obey Prophet Muhammad and to follow his illustrious example of behavior and conduct. As such, the *Sunnah* of Prophet Muhammad is religiously authoritative and binding on all Muslims. The following Qur'anic passages are among the many that illustrate the authoritative nature of the *Sunnah*.

> Say: "If ye do love Allah, follow me: Allah will love you and forgive you your sins; for Allah is oft-forgiving, most merciful." Say: "Obey Allah and His messenger": but if they turn back, Allah loveth not those who reject faith. (*Qur'an* 3: 31-32)

> And obey Allah and the messenger; that ye may obtain mercy. (*Qur'an* 3: 132)

> Those are limits set by Allah; those who obey Allah and His messenger will be admitted to Gardens with rivers flowing beneath, to abide therein (forever) and that will be the supreme achievement. But those who disobey Allah and His messenger and transgress His limits will be admitted to a fire, to abide therein: and they shall have a humiliating punishment. (*Qur'an* 4: 13)

On that day those who reject faith and disobey the messenger will wish that the earth were made one with them: but never will they hide a single fact from Allah! (*Qur'an* 4: 42)

O ye who believe! Obey Allah, and obey the messenger, and those charged with authority among you. If ye differ in anything among yourselves, refer it to Allah and His messenger, if ye do believe in Allah and the last day: that is best, and most suitable for final determination. (*Qur'an* 4:59)

We sent not a messenger, but to be obeyed, in accordance with the will of Allah...But no, by the Lord, they can have no (real) faith, until they make thee judge in all disputes between them, and find in their souls no resistance against thy decisions, but accept them with the fullest conviction. (*Qur'an* 4: 64a, 65)

He who obeys the messenger, obeys Allah; but if any turn away, We have not sent thee to watch over their (evil deeds). (*Qur'an* 4: 80)

If anyone contends with the messenger even after guidance has been plainly conveyed to him, and follows a path other than that becoming to men of faith, We shall leave him in the path he has chosen, and land him in hell — what an evil refuge! (*Qur'an* 4: 115)

Obey Allah, and obey the messenger, and beware (of evil): if ye do turn back, know ye that it is Our messenger's duty to proclaim (the message) in the clearest manner. (*Qur'an* 5: 92)

...the unlettered prophet...commands them what is just and forbids them what is evil; he allows them as lawful what is good (and pure) and prohibits them from what is bad (and impure); he releases them from their heavy burdens and from the yokes that are upon them. So it is those who believe in him, honor him, help him, and follow the light which is sent down with him — it is they who will prosper...So believe in Allah and His messenger, the unlettered prophet, who believeth in Allah and His words: follow him that (so) ye may be guided." (*Qur'an* 7: 157, 158b)

Say: "Obey Allah, and obey the messenger: but if ye turn away, he is only responsible for the duty placed on him and ye for that placed on you. If ye obey him, ye shall be on right guidance. The messenger's duty is only to preach the clear (message)...So establish regular prayer, and give regular charity, and obey the messenger; that ye may receive mercy. (*Qur'an* 24: 54, 56)

So take what the messenger assigns to you, and deny yourselves that which he withholds from you. And fear Allah; for Allah is strict in punishment. (*Qur'an* 59: 7b)

We have indeed in the messenger of Allah a beautiful pattern (of conduct) for any one whose hope is in Allah and the final day, and who engages much in the praise of Allah. (*Qur'an* 33: 21)

Verily those who plight their fealty to thee do no less than plight their fealty to Allah... (*Qur'an* 48: 10a)

A Muslim is to follow the *Sunnah* or religious teaching and customary religious practice of Prophet Muhammad. However, the key adjective "religious" should not be too quickly overlooked. That the Prophet spoke Arabic as his only known language is an "accident of history", and it is not incumbent upon Muslims to know and speak only Arabic. That the Prophet reportedly loved the taste of honey does not mean that all Muslims must learn to love honey. That the Prophet reportedly snored does not make it necessary that all Muslims snore. Clearly, acts of Prophet Muhammad that are easily explained on the sole basis of history and culture do not have the same binding authority on Muslims as his customary religious practice and his religious instructions. However, a caveat is necessary at this point, as it can be tempting for a person to begin dismissing the actual religious teaching and practice of the Prophet based on nothing more than subjective intuition that the act or statement in question was culturally determined or was precipitated by a specific historical situation that no longer applies. As such, the devout Muslim must be quite cautious in dismissing acts or sayings of the Prophet as being specific to a given time and place.

C2. *SUNNAH* AND *AHADITH*

Given that Muslims are to follow the *Sunnah* of Prophet Muhammad as their second source of religious instruction and authority, how are Muslims to know what was the actual *Sunnah* of Prophet Muhammad? The answers are to be found in the *Ahadith* (singular =*Hadith*), which are narratives concerning what Prophet Muhammad reportedly said and did. (Occasionally, *Ahadith* report on what a companion of Prophet Muhammad said and did.) However, let us be clear that it is the actual *Sunnah* of Prophet Muhammad that is religiously authoritative and binding upon Muslims, not the *Ahadith per se*. Not all *Ahadith* were created equal. Some appear to have a stronger provenance than others, and some *Ahadith* were clearly fabricated, an historical fact that leads to the all-important topic of the provenance and authenticity of any given *Hadith*.

C3. PROVENANCE AND AUTHENTICITY OF THE *AHADITH*

In the first few centuries after the death of Prophet Muhammad, certain theological and doctrinal differences inevitably developed among different groups within the Muslim *Ummah*. Typically, these differences arose either because of differing interpretations of various Qur'anic passages, or because the *Qur'an* did not specifically address a given issue. In such instances, the *Ummah* attempted to turn to the *Sunnah* of Prophet Muhammad for guidance. In some cases, this was relatively easy to do, as various *Sahabah* had preserved in written form the *Ahadith* for which they served as the primary narrator. For example, 'Abd Allah ibn 'Amr wrote *Ahadith* of Prophet Muhammad, which 'Abd Allah had heard witnessed, in his *Saadqa*. 'Abd Allah ibn 'Abbas wrote a collection of *Ahadith*. Abu Huraira had Hammam ibn Munabbah reduce to written form the *Ahadith* witnessed by Abu Huraira. Jabir ibn 'Abd Allah had his personally witnessed *Ahadith* recorded in written form by Wahab Tabai. Anas ibn Malik also wrote down the *Ahadith* that he personally witnessed. However, many *Ahadith* were initially preserved only in oral form, and the provenance of such *Ahadith* was not always optimally reliable.

Unfortunately, the desire to prevail in a theological or doctrinal discussion sometimes led an individual to fabricate an oral *Hadith* in order to bolster his ideological position. Given this proclivity, and given the natural frailties of human memory, the fabrication of *Ahadith* almost became a cottage industry, and many otherwise genuine *Ahadith* became infected with some measure of distortion. What was needed was some system of sorting through and separating the genuine from the distorted and fabricated *Ahadith*. In response to this need, the early scholars of Islam developed the academic discipline of *Ahadith* science, which developed a thorough and all-encompassing process for analyzing the provenance and authenticity of *Ahadith*.

Any given *Hadith* consists of two component parts: an *Isnad* (plural = *Asanid*); and a *Matn*. The first part of any *Hadith* was the *Isnad*, which consisted of the chain of transmission of an oral *Hadith* from the person who actually heard or saw the Prophet say or do something, to the person he told it to, to the person that person told it to, and so forth, on down to the person who actually recorded the *Hadith* in written form. For example, a hypothetical *Isnad* might report that X received it from Y, who received it from Z, that Z heard the Prophet say... (Note: in the interest of brevity, in the *Ahadith* quoted in this book, the entire *Isnad* has typically not been reported, although the original narrator is almost always mentioned.) As can be quickly seen, the *Isnad* is fairly comparable to the chain of ownership that art experts establish in order to verify the provenance of a painting or other work of art. Clearly, the *Isnad* was tailor-made to serve as an objective tool in establishing the authenticity of *Ahadith*. However, the *Matn*, which comprised the actual narrative portion of a *Hadith*, was also developed as a tool of *Hadith* verification.

As previously noted, the *Isnad* was ideally suited to serve as a crucial building block in establishing the provenance of any given *Hadith*. However, for the *Isnad* to be a truly effective tool, it was first necessary to develop biographies of all the individuals mentioned in all the *Asanid* of the various *Ahadith*. This was a monumental, but crucial, task, eventually entailed developing biographies on about 13,000 transmitters of *Ahadith*, and was a pivotal development within *Ahadith* science. Early examples of these collections of biographies include: (1) *Kitab Al-Tabaqat Al-Kabir* (the great book of classes) by Muhammad ibn Sa'd (784-845 CE), which contained about 4,250 biographical entries; (2) *Al-Tarikh Al-Kabir* (the large history) by Abu 'Abd Allah Muhammad ibn Isma'il ibn Ibrahim Al-Bukhari Al-Jufi' (810-870 CE); (3) the biographical dictionary of Ibn Al-Athir (d. 1233 CE); and (4) the biographical dictionary of Al-Dhahabi (d. 1348 CE).

With the development of these biographies, it became possible to determine whether two given individuals had ever been in the same place at the same time, which was an obvious and necessary prerequisite for the one to have told the other a *Hadith*. To return to the previous hypothetical example of an *Isnad* involving X, Y, and Z, this aspect of *Isnad* verification required that Y and Z had both been present at the same place at the same time, that X and Y had both been present at the same place at the same time, and that the possible meeting of X and Y had come after the possible meeting of Y and Z. In this way, the science of *Isnad* verification began to be developed.

The above aspect of *Isnad* verification established whether or not it was possible that Z could have told Y a *Hadith*, and that Y could have later told the *Hadith* to X. However, that was not the only criterion used in *Isnad* verification. By recourse to the biographies of the various transmitters, the transmitters were also categorized according to memory skills, personal integrity, honesty, truthfulness, religious knowledge, language skills, etc. Summing across these different dimensions, each transmitter was categorized as to his personal reliability as a transmitter. Thus, two interrelated aspects of *Isnad* verification were developed: (1) the possibility of a *Hadith* being transmitted along a specified chain of transmission; and (2) the reliability of each individual link of transmission in the *Isnad*. To be accepted as authentic, two hurdles had to be past. Firstly, the chain of transmission had to be possible. Secondly, the chain of transmission had to be sound and acceptable, and the strength of that chain of transmission could be no more reliable than the weakest link of reliability in that chain.

The second aspect of *Ahadith* verification involved analysis of the *Matn* or narrative content of the *Hadith*. Was the *Matn* of a given *Hadith* consistent with the *Qur'an*? Was the *Matn* consistent with other, already verified *Ahadith*? Finally, combining *Isnad* and *Matn* analysis, one could ask whether the *Matn* was independently verified by other *Asanid*, which had no overlap with the *Isnad* under consideration?

Using the twin criteria of *Isnad* and *Matn* analysis, *Ahadith* were then classified into those that were: (1) *Sahih* or sound; (2) *Hasan* or good; (3) *Daif* or weak; or (4) fabricated. The latter two categories of *Ahadith* (*Daif* and fabricated) are never used in Islamic law and jurisprudence, nor are they considered to be an acceptable source for religious guidance. Several elaborations of the above four-fold classification system were developed over time, however a discussion of such elaborations goes well beyond a simple introduction to the concept of *Ahadith*.

C4. MAJOR COLLECTIONS OF *AHADITH*

Over the first three centuries following the death of Prophet Muhammad, many *Ahadith* scholars categorized the various *Ahadith*, and compiled the *Sahih Ahadith* into major collections. Over time, six of these collections of *Sahih Ahadith* came to be almost universally regarded within Sunni Islam as being religiously authoritative and are referred to as the *Al-Kutub Al-Sittah,* i.e., the six books. These six collections may be considered to be the six "standard" collections of *Ahadith*.

(1) Abu 'Abd Allah Muhammad ibn Isma'il ibn Ibrahim Al-Bukhari Al-Jufi' was born in 810 CE in Bukhara, in what is now Uzbekistan, and died in 870 CE. As a teen, he made the pilgrimage to Makkah and began to gather and collect various *Ahadith*. He subsequently was a student of Malik. Before beginning his classic compilation of *Ahadith*, he wrote *Al-Tarikh Al-Kabir* (the large history), which contains biographies of many of the transmitters and narrators of *Ahadith*, and became one of the pioneering scholars in that aspect of *Ahadith* studies. His *Kitab Al-Jami' Al-Sahih* (referenced in the current text as *Al-Bukhari*) was a monumental work that occupied 16 years of his life. Sifting through over 600,000 *Ahadith*, and applying the most rigorous standards of judging authenticity, Al-Bukhari included only 2,762 *Ahadith* (over 7,000 if one counts repetitions and parallels) in his collection. A somewhat more conservative counting of repetitions and parallels would credit this collection with about 4,000 *Ahadith* that are not repeated. Many of these *Ahadith* can be found in one or another of the other five "standard" collections, and all were arranged according to subject matter, explaining why many *Ahadith* were repeated, as they related to more than one main theme. His collection is the one that enjoys the widest acceptance and authority within the Muslim *Ummah*. Al-Bukhari's collection can be found in a nine-volume English translation.

(2) Abu Al-Husain 'Asakir Al-Din Muslim ibn Al-Hajjaj Al-Qushayri Al-Naisabori was born circa 820 CE in Al-Naisabor, a city now within the confines of the country of Iran. He died in 875

CE in the city of his birth. He began studying *Ahadith* at age 12, studied under Ahmad ibn Hanbal Al-Shaybani and others, and journeyed throughout Arabia, Egypt, Syria, and Iraq in search of authentic *Ahadith*. His *Al-Jami' Al-Sahih* (referenced as *Muslim* within the current text) was derived from about 300,000 *Ahadith*, which he sifted through and sorted with meticulous care and judgment before arriving at about 4,000 *Ahadith*, which he included as *Sahih* in his collection and listed by subject matter. His collection is typically considered second only to that of Al-Bukhari's in acceptance and authority, and most of the *Ahadith* in Muslim's collection can be found in one or another of the other five "standard" collections. Muslim's collection can be found in a four-volume English translation.

(3) Abu Dawud Sulayman ibn Al-Ashath Al-Azdi Al-Sijistani was born circa 818 CE and died circa 889 CE. He was a student of Ahmad ibn Hanbal Al-Shaybani. In his *Kitab Al-Sunan* (referenced as *Abu Dawud* within the current text), Abu Dawud applied stringent and rigorous evaluation to *Ahadith*, winnowing down from about 500,000 *Ahadith* to about 4,800 *Ahadith*, which he listed by subject matter. Many of these approximately 4,800 *Ahadith* can also be found within the other five "standard" collections. Abu Dawud's classic collection, which took 20 years to produce, can be found in a three-volume English translation.

(4) Abu 'Isa Muhammad ibn 'Isa ibn Sawrah ibn Shaddad Al-Tirmidhi (824-892 CE) has been variously reported to have been born in Makkah and in what is now Uzbekistan. He was a student of Abu Dawud. He authored *Al-Jami'Al-Kabir*, aka *Al-Jami' Al-Sahih* and *Sunan Al-Tirmidhi* (referenced as *Al-Tirmidhi* within the current text). This collection includes almost 4,000 *Ahadith*, most of which can be found in one or another of the other five "standard" collections.

(5) Abu 'Abd Al-Rahman Ahmad ibn Shu'ayb ibn 'Ali Al-Khursani Al-Nasa'i was born circa 830 at Nasa, a town in Khurasan, and died circa 916 CE in the vicinity of Damascus, Syria. He was a student of Abu Dawud, and authored *Al-Sunan Al-Mujtaba*, aka *Al-Sunan Al-Nasa'i*. Many of these *Ahadith* can also

be found in one or another of the other five "standard" collections.

(6) Abu 'Abd Allah Muhammad Yazeed Al-Rabi Al-Qazwini, aka ibn Majah, was born in 824 CE at Qazwin and died in 886 CE. He was a student of Abu Dawud. His collection of *Ahadith*, while generally considered to be one of the six "standard" collections, was clearly the most lax of the six in verifying *Ahadith*. His collection includes 4,341 *Ahadith*, of which 3,002 may be found in one of the other five "standard" collections. Unfortunately, of these 4,341 *Ahadith*, some scholars consider as many as 613 to be *Daif Ahadith*, and as many as 99 to have been fabricated by unknown perpetrators.

Over and above these six "standard" collections of *Ahadith*, there are several other collections that are worthy of notice. The *Musnad* of Ahmad ibn Hanbal Al-Shaybani (780-855 CE) was the first of the great compilations of *Ahadith*, and has its *Ahadith* arranged by the original narrator, rather than by thematic material. The *Al-Muwatta* (referenced within the current text as *Malik*) of Malik ibn Anas ibn Malik ibn Abu 'Amr Al-Asbahi (circa 712-795 CE) enjoys a reputation equal to if not surpassing some of the six "standard" collections. The *Mishkat Al-Masabih* of Wali Al-Din Muhammad ibn 'Abd Allah Al-Khajib Al-Tibrizi is an important reworking of Abu Muhammad Al-Husain ibn Mas'ud ibn Muhammad Al-Farra' Al-Baghawi's classic *Masabih Al-Sunnah*, contains about 5,945 *Ahadith*, including repetitions and parallels, and is available in a four-volume English translation. The *Riyad Al-Saliheen* and the *Forty Ahadith of Al-Nawawi* (the latter referenced as *Al-Nawawi* within the current text) are two very important collections, both of which were authored by Muhi Al-Din Abu Zakariya Yahya ibn Sharaf Al-Hizami Al-Nawawi (1233-1277 CE), and both of which are available in English translations.

C5. *AHADITH* AND THE *BIBLE*

While the concept of *Ahadith* may initially appear to be somewhat new to non-Muslim and Western readers, there are remarkable parallels to *Ahadith* in the gospels of the *New Testament*. Analysis of the four canonical gospels reveals that each gospel can be broken down into a series of individual pericopes, which are often drawn from earlier written sources, and which are linked together within the fabric of the gospel through editorial statements of transition from one pericope to another. These individual pericopes typically allege to be statements about what Prophet Jesus said or did, and thus conform to the *Ahadith* literature as found in Islam. The crucial difference between the *Ahadith* of Islam and the pericopes of the four gospels is that the former includes an *Isnad* providing the provenance of each individual *Hadith*, as well as the *Matn* or narrative material, while the latter provides only the narrative material and lacks an *Isnad* demonstrating acceptable provenance. This difference is crucial in that modern Biblical scholarship rather unanimously rejects the proposition that any of the four canonical gospels was actually written by anyone who was an eyewitness to the events being described.

D. SUMMARY

Islam rests about the twin foundations of the *Qur'an* and the *Sunnah*. The former consists of a verbatim recording of the divine revelations given to Prophet Muhammad through Gabriel, and its accurate preservation was guaranteed by Allah. As such, the *Qur'an* is the highest religious authority available to Muslims. In contrast, the *Sunnah* consists of Prophet Muhammad's teaching and typical pattern of conduct regarding religious matters. The *Sunnah* was preserved within the *Ahadith* literature, and elaborate and demanding criteria were developed by the early scholars of the Muslim *Ummah* in order to: authenticate the provenance of individual *Hadith*; and verify whether or not a given *Hadith* accurately preserved the *Sunnah* of Prophet Muhammad. As such, within Islam, the *Sunnah* is second only to the *Qur'an* as a source of religious authority and guidance.

Notes

16. Siddiqui AH (1991), page 287.

17. Varied sequences of Arabic letters are found at the start of 29 *Surat* (chapters) of the *Qur'an*, and are known as *Fawatih* (detached letters). The meaning of these "detached letters" in such a context is basically unknown. "*Alif*", "*Lam*", and "*Ra*" are examples of this phenomenon.

Chapter 5
Articles of Faith

A. INTRODUCTION

Upon completion of the final revelation to Prophet Muhammad, the basic belief system of Islam could be codified into five primary articles of faith, all of which are specifically mentioned in the *Qur'an*. (1) Muslims believe that there is no god but Allah. (2) Muslims believe in all the messengers and prophets of Allah. (3) Muslims believe in all the scriptures and revelations of Allah as they were delivered in their original form. (4) Muslims believe in the angels of Allah without attributing to the angels any partnership with Allah. (5) Muslims believe in life after death and in an ultimate Day of Judgment. To these five articles of faith, one can add a sixth, which is mentioned in several *Ahadith*, i.e., Muslims believe in the timeless knowledge of Allah and in His power to plan and execute His plans. In what follows, each of these six articles of faith is discussed in somewhat greater depth.

B. BELIEF IN ALLAH

B1. THE ONENESS OF ALLAH (*TAWHEED*)

The first article of faith in Islam is belief in Allah. As the term Allah, i.e., the One God, implies, the belief in Allah is a stringent and severe monotheism. Allah is the One God. There is no other. As such, Allah is not the god of just one selected nation or ethnic group. Allah is the god of all mankind, of all life forms, of all creation, and of all worlds.

> Praise be to Allah, the cherisher and sustainer of the worlds. (*Qur'an* 1: 2)

> He is the Living (One): there is no god but He: call upon Him, giving Him sincere devotion. Praise be to Allah, Lord of the worlds. (*Qur'an* 40: 65)

Allah is not simply a nationalistic or ethnic god among a plurality of gods, as at least some of the early Israelites appear to have maintained and as at least one reading of the following *Old Testament* verse appears to imply. In that regard, it should be noted that the following verse, the first of the so-called Ten Commandments, does not deny the existence of other gods, but merely prioritizes which god is to be worshipped by the children of Israel, and establishes a preferred tribal deity, i.e., "the god of Abraham, Isaac, and Jacob".

> I am the Lord your God, who brought you out of the land of Egypt, out of the house of slavery; you shall have no other gods before me. (*Exodus* 20: 2; *Deuteronomy* 5: 6)

However, not only is Allah One without equal and without peer, Allah is One in His unity. His unity admits and allows no partners or associates. His unity leaves no room for any triune conceptualization of the deity, which results in sectarian divisions and in endless theological squabbling about such issues as: is it three persons in one substance or three persons of similar substance; how does one really define person and substance; how does each of three persons in one substance keep its separate identity without beginning to sound like a textbook example of multiple personality disorder; which person of the unified substance preceded which other persons; which person of the unified substance begat which other person; if one person begat another person, did not the first person precede the second person, implying a time when the second person did not exist; which person of the unified substance directed which other person to do what, e.g., to create the world and universe, and does this not imply that one person is subordinate to another person; are the three persons of the unified substance equal or unequal; do each of the three persons of the unified substance share in the being of the other persons, or are they rigidly separated; etc.

Issues such as the above have resulted in fruitless and repetitious debate, as well as multiple schisms, within Christianity for almost 2,000 years. Ritualistic and liturgical formulae and creeds, such as the statement that the Son proceeded from the Father and the Holy Spirit proceeded from the Father and the Son, raise far more questions than they answer and have led to major sectarian divisions within Christianity.

In Islam, Allah is One, i.e., One without peer, and One in absolute unity. He is not One among many, nor even One among others, but One in total uniqueness. His very uniqueness defies total comprehension by the limited intellect of mortal man. He is without beginning and without end, and there is nothing comparable to Him. Allah is the One God besides Whom there is no other. The most perfect, beautiful, and sublime expression of this Oneness of Allah is to be found in the 112th *Surah* (chapter) of the *Qur'an*.

> In the name of Allah, most gracious, most merciful. Say: "He is Allah, the One and Only; Allah, the eternal, absolute; He begetteth not, nor is He begotten; and there is none like unto Him." (*Qur'an* 112: 1-4)

B2. THE NATURE OF ALLAH

As noted previously, Allah is utterly unique. His divine nature cannot be encapsulated by the limited intellect of man. Any systematic attempt to do so can only lead to distortion, minimization, and the limiting of Allah to the finite limits of man's cognitive and conceptual abilities. If the attempt is made, one simultaneously attempts to limit the Unlimited and to elevate the intellect of man to some sort of co-equal status with Allah.

> That is Allah, your Lord! There is no god but He, the creator of all things; then worship ye Him; and He hath power to dispose of all affairs. No vision can grasp Him. But His grasp is over all vision: He is above all comprehension, yet is acquainted with all things. (*Qur'an* 6: 102-103)

However, the *Qur'an* does provide some guidance about the nature of Allah. Besides *Surah* 112, which was quoted above, the following passages are also relevant to the present discussion.

In the name of Allah, most gracious, most merciful. Praise be to Allah the cherisher and sustainer of the worlds; most gracious, most merciful; master of the Day of Judgment. (*Qur'an* 1: 1-4)

Whatever is in the heavens and on earth — let it declare the praises and glory of Allah: for He is the exalted in might, the wise. To Him belongs the dominion of the heavens and the earth: it is He Who gives life and death: and He has power over all things. He is the first and the last, the evident and the hidden: and He has full knowledge of all things. He it is Who created the heavens and the earth in six days, and is moreover firmly established on the throne (of authority). He knows what enters within the earth and what comes forth out of it, what comes down from heaven and what mounts up to it. And He is with you wheresoever ye may be. And Allah sees well all that ye do. To Him belongs the dominion of the heavens and the earth: and all affairs are referred back to Allah. He merges night into day, and He merges day into night; and He has full knowledge of the secrets of (all) hearts. (*Qur'an* 57: 1-6)

Allah is He, than Whom there is no other god — Who knows (all things) both secret and open; He, most gracious, most merciful. Allah is He, than Whom there is no other god — the sovereign, the Holy One, the source of peace (and perfection), the guardian of faith, the preserver of safety, the exalted in might, the irresistible, the supreme: glory to Allah! (High is He) above the partners they attribute to Him. He is Allah, the creator, the evolver, the bestower of forms (or colors). To Him belong the most beautiful names: whatever is in the heavens and earth, doth declare His praises and glory; and He is the exalted in might, the wise. (*Qur'an* 59: 22-24)

In addition, one can derive some knowledge of the nature of Allah by reference to His 99 names, as detailed in the following *Hadith*.

Abu Huraira narrated that Allah's Messenger (peace be upon him) said, "Allah Most High has ninety-nine names. He who retains them in his memory will enter Paradise. He is Allah, other than Whom there is no god, the Compassionate, the Merciful, the King, the Holy, the Source of Peace, the Preserver of Security, the Protector, the Mighty, the Overpowering, the Great in Majesty, the Creator, the Maker, the Fashioner, the Forgiver, the Dominant, the Bestower, the Provider, the Decider, the Knower, the Withholder, the Plentiful Giver, the Abaser, the Exalter, the Honorer, the Humiliator, the Hearer, the Seer, the Judge, the Just, the Gracious, the Informed, the Clement, the Incomparably Great, the Forgiving, the Rewarder, the Most High, the Most Great, the Preserver, the Sustainer, the Reckoner, the Majestic, the Generous, the Watcher, the Answerer, the Liberal, the Wise, the Loving, the Glorious, the Raiser, the Witness, the Real, the Trustee, the Strong, the Firm, the Patron, the Praiseworthy, the All-Knowing, the Originator, the Restorer to Life, the Giver of Life, the Giver of Death, the Living, the Eternal, the Self-sufficient, the Grand, the One, the Single, He to Whom men repair, the Powerful, the Prevailing, the Advancer, the Delayer, the First, the Last, the Outward, the Inward, the Governor, the Sublime, the Amply Beneficent, the Accepter of Repentance, the Avenger, the Pardoner, the Kindly, the Ruler of the Kingdom, the Lord of Majesty and Splendour, the Equitable, the Gatherer, the Independent, the Enricher, the Depriver, the Harmer, the Benefactor, the Light, the Guide, the First Cause, the Enduring, the Inheritor, the Director, the Patient." (*Al-Tirmidhi, Hadith* # 2285; see also *Mishkat Al-Masibah*, pages 483-484)

C. BELIEF IN THE PROPHETS AND MESSENGERS OF ALLAH

C1. BELIEF IN ALL THE PROPHETS AND MESSENGERS

Muslims believe in all the messengers and prophets of Allah. Further, Muslims believe that Allah has provided a messenger to every people. At one time or another, every people or nation of people has received revelation from Allah through its own messenger of Allah. There are many verses in the *Qur'an*, which attest to this basic truth. Perhaps, the following verses are among the most direct in making this point.

> Before thee We sent (messengers) to many nations, and We afflicted the nations with suffering and adversity, that they might learn humility. (*Qur'an* 6: 42)

> Verily, We have sent thee in truth, as a bearer of glad tidings, and as a warner: and there never was a people, without a warner having lived among them (in the past). (*Qur'an* 35: 24)

> To every people (was sent) a messenger: when their messenger comes (before them), the matter will be judged between them with justice, and they will not be wronged. (*Qur'an* 10: 47)

> For we assuredly sent amongst every people a messenger, (with the command), "Serve Allah and eschew evil": of the people were some whom Allah guided, and some on whom error became inevitably (established). So travel through the earth, and see what was the end of those who denied (the truth). (*Qur'an* 16: 36)

Many of these messengers and prophets may no longer be known to modern man. However, numerous prophets and messengers are directly mentioned in the *Qur'an*, including many familiar to Christians and to Jews, including Adam, Noah, Abraham, Lot, Ismael, Isaac, Jacob, Joseph, Job, Moses, Aaron,

David, Solomon, Elijah, Elisha, Jonah, John the Baptist, and Jesus. In addition, the *Qur'an* names several prophets not directly mentioned in the *Bible*, including Shu'ayb of the Midianites (Madyan), Hud of the 'Ad, Salih of the Thamud, and Muhammad. There were many prophets and messengers, and a Muslim is not free to pick and chose among the prophets and messengers of Allah. A Muslim must acknowledge all of the prophets and messengers of Allah of which he is aware, e.g., those specifically mentioned in the *Qur'an*.

> Those who deny Allah and His messengers, and (those who) wish to separate Allah from His messengers, saying: "We believe in some but reject others": and (those who) wish to take a course midway — they are in truth (equally) unbelievers; and We have prepared for unbelievers a humiliating punishment. (*Qur'an* 4: 150-151)

C2. THE NATURE OF THE MESSAGE

Each prophet and messenger was granted inspiration and revelation from Allah. As time passed, because of the nature of the progressive revelation of Allah, earlier revelations were sometimes abrogated, modified, or expanded.[18] However, it must be stressed that Islam adamantly rejects the notion that Allah in any way evolved, as this would imply some earlier time in which Allah was limited or incomplete. The evolution under discussion is limited to what Allah has revealed. In short, the revelation of Allah evolved, consistent with man's evolving readiness to receive that revelation. The following verses of the *Qur'an* serve to highlight and confirm this concept of progressive revelation.

> O People of the Book! There hath come to you Our messenger, revealing to you much that ye used to hide in the book, and passing over much (that is now unnecessary): there hath come to you from Allah a (new) light and a perspicuous book— wherewith Allah guideth all who seek His good pleasure to

ways of peace and safety, and leadeth them out of darkness, by His will, unto the light — guideth them to a path that is straight. (*Qur'an* 5: 15-16)

None of Our revelations do We abrogate or cause to be forgotten, but We substitute something better or similar: knowest thou not that Allah hath power over all things. (*Qur'an* 2 :106)

This Qur'an is not such as can be produced by other than Allah; on the contrary it is a confirmation of (revelations) that went before it, and a fuller explanation of the book — wherein there is no doubt — from the Lord of the worlds. (*Qur'an* 10: 37)

We did send messengers before thee, and appointed for them wives and children: and it was never the part of a messenger to bring a sign except as Allah permitted (or commanded). For each period is a book (revealed). Allah doth blot out or confirm what He pleaseth: with Him is the mother of the book. (*Qur'an* 13: 38-39)

However, consistent throughout all these revelations, which were given to different prophets at different times, the central theme was the Oneness of Allah (*Tawheed*). Only Allah is worthy of worship. No matter the messenger, no matter the setting, and no matter the progressive nature of the revelation, the fundamental truth of the Oneness of Allah was the pivotal point of the message provided by Allah. This fact is explicitly stated by Allah in the following verse from the *Qur'an*.

Not a messenger did We send before thee without this inspiration by Us to him: that there is no god but I; therefore worship and serve Me. (*Qur'an* 21: 25)

C3. MAKE NO DISTINCTIONS AMONG THEM

Not only are Muslims to believe in all of the prophets and messengers of Allah, but Muslims are specifically commanded by Allah to make no hierarchical distinctions among His prophets and messengers, even though Allah may have bestowed certain gifts upon one prophet or messenger and not upon another, and even though Allah may have preferred one prophet or messenger to another.

> Those Messengers We endowed with gifts, some above others: to one of them Allah spoke; others He raised to degrees (of honor); to Jesus, the son of Mary, We gave clear (signs), and strengthened him with the Holy Spirit. (*Qur'an* 2: 253a)

Nonetheless, a Muslim has neither the religious freedom nor the knowledge to elevate one messenger above another. A Muslim is to honor all of Allah's messengers and prophets equally. Unfortunately, some Muslims, in their zeal to honor Prophet Muhammad, appear to lose sight of this Qur'anic injunction. However, the non-Muslim observer of such zealousness should not be misled by the behavior or statements of Muslims, which appear to contradict the non-discriminatory way in which all Muslims are to respect and honor all of Allah's prophets and messengers. The words of Allah, as recorded in the *Qur'an*, are quite clear.

> Say ye: "We believe in Allah, and the revelation given to us, and to Abraham, Ismail, Isaac, Jacob, and the tribes, and that given to Moses and Jesus, and that given to (all) prophets from their Lord: we make no difference between one and another of them: and we bow to Allah (in Islam). (*Qur'an* 2: 136; see also 3: 84)

> The Messenger believeth in what hath been revealed to him from his Lord, as do the men of faith. Each one (of them)

believeth in Allah, His angels, His books, and His messengers. "We make no distinction (they say) between one and another of His messengers." And they say: "We hear, and we obey: (we seek) Thy forgiveness, our Lord, and to Thee is the end of all journeys." (*Qur'an* 2: 285)

Those who deny Allah and His messengers, and (those who) wish to separate Allah from His messengers, saying: "We believe in some but reject others": and (those who) wish to take a course midway — they are in truth (equally) unbelievers; and We have prepared for unbelievers a humiliating punishment. To those who believe in Allah and His messengers and make no distinction between any of the messengers, We shall soon give their (due) rewards: for Allah is oft-forgiving, most merciful. (*Qur'an* 4: 150-152)

Furthermore, the words of Prophet Muhammad on this subject are equally clear and unambiguous. As narrated by both Abu Said Al-Khudri and Abu Huraira (*Al-Bukhari, Ahadith # 3: 594-595; 4: 620,626; 6: 162; 8: 524; 9: 564*), Prophet Muhammad specifically instructed his companions that they were not to assign to any one prophet, including himself, superiority over any other of Allah's prophets.

Narrated Abu Huraira: "...The Prophet...said, 'Don't give superiority to any prophet among Allah's prophets...'" (*Al-Bukhari, Hadith # 4: 626*)

Narrated Abu Sa'id Al-Khudri: "...The Prophet said, 'Do not give me superiority over the other prophets...'" (*Al-Bukhari, Hadith # 6: 162*)

C4. THE PROPHETS AND MESSENGERS ARE MEN

Concomitant with the above point, it should also be stressed that the prophets and messengers of Allah are not in any way, shape, or form to be considered as partners with Allah. In Islam, there is no room for any triune god or for any attempt to dress polytheism in the clothing of monotheism. Islam is the religion perfected by Allah, not by Prophet Muhammad nor by any other of the prophets and messengers of Allah. The prophets and messengers, while chosen by Allah, were merely tools, which were used by Allah. They were not divine or semi-divine. This is consistent with the words attributed to Prophet Jesus in the *Bible*:

> Very truly, I tell you, servants are not greater than their master, nor are messengers greater than the one who sent them. (*John* 13:16)

The messengers and prophets of Allah were simply men upon whom Allah had conferred His inspiration. This was true of Prophet Muhammad and of every prophet and messenger who came before him.

> Before thee, also, the messengers We sent were but men, to whom We granted inspiration: if ye realise this not, ask of those who possess the message. Nor did We give them bodies that ate no food, nor were they exempt from death. (*Qur'an* 21: 7-8)

> And the messengers whom We sent before thee were all (men) who ate food and walked through the streets... (*Qur'an* 25: 20a)

In the case of Prophet Muhammad, this is even more emphatically attested by the following verses from the *Qur'an*.

> Muhammad is no more than a messenger: many were the messengers that passed away before him. If he died or were slain, will ye then turn back on your heels? If any did turn back on his heels, not the least harm will he do to Allah; but Allah (on the other hand) will swiftly reward those who (serve him) with gratitude. (*Qur'an* 3: 144)

Say: "Glory to my Lord! Am I aught but a man — a messenger. What kept men back from belief when guidance came to them, was nothing but this: they said" Has Allah sent a man (like us) to be (His) messenger?" (*Qur'an* 17: 93b-94)

Say: "I am but a man like yourselves, (but) the inspiration has come to me that your God is One God: whoever expects to meet his Lord, let him work righteousness, and, in the worship of his Lord, admit no one as partner." (*Qur'an* 18:110)

Say thou: "I am but a man like you: it is revealed to me by inspiration, that your God is One God: so stand true to Him, and ask for His forgiveness." And woe to those who join gods with Allah — (*Qur'an* 41:6)

Various *Ahadith* also affirm the complete humanity of Prophet Muhammad while denying any pretense at divinity. The following two examples are noteworthy in that respect.

At the time of the Prophet there was a hypocrite who rendered so much harm to the believers that some of them summoned the others to ask the help of the Prophet against him. When the Prophet, peace be upon him, heard of it, he said: "No man may seek my help. Only the help of Allah is worthy of being sought." (*Kitab Al-Tawhid,* page 43)

'Umar reported that the Prophet, peace be upon him, said: "Do not aggrandize me as the Christians aggrandized the son of Maryam. I am but a creature. Call me the creature of Allah, His servant and messenger." (*Kitab Al-Tawhid*, pages 60-61. See also the parallel version of this *Hadith* in *Al-Bukhari, Hadith #* 4:656.)

Having stressed the point that the prophets and messengers were only men, it also needs to be acknowledged that the prophets were men of extraordinary character, piety, spirituality, and faith. This Islamic view of the prophets and messengers stands in sharp contrast to the Judaea-Christian scriptures, in which the prophets are frequently portrayed as spiritual leaders with feet of clay, lusting and sinning as frequently as those to whom they preached. However, Allah, Himself, has assured mankind that no prophet could betray the revelation and inspiration given to him.

No prophet could (ever) be false to his trust. (*Qur'an* 3:161a)

Does this mean that the prophets were perfect? Of course not, as nothing is perfect other than Allah. Does this mean that the prophets were never tempted? No, as Allah's own words indicate the very opposite.

Never did We send a messenger or a prophet before thee, but, when he framed a desire, Satan threw some (vanity) into his desire: but Allah will cancel anything (vain) that Satan throws in, and Allah will confirm (and establish) His signs: for Allah is full of knowledge and wisdom. (*Qur'an* 22: 52)

Perchance thou mayest (feel the inclination) to give up a part of what is revealed unto thee, and thy heart feeleth straitened lest they say, "Why is not a treasure sent down unto him, or why does not an angel come down with him?" But thou art there only to warn! It is Allah that arrangeth all affairs! (*Qur'an* 11: 12)

Does this mean that a prophet could never make a mistake? No, as clearly stated in the *Qur'an* with regard to: an example of rushing to judgment between two disputants by Prophet David (*Qur'an* 38: 21-25); and an example of Prophet Muhammad ignoring the questioning of a blind man, Ibn Um Makhtum, interested in Islam, due to the Prophet's preoccupation in attempting to persuade a person of substance and influence into Islam.

(The Prophet) frowned and turned away, because there came to him the blind man (interrupting), but what could tell thee but that perchance he might grow (in spiritual understanding)? Or that he might receive admonition, and the teaching might profit him? As to one who regards himself as self-sufficient, to him dost thou attend; though it is no blame on thee if he grow not (in spiritual understanding). But as to him who came to thee striving earnestly, and with fear (in his heart), of him wast thou unmindful. By no means (should it be so)! For it is indeed a message of instruction: therefore let whoso will keep it in remembrance. (*Qur'an* 80: 1-12)

However, such mistakes were a far cry from the immorality frequently attributed to the prophets by the *Bible*, and do not imply that the prophets and messengers made mistakes when it came to points of religious doctrine and belief. Clearly, despite occasional minor mistakes, the prophets were exemplary individuals, and were excellent guides to follow. This very point is stated in the *Qur'an*, where Allah talks about the examples of Prophets Abraham and of Muhammad.

Abraham was indeed a model. Devoutly obedient to Allah, (and) true in faith, and he joined not gods with Allah. He showed his gratitude for the favors of Allah, Who chose him, and guided him to a straight way. And We gave him good in this world, and he will be, in the hereafter, in the ranks of the righteous. So We have taught thee the inspired (message), "Follow the ways of Abraham the true in faith, and he joined not gods with Allah." (*Qur'an* 16: 120-123)

We have indeed in the messenger of Allah a beautiful pattern (of conduct) for any one whose hope is in Allah and the final day, and who engages much in the praise of Allah. (*Qur'an* 33: 21)

As such, Muslims do utilize the model, i.e., actual sayings and behavior (*Sunnah*), of Prophet Muhammad as an example that should be followed and as being religiously authoritative, without elevating such behavior to the status of having the same significance or importance as the literal words of Allah, i.e., the *Qur'an*.

C5. THE SEAL OF THE PROPHETS

While Muslims are forbidden to differentiate among the prophets and messengers of Allah in any hierarchical manner, and while all such prophets and messengers are to be seen as only men, however virtuous, the *Qur'an* specifically states that Prophet Muhammad was the last of the prophets and messengers of Allah. In that respect, Allah refers to Prophet Muhammad as the "seal of the prophets". This phrase is sometimes understood by non-Muslims and by Westerners to imply some sort of hierarchical significance to the prophethood of Muhammad. However, such an understanding is erroneous. Just as the last thing to be placed on a formal document is the signatory seal, Prophet Muhammad is "the seal of the prophets", meaning that he was the last prophet and messenger of Allah. With the revelation given to Prophet Muhammad, the revelation of Allah has ended, earlier revelations have been modified or abrogated, and Islam has been perfected.

> Muhammad is not the father of any of your men, but (he is) the messenger of Allah, and the seal of the prophets: and Allah has full knowledge of all things. (*Qur'an* 33: 40)

D. BELIEF IN THE BOOKS OF ALLAH

D1. INTRODUCTION

Muslims believe in all of the revealed books of Allah. This includes both the *Qur'an* and earlier books of revelation given by Allah to His various messengers. While all of Allah's prophets received divine inspiration and revelation, some of those prophets were given an actual book of revelation. Those, who were given such a book, are frequently referred to as the messengers of Allah.[19] The *Qur'an* notes five such books of revelation: the book given to Prophet Abraham[20]; the book (*Torah* or *Law*) given to Prophet Moses[21]; the book (*Zabur* or *Psalms*) given to Prophet

David[22]; the book (*Injil* or *Gospel*) given to Prophet Jesus [23]; and the book (*Qur'an*) given to Prophet Muhammad.[24]

> Or do they envy mankind for what Allah hath given them of His bounty? But We had already given the people of Abraham the book and wisdom, and conferred upon them a great kingdom. (*Qur'an* 4:54)

> ...and to David We gave the Psalms. (*Qur'an* 4:163)

> And in their footsteps we sent Jesus the son of Mary, confirming the Law (Torah) that had come before him: We sent him the Gospel: therein was guidance and light, and confirmation of the Law (Torah) that had come before him: a guidance and an admonition to those who fear Allah. (*Qur'an* 5:46)

Muslims believe that all those books, as they were delivered in their original form to the messenger, who then imparted them to mankind, were the actual, literal words of Allah. However, the operative phrase is "as they were delivered in their original form".

D2. THE CORRUPTION OF EARLIER BOOKS

With regard to the book of Prophet Abraham, such a book is no longer known to exist, and no trace of such a book has been left to modern man. However, the book of *Jubilees* (45:14-16), a Jewish religious writing of the third or second century BCE, appears to refer to this book of Abraham, when it notes that, upon his death, Prophet Jacob left his books and the books of his fathers, i.e., Isaac and Abraham, to his son Levi.

With regard to the book of Prophet Moses, the received *Torah* as found in the current Biblical books of *Genesis, Exodus, Leviticus, Numbers,* and *Deuteronomy* is a far cry from the original *Torah*, although traces and elements of the original *Torah* may continue to be found, scattered here and there in the received *Torah*. In fact, Biblical analysis by Christian scholars has clearly demonstrated that: these five books of the received *Torah* did not reach their present form until late in the fifth century BCE, i.e., around 1,000 years after Prophet Moses; and that these books are compilations from earlier written sources, known as J, E, P, and D.

Likewise, the current Biblical book of *Psalms* little resembles the original *Psalms* of Prophet David, although occasional chapters or verses in the received *Psalms* may be part of the original *Psalms*. Of note, this Islamic belief finds significant support from Christian scholars and commentators on the *Psalms*.

Finally, it must be noted that the original *Gospel* of Prophet Jesus can nowhere be found in the corpus of the *Bible*, although various Biblical sayings attributed to Prophet Jesus may represent preserved fragments from the original *Gospel* or *Injil*. The original *Gospel* of Prophet Jesus would have been a word-for-word repetition of the words of Allah. In that regard, it may have been similar to *Q* (a lost collection of the sayings of Prophet Jesus utilized by *Matthew*, *Luke*, and *Thomas*) or to the apocryphal gospel of *Thomas*, both of which were books of the sayings of Prophet Jesus. In contrast, the current canonical gospels of *Matthew, Mark, Luke,* and *John* are basically small biographies of Jesus. The canonical gospels are merely the writings about Prophet Jesus by anonymous authors, to which the later Christian churches assigned the names of various disciples of Prophet Jesus or of followers of the disciples of Prophet Jesus. They certainly are not books that claim to be the word-for-word rendition of Prophet Jesus, whereby he quotes the words of Allah.

Numerous passages of the *Qur'an* refer to man's distortion and alteration of the previous books of revelation from Allah.[25] These passages consistently note that the received books being utilized by the People of the Book, i.e., by Jews and Christians, do not conform to the original revelations that were given. The following verses from the *Qur'an* are among the more direct in addressing this distortion of the prior books of Allah.

> Can ye (O ye men of faith) entertain the hope that they will believe in you? — seeing that a party of them heard the word of Allah, and perverted it knowingly after they understood it...Then woe to those who write the book with their own

hands, and then say: "This is from Allah," to traffic with it for a miserable price! — woe to them for what their hands do write, and for the gain they make thereby. (*Qur'an* 2: 75,79)

There is among them a section who distort the book with their tongues: (as they read) you would think it is a part of the book, but it is no part of the book; and they say, "That is from Allah," but it is not from Allah: it is they who tell a lie against Allah, and (well) they know it. (*Qur'an* 3: 78)

And remember Allah took a covenant from the People of the Book, to make it known and clear to mankind, and not to hide it; but they threw it away behind their backs, and purchased with it some miserable gain! And vile was the bargain they made! (*Qur'an* 3:187)

But because of their breach of their covenant, We cursed them, and made their hearts grow hard: they change the words from their (right) places and forget a good part of the message that was sent them, nor wilt thou cease to find them — barring a few — ever bent on (new) deceits: but forgive them, and overlook (their misdeeds): for Allah loveth those who are kind. From those, too, who call themselves Christians, We did take a covenant, but they forgot a good part of the message that was sent them: so We estranged them, with enmity and hatred between the one and the other, to the Day of Judgment. And soon will Allah show them what it is they have done. (*Qur'an* 5: 13-14)

No just estimate of Allah do they make when they say: "Nothing doth Allah send down to man (by way of revelation)": say: "Who then sent down the book which Moses brought? — a light and guidance to man: but ye make it into (separate) sheets for show, while ye conceal much (of its contents): therein were ye taught that which ye knew not — neither ye nor your fathers." Say: "Allah (sent it down)": then leave them to plunge in vain discourse and trifling. (*Qur'an* 6: 91)

The reader who is coming from a Judaeo-Christian religious background may well object to these Qur'anic passages that maintain that the books of the *Bible* have been adulterated. However, it is not just the *Qur'an* that speaks of the distortion and alteration of prior books of revelation. The Biblical book of *Jeremiah* clearly states that the scribes of the ancient Israelites altered the revealed scriptures given to the Israelites by Allah, and thus changed them "into a lie".

> How can you say, "We are wise and the law of the Lord is with us," when, in fact, the false pen of the scribes has made it into a lie? (*Jeremiah* 8: 8)

D3. THE INVIOLABILITY OF THE *QUR'AN*

In contrast to the prior books of revelation, the incorruptibility of the *Qur'an* was guaranteed by Allah. The revelation of Allah to Prophet Muhammad, across a span of approximately 22 years, is preserved without blemish in the *Qur'an*. As such, the *Qur'an* remains a true and unadulterated recording of the literal words of Allah. As recorded in the *Qur'an*, Allah's own promise to Prophet Muhammad illustrates that the integrity of the *Qur'an* will remain inviolate for all time.

> Say: "Shall I seek for judge other than Allah? — when He it is Who hath sent unto you the book, explained in detail." They know full well, to whom We have given the book, that it hath been sent down from thy Lord in truth. Never be then of those who doubt. The word of thy Lord doth find its fulfillment in truth and in justice: none can change His words: for He is the one Who heareth and knoweth all. (*Qur'an* 6: 114-115)

> We have, without doubt, sent down the message; and We will assuredly guard it (from corruption). (*Qur'an* 15: 9)

> And recite (and teach) what has been revealed to thee of the book of thy Lord: none can change His words, and none wilt thou find as a refuge other than Him. (*Qur'an* 18:27)

Those who reject the message when it comes to them (are not hidden from Us). And indeed it is a book of exalted power. No falsehood can approach it from before or behind it: it is sent down by One full of wisdom, worthy of all praise. (*Qur'an* 41: 41-42)

Nay, this is a glorious Qur'an (inscribed) in a tablet preserved. (*Qur'an* 85: 21-22)

In closing this brief discussion of the Muslim's belief in the books of Allah, it needs to be reemphasized that the *Qur'an* is a true and accurate recording of Prophet Muhammad's verbatim quotation of the words delivered to him from Allah. Therefore, the *Qur'an* does not consist of the words of Prophet Muhammad, but of Allah. The *Qur'an* does not even consist of the words of Prophet Muhammad as inspired by Allah. Likewise, the *Qur'an* is not Prophet Muhammad's interpretation of the words or message of Allah. The *Qur'an* consists solely of the words of Allah.

Verily this is a revelation from the Lord of the worlds: with it came down the Spirit of Faith and Truth—to thy heart and mind, that thou mayest admonish in the perspicuous Arabic tongue. (*Qur'an* 26: 192-195)

E. BELIEF IN THE ANGELS OF ALLAH
E1. ANGELS AS A CLASS OF CREATION

Muslims believe in the angels of Allah without in any way attributing to the angels any partnership with Allah.

...it is righteousness—to believe in Allah and the Last Day, and the angels... (*Qur'an* 2:177)

Having noted the above, it must be stated that the angels are no more than creations of Allah. In that regard, they can be compared to the jinn and to man.

'Aisha reported that Allah's Messenger (may peace be upon him) said: "The angels were born out of light and the jinns were born out of the spark of fire and Adam was born as he has been defined (in the Qur'an) for you (i.e., he was fashioned out of clay). (*Muslim, Hadith # 7134*)

Given the above *Hadith*, given the confusion that typically exists among non-Muslims and Westerners about the Islamic view of these three classes of creation, and given the differences between Muslims and those of the Judaea-Christian persuasion about the role of Satan, it may be profitable to digress for a moment. This digression allows one to consider briefly the similarities and differences to be found among these three classes of creation, i.e., the angels, the jinn, and mankind.

E2. OF ANGELS, JINN, AND MEN

As the above *Hadith* reveals, the angels were created from light, the jinn from fire, and mankind, through Adam, from dirt or clay. Several passages from the *Qur'an* also indicate that the jinn were created from fire, while Adam was created from dirt or clay.[26]

We created man from sounding clay, from mud moulded into shape; and the jinn race, We had created before, from the fire of a scorching wind. (*Qur'an* 15: 26-27)

He created man from sounding clay like unto pottery, and He created jinns from fire free of smoke: then which of the favors of your Lord will ye deny? (*Qur'an* 55: 14-16)

As such, all three classes of beings are mere creations of Allah. While it may be true that the angels and the jinn have been granted certain powers by Allah, which have not been granted to mankind, the angels and jinn remain no more than creations of Allah. None of the three classes can claim any divinity, and none are to be considered associates of or partners with Allah. Such a conceptualization would constitute a direct denial of the Oneness of Allah, and is thus expressly forbidden in Islam. Likewise, one may not pray to any of the creations of Allah, whether angel or not, even to the extent of asking such a creation to make intercession between oneself and Allah. One prays directly to Allah without intermediaries.

> How many so ever be the angels in the heavens, their intercession will avail nothing except after Allah has given leave for whom He pleases and that he is acceptable to Him. (*Qur'an* 53:26)

With regard to these three classes of creation, Allah endowed only the jinn and mankind with the gift of free will. Among both the jinn and mankind, there were and are believers and non-believers, i.e., those who choose to submit to Allah and those who choose not to submit. This distinction between believers and non-believers cannot be made with regard to the angels. All angels are believers, because they are not free to choose otherwise. As such, Islam rejects the concept of fallen angels as portrayed in the Judaeo-Christian tradition.

E3. SATAN OR IBLIS

If there are no fallen angels, how does Islam account for Satan? According to the *Qur'an*, Satan, also known as Iblis, was a particularly powerful jinn. This identification of Satan with the jinn can be made both directly and indirectly. The indirect identification is based upon those Qur'anic passages, in which Iblis refers to himself as having been created from fire by Allah (*Qur'an* 7: 11-12; 38: 76), which links the creation of Iblis with the creation of the jinn. However, one does not have to rely upon this indirect identification. A direct identification of Iblis as being one of the jinn is specifically stated in the *Qur'an*. This verse is quoted immediately below.

> Behold! We said to the angels, "Bow down to Adam": they bowed down except Iblis. He was one of the Jinns, and he broke the command of his Lord. (*Qur'an* 18: 50a)

The story of the "fall" of Iblis or Satan is told in greater detail in other passages (*Qur'an* 7: 11-18; 15: 28-43; 17: 61-65; 38: 71-85).

To summarize, after making Adam from clay, Allah ordered the angels to bow down to Adam. The angels did so. However, Iblis, who happened to be near a company of angels at that time, refused to bow down, claiming that he was better than Adam. Adam had only been fashioned from clay, while Iblis had been created from fire. As such, Iblis believed that he was Adam's superior, and Iblis' own arrogance and pride resulted in his choosing to disobey Allah. Caught disobeying Allah and about to be punished by Him, Iblis begged that the punishment be withheld until the Day of Judgment. Allah granted this request, and Iblis then vowed to spend his time between then and the Day of Judgment in attempting to lead mankind and the jinn away from true submission to Allah. However, it is a great mercy to mankind that Allah specifically stipulated that Iblis would have no power over those who submit fully to Allah.

> Behold! thy Lord said to the angels: "I am about to create man, from sounding clay, from mud molded into shape; when I have fashioned him (in due proportion) and breathed into him of My spirit, fall ye down in obeisance unto him." So the angels prostrated themselves, all of them together; not so Iblis: he refused to be among those who prostrated themselves. (Allah) said: "O Iblis! What is your reason for not being among those who prostrated themselves?" (Iblis) said: "I am not one to prostrate myself to man, whom Thou didst create from sounding clay, from mud molded into shape." (Allah) said: "Then get thee out from here: for thou art rejected, accursed. And the curse shall be on thee till the Day of Judgment." (Iblis) said: "O my Lord! give me then respite till the day the (dead) are raised." (Allah) said: "Respite is granted thee—till the day of the time appointed." (Iblis) said: "O my Lord! because Thou hast put me in the wrong, I will make (wrong) fair-seeming to them on the earth, and I will put them all in the wrong — except Thy servants among them, sincere and purified (by Thy grace)." (Allah) said: "This (way of my sincere servants) is indeed a way that leads

straight to Me. For over My servants no authority shalt thou
have, except such as put themselves in the wrong and follow
thee." And verily, hell is the promised abode for them all!
(*Qur'an* 15: 28-43)

E4. NAMES OF THE ANGELS

Four angels are mentioned by name in the *Qur'an*. These
are Gabriel (Jibril), Michael, Harut, and Marut.[27] Of these four,
both Gabriel and Michael are mentioned in the *Bible*.[28] Of some
linguistic interest, both Gabriel (Hebrew=Gabri'el) and Michael
(Hebrew=Myka'el) incorporate the Semitic *El* at the end of
their names. Thus, the name Gabriel can be translated as "man of
God (Allah)" or as "God (Allah) has shown Himself strong", while
Michael can be translated as "who is like God (Allah)?", implying
that there is none like Allah, and thus emphasizing the Oneness
of Allah.

E5. THE ROLE OF THE ANGELS

The *Qur'an* specifically mentions several different roles
fulfilled by the angels of Allah. These roles include, but are not
limited to: removing the souls from men after death; recording
man's every deed, both good and bad, in order to provide a record
by which each man will be judged on the Day of Judgment;
protecting men; running errands of mercy; praying for forgiveness
from Allah for all of mankind; providing occasional trials to test
mankind; praising and worshipping Allah; and serving as the
transmitters of Allah's revelation to His prophets and messengers.

E6. GABRIEL

With regard to this last point, the *Qur'an* identifies Gabriel as
being the messenger angel who serves as the one who provides
the words of Allah to His prophets and messengers.[29]

Say: whoever is an enemy to Gabriel — for he brings down
the (revelation) to thy heart by Allah's will, a confirmation

of what went before, and guidance and glad tidings for those who believe — whoever is an enemy to Allah and His angels and prophets, to Gabriel and Michael — Lo! Allah is an enemy to those who reject faith. (*Qur'an* 2: 97-98)

It may be noted that this same role of being the bearer of Allah's revelation and inspiration is assigned to Gabriel in several passages from the *Bible*, including those from both the *Old* and *New Testament* — see *Daniel* 8:16; 9:21-27; and *Luke* 1:11-38. As such, the concept of Gabriel as the messenger angel who brings Allah's revelation and inspiration to His prophets and messengers is a concept that is common to Judaism, Christianity, and Islam.

Having established that the scriptures of Judaism, Christianity, and Islam all hold that it is Gabriel who, among the angels, transmits Allah's divine revelation to His human messengers and prophets, one is now in a position to further identify Gabriel according to certain titles. These titles are occasionally used in the *Qur'an* in place of Gabriel's name, especially when discussing Gabriel's role as the transmitter of Allah's revelation. In several passages in the *Qur'an*,[30] Gabriel is simply referred to by the title of *Al-Ruh*, which can be translated as "the spirit". Somewhat more specifically, Gabriel is referred to as *Al-Ruh Al-Amin*.

Verily this is a revelation from the Lord of the worlds: with it came down the Spirit of Faith and Truth — (*Qur'an* 26: 192-193)

In the above quotation from the meaning of the *Qur'an*, *Al-Ruh Al-Amin* has been rendered as "Spirit of Faith and Truth". A somewhat more literal translation might be "Spirit of Trustworthiness". However, the most appropriate translation is perhaps simply "Spirit of Truth".

Several Biblical passages in the gospel of *John* address the concept of the Spirit of Truth, and traditional Christian interpretation identifies this Spirit of Truth with the Holy Spirit.

And I will ask the Father, and he will give you another Advocate, to be with you forever. This is the Spirit of truth, whom the world cannot receive, because it neither sees him nor knows him. You know him, because he abides with you, and he will be in you. (*John* 14: 16-17)

When the Advocate comes whom I will send to you from the Father, the Spirit of truth who comes from the Father, he will testify on my behalf. (*John* 15: 26)

When the Spirit of truth comes, he will guide you into all the truth; for he will not speak on his own, but will speak whatever he hears, and he will declare to you the things that are to come. (*John* 16: 13)

These Biblical passages clearly associate the Spirit of Truth with the bringing of Allah's revelation and inspiration, and it is noted that the Spirit of Truth "will not speak on his own, but will speak whatever he hears" from Allah. In other words, these verses from *John*: clearly imply that the Spirit of Truth, i.e., the Holy Spirit, is subordinate to Allah and not a partner with Him, in that the Spirit of Truth "will not speak on his own, but will speak whatever he hears" from Allah; and assign the same function, i.e., the bringing of revelation, to Gabriel and to the Spirit of Truth, i.e., the Holy Spirit. Thus, it is implied that Gabriel is the Spirit of Truth, and that the Spirit of Truth is the Holy Spirit. If Gabriel is the bearer of revelation, if the Spirit of Truth is the bearer of revelation, and if the Holy Spirit is the Spirit of Truth, then Gabriel is the Holy Spirit. The mathematical logic of this identification can be readily summarized as: G (Gabriel) = B (bearer of revelation); ST (Spirit of Truth) = B (bearer of revelation); HS (Holy Spirit) = ST (Spirit of Truth); therefore G (Gabriel) = HS (Holy Spirit).

This identification is made quite clearly merely by contrasting two verses from the *Qur'an*, each of which discusses the bearer of Allah's revelation to Prophet Muhammad. In the first verse, Gabriel is identified by name as being the bearer of revelation to Prophet Muhammad. In the second verse, Gabriel is identified by his title, i.e., the Holy Spirit, as being the bearer of revelation to Prophet Muhammad. In that second verse, *Al-Ruh Al-Qudusi* is translated quite literally as "Holy Spirit".

> Say: whoever is an enemy to Gabriel — for he brings down the (revelation) to thy heart by Allah's will, a confirmation of what went before. And guidance and glad tidings for those who believe — (*Qur'an* 2: 97)

> Say, the Holy Spirit has brought the revelation from thy Lord in truth, in order to strengthen those who believe, and as a guide and glad tidings to Muslims. (*Qur'an* 16:102)

In summary, Gabriel is none other than the Holy Spirit. While traditional Christianity has elevated Gabriel under his title of Holy Spirit to a partnership with Allah in a triune godhead, Islam reaffirms the Oneness of Allah, vigorously resists any polytheistic ideology, and continues to see Gabriel as merely an angel of Allah.

F. BELIEF IN THE DAY OF JUDGMENT

F1. INTRODUCTION

As is the case in Judaism and Christianity, belief in an eventual Day of Judgment is a central article of belief in Islam. While there are certain similarities among the Jewish, Christian, and Islamic conceptions of the Day of Judgment, there are also distinct differences. An in-depth analysis of the Day of Judgment from the Islamic perspective, not to mention from the vantage point of comparative religions, is outside the scope and framework of this modest essay. As such, only a few issues concerning the Islamic belief in the Day of Judgment will be covered in the space below.

F2. THE TIME

As repeatedly stated in the *Qur'an*, the timing of the Day of Judgment is knowledge that rests solely with Allah. No man, no jinn, no angel, and no prophet or messenger has that knowledge.

During his ministry, Prophet Muhammad was asked repeatedly about the timing of the Day of Judgment. In response to such questioning, Allah provided the following revelations to Prophet Muhammad through the angel Gabriel.

They ask thee about the (final) Hour—when will be its appointed time? Say: "The knowledge thereof is with my Lord (alone): none but He can reveal as to when it will occur. Heavy were its burden through the heavens and the earth. Only, all of a sudden will it come to you." They ask thee as if thou wert eager in search thereof: say: "The knowledge thereof is with Allah (alone), but most men know not." (*Qur'an* 7: 187)

They ask thee about the Hour — "When will be its appointed time?" Wherein art thou (concerned) with the declaration thereof? With thy Lord is the limit fixed therefor. Thou art but a warner for such as fear it. (*Qur'an* 79:42-45)

Men ask thee concerning the Hour: say, "The knowledge thereof is with Allah (alone)": and what will make thee understand? — perchance the Hour is nigh! (*Qur'an* 33: 63)

Say: "As to the knowledge of the time, it is with Allah alone: I am (sent) only to warn plainly in public." (*Qur'an* 67: 26)

Verily the knowledge of the Hour is with Allah (alone). (*Qur'an* 31: 34a)

And blessed is He to Whom belongs the dominion of the heavens and the earth, and all between them: with Him is the knowledge of the Hour (of Judgment): and to Him shall ye be brought back. (*Qur'an* 43: 85)

As a brief digression, it is instructive to note the similarity of the wording of these revelations to Prophet Muhammad with the

Biblical report of the words of Prophet Jesus about the same issue.

But about that day and hour no one knows, neither the angels of heaven, nor the Son, but only the Father. (*Matthew* 24: 36; *Mark* 13: 32)

Even with the inappropriate capitalization of the word "son" by the *Bible* translators, the Biblical statement is remarkably similar in conceptual content to those recorded in the *Qur'an*.

F3. THE PRECURSORS

Notwithstanding the fact that no one knows the timing of the Day of Judgment except Allah, the coming of the Day of Judgment is inevitable.[31]

The Hour will certainly come: therein is no doubt: yet most men believe not. (*Qur'an* 40: 59)

Verily, the doom of thy Lord will indeed come to pass — there is none can avert it — on the Day when the firmament will be in dreadful commotion, and the mountains will fly hither and thither. (*Qur'an* 52: 7-10)

The unbelievers think that they will not be raised up (for judgment), say: "Yea, by my Lord, ye shall surely be raised up: then shall ye be told (the truth) of all that ye did. And that is easy for Allah." (*Qur'an* 64: 7)

With regard to the Day of Judgment, some of the signs that herald its coming were reported by Prophet Muhammad and recorded as *Ahadith*. Among these signs are: various "natural" disasters; the greatest of wars; and the reordering of some of the laws of nature. In addition to these signs, the following signs of the impending Day of Judgment will occur in rough chronological order: the coming of the Antichrist (or Dajjal); the descent of Prophet Jesus back to earth, where he will slay the Antichrist and rule before dying; the release of and war with Gog and Magog;

and the coming of a pleasant wind, associated with the death of every living Muslim, leaving the world to the unbelievers.[32]

The following two *Ahadith* give a succinct account of some of these events, many of which will probably seem quite familiar to Christian readers, as these events are quite consistent with traditional Christian teaching about the end of time. Noteworthy in that regard are the appearance of the Antichrist and the return of Prophet Jesus to rule over the earth for a specified length of time.

Hudhaifa b. Usaid Ghifari reported: "Allah's Messenger (may peace be upon him) came to us all of a sudden as we were (busy in a discussion). He said: 'What do you discuss about?' They (the Companions) said: 'We are discussing about the Last Hour.' Thereupon he said: 'It will not come until you see ten signs before', and (in this connection) he made mention of the smoke, Dajjal, the beast, the rising of the sun from the west, the descent of Jesus son of Mary (Allah be pleased with him), the Gog and Magog, and land-slidings in three places, one in the east, one in the west and one in Arabia at the end of which fire would burn forth from the Yemen, and would drive people to the place of their assembly." (*Muslim, Hadith # 6931*)

Abu Huraira reported the Prophet (may peace be upon him) as saying: "There is no prophet between me and him, that is, Jesus (peace be upon him). He will descend (to the earth). When you see him, recognize him: a man of medium height, reddish fair, wearing two light yellow garments, looking as if drops were falling down from his head though it will not be wet. He will fight the people for the cause of Islam. He will break the cross, kill swine, and abolish jizyah. Allah will perish all religions except Islam. He will destroy the Antichrist and will live on the earth for forty years and then he will die. The Muslims will pray over him." (*Abu Dawud, Hadith # 4310*)

(Note: *Jizyah* is a tax imposed by a Muslim state on non-Muslims who chose to remain non-Muslims while continuing to reside in the Muslim state. In return for *Jizyah*, the non-Muslim is exempted from certain obligations to the state, e.g., military service and the *Zakat* tax, but still continues to enjoy the protection of the state. Typically, the *Jizyah* tax is no more than, and often less than, what a Muslim resident of the state would pay. A personal example from the author's family history illustrates this point. The author's great grandfather, Abraham Dirks, emigrated from Russia to the Khanate of Khiva, in what is now Uzbekistan, during the early 1880s. Abraham Dirks was a Mennonite, one of the Anabaptist denominations within Christianity, who was searching for the religious freedom to practice his faith unhampered by state interference. He had been unable to find that religious freedom in Christian Russia. However, in the Khanate of Khiva, which was a Muslim country, Abraham Dirks, his parents, and his siblings were granted religious freedom by the Muslim ruler, and were even given free agricultural land for farming, with such land being irrigated by a system of canals. In return, Abraham Dirks and his family had to pay the *Jizyah*, which was set at 05% of the yearly harvest and the giving to the state of 12 days of free labor per year per adult male. Of note, a Muslim resident of the state, who may not have been given any land by the state, would have still been required to give 05% of the produce from his irrigated land in *Zakat* (see chapter VI, section E), and would still have been liable for military conscription etc. As can be seen, Abraham Dirks, as a Christian immigrant to a Muslim state, was not only granted religious freedom and free agricultural land by the Muslim state, but was actually taxed at a rate comparable to that paid by a Muslim resident of the state.)

Somewhat less dramatic signs of the coming Day of Judgment are narrated in the following *Hadith*.

He (the inquirer) again said: "Inform me about the hour (of the Doom)." He (the Holy Prophet) remarked: "One who is inquired knows no more than the one who is inquiring (about

it)." He (the inquirer) said: "Tell me some of its indications."
He (the Holy Prophet) said: "That the slave-girl will give birth
to her mistress and master, that you will find barefooted,
destitute shepherds of goats vying with one another in the
construction of magnificent buildings." (*Muslim, Hadith # 1*)

In the face of the enormous economic and lifestyle changes
that have taken place in the petroleum-producing parts of the
Arab world in the last 50 years, secondary to the influx of massive
quantities of "petrodollars", the last part of the above quoted
Hadith should give the reader some pause. Skeptics may wish
to ponder how it was that Prophet Muhammad could have so
accurately predicted events that were still over 1,300 years in
the future. However, despite the obvious fulfillment of one aspect
of the above *Hadith*, knowledge of the Hour remains solely in
the possession of Allah.

F4. THE TRUMPET BLASTS

With the death of every believing Muslim, there will be no one
remaining on earth with a belief in the eventual Day of Judgment
that was ordained by Allah. As such, despite whatever precursors
may previously have been mentioned about the Day of Judgment
and despite however many of those precursors were recognized
by believing Muslims prior to their death, the Hour will come with
unexpected suddenness to the unbelievers who remain living upon
the earth.[33]

> Do they only wait for the Hour — that it should come on them
> all of a sudden, while they perceive not? (*Qur'an* 43: 66)

> Further, they say, "When will this promise (come to pass), if
> what ye say is true?" They will not (have to) wait for aught but
> a single blast: it will seize them while they are yet disputing
> among themselves! No (chance) will they then have, by will,
> to dispose (of their affairs), nor to return to their own people!
> (*Qur'an* 36: 48-50)

At the first trumpet blast, all living creatures, except possibly a few spared by Allah, will die or lose the normal functioning of life. At the second trumpet blast, there will be a general, bodily resurrection of all the dead and a reunion of body and soul.[34]

> The trumpet will (just) be sounded, when all that are in the heavens and on earth will swoon, except such as it will please Allah (to exempt). Then will a second one be sounded, when, behold, they will be standing and looking on! (*Qur'an* 39: 68)

> The trumpet shall be sounded, when behold! from the sepulchers (men) will rush forth to their Lord! (*Qur'an* 36: 51)

> And the trumpet shall be blown: that will be the Day whereof warning (had been given). And there will come forth every soul: with each will be an (angel) to drive, and an (angel) to bear witness. (*Qur'an* 50: 20-21)

However, it will be a far different earth and universe to which the resurrected return. The mountains will be vanished, being uprooted and scattered as dust. The clouds will be no more. The sky will be made flimsy and will be torn asunder. The heavens will be opened.[35]

> Then, when one blast is sounded on the trumpet, and the earth is moved, and its mountains, and they are crushed to powder at one stroke — on that Day shall the (great) event come to pass, and the sky will be rent asunder, for it will that Day be flimsy, and the angels will be on its sides, and eight will, that Day, bear the throne of thy Lord above them. (*Qur'an* 69: 13-17)

Each person will be handed a copy of the book of his recorded deeds in life, which was meticulously kept by the two angels who accompanied him throughout his mortal life. Those blessed believers who have led a virtuous and righteous life will be given their book in their right hands. Those unfortunate wretches who have been found wanting will be given their book in their left hands.[36]

> That Day shall ye be brought to judgment: not an act of yours that ye hide will be hidden. Then he that will be given his record in his right hand will say: "Ah here! Read ye my record! I did really understand that my account would (one day) reach me!" And he will be in a life of bliss, in a garden on high ... And he that will be given his record in his left hand, will say: "Ah! Would that my record had not been given to me! And that I had never realized how my account (stood)! Ah! Would that (death) had made an end of me! Of no profit to me has been my wealth! My power has perished from me!"... (*Qur'an* 69: 18-22,25-29)

The Judgment of Allah will then proceed.

F5. THE JUDGMENT

In the Jewish tradition, the Final Judgment is based upon one's acts and deeds. The issue of faith or belief does not really enter into the equation. In the Christian tradition, the Final Judgment is based upon one's faith. While lip service is sometimes paid to the issue of the righteousness and piety of one's life on earth, the bottom line remains that if one has sufficient faith, one "passes". If not, one "fails". Unfortunately, this doctrine is often used by Christians for rationalizing the commission of sinful or questionable behavior. "No matter my behavior in this instance, my faith will still save me."

The Islamic view of the Final Judgment stands in sharp contrast to that of both Judaism and Christianity. In Islam, belief is a necessary condition for final reward and salvation, but it is not a sufficient condition, in and of itself. If belief was present during earthly life, judgment then devolves to the individual merits and demerits of the judged. At this point, the individual's book of deeds in life, as previously listed by the recording angels, firmly enters into the equation.[37] Given human nature, it is to the extreme good fortune of mankind, that this analysis of one's merits and demerits is tempered by the abundant mercy of Allah.

> He that doeth good shall have ten times as much to his credit: he that doeth evil shall only be recompensed according to his evil: no wrong shall be done unto (any of) them. (*Qur'an* 6: 160)

However, unbelief is a sufficient condition, in and of itself, for punishment and damnation.

> And the earth will shine with the glory of its Lord: the record (of deeds) will be placed (open); the prophets and the witnesses will be brought forward; and a just decision pronounced between them; and they will not be wronged (in the least). And to every soul will be paid in full (the fruit) of its deeds; and (Allah) knoweth best all that they do. The unbelievers will be led to hell in crowd: until, when they arrive there, its gates will be opened. And its keepers will say, "Did not messengers come to you from among yourselves rehearsing to you the signs of your Lord, and warning you of the meeting of this Day of yours?" The answer will be: "True: but the decree of punishment has been proved true against the unbelievers!" (To them) will be said: "Enter ye the gates of hell, to dwell therein: and evil is (this) abode of the arrogant!" And those who feared their Lord will be led to the garden in crowds: until behold, they arrive there; its gates will be opened; and its keepers will say: "Peace be upon you! Well have ye done! Enter ye here, to dwell therein." They will say: "Praise be to Allah, Who has truly fulfilled His promise to us, and has given us (this) land in heritage: we can dwell in the garden as we will: how excellent a reward for those who work (righteousness)!" (*Qur'an* 39: 69-74)

(The sentence will be:) "Throw, throw into Hell every contumacious rejecter (of Allah)! — who forbade what was good, transgressed all bounds, cast doubts and suspicions; who set up another god beside Allah: throw him into a severe penalty." (*Qur'an* 50: 24-26)

When unbelief is present, the individual's motive for any good deed can never be the proper motive, i.e., doing something for the sake of Allah. It is only when some act is done for the sake of Allah that the act is truly and actually good. If done for human-itarian reasons, if done out of some philosophical sense of right and wrong, or if done for baser reasons, the act fails to pass muster as being good. Given this conceptualization, it is easy to see that: belief is a necessary condition for salvation, for without belief there can be no action for the sake of Allah; and the ultimate test of one's individual actions is extremely stringent and severe, although meticulously fair. This notion is eloquently and unequivocally illustrated in the following verses from the *Qur'an*.

> Say: "Shall We tell you of those who lose most in respect of their deeds? — those whose efforts have been wasted in this life while they thought that they were acquiring good by their works?" They are those who deny the signs of their Lord and the fact of their having to meet Him (in the hereafter): vain will be their works, nor shall We, on the Day of Judgment, give them any weight. That is their reward, hell; because they rejected faith, and took My signs and My messengers by way of jest. (*Qur'an* 18: 103-106)

This point finds additional expression in several *Ahadith* of Prophet Muhammad. Perhaps, the most dramatic such example can be seen when Prophet Muhammad implied that the Antichrist was less of a threat to a believer, than was the believer doing an otherwise virtuous act for the wrong reason.

> Allah's Messenger, peace be upon him, came out to them when they were discussing the Antichrist, and asked if they would like him to tell what caused him more fear for them than the Antichrist. They replied that they certainly

would, so he said, "Latent polytheism, meaning that a man will stand up and pray and lengthen his prayer because he sees someone looking at him." (*Al-Tirmidhi, Hadith #* 5333)

Worshipful prayer to Allah is one of the most virtuous acts a person can undertake. However, if a person lengthens that prayer for show or for praise because someone is watching him, he is in essence performing that prayer for the sake of show or praise and not for the sake of Allah. Further, there is a subtle implication that he has compromised his belief in the Oneness of Allah by assigning a weight to the onlooker's praise or commendation, which is equal to or superior to the weight that he is assigning to Allah. (Within the framework of Islamic law (*Shariah*), this type of action is known as *Riyaa*, i.e., to perform acts that are pleasing to Allah, with the intention of pleasing others than Allah.)

A second example from the *Ahadith* of Prophet Muhammad may help make the matter even clearer.

Allah's Apostle, peace be upon him, said, "The reward of deeds depends upon the intention, and every person will get the reward according to what he has intended. So, whoever emigrated for Allah and His Apostle, then his emigration was for Allah and His Apostle. And whoever emigrated for worldly benefits, or for a woman to marry, his emigration was what he emigrated for." (*Al-Bukhari, Hadith #* 1: 51; see also *Muslim, Ahadith #* 4692-4693; and *Abu Dawud, Hadith #* 2195)

As a brief digression for Christian readers, one notes the essential similarity of thought between: the Qur'anic passage and the two *Ahadith* quoted above; and the alleged words of Prophet Jesus, as reported in *Matthew*.

Beware of practicing your piety before others in order to be seen by them; for then you have no reward from your Father in heaven. So whenever you give alms, do not sound a trumpet before you, as the hypocrites do in the synagogues and in the streets, so that they may be praised by others.

Truly I tell you, they have received their reward. But when you give alms, do not let your left hand know what your right hand is doing, so that your alms may be done in secret; and your Father who sees in secret will reward you. And whenever you pray, do not be like the hypocrites; for they love to stand and pray in the synagogues and at the street corners, so that they may be seen by others. Truly I tell you, they have received their reward. But whenever you pray, go into your room and shut the door and pray to your Father who is in secret; and your Father who sees in secret will reward you. (*Matthew* 6: 1-6)

As an additional thought, given the stringency of the nature of this test of one's deeds and actions, one might well wonder how anyone could possibly pass this test. The simple answer is that mankind, even while being judged by Allah, is dependent upon the mercy of Allah. Furthermore, it is a promise and a mercy of Allah that no matter how severe the trials one may undergo during one's earthly life, those trials will never exceed one's potential to bear them.

On no soul doth Allah place a burden greater than it can bear. It gets every good that it earns, and it suffers every ill that it earns. (Pray:) "Our Lord! Condemn us not if we forget or fall into error; our Lord! lay not on us a burden like that which Thou didst lay on those before us; our Lord! lay not on us a burden greater than we have strength to bear, blot out our sins, and grant us forgiveness. Have mercy on us. Thou art our protector; help us against those who stand against faith." (*Qur'an* 2: 286)

Further, one notes that each person is judged on his own merits and demerits. Unlike the Christian concept of Final Judgment, there is no salvation through the sacrifice of another, and there is no "atonement in the blood". Each person must stand on his/her own two feet before Allah, and each person must answer for his/her own conduct and belief.

On that day shall no intercession avail except for those for whom permission has been granted by (Allah) most gracious and whose word is acceptable to Him. (*Qur'an* 20: 109)

Again, what will explain to thee what the Day of Judgment is? (It will be) the day when no soul shall have power (to do) aught for another: for the command, that day, will be (wholly) with Allah. (*Qur'an* 82: 18-19)

Say: "Shall I seek for (my) cherisher other than Allah, when He is the cherisher of all things (that exist)? Every soul draws the need of its acts on none but itself: no bearer of burdens can bear the burden of another. Your goal in the end is towards Allah: He will tell you the truth of the things wherein ye disputed." (*Qur'an* 6:164)

The judgment of Allah will be scrupulously just and fair, and His justice will be perfect justice.

F6. REWARD AND PUNISHMENT

The traditional Christian perspective of the judgment of Allah is that it is a "pass-fail" test. One either passes, i.e., receives heaven, or one fails, i.e., enters hell. The Islamic view is rather more sophisticated and complex, and emphasizes a level of fairness beyond that seen in the Christian perspective. In that regard, it is first noted that some individuals may first be punished in hell for a while before Allah's mercy allows them to enter heaven. Secondly, in the Islamic belief system, heaven is multi-leveled, as is hell. While the gulf between "passing" and "failing" is enormous and while the consequences of that gulf are beyond the actual comprehension of the mind of man, there are different degrees of reward in heaven, and there are different degrees of punishment in hell.

Such in truth are the believers: they have grades of dignity with their Lord, and forgiveness, and generous sustenance... (*Qur'an* 8: 4)

In this way, each person "gets every good that it earns, and it suffers every ill that it earns" (*Qur'an* 2: 286a).

The rewards of heaven and the punishment of hell are both physical and spiritual. In regard to the bliss of heaven, one notes the following passages from the *Qur'an*.

> Verily the companions of the garden shall that day have joy in all that they do; they and their associates will be in groves of (cool) shade, reclining on thrones (of dignity); (every) fruit (enjoyment) will be there for them; they shall have whatever they call for; "Peace!"— a word (of salutation) from a Lord most merciful. (*Qur'an* 36: 55-58)

> And he will be in a life of bliss, in a garden on high, the fruits whereof (will hang in bunches) low and near. "Eat ye and drink ye, with full satisfaction; because of the (good) that ye sent before you, in the days that are gone!" (*Qur'an* 69: 21-24)

> Verily for the righteous there will be a fulfillment of (the heart's) desires; gardens enclosed, and grapevines; companions of equal age; and a cup full (to the brim). (*Qur'an* 78: 31-34)

> The righteous (will be) amid gardens and fountains (of clear-flowing water). (Their greeting will be): "Enter ye here in peace and security." And We shall remove from their hearts any lurking sense of injury: (they will be) brothers (joyfully) facing each other on thrones (of dignity). There no sense of fatigue shall touch them, nor shall they (ever) be asked to leave. (*Qur'an* 15: 45-48)

> But the sincere (and devoted) servants of Allah — for them is a sustenance determined, fruits (delights); and they (shall enjoy) honor and dignity, in gardens of felicity, facing each other on thrones (of dignity): round will be passed to them a cup from a clear-flowing fountain, crystal-white, of a taste delicious to those who drink (thereof), free from headiness;

nor will they suffer intoxication therefrom. And besides them will be chaste women; restraining their glances, with big eyes (of wonder and beauty). As if they were (delicate) eggs closely guarded. (*Qur'an* 37: 40-49)

The *Qur'an* describes the curse and punishment of hell in even more graphic terms, as witnessed by the following.

(The stern command will say): "Seize ye him and bind ye him, and burn ye him in the blazing fire. Further, make him march in a chain, whereof the length is seventy cubits! This was he that would not believe in Allah most high, and would not encourage the feeding of the indigent! So no friend hath he here this day. Nor hath he any food except the corruption from the washing of wounds, which none do eat but those in sin." (*Qur'an* 69: 30-37)

Truly hell is as a place of ambush — for the transgressors a place of destination: they will dwell therein for ages. Nothing cool shall they taste therein, nor any drink, save a boiling fluid and a fluid, dark, murky, intensely cold — a fitting recompense for them...for no increase shall We grant you, except in punishment. (*Qur'an* 78: 21-26,30b)

In front of such a one is hell, and he is given for drink, boiling fetid water. In gulps will he sip it, but never will he be near swallowing it down his throat: death will come to him from every quarter, yet will he not die: and in front of him will be a chastisement unrelenting. (*Qur'an* 14: 16-17)

G. BELIEF IN *AL-QADAR*

G1. INTRODUCTION

There are some words that one is better off not translating into another language, because any such translation is likely to result in miscommunication and in misinformation, secondary to the cultural or religious baggage that necessarily accompanies the conceptual meaning of the word in its translated form.

Any attempt to translate *Al-Qadar* into English runs that very risk. For example, prior authors have occasionally translated *Al-Qadar* as predestination. In many respects, this is a most unfortunate translation, as the typical Occidental Christian's understanding of predestination is so shaped by the legacy of Calvinistic theology that there is probably no escaping a prejudicial understanding and conceptualization of *Al-Qadar*. Other attempts to translate *Al-Qadar*, e.g., divine destiny, minimize the risk of miscommunication without eliminating that risk. In an attempt to prevent the reader from misconceptualizing the Islamic principle of *Al-Qadar*, the present author has elected not to use any translation of the term, although the author notes that *Al-Qadar* has as its root meaning the notion of measure, balance, or set amount.

> Verily, all things have We created in proportion and measure (*Qadar*). (*Qur'an* 54: 49)

Complicating the problem still further is the fact that the principle of *Al-Qadar* is quite complex and has multiple levels of meaning. In what follows, several different levels of meaning are briefly explored. This exploration of the meaning of *Al-Qadar* is necessarily somewhat superficial and incomplete. A full treatment of the issue would require multiple volumes, and would fall far outside the scope of this modest chapter.

G2. NATURAL LAW AND ALLAH

One aspect of *Al-Qadar* can be found in the natural laws that govern the running of the universe. Secondary to and consistent with Allah's divine plan and will, each aspect of creation has its assigned measure and set amount. The laws of mathematical probability, geology, navigation, genetics, agricultural husbandry, gravity, movement, physics, etc. are merely manifestations of the concept of *Al-Qadar*. The composition of each atom is governed by natural law. The earth has a set rotation upon its axis. Each planet has its set orbit around a star. Each star has its set movement within a galaxy. All aspects of creation are governed by natural laws that are merely reflections of the will of Allah. Numerous examples of this aspect of *Al-Qadar* are listed in the *Qur'an*.

> It is Allah Who causeth the seed grain and the date stone to split and sprout ... He it is that cleaveth the daybreak (from the dark): He makes the night for rest and tranquillity, and the sun and moon for the reckoning (of time): Such is the judgment and ordering of (Him), the exalted in power, the omniscient. It is He Who maketh the stars (as beacons) for you, that ye may guide yourselves, with their help, through the dark spaces of land and sea: We detail Our signs for people who know...It is He Who sendeth down rain from the skies; with it We produce vegetation of all kinds: from some We produce green (crops), out of which We produce grain, heaped up (at harvest); out of the date palm and its sheaths (or spathes) (come) clusters of dates hanging low and near: and (then there are) gardens of grapes, and olives, and pomegranates, each similar (in kind) yet different (in variety)... (*Qur'an* 6: 95a, 96-97, 99a-b)

> It is Allah Who hath created the heavens and the earth and sendeth down rain from the skies, and with it bringeth out fruits wherewith to feed you: it is He Who hath made the ships subject to you, that they may sail through the sea by His command. And He hath made subject to you the sun and the moon, both diligently pursuing their courses: and the night and the day hath He (also) made subject to you. (*Qur'an* 14: 32-33)

> The sun and the moon follow courses (exactly) computed; and the herbs and the trees — both (alike) bow in adoration. (*Qur'an* 55: 5-6)

> And a sign for them is the night: We withdraw therefrom the day, and behold they are plunged in darkness; and the sun runs its course for a period determined for it; that is

the decree of (Him), the exalted in might, the all-knowing. And the moon — We have measured for it mansions (to traverse) till it returns like the old (and withered) lower part of a date stalk. It is not permitted to the sun to catch up to the moon, nor can the night outstrip the day: each (just) swims along in (its own) orbit (according to law). (*Qur'an* 36: 37-40)

It is He Who created the night and the day, and the sun and the moon: all (the celestial bodies) swim along, each in its rounded course. (*Qur'an* 21: 33)

Verily, all things have We created in proportion and measure. (*Qur'an* 54: 49)

Glorify the name of thy Guardian-Lord Most High, Who hath created, and further, given order and proportion; Who hath ordained laws. And granted guidance; and Who bringeth out the (green and luscious) pasture, and then doth make it (but) swarthy stubble. (*Qur'an* 87: 1-5)

G3. THE FOREKNOWLEDGE OF ALLAH

A second aspect of *Al-Qadar* is the foreknowledge of Allah. Allah knows all things, whether they are past, present, or future. Allah is above and beyond the human concept of time. More specifically, Allah knows each hope, each desire, and each action of any given person before that hope, desire, or action has even transpired. He knows the eventual length of each person's life and the end result of that person on the Day of Judgment. Furthermore, that foreknowledge has existed with Allah throughout all of eternity, and has been written down and recorded.

With Him are the keys of the unseen, the treasures that none knoweth but He, He knoweth whatever there is on the earth and in the sea. Not a leaf doth fall but with His knowledge: there is not a grain in the darkness (or depths) of the earth, nor anything fresh or dry (green or withered), but is (inscribed) in a record clear (to those who can read). (*Qur'an* 6: 59)

Knowest thou not that Allah knows all that is in heaven and on earth? Indeed, it is all in a record, and that is easy for Allah. (*Qur'an* 22: 70)

No misfortune can happen on earth or in your souls, but is recorded in a decree before We bring it into existence: that is truly easy for Allah. (*Qur'an* 57: 22)

G4. THE WILL OF ALLAH AND THE FREE WILL OF MAN

As noted previously, *Al-Qadar* has at times been translated as predestination, implying that all the actions and intentions of each member of the human race are subject to a fatalistic determination outside of the boundaries of any exercise of human free will. While Allah has complete foreknowledge of each and every human action and intention, and in that sense alone is each such action and intention foreordained, it is not the case that *Al-Qadar* is an abrogation of human free will. It is, instead, an affirmation of the free will of each and every person.

Precisely because of the will of Allah, humans and jinn have been granted the gift of choice. They have been granted free will via the will of Allah. While there is no way in which any man can act against the will of Allah, it is not the case that Allah wills whatever the individual human wills. Rather, Allah wills that man be free to will as he chooses. If it were otherwise, there would be no free will, as the *Qur'an* is quite precise in declaring that whatever Allah wills immediately springs into existence. Whatever Allah wills is an accomplished fact.

He (Gabriel) said: "Even so: Allah createth what He willeth: when He hath decreed a plan, He but saith to it, 'Be', and it is!" (*Qur'an* 3: 47b)

(Inevitably) cometh (to pass) the command of Allah...
(*Qur'an* 16: 1a)

And He is the oft forgiving, full of loving kindness, Lord of the throne of glory, Doer (without let) of all that He intends. (*Qur'an* 85: 14-16)

There is evil, adversity, and trauma in the world. Does Allah will the existence of such misfortune on a case-by-case basis? No, but Allah does will certain natural laws and probability systems to exist, and Allah does will that mankind and the jinn have free will. Given such natural laws and probabilities and given the free will of mankind and of the jinn, evil, adversity, and trauma are sure to exist. In this sense and, barring divine intervention in some direct and miraculous manner (see below), in this sense alone, Allah wills the prerequisites for such misfortune.

G5. THE LIMITS OF FREE WILL

Mankind and the jinn have been granted free will by the will of Allah. It is this free will that serves as one of the basic cornerstones for the eventual Day of Judgment. Without the free will of man, Allah's ultimate judgment would be an arbitrary dispensation of reward and punishment. However, there are certain necessary limits that accompany the free will of man. While as a general rule man is free to choose as he wishes, his ability to carry out that choice in actual behavior is necessarily limited. One may wish to run a three-minute mile or to high jump 10 feet into the air or to throw a baseball 110 miles per hour. One is free to choose to do so. However, the actual behavior of doing so may not be allowed or might not happen. One may simply not have the requisite physical skills and abilities to carry out the behavior in question. Has one's free will been compromised? Obviously, there has been no limitation placed on one's intention or choice, but one's behavioral and physical skills are limited by events and considerations that we as humans simply do not control. In recognition of this fact, Muslims typically say *Insha'Allah* (Allah willing) after expressing any intention to do something. In this manner, Muslims routinely acknowledge that everything is contingent upon Allah in the final analysis.

However, even when and where man has the actual physical ability to do something, the results expected from that action might not occur. One may choose to become wealthy or famous, not that these are laudable goals in their own right, and then proceed to act in such a manner as to optimize the probabilities of achieving those goals. However, the anticipated results may not accrue. Such limitations were even the case for Prophet Muhammad and for the success or failure of his ministry.

> But thou art there only to warn! It is Allah that arrangeth all affairs. (*Qur'an* 11: 12b)

> At the Battle of Uhud, the Prophet was hit and one of his molars was broken. Despondently, he exclaimed: "How can a people succeed who hit their prophet?" In the following moment, the verse was revealed: "The matter is not yours to control at all." (*Kitab Al-Tawhid.* The Qur'anic verse referred to is 3:128)

Do these limitations mean that mankind is doomed to a mindless determinism? The answer is a resounding no. Do these limitations mean that mankind should retire into a resigned fatalism? Absolutely not! These limitations in no manner obviate man's duty to make a good-faith effort and to attempt to act accordingly. However, if the anticipated or hoped for results do not transpire, it is an act of faith and submission to accept what has happened. Allah willing, that which is good will be achieved. However, whether the anticipated results accrue or not, the Muslim's proper response is *Al-Hamdulillah*, i.e., praise be to Allah.

G6. DIVINE INTERVENTION

Finally, it must be acknowledged that Allah has no limitations on His power. He may intervene or not intervene into the affairs of mankind as He chooses. As such, the possibility must always be acknowledged that Allah may choose to set aside the natural laws of His creation. Further, He may chose to alter the choices, abilities, skills, and behavior of any given person at any given moment in time. In the final analysis, everything is contingent upon the will of Allah. The insignificance of mankind in relationship to the glory, exaltation, and power of Allah is such as to make it a complete folly for mankind to assume it has complete knowledge of the will of Allah.

> That is Allah, your Lord! There is no god but He, the creator of all things; then worship ye Him; and He hath power to dispose of all affairs. No vision can grasp Him. But His grasp is over all vision: He is above all comprehension, yet is acquainted with all things. (*Qur'an* 6:102-103)

H. SUMMARY

To summarize briefly, the articles of Islamic faith are as follows. (1) Muslims believe that there is no god but Allah and that only Allah is worthy of worship. The essential Oneness of Allah (*Tawheed*) precludes His having any associates or partners. (2) Muslims believe in all the messengers and prophets of Allah without differentiating hierarchically among them and without elevating them beyond their human nature. (3) Muslims believe in all the scriptures and revelations from Allah as they were delivered in their original form. However, only the last book from Allah, i.e., the *Qur'an*, continues to exist on earth in its original and pristine form. (4) Muslims believe in the angels of Allah, but realize that they are no more than one of Allah's creations. (5) Muslims believe in life after death, in an ultimate Day of Judgment, and in a hereafter containing both a heaven and a hell. (6) Muslims believe in the timeless knowledge of Allah and in His power to plan and execute His plans.

Five of the six articles of faith are succinctly listed in the following verse from the *Qur'an*, while all six are enumerated in an *Hadith* narrated by 'Abd Allah ibn 'Umar ibn Al-Khattab.

It is not righteousness that ye turn your faces towards East or West; but it is righteousness — to believe in Allah and the Last Day, and the angels, and the book, and the messengers... (*Qur'an* 2: 177a)

...My father 'Umar b. Khattab told me: "One day we were sitting in the company of the Messenger of Allah (may peace be upon him) when there appeared before us a man dressed in extremely white clothes, his hair extraordinary black. There were no signs of travel on him. None amongst us recognized him. At last he sat with the Apostle (peace be upon him). He knelt before him, placed his palms on his thighs, and... said: 'Inform me about Iman (faith).' He (the Holy Prophet) replied: 'That you affirm your faith in Allah, in His angels, in His Books, in His Apostles, in the Day of Judgment, and you affirm your faith in the Divine Decree to good and evil.'... Then he (the inquirer) went on his way... He (the Holy Prophet) remarked: 'He was Gabriel (the angel). He came to you in order to instruct you in matters of religion.'" (*Muslim, Hadith* # 1; see parallels in *Al-Bukhari, Ahadith* 1:47 and 6: 300, as well as in *Al-Nawawi, Hadith* # 2)

Notes

18. *Qur'an* 2:106; 3:23,50,93; 4:44,160; 5:3,15-16; 6:145-146; 10:37; 13:38-39.

19. The word "messenger" can also be used to refer to the angel who, upon the instructions of Allah, gave the revelation to the prophet.

20. *Qur'an* 4:54; 53:36-37; 87:19.

21. *Qur'an* 2:87; 3:3; 5:44; 6:91,154; 11:17,110; 17:2; 23:49; 25:35; 28:43; 32:23; 37:114-118; 40:53; 41:45; 46:12; 53:36; 87:19.

22. *Qur'an* 4:163; 17:55; 21:105.

23. *Qur'an* 3:3,45-48; 5:46,110; 57:27.

24. *Qur'an* 3:7; 4:105,113,127,140; 5:48; 6:92; 7:2; 10:37; 11:1-4; 12:1-3; 13:1; 14:1; 16:64,89; 18:1,27; 27:1-6; 32:2-3; 38:29; 39:1-2,41; 40:2; 41:2-4; 56:75-80.

25. *Qur'an* 2:75-79,101; 3:23-24,71,78,187; 4:46; 5:12-15,41,44; 6:91; 10:93; 11:110; 15:90; 41:45; 62:5.

26. *Qur'an* 3:59; 6:2; 7:11-12; 15:26-33; 17:61; 18:50; 32:7; 37:11; 38:71-76; 55:14-15.

27. *Qur'an* 2:97-98, 102; 66:4.

28. *Daniel* 8:16; 9:21; 10:13,21; 12:1; *Luke* 1:19,26; *Jude* 1:9; *Revelation* 12:7.

29. *Qur'an* 2:97, 102; 4:97; 6:61, 93; 8:50; 16:2; 42:5; 47:27; 50:16-17; 79:1-5; 82:10-12.

30. *Qur'an* 70:4; 78:38; 97:4.

31. *Qur'an* 34:3-5; 40:59; 51:5-6,12-14; 52:7-10; 56:1-7; 64:7.

32. (A) *Muslim, Ahadith* #293, 6931-6934, 7005-7015, 7023. (B) *Abu Dawud, Ahadith* #2478, 2526, 4230, 4232, 4281-4283, 4310 (C) *Al-Tirmidhi, Ahadith* #1761, 3553. (D) *Al-Bukhari, Ahadith* #3:425,656; 4:657,658.

33. *Qur'an* 7:187; 16:77; 36:48-50; 43:66; 54:50

34. *Qur'an* 20:102-104; 23:100-101; 27:87; 36:51; 39:68; 50:20-21; 69:13-18; 78:18.

35. *Qur'an* 20: 105-106; 27: 88; 69: 13-16; 78: 18-20.

36. *Qur'an* 39: 69; 50: 20-23; 69: 18-37; 78: 29.

37. *Qur'an* 23: 102-103; 27: 89-90; 36: 54; 39: 70; 69: 19-37.

Chapter 6
Pillars of Practice

A. INTRODUCTION

Given the six articles of faith enumerated in the preceding chapter, the application of faith in daily life can be summarized into what has been called the Five Pillars of Islam. (1) The first pillar is the *Shahadah* or testimonial of faith, i.e., testifying that there is no god but Allah and that Muhammad is the messenger of Allah. (2) The second pillar is *Salat*, i.e., to perform the five obligatory prayers every day at their stated times. (3) The third pillar is *Sawm*, i.e., to fast during the Islamic month of *Ramadan*. (4) The fourth pillar is *Zakat* or the mandatory payment to approved charity of a set percentage of one's economic surplus. (5) The fifth pillar is to make the *Hajj* pilgrimage to Makkah at least once in one's adult lifetime, if one is financially and physically capable of doing so.

B. *SHAHADAH*

The first pillar of practice is the *Shahadah*, or testimonial of faith. In simple English translation, the *Shahadah* consists of saying: "I testify that there is no god but Allah, and I testify that Muhammad is the messenger of Allah". As belief in Allah and belief in the prophets and messengers of Allah have been discussed in the previous chapter, that discussion is not repetitiously stated at this time. Suffice it to say that anyone who honestly says the *Shahadah* with comprehension and understanding is a Muslim.

Given the previous discussion of the etymology of the word "Allah" (see chapter I, section C), most Christians and Jews who bother to think about the *Shahadah* would probably conclude that they would have no difficulty saying and meaning the first part of the *Shahadah*, i.e., there is no god but Allah. However, those Christians who actually believe in a triune godhead should be warned that the first part of the *Shahadah* incorporates by implication the concept of *La Sharika*, i.e., no partners or associates with Allah. The *Tawheed* or Oneness of Allah is absolute, and there is no maneuvering room or fudge factor with regard to this concept.

However, the stumbling block in the *Shahadah* for most Christians and Jews consists of testifying to the fact that Prophet Muhammad was the messenger of Allah. While it must be emphasized that this phrase does not imply that Prophet Muhammad was the only messenger of Allah, this phrase still remains a gulf separating Islam from Christianity and Judaism. Allah willing, each Christian and Jew who is reading this chapter will find his or her own way to bridge this gulf.

One final point does need to be made before leaving this abbreviated discussion of *Shahadah*. In accepting Prophet Muhammad as a messenger of Allah, one must by implication accept the *Qur'an* as the revealed words of Allah.

C. *SALAT*

C1. PRAYER

The second pillar of practice is to perform the daily prayers of worship, i.e., *Salat*. The importance of establishing regular prayer is repeatedly stressed in the *Qur'an*. The English translations of a few of those Qur'anic injunctions are quoted below.

> And be steadfast in prayer; practice regular charity; and bow down your heads with those who bow down (in worship). (*Qur'an* 2: 43)

> Guard strictly your (habit) of prayers, especially the middle prayer; and stand before Allah in a devout (frame of mind). (*Qur'an* 2 :238)

Say: "Allah's guidance is the (only) guidance, and we have been directed to submit ourselves to the Lord of the worlds — to estalish regular prayers and to fear Allah: for it is to Him that we shall be gathered together." (*Qur'an* 6: 71b-72)

And establish regular prayers at the two ends of the day and at the approaches of the night: for those things that are good remove those that are evil: be that the word of remembrance to those who remember (their Lord): (*Qur'an* 11: 114)

Establish regular prayers — at the sun's decline till the darkness of the night, and the morning prayer and reading: for the prayer and reading in the morning carry their testimony. And pray in the small watches of the morning: (it would be) an additional prayer (or spiritual profit) for thee: soon will thy Lord raise thee to a station of praise and glory. (*Qur'an* 17: 78-79)

Therefore be patient with what they say, and celebrate (constantly) the praises of thy Lord before the rising of the sun, and before its setting; yea, celebrate them for part of the hours of the night, and at the sides of the day: that thou mayest have (spiritual) joy. (*Qur'an* 20: 130)

O ye who believe! Bow down, prostrate yourselves, and adore your Lord; and do good; that ye may prosper. (*Qur'an* 22: 77)

So establish regular prayer and give regular charity; and obey the messenger; that ye may receive mercy. (*Qur'an* 24: 56)

So (give) glory to Allah, when ye reach eventide and when ye rise in the morning; yea, to Him be praise, in the heavens and on earth; and in the late afternoon and when the day begins to decline. (*Qur'an* 30: 17-18)

Turn ye back in repentance to Him, and fear Him: establish regular prayers, and be not ye among those who join gods with Allah — (*Qur'an* 30: 31)

Several points need to be emphasized with regard to *Salat*. Firstly, *Salat* is obligatory, not voluntary. Secondly, *Salat* is primarily a prayer of worship, and is not a prayer of supplication or of personal communication, which is called *Dua*, although *Dua* may be appended to or incorporated into the *Salat*. Thirdly, as such, *Salat* takes a set form. Fourthly, there are five set times in every day at which *Salat* must be said. In what follows, these points are briefly discussed.

(1) *Salat* is obligatory on every Muslim who has reached 10 years of age.[38] However, there are certain exceptions to and modifications of this rule. Without going into in-depth, explanatory detail, it is noted that there are those who are excused from, and in some cases even prohibited from, performing *Salat*. These include the feeble minded, the mentally insane, and those in certain states of ritual impurity (e.g., menstruating women, post-partum women, etc.).[39] Further, the obligatory nature of *Salat* is eased for those upon whom *Salat* would be especially difficult, e.g., the traveler, the person who is in a state of personal danger from his or her surroundings, the seriously ill, etc.[40] In such cases, if certain conditions are met, *Salat* may be shortened, or may be modified as to the nature of the ritual positions assumed in performing *Salat*, or two different *Salat* may be said one after the other, instead of waiting for the appointed time of each.

(2) *Salat* is a prayer of worship. It is an act of worshipping Allah. For Christians, who are used to conceptualizing prayer as a time of personal communication with the deity, *Salat* may seem somewhat impersonal and lacking in personal gratification. In this regard, it must be re-emphasized that *Salat* is an obligatory act of worshipping Allah. However, *Salat* is not a substitute for personal communication with Allah, nor is it a replacement for supplicating to Allah. Such personal communication and supplication is known

in Islam as *Dua*, and can be made at any time of the day or night. *Salat* is not a substitute for *Dua*. They are two different concepts and two different acts. The former is a required act of worship, while the latter is voluntary and has a more personal meaning.

(3) The following description of *Salat* is necessarily somewhat superficial, and is intended only to give the non-Muslim a general idea of *Salat*. To begin with, it is noted that one should approach *Salat* with the intention of performing *Salat* and of worshipping Allah. The *Salat* consists of units (one unit is a *Raka*; plural is *Rakat*) of prayer, with the number of units varying, depending upon which *Salat* is being performed. Each *Raka* consists of various postures, which are taken in a set sequence. For odd numbered *Rakat*, the sequential postures are: standing with right hand placed over left (or both hands hanging down at the sides for those who follow the Maliki school); bowing with hands on knees; standing; prostrating with hands placed on the ground between shoulder and ear level; kneeling with hands and forearms resting on knees and thighs; and prostrating with hands placed on the ground between shoulder and ear level. For even numbered *Rakat* and for the third and final *Raka* of *Maghrib Salat*, there is a final kneeling after the last prostration. The *Salat* begins by raising both hands upward to the ears in the standing posture and saying *Allahu Akbar*, i.e., Allah is greater. The *Salat* ends while in a kneeling posture by turning the face to the right shoulder and saying *Al-Salam 'Alaykum Wa Rahmatullah*, i.e., may the peace and mercy of Allah be upon you, and then by turning the face to the left shoulder and repeating the phrase. *Allahu Akbar* is said when changing positions.

During the standing postures at the start of each *Raka*, one recites from the *Qur'an*, always beginning by saying the first *Surah* (chapter) of the *Qur'an*. This recitation is audible for the first two *Rakat* of the first, fourth, and fifth *Salat* of the day. It is said silently at all other times, with the exception of certain specified *Salat*, e.g., the Friday noon prayer when said in congregation. During the bowing and prostration postures, one offers set phrases of praise to Allah. During the kneeling posture, one asks for forgiveness in a set manner. During the final kneeling posture of the even numbered

Rakat, one offers additional aspects of the *Salat*, including a testimonial of faith.

(4) *Salat* is mandated on all Muslims at five different times each day. The *Fajr* prayer is to be said before dawn, and consists of two *Rakat*. *Dhur* is said just after true noon, and consists of four *Rakat*. *'Asr* is said just after halfway between true noon and sunset, and consists of four *Rakat*. *Maghrib* is said just after sunset, and consists of three *Rakat*. *'Isha* is said after the true darkness of night begins, and consists of four *Rakat*. These five prayers are obligatory and mandatory. In addition to these obligatory prayers, there are a number of voluntary or supplementary prayers of worship (*Salat*), which are highly encouraged and for which Muslims have the example of Prophet Muhammad. These include prayers just before *Fajr*, prayers just before and after *Dhur*, prayers after *Maghrib*, prayers after *'Isha*, prayers in the middle of the night, and prayers of respect upon entering a mosque. Additional prayers of worship are encouraged during the Islamic month of *Ramadan*, during the *'Eid* holidays, and at certain other special times. As noted previously, over and above *Salat*, prayers of *Dua* may be offered at any time, and are highly encouraged acts within Islam.

(5) It is preferable that *Salat* be said in congregational prayer at the mosque (this is especially true for the Friday noon prayer, and especially true for men), and the rewards of congregational prayer are said to be twenty-five times greater than that of individual prayer.

> Narrated Abu Huraira, may Allah accept him: The Prophet, peace be upon him, said: "The prayer offered in congregation is twenty-five times more superior (in reward) than the prayer offered alone in one's house or in a business center, because if one performs ablution and does it perfectly, and then proceeds to the mosque with the sole intention of praying, then for each step which he takes towards the mosque, Allah upgrades him a degree in reward and (forgives) crosses out one sin, till he enters the mosque. When he enters the mosque he is considered in prayer as long as he is waiting for the prayer, and the angels keep on asking for Allah's forgiveness

for him, and they keep on saying: 'O Allah! be merciful to him,
O Allah! Forgive him'"... (*Al-Bukhari, Hadith* # 1:466. See also
Al-Bukhari, Ahadith # 1:619-621; 3:330; and 6:241)

However, *Salat* can be said individually, either at home, at
work, or almost anywhere one happens to be.

C2. ABLUTION

As an act of worship and respect, each Muslim is to make
ritual ablution (*Wudu*) before performing *Salat*. Following sexual
intercourse or the completion of menses, the entire body is to be
bathed. Usually, however, ritual ablution is confined to washing
certain prescribed parts of the body. The following injunction
from the *Qur'an* addresses these points.

> O ye who believe! When ye prepare for prayer, wash your
> faces, and your hands (and arms) to the elbows; rub
> your heads (with water); and (wash) your feet to the ankles.
> If ye are in a state of ceremonial impurity, bathe your whole
> body. But if ye are ill, or on a journey, or one of you cometh
> from offices of nature, or ye have been in contact with women,
> and ye find no water, then take for yourselves clean sand or
> earth, and rub therewith your faces and hands. Allah doth
> not wish to place you in a difficulty, but to make you clean,
> and to complete His favor to you, that ye may be grateful.
> (*Qur'an* 5: 6)

Based upon the example of the practice of Prophet
Muhammad, Muslims actually perform a somewhat more
elaborate ablution than that specified in the above injunction
from the *Qur'an*. This ablution consists of: washing the hands;
rinsing out the mouth; rinsing out the nose; washing the face;
washing the forearms to the elbows; washing or wetting the hair;
washing the ears; washing the back of the neck; and washing
the feet. Various aspects of this practice of performing *Wudu* are
covered extensively in the *Ahadith* literature.[41] Where and when

water is not available for performing *Wudu*, a substitute ablution may be performed with clean dirt.

C3. WORSHIP

As repeatedly stressed earlier, *Salat* is an act of worship. Obviously, *Salat* is not the only act of worship that can and should be made, but it is an obligatory one. As noted in the *Qur'an*, the very purpose of man's existence is to serve and worship Allah.

Not a messenger did We send before thee without this inspiration sent by Us to him: that there is no god but I; therefore worship and serve Me. (*Qur'an* 21: 25)

Did I not enjoin on you, O ye children of Adam, that ye should not worship Satan; for that he was to you an enemy avowed? — And that ye should worship Me, (for that) this was the straight way? (*Qur'an* 36: 60-61)

That is Allah, your Lord! There is no god but He, the creator of all things; then worship ye Him; and He hath power to dispose of all affairs. (*Qur'an* 6: 102)

I have only created jinns and men, that they may serve Me. (*Qur'an* 51: 56)

D. *SAWM*

D1. INTRODUCTION

The third pillar of practice is *Sawm*, i.e., fasting, during the Islamic month of *Ramadan*. The *Qur'an* directly prescribes and addresses the issues surrounding this third pillar of practice.

O ye who believe! Fasting is prescribed to you as it was prescribed to those before you, that ye may (learn) self-restraint...Ramadan is the (month) in which was sent down the Qur'an, as a guide to mankind, also clear (signs) for guidance and judgment (between right and wrong).

So every one of you who is present (at his home) during that month should spend it in fasting... (*Qur'an* 2:183,185a)

D2. *RAMADAN* AND THE ISLAMIC CALENDAR

Unlike the solar calendar of the West, the Islamic calendar is a lunar calendar consisting of 12 months. Of these lunar months, the eighth is *Sha'ban*, the ninth is *Ramadan*, and the tenth is *Shawwal*. Because the Islamic calendar is lunar, each Islamic year is approximately 11 days shorter than each solar year. Thus, every year on the Gregorian calendar, *Ramadan* occurs abou 11 days earlier than the year before. Each year, *Ramadan* begins on the sighting of the first sliver of the crescent of the new moon following the month of *Sha'ban*. It continues until the sighting of the first sliver of the crescent of the next new moon. In this way, *Ramadan* is always either 29 or 30 days in length.

> Narrated Abu Huraira, may Allah accept him: "The Prophet, peace be upon him, or Abul-Qasim,[42] peace be upon him, said, 'Start fasting on seeing the crescent (of Ramadan), and give up fasting on seeing the crescent (of Shawwal), and if the sky is overcast (and you cannot see it), complete thirty days of Sha'ban'". (*Al-Bukhari, Hadith* # 3: 133; see also *Al-Bukhari, Ahadith* # 3: 130-132)

D3. WHY FAST

Why do Muslims fast during the month of *Ramadan*? *Insha'Allah*, there are a number of benefits from such fasting: spiritual purification; potential health benefits, especially in a Western society tending towards corpulence; increased self-discipline and self-restraint; increased focus on and study of one's religion; a heightened sense of Muslim community, with Muslims across the world fasting together; an increased empathy for the poor and hungry; etc. However, none of these is the primary reason that Muslims fast during *Ramadan*. The simple reason that Muslims fast during *Ramadan* is that it is an order of Allah. This directive is eloquently stated in the following verses from *Surah Al-Baqarah*.

> O ye who believe! Fasting is prescribed to you as it was prescribed to those before you, that ye may (learn) self-restraint — (fasting) for a fixed number of days; but if any of you is ill or on a journey, the prescribed number (should be made up) from days later. For those who can do it (with hardship), is a ransom, the feeding of one that is indigent but he that will give more, of his own free will — it is better for him. And it is better for you that ye fast, if ye only knew. *Ramadan* is the (month) in which was sent down the *Qur'an*, as a guide to mankind, also clear (signs) for guidance and judgment (between right and wrong). So every one of you who is present (at his home) during that month should spend it in fasting, but if any one is ill, or on a journey, the prescribed period (should be made up) by days later. Allah intends every facility for you; He does not want to put you to difficulties. (He wants you) to complete the prescribed period, and to glorify Him in that He has guided you; and perchance ye shall be grateful. (*Qur'an* 2: 183-185)

D4. THE LIMITS OF FASTING

Before turning to what exactly is entailed in fasting during the month of *Ramadan*, it may be helpful to focus on the limits regarding fasting, which are mentioned in the above passage from the *Qur'an*. It is a mercy from Allah that a number of people are specifically excluded from the obligation to fast, or are given an option as to whether to fast or not. By and large, such individuals are those for whom fasting would be a physical risk, e.g., the Qur'anic passage refers to the ill and to those who are traveling. To this list, one might add pregnant women and those women who are nursing, as in either case, fasting by the mother may be a physical risk for the child. Likewise, the aged may be considered to be at physical risk. If able, all such individuals are to make up their fasting, day for day, at a later time. In the case of chronic physical risk, the individual is to substitute for fasting by feeding the poor, one day for every day not fasting. As such, the reader can see that no individual is burdened with an obligation that is too big for that person to bear.

D5. THE FAST

Fasting begins each day at the first light of dawn, prior to the time of *Salat Fajr*, and continues until the completion of sunset, i.e., the time of *Salat Maghrib*. As such, the day of fasting is longer when *Ramadan* occurs in the summer and shorter in the winter. During the time of fasting, food, drink, sexual activity, tobacco, gum, and the ingestion of any and all substances are prohibited. Frivolous and worldly talk is discouraged, and Muslims are to be especially vigilant in focusing on the spiritual aspects of their lives. Each day during *Ramadan*, a Muslim is encouraged to read 1/30th of the *Qur'an*, so that by the completion of the month of Ramadan, the entire *Qur'an* will have been read with a receptive and meditative attitude. Furthermore, throughout the entire month of *Ramadan*, it is preferable for Muslims to participate in a series of supplemental prayers each night following *Salat Al-'Isha*.

D6. *RAMADAN* AND REVELATION

Over and above fasting, *Ramadan* holds a special place in the Islamic calendar, for tradition holds that it was during the last ten days of the month of *Ramadan* that revelation was first given to Prophet Muhammad. Within Islam, the time of this first revelation is referred to as the Night of *Qadr*, i.e., the night of power. A chapter in the *Qur'an* by the name of *Al-Qadr* reads:

> We have indeed revealed this (message) in the night of power: and what will explain to thee what the night of power is? The night of power is better than a thousand months. Therein come down the angels and the Spirit by Allah's permission, on every errand: peace!...this until the rise of morn! (*Qur'an* 97: 1-5)

The following English translation of the meanings of several *Ahadith* provide additional references for this tradition.

Narrated Ibn 'Abbas: "The Prophet said: 'Look for the Night of *Qadr* in the last ten nights of Ramadan'". (*Al-Bukhari, Hadith # 3: 238*; see also *Al-Bukhari, Ahadith 3:237,239*)

Narrated Abu Salama: "...In the morning of the 20th of Ramadan, the Prophet delivered a sermon saying, '...I have been shown the Night of Qadr, but have forgotten its date, but it is in the odd nights of the last ten nights..." (*Al-Bukhari, Hadith # 1: 777*)

Scholars hold different opinions as to the night, which is the Night of Qadr. Some are of the opinion that it is the 21st, some say the 23rd, others say the 25th, and still others say it is the 29th. Some say that it varies from year to year, but is always among the last ten nights of Ramadan. Most scholars, though, vouch for the 27th. Ahmad recorded, with a Sahih chain, from Ibn 'Umar that the Prophet said: "He who likes to seek that night should do so on the 27th." Ubayy ibn K'ab said: "By Allah, and there is no god but He, it is during Ramadan — and he swore to that — and by Allah, I know what night it is. It is the night during which the Prophet ordered us to make prayers, the night of the 27th. Its sign is that the sun rises in the morning white and without any rays." This is related by Muslim, Abu Dawud, Ahmad, and by Al-Tirmidhi who called it Sahih. (*Fiqh Al-Sunnah*, volume 3, page 145a)

Tradition further holds that every *Ramadan* following the initial Night of *Qadr*, and throughout the remainder of the lifetime of Prophet Muhammad, the angel Jibril (Gabriel) would rehearse the *Qur'an* with Prophet Muhammad.

Narrated Ibn 'Abbas: "Allah's Apostle was the most generous of all the people, and he used to be more generous in the month of Ramadan when Gabriel used to meet him. Gabriel used to meet him every night in Ramadan to study the Holy Qur'an carefully together. Allah's Apostle used to become more generous than the fast wind when he met Gabriel." (*Al-Bukhari, Hadith* #4:443; also see *Al-Bukhari, Ahadith* # 1:5, 3:126, 4:754, and 6:519)

D7. THE REWARDS OF *RAMADAN*

As might already be gathered from the preceding discussion, tradition holds that there are numerous rewards and virtues associated with the month of *Ramadan*. A brief synopsis of these are noted in *Fiqh Al-Sunnah*, with the current author's editorial insertions included in square brackets.

Abu Huraira reported that the Prophet, upon whom be peace, said: "The blessed month [Ramadan] has come to you. Allah has made fasting during it obligatory upon you. During it, the gates to Paradise are opened and the gates to hellfire are locked, and the devils are chained. There is a night [Night of Qadr] (during the month) which is better than a thousand months. Whoever is deprived of its good is really deprived (of something great)." This is related by Ahmad, Al-Nasa'i, and Al-Baihaqi. 'Arfajah testifies to this: "We were with 'Utbah ibn Farqad while he was discussing Ramadan. A companion of the Prophet entered upon the scene. When 'Utbah saw him, he became shy and stopped talking. The man (the companion) spoke about Ramadan, saying: 'I heard the Messenger of Allah say during Ramadan: 'The gates of Hell are closed, the gates of Paradise are opened, and the devils are in chains. An angel calls out: 'O you who intend to do good deeds, have glad tidings. O you who intend to do evil, refrain, until Ramadan is completed.''"

Muslim relates that Abu Huraira reported the Prophet saying: "The time between the five prayers, two consecutive Friday prayers, and two consecutive Ramadans are expiations for all that has happened during that period, provided that one has avoided the grave sins."

Abu Sa'id Al-Khudri reported that the Prophet, upon whom be peace, said: "Whoever fasts the month of Ramadan, obeying all of its limitations and guarding himself against what is forbidden, has in fact atoned for any sins he committed before it." Ahmad and Al-Baihaqi related this hadith with a good chain.

Abu Huraira reported that the Prophet, upon whom be peace, said: "Whoever fasts the month of Ramadan with faith and seeks Allah's pleasure and reward will have his previous sins forgiven." This hadith is related by Ahmad and the compilers of the *sunan*. (*Fiqh Al-Sunnah*, volume 3, page 109)

E. *ZAKAT*

E1. INTRODUCTION

Zakat refers to obligatory charity. Both obligatory and voluntary charity are concepts that are repeatedly endorsed in the *Qur'an*.

And be steadfast in prayer and regular in charity... (*Qur'an* 2:110a)

...it is righteousness — to believe in Allah and the Last Day, and the angels, and the Book, and the messengers; to spend of your substance, out of love for Him, for your kin, for orphans, for the needy, for the wayfarer, for those who ask, and for the ransom of slaves; to be steadfast in prayer, and practice regular charity... (*Qur'an* 2: 177b)

And spend of your substance in the cause of Allah, and make not your own hands contribute to (your) destruction; but do good; for Allah loveth those who do good. (*Qur'an* 2:195)

They ask thee what they should spend (in charity), Say: "Whatever ye spend that is good, is for parents and kindred and orphans and those in want and for wayfarers". And whatever ye do that is good — Allah knoweth it well. (*Qur'an* 2: 215)

They ask thee how much they are to spend; say: "What is beyond your needs." Thus doth Allah make clear to you His signs: in order that ye may consider — (*Qur'an* 2: 219b)

O ye who believe! spend out of (the bounties) We have provided for you... (*Qur'an* 2: 254a)

For those who give in charity, men and women, and loan to Allah a beautiful loan, it shall be increased manifold (to their credit), and they shall have (besides) a liberal reward. (*Qur'an* 57: 18)

And spend something (in charity) out of the substance which We have bestowed on you, before death should come to any of you and he should say, "O my Lord! why didst thou not give me respite for a little while? I should then have given (largely) in charity, and I should have been one of the doers of good." (*Qur'an* 63: 10)

So fear Allah as much as ye can; listen and obey; and spend in charity for the benefit of your own souls. And those saved from the covetousness of their own souls — they are the ones that achieve prosperity. If ye loan to Allah a beautiful loan, He will double it to your (credit), and He will grant you forgiveness: for Allah is most ready to appreciate (service), most forbearing — (*Qur'an* 64: 16-17)

E2. *ZAKAT* VS. TITHING

Zakat has often been compared by Western writers to the Judaeo-Christian concept of tithing. However, such a comparison is highly misleading for several reasons. In what follows, the concept of *Zakat* is explained by contrasting it with tithing, the latter of which was mandated in several passages in the received *Torah*, e.g., in *Deuteronomy* 14:22-29 and in *Numbers* 18:21-32. In making these comparisons, the following contrasts are generalizations, which ignore the special rules of *Zakat* that apply to agricultural produce, livestock, etc. However, these are considerations that affect few Occidentals.

(1) Tithing is based upon one's yearly income, while *Zakat* is based upon one's economic surplus that has been held for one year.

(2) Given # 1, tithing is obligatory on every Christian and Jew who has any income, although this is honored by Christians more as the exception, than the rule. In contrast, *Zakat* is obligatory only upon those Muslims with an economic surplus.

(3) Tithing is based upon a formula of giving 10.0% of one's income. In fact, the word tithe comes from the Old English, meaning the tenth part. In contrast, *Zakat* is based upon a formula of giving 02.5% of one's economic surplus.

(4) Tithes are to be given to the relevant ecclesiastical authority, i.e., the church for Christians, where the money is used to support various building programs (e.g., bricks and mortar for new churches), to pay ministerial and staff salaries, and to otherwise cover the expenses of running the church. Only if the church has an economic surplus does some portion of the tithes go to charity. (In ancient Judaism, the entire tithe was meant for the support of the Levites and the priestly class.[43]) In contrast, it is preferred that *Zakat* go directly from the hand of the one who is giving to the hand of the person in need. This implies that every Muslim has a responsibility to know which of his brothers and sisters are in need. In addition, there are certain approved programs to which *Zakat* can be given.

A couple of hypothetical examples may solidify the contrast between *Zakat* and tithing. As a first example, consider a Christian family consisting of father, mother, and three children, whose yearly income is $15,000. After deducting reasonable expenses, such as rent, food, medical bills, educational bills, etc., the family will probably have no economic surplus, and will probably be in debt. Under a strict interpretation of the Judaeo-Christian concept of tithing, the family is still obligated to turn over $1,500 each year to the church, thus increasing their debt load. In contrast, consider a Muslim family of five with exactly the same income and expenses. Under the rules of *Zakat*, since there is no economic surplus, no *Zakat* is due from the family. Further, because the family has incurred debt in maintaining a subsistence level of existence, the family is actually eligible to receive *Zakat* from those who have an economic surplus!

As a second example, posit a Christian family consisting of a father, a mother, and two children, whose yearly income is $100,000. By the rules of tithing, the family should give $10,000, presumably to the church. In contrast, consider a Muslim family of four with exactly the same income and expenses. Reasonable living expenses (rent, food, clothing, transportation, mandatory taxes, mandatory social security payments — assuming an American family, medical bills, etc.) might easily run up to $60,000, leaving an economic surplus of $40,000. If the family were able to hold that economic surplus for one full year, they would then need to pay $1,000 in *Zakat*, preferably to some Muslim brother or sister in need.

E3. *ZAKAT* VS. *SADAQAH*

Zakat is obligatory charity, i.e., what a Muslim having an economic surplus must pay in charity to the needy. However, a Muslim is encouraged to give additional charity, over and above what is mandatory. This additional charity is totally voluntary, and is known as *Sadaqah*.

F. HAJJ

F1. INTRODUCTION

Because the rites of the *Hajj* pilgrimage have so many points of interface with the Judaeo-Christian tradition, and because this introduction to Islam is primarily written for the Judaeo-Christian reader, the author has covered this pillar of practice in far more detail than he has the preceding four pillars.

The fifth pillar of the practice of Islam is making the pilgrimage to Makkah to perform the rites of *Hajj* at their appointed times during the Islamic month of *Dhul-Hijjah*. Performance of the *Hajj* is incumbent upon every adult Muslim who has the financial and physical ability to do so. This obligation is specified in the following passage from the *Qur'an*, in which Makkah is referred to by an older variant of its name, i.e., Bakka.

> The first house (of worship) appointed for men was that at Bakka; full of blessing and of guidance for all kinds of beings: in it are signs manifest; (for example), the Station of Abraham; whoever enters it attains security; pilgrimage thereto is a duty men owe to Allah — those who can afford the journey; but if any deny faith, Allah stands not in need of any of His creatures. (*Qur'an* 3: 96-97)

The origins of the prescribed pilgrimage to Makkah trace to Prophet Abraham (Ibrahim). Following the building of the Ka'ba (literally "cube"; the Ka'ba is also known as Sacred House and Ancient House) at Makkah by Prophets Abraham and Ismael (*Qur'an* 2:127; 22:26), Allah prescribed the pilgrimage to Makkah as a duty upon the believers.

> Behold! We gave the site, to Abraham, of the (Sacred) House, (saying): "Associate not anything (in worship) with Me; and sanctify My House for those who compass it round, or stand up, or bow, or prostrate themselves (therein in prayer). And proclaim the pilgrimage among men: they will come to thee on foot and (mounted) on every kind of camel, lean on account

of journeys through deep and distant mountain highways; that they may witness the benefits (provided) for them, and celebrate the name of Allah, through the days appointed, over the cattle which He has provided for them (for sacrifice): then eat ye thereof and feed the distressed ones in want. Then let them complete the rites prescribed for them, perform their vows, and (again) circumambulate The Ancient House". Such (is the pilgrimage): whoever honors the sacred rites of Allah, for him it is good in the sight of his Lord... (*Qur'an* 22: 26-30a)

Although the rites of the *Hajj* are rich in symbolic meaning, as will be seen below, the correct performance of the *Hajj* can never be reduced to mere ritual. One must also have the correct intention, attitude, and conduct in performing *Hajj*.

For Hajj are the months well known. If anyone undertakes that duty therein, let there be no obscenity, nor wickedness, nor wrangling in the Hajj. And whatever good ye do, (be sure) Allah knoweth it. And take a provision (with you) for the journey, but the best of provisions is right conduct. So fear Me, O ye that are wise. (*Qur'an* 2: 197)

F2. THE SYMBOLIC MEANING OF *HAJJ*

There are a number of rituals of *Hajj* and '*Umrah*. Each ritual, the performance of the ritual, and the order or progression of the rituals is based upon the manner in which Prophet Muhammad performed *Hajj* in 632 CE. While these rituals may seem foreign and somewhat incomprehensible to non-Muslims, most of these rituals have a symbolic meaning that can be traced back to events in the lives of Prophets Adam and Abraham. In what follows, several of these rituals are explained, as well as their relevant symbolic origins. The rituals that will be considered are those of Arafat, *Hadi*, Maqam Ibrahim, *Ramy, Sa'e, Talbiyah, Tawaf*, and Zamzam. In addition, a brief description is given regarding the Black Stone of Makkah.

ARAFAT. The ritual of Arafat is performed on the ninth of *Dhu'l-Hijja*, and is the most important of the rituals of *Hajj*. It is recorded that Prophet Muhammad said, "Arafat is *Hajj*" (e.g. *Abu Dawud, Hadith* # 1944). Arafat is an area about 12 miles SSE of Makkah, and includes Jebel Rahman (Mount of Mercy). The origins of the Arafat ritual go back to Prophet Adam and to Eve. With regard to that point, it is important to note that according to traditional Islamic belief the Garden of Eden was not located on earth.

> We said: "O Adam! Dwell thou and thy wife in the Garden; and eat of the bountiful things therein as (where and when) ye will; but approach not this tree, or ye run into harm and transgression." Then did Satan make them slip from the (Garden), and get them out of the state (of felicity) in which they had been. We said: "Get ye down, all (ye people), and with enmity between yourselves. On earth will be your dwelling place and your means of livelihood — for a time." (*Qur'an* 2: 35-36)

After their expulsion from the Garden of Eden, Adam and Eve were placed on earth, but they were separated by a vast distance. Because of their supplications and prayers to Him, Allah allowed them to find each other and to reunite at the Mount of Mercy in Arafat. As such, the ritual of Arafat consists of constantly approaching Allah in prayers of supplication, giving praise and thanksgiving, and reading from the *Qur'an*. This activity continues between noon and sunset on the ninth of *Dhu'l-Hijja*. In this way, *Hajjis* commemorate the thanksgiving offered by Adam and Eve upon their reunion on earth.

Arafat is also quite important to Muslims, because it was on the day of Arafat, i.e., the ninth of *Dhu'l-Hijja*, that Allah sent the final revelation to Prophet Muhammad, which revelation perfected and completed the religion of Islam. This revelation finds verbatim expression in the *Qur'an*, the key phrase of which is quoted below.

> This day have I perfected your religion for you, completed My favor upon you, and have chosen for you Islam as your religion. (*Qur'an* 5:3, in part)

BLACK STONE OF MAKKAH. When Prophets Abraham and Ismael built the original building known as the Ka'ba (see Maqam Ibrahim below), one of the stones used in its construction was the famous Black Stone of Makkah, i.e., *Hajr Al-Aswad*. According to Islamic tradition, the Black Stone was brought from heaven to earth by the angel Gabriel, and was given by Gabriel to Prophets Abraham and Ismael for use in constructing the Ka'ba. The Prophet reportedly said (*Al-Tirmidhi, Hadith # 2577*) that the stone was originally whiter than milk, but was turned black by a sinful mankind.

HADI. Hadi refers to a sacrificial animal, and the ritual of *Hadi* consists of making an animal sacrifice in Mina on the 10th of *Dhu'l-Hijja*. For each individual, the sacrifice consists of one lamb or goat. However, seven *Hajjis* may go together to sacrifice either one camel or one cow, instead of making individual sacrifices. Originally, the meat from the sacrifice was given to the poor of Makkah, as well as being eaten by the *Hajjis*. With approximately 2,000,000 *Hajjis* making *Hajj* every year, it is physically impossible for 2,000,000 individual sacrifices to be carried out and for that much meat to be distributed to the poor of Makkah. Today, most *Hajjis* purchase a sacrificial animal, which is then sacrificed for them at a large slaughtering house in Mina. The meat from this sacrifice is then sent to the poor throughout the Muslim countries of the world.

The act of sacrifice on the 10th of *Dhu'l-Hijja* has its origins in the stories of Abraham. The Biblical account of the relevant event is found in *Genesis*, and is quoted below (bold face added).

After these things God tested Abraham. He said to him, "Abraham!" And he said, "Here I am." He said, "Take your son, **your only son**, Isaac, whom you love, and go to the land of Moriah, and offer him there as a burnt offering on one of the mountains that I shall show you." So Abraham rose early in the morning, saddled his donkey, and took two of his young men with him, and his son Isaac; he cut the wood for the burnt offering, and set out and went to the place in the distance that God had shown him. On the third day Abraham looked up and saw the place far away...When they came to the place that God had shown him, Abraham built an altar there and laid the wood in order. He bound his son Isaac, and laid him on the altar, on top of the wood. Then Abraham reached out his hand and took the knife to kill his son. But the angel of the Lord called to him from heaven, and said, "Abraham, Abraham!" And he said, "Here I am." He said, "Do not lay your hand on the boy or do anything to him; for now I know that you fear God, since you have not withheld your son, **your only son**, from me." And Abraham looked up and saw a ram, caught in a thicket by its horns. Abraham went and took the ram and offered it up as a burnt offering instead of his son. (*Genesis* 22: 1-4, 9-13)

The Islamic tradition regarding the sacrifice of Prophet Abraham is in essential agreement with the *Genesis* account, but there are a few important differences. First, the Islamic tradition holds that the sacrifice was made in Mina, not in Moriah. Second, the Islamic tradition holds that it was Prophet Ismael, not Prophet Isaac, who was to be sacrificed. The Islamic tradition maintains that there have been numerous corruptions of the *Bible* over time and that the references to Prophet Isaac in *Genesis* 22 are illustrations of such corruptions of the original text. For example, Muslim scholars note that *Genesis* 22 twice refers to the intended sacrificial victim as being Prophet Abraham's "only son". As *Genesis* 16:15 clearly states that Prophet Ismael was born when Prophet Abraham was 86 years old and as *Genesis* 21:5 clearly states that Prophet Isaac was not born until Prophet Abraham was 100 years old, it stands to reason that Prophet Ismael was Prophet Isaac's senior by 14 years and that the only time Prophet Abraham had an only son was after the birth of Prophet Ismael and before the birth of Prophet Isaac. (Note: this cannot be explained away by positing that Prophet Ismael died before the sacrifice, because *Genesis* 25:7-9 clearly states that both Prophet Ismael and Prophet Isaac buried Prophet Abraham.)

As Abraham sacrificed a ram at Mina in exchange for Ismael, so *Hajjis* sacrifice a lamb as part of their *Hajj*.

MAQAM IBRAHIM. While the Ka'ba has been built and rebuilt on several occasions, the *Qur'an* specifically states that the foundations of the Ka'ba were built by Prophets Abraham and Ismael.

> And remember Abraham and Isma'il raised the foundations of the House (with this prayer): "Our Lord! Accept (this service) from us: for Thou art the all-hearing, the all-knowing." (*Qur'an* 2: 127)

According to *Al-Bukhari* (*Ahadith* # 4: 583-584), Prophet Abraham had to stand on a rock on the ground, in order to lift a rock high enough to place it on the highest row of rocks comprising the walls of the Ka'ba. The rock on which Abraham stood is known as Maqam Ibrahim (the station of Abraham). In remembrance of this event, the *Qur'an* directs Muslims to pray behind the Maqam Ibrahim.

> Remember We made the House a place of assembly for men and a place of safety; and take ye the station of Abraham as a place of prayer; and We covenanted with Abraham and Isma'il that they should sanctify My House for those who compass it round, or use it as a retreat, or bow, or prostrate themselves (therein in prayer). (*Qur'an* 2: 125)

As such, upon completion of *Tawaf* (see below), a Muslim is directed to offer prayer behind Maqam Ibrahim.

RAMY. As already noted, Islamic tradition holds that Abraham was directed to sacrifice his son, Ismael, and that this sacrifice was to take place at Mina. Al-Tabari (1987) reports that on his way from Makkah to Mina with Ismael, Abraham was several times tempted by Satan not to sacrifice Ismael. As each such temptation was presented, Abraham rejected the temptation, and symbolically drove Satan off by throwing small stones at him.

This aspect of the Abrahamic tradition in symbolized in *Hajj* by the act of *Ramy*, or the stoning of a series of three stone pillars (Jamarat Al-'Aqaba, Jamarat Al-Wusta, and Jamarat Al-Sughra) in Mina. The first act of *Ramy* occurs on the 10th of *Dhu'l-Hijja*, when one arrives back in Mina from Muzdalifeh. At this time, only the largest (Jamarat Al-'Aqaba) of the three stone pillars is stoned, and one throws seven small stones one at a time, each stone being the size of a large pea. With each throw, one says *Allahu Akbar* (Allah is greater). On the 11th, 12th, and possibly 13th of *Dhu'l-Hijja*, one repeats the act of *Ramy*. However, on these days, all three pillars are stoned, beginning with Jamarat Al-Sughra, and ending with Jamarat Al-'Aqabah. Each pillar is stoned seven times during each stoning, and with each throw one says *Allahu Akbar*.

SA'E. The act of *Sa'e* is also symbolic of an event in the Abrahamic tradition. According to the Biblical account of *Genesis* 21:8-13, after the weaning of Isaac, which would make Ismael about 16 years old, Sarah grew jealous of Ismael when she saw him playing with Isaac. As such, she requested that Abraham drive Hagar and Ismael away. Abraham was reportedly distressed by this request, but Allah assured Abraham that he should follow Sarah's request. The Biblical story then continues in *Genesis* with the following account.

> So Abraham rose early in the morning, and took bread and a skin of water, and gave it to Hagar, **putting it on her shoulder, along with the child**, and sent her away. And she departed, and wandered about in the wilderness of Beersheba. When the water in the skin was gone, **she cast the child under one of the bushes.** Then she went and sat down opposite him a good way off, about the distance of a bowshot; for she said, "Do not let me look on the death of the child." And as she sat opposite him, she lifted up her voice and wept. And God heard the voice of the boy; and the angel of God called to Hagar from heaven, and said to her, "What troubles you, Hagar? Do not be afraid; for God has heard

the voice of the boy where he is. Come, **lift up the boy and hold him fast with your hand**, for I will make a great nation of him." Then God opened her eyes and she saw a well of water. She went, and filled the skin with water, and gave the boy a drink. (*Genesis* 21: 14-19)

In the above quotation, boldface type has been added to key phrases that illustrate the impossibility of the *Genesis* account of Ismael being about 16 years old at the time. Hagar variously carries Ismael on her shoulder, casts him under a bush, and lifts him up and holds him fast with one hand. These simply are not actions one does with a 16-year-old. Rather, they are actions one might do with an infant. This observation serves as the introduction to the Islamic tradition regarding the above event.

The Islamic tradition, as recorded in *Ahadith* 4: 583-584 of *Al-Bukhari*, preserves an independent account of the separation of Hagar and Ismael from Abraham. Among the differences to be found in the Islamic tradition are the following. (1) The event takes place when Ismael is an infant, before he is weaned, and many years before the birth of Isaac. (2) Rather than Abraham sending his wife and son out of camp on their own, he accompanies them to a place where he eventually leaves them. (3) That place is not Beersheba, but is Makkah, which was then an isolated, barren, and desert valley devoid of civilization. (4) At Makkah, Abraham leaves Hagar and Ismael with only a skin of water and a bag of dates, entrusting their care and survival to Allah. (5) Abraham then returns to Sarah in the Negev of Palestine.

As in the Biblical account, the Islamic tradition notes that Hagar's skin of water is soon emptied. As recorded in *Ahadith* 4:583-584 of *Al-Bukhari*, she and her infant son begin to suffer early dehydration and starvation. This continues to the point where: (1) Hagar's milk supply dries up, and she is no longer able to nurse Ismael; and (2) Ismael begins his death throes. At that point, Hagar frantically begins to look around her for any possible help. Seeing a hill (Safa) a little way in the distance, she desperately climbs to the top of the hill to look for any possible caravan that might be passing by. Seeing none, she climbs down the hill. However, rather than returning to Ismael, she walks to an adjoining hill (Marwah) about 450 meters from Safa. Along the way, despite her weakened physical condition, she inexplicably begins to run for part of the way. Climbing Marwah, she again finds no sign of a passing caravan. She then retreats from Marwah, only to climb Safa again. Still, there is no sign of possible help. In her frantic and desperate state, she then climbs Marwah for a second time, climbs Safa for a third time, climbs Marwah for a third time, climbs Safa for a fourth time, and finally climbs Marwah for a fourth time. Each time she travels from Safa to Marwah, she inexplicably runs for part of the distance.

The above account of Hagar moving back and forth between Safa and Marwah for a total of seven times provides the symbolic meaning of *Sa'e*. Thus, *Sa'e* consists of climbing up Safa, and then traveling back and forth between Safa and Marwah seven times, running part of the way each time one goes from Safa to Marwah. *Sa'e* ends on the fourth ascent of Marwah. During both *'Umra* and *Hajj*, the *Hajji* is required to perform the act of *Sa'e* at set times, thus commemorating and symbolically re-enacting Hagar's desperate attempt to save Ismael. (Note: for the ease of close to two million *Hajjis* attempting to perform *Sa'e* at roughly the same time, the Kingdom of Saudi Arabia has enclosed both hills and the distance between them within the two-story structure of the Grand Mosque. Thus, counting the roof surface, there are three levels on which *Hajjis* may simultaneously perform *Sa'e*.) The rite of *Sa'e* is consistent with the following verse from the *Qur'an*.

> Behold! Safa and Marwah are among the symbols of Allah. So, if those who visit the House in the season or at other times, should compass them round, it is no sin in them. And if anyone obeyeth his own impulse to good — be sure that Allah is He Who recognizeth and knoweth. (*Qur'an* 2: 158)

As to what happened when Hagar ascended Marwah for the

last time, that part of the narrative is presented below under the topic of Zamzam.

TALBIYAH. While journeying to Makkah, and at frequent and various times during the course of *Hajj*, *Hajjis* are encouraged to recite the *Talbiyah*.

> *Labbayk Allahumma Labbayk. Labbayk La Sharika Laka Labbayk. Innal Hamda Wannimata Laka Walmulk. La Sharika Lak.*

The *Talbiyah* can be roughly translated as follows.

> Here I am, O Allah, at Your service, here I am. Here I am, You (are One, and) have no partner, here I am. Truly, all praise and provision are Yours, and so is the dominion and sovereignty. You (are One, and) have no partner.

TAWAF. *Tawaf* consists of circumambulating the Ka'ba seven times in a counter-clockwise direction. Al-Tabari (1989) notes that the act of *Tawaf* at what would later become the eventual site of the Ka'ba was first practiced as an act of worship of Allah by Adam. During both *'Umrah* and *Hajj*, the *Hajji* is required to perform *Tawaf* at certain set times. At such times, up to two million people, body pressed to body, will be simultaneously circumambulating around the Ka'ba.

> Behold! We gave the site, to Abraham, of the (Sacred) House, (Saying): "Associate not anything (in worship) with Me; and sanctify My House for those who compass it round, or stand up, or bow, or prostrate themselves (therein in prayer). (*Qur'an* 22: 26, in part)

> Then let them complete the rites prescribed for them, perform their vows, and (again) circumambulate The Ancient House. (*Qur'an* 22: 29)

It should be noted that counter-clockwise circumambulation also finds expression in the Jewish tradition, reaching back at least 3,000 years into the distant past. For example, one notes the rituals surrounding the Feast of Booths or Tabernacles (Hebrew=*Sukkot*), also known as the Festival of Ingathering (Hebrew=*Hag ha-Asif*). The Feast of Booths was the celebration of the fall fruit and olive harvest in ancient Israel, lasted for seven days, and was the most important of the three pilgrim festivals in ancient Israel. According to the rituals prescribed for this feast in the *Mishna* tractate *Sukka*, the Jewish priests made a daily circumambulation of the altar at the temple in Jerusalem (or of the synagogue dais in non-temple times) and a seven-fold circuit of the altar at the temple in Jerusalem (or of the synagogue dais in non-temple times) on the last day of the festival.

ZAMZAM. Returning to the Islamic account (*Al-Bukhari, Ahadith* #4:538-584) of Hagar and Ismael having been left in Makkah by Abraham, the current report of that story had previously ended with the account of Hagar having climbed Marwah for the fourth time. One can now continue the narrative by noting that when Hagar stood on Marwah for the fourth time, she heard a voice. Looking down into the valley by where Ismael was dying under the scrub bush, she saw the angel Gabriel standing there. Gabriel then struck the ground with the heel of his foot. Where his foot hit, water came gushing up out of the ground. Despite her precarious and weakened state, Hagar struggled down off Marwah, and hurried as best she could to Ismael and to the newly formed Well of Zamzam. She scooped the running water into her water skin, and drank her fill. Miraculously, her milk supply returned, and she suckled Ismael, who was unexpectedly revived by his mother's milk.

The Biblical account in *Genesis* limits the above narrative to a single verse, which is quoted below.

Then God opened her eyes and she saw a well of water. She went, and filled the skin with water, and gave the boy a drink. (*Genesis* 21: 19)

As can be seen, the *Genesis* account is extremely sparse, and omits much of the detail found in the Islamic tradition. However, *Psalms* refers to the Well of Zamzam, although not by name, and specifically locates it in Baca, an early variant of the name Makkah.

> Happy are those whose strength is in you, in whose heart are the highways to Zion. As they go through the valley of Baca they make it a place of springs; the early rain also covers it with pools. (*Psalms* 84: 5-6)

Rather miraculously, the Well of Zamzam continues to exist some 4,000 years after its founding by the angel Gabriel, and it continues to be a source of plentiful water, serving close to two million *Hajjis* each year, as well as serving the residents of Makkah. With the expansion of the Grand Mosque over the years, the Well of Zamzam has come to be located within the actual walls of the Grand Mosque, and is about halfway between the Ka'ba and Safa.

In remembrance of Allah having saved Hagar and Ismael through Gabriel's digging of the Well of Zamzam, it is tradition that *Hajjis* drink from the Well of Zamzam immediately after performing the post *Tawaf* prayers behind the Maqam Ibrahim.

F3. TYPES OF *HAJJ*

There are three types of *Hajj*, including *Hajj Al-Ifrad, Hajj Al-Qiran*, and *Hajj Al-Tamattu*. *Hajj Al-Ifrad* consists of making *Hajj*, i.e., the major pilgrimage, without making *'Umrah*, i.e., the minor pilgrimage. *Hajj Al-Qiran* consists of making *'Umrah* and *Hajj* as one continuous act. *Hajj Al-Tamattu* consists of making *'Umrah*, taking a break from the pilgrimage, and then making *Hajj*. As *Hajj Al-Tamattu* is probably the most commonly performed of the three types of *Hajj*, it is presented below.

F4. *HAJJ AL-TAMMATU*

Hajj Al-Tamattu consists of the following steps: (1) performing *'Umrah*, i.e., the minor pilgrimage, at some point in the three months of *Hajj*, but before the actual rites of *Hajj* begin in the third month of *Hajj*; (2) taking a break from the rites of pilgrimage; and (3) then performing *Hajj*, i.e., the major pilgrimage, beginning on the eighth of *Dhu'l-Hijja*. *Hajj Al-Tamattu* is one of the three forms of *Hajj*, and is fulfillment of the following injunction from the *Qur'an*.

> And complete the *Hajj* or *'Umrah* in the service of Allah. (*Qur'an* 2: 196)

'UMRAH. As one approaches Makkah from any direction, one first reaches a point of *Miqat*. There are five exact points of *Miqat* (Al-Juhfah, Dhul-Hulaifah, Dhat-'irq, Qarn Al-Manazil, and Yalamlam), each being somewhere between 45 and 450 kilometers from Makkah. At the *Miqat*, or before reaching the *Miqat*, one must enter the state of *Ihram*. Entering the state of *Ihram* consists of the following steps: (1) removal of all superfluous body hair; (2) bathing; (3) putting on *Ihram* clothing (see below); (4) stating the intention to perform the *'Umrah* portion of *Hajj Al-Tamattu*, i.e., *Labbayk Allahumma 'Umrah Mutamati'an Biha 'Ilal Hajj* (I am responding to you, my Lord, by *'Umrah* with *Tamattu Hajj*); and (5) maintaining the state of *Ihram* (see below) until the completion of the rites of *'Umrah*.

Ihram clothing differs between men and women. For men, *Ihram* clothing consists of two clean, white seamless pieces of cloth. One piece is wrapped around the lower body, beginning well above the navel, and extending down below the knees. One then rolls the top portion of this cloth down to just above the navel, in order to create a "belt" to hold the garment in place. The second piece of cloth is worn over the upper body. Sandals or thongs may also be worn, so long as they have absolutely no stitching or sewing. These three articles (lower cloth, upper cloth, and sandals) are the only clothing that one may wear, and none of them may be stitched or sewn. In this way, i.e., in the state of *Ihram*, all men approach Allah dressed identically. No matter their state in life, no matter their wealth or poverty, no matter their power or helplessness, each man comes before Allah dressed no differently than his brothers. One is reminded that all men are equal before Allah, differing only in piety and faith. One is reminded that the temporal, secular, and financial differences that attempt to divide men in this earthly life are in reality of no consequence. The *Ihram* clothing for women consists of more regular clothing: normal underwear; a loose, ankle-length dress, which is modest and which hides one's figure; and a *Hijab* (scarf) to cover one's hair completely. During *Ihram*, a woman is prohibited from covering her hands or face, i.e., she is not allowed to veil.

While in the state of *Ihram*, one is prohibited from shaving, cutting hair, clipping nails, using perfumes or colognes, killing or hunting animals, sexual intercourse, making or entertaining a marriage proposal, and entering into a marriage contract.

Having entered into the state of *Ihram* at or before reaching a *Miqat*, one is directed to journey to Makkah in the most direct and expedient manner. Upon arriving at Makkah, one is ready to begin the rites of *'Umrah*, preferably after bathing and making formal ablution (*Wudu*). The rites of *'Umrah* are then performed in the following sequential steps.

Firstly, the Grand Mosque is entered, and *Tawaf* is performed around the Ka'ba. In performing *Tawaf*, one begins at the corner of the Ka'ba containing the Black Stone of Makkah, and says *Allahu Akbar* (Allah is greater). Each time one approaches the Black Stone during a circumambulation, one intones from *Qur'an* 2:201:

> *Rabana Atina Fi Al-Dunya Hasanata Wa Fi Al-Akhirati Hasanata Wa Qina'atdaba Al-Nar.*

A translation of which would be:

> Our Lord! give us good in this world and good in the Hereafter, and defend us from the torment of the Fire.

Each time the Black Stone is actually reached, one again says *Allahu Akbar*. In addition, there are certain rituals regarding how the upper cloth of the male *Hajji* is to be worn during the different rounds of *Tawaf*, as well as regarding the pace of movement in the different circumambulations comprising the *Tawaf* (male *Hajjis* perform the first three rounds at an increased speed). Throughout the entire *Tawaf*, each *Hajji* is to praise Allah, make supplication to Allah, and quote the *Qur'an* on a continuous basis.

Secondly, upon completion of *Tawaf*, one prays a two-*Rakat* prayer that includes reciting the appropriate Qur'anic passages, giving praise to Allah, begging forgiveness from Allah, etc., at their appropriate times. Preferably, this prayer is given behind the Maqam Ibrahim. However, wherever one may happen to be when performing this prayer, the *Hajji* must be facing the Ka'ba. (All Muslims face the Ka'ba for each and every prayer they make, wherever they may happen to be.)

Thirdly, one then walks over to the Well of Zamzam, where one drinks one's fill of this water that has continued to flow for over 4,000 years.

Fourthly, having drunk at Zamzam, one now walks to Safa. Arriving on Safa, the *Hajji* intones *Allahu Akbar* three times, and makes supplication to Allah. One then performs the rite of *Sa'e,* traveling back and forth between Safa and Marwah a total of seven times. Each time the male *Hajji* moves from Safa to Marwah, he runs part of the way in commemoration of Hagar's running for part of the way between these two hills. Throughout the entire rite of *Sa'e*, *Hajjis* praise Allah, and make supplication to Allah. One ends *Sa'e* on Marwah, having traveled a total of about 1.9 miles throughout *Sa'e*.

Fifthly, the male *Hajji* either shaves his head or cuts his hair. The female *Hajja* simply cuts her hair.

Sixthly, 'Umrah has now been completed. The state of *Ihram* for 'Umrah has now ended, and *Hajjis* may return to their normal dress as soon as convenient.

HAJJ. The *Hajj* portion of the rites of *Hajj Al-Tamattu* begins in the morning of the eighth of *Dhul-Hijjah*. The rites of *Hajj* consist of the following steps.

Firstly, on the morning of the eighth of the Islamic month of *Dhul-Hijjah*, one enters the state of *Ihram*, as one had previously done for *'Umrah*. However, this time the intention of *Ihram* is stated as *Labbayka Allahumma Hajjan* (O Allah, I am responding to Your call by making *Hajj*). The *Hajji* then prays a two-*Rakat* prayer, and journeys from Makkah to Mina, which is about five to six kilometers east of Makkah. Along the way, the *Hajji* recites the *Talbiyah*, and is to arrive at Mina before noon.

Secondly, one stays at Mina from before noon on the eighth of *Dhul-Hijjah* until sunrise on the ninth of *Dhul-Hijjah*. The *Hajjis'* only obligation during this time is to perform the five daily prayers of Islam. However, those prayers that usually consist of four *Rakat* (*Dhur* at noon, *'Asr* at mid-afternoon, and *'Isha* after the true darkness of night) are shortened to two *Rakat* each. *Fajr* (pre-sunrise prayer) remains two *Rakat*, and *Maghrib* (sunset prayer) remains three *Rakat*.

Thirdly, at sunrise on the ninth of *Dhul-Hijjah*, one journeys from Mina to Arafat, which is about 20 kilometers southeast of Makkah. Along the way, the *Hajjis* continually recite *Talbiyah* and say *Allahu Akbar*.

Fourthly, at Arafat, the rites of Arafat are performed. These consist of: (1) listening to the *Khutbah* (sermon) at Masjid Namira (Namira Mosque); (2) praying the *Dhur* and *'Asr* prayers one right after the other at the time of *Dhur*, and shortening each prayer to two *Rakat*; (3) spending all afternoon praising and glorifying Allah, asking Allah for forgiveness, and repenting to and supplicating Allah; (4) leaving Arafat for Muzdalifah (about eight to nine kilometers north of Arafat) after sunset, and reciting *Talbiyah* quietly along the way.

Fifthly, at Muzdalifah, the *Hajjis* pray the *Maghrib* and *'Isha* prayers one right after the other, shortening the *'Isha* prayer to two *Rakat*. One then scrounges around to find seven pebbles, which will be used back at Mina for the stoning (*Ramy*) of Jamarat Al-Aqabah. After midnight, certain *Hajjis* (women, the old, and the weak), as well as those needed to accompany them (e.g., a husband accompanies his wife), are allowed to begin the journey back to Mina. Other *Hajjis* must wait until the pre-sunrise prayer.

Sixthly, arriving back at Mina on the 10th of *Dhul-Hijjah*, the *Hajjis* perform the rite of *Ramy*, limiting their stoning to Jamarat Al-Aqabah.

Seventhly, after sunrise on the 10th of *Dhul-Hijjah* (any time after sunrise on the 10th until sunset on the 13th), the rite of *Hadi* is performed, and the sacrifice is made and offered. The *Hajji* then travels to Makkah to perform the rites of *Tawaf* and *Sa'e* as previously done during '*Umrah*, followed by shaving the head or cutting the hair. At this point, the state of *Ihram* has ended. (Actually, the three rites of *Hadi*, *Tawaf* and *Sa'e*, and the hair cutting can be performed in any order, although *Tawaf*, *Sa'e*, and the ritual hair cutting must be performed on the 10th of *Dhul-Hijjah*. If *Tawaf* and *Sa'e* are completed after the other two rites, a partial release from *Ihram* exists after completing *Hadi* and the hair cutting. In this partial release from *Ihram*, the *Hajji* may engage in all normal activities, except for sexual intercourse. The *Hajji* will then only be fully released from *Ihram* after performing *Tawaf* and *Sa'e*.)

Eighthly, returning from Makkah to Mina, the *Hajjis*' only obligations are as follows: (1) to pray the five daily prayers, shortening those prayers that are normally four *Rakat* to two *Rakat*; and (2) to perform the rite of *Ramy* after true noon on the 11th, 12th, and possibly 13th of *Dhul-Hijjah*. Each time during *Ramy*, the order of stoning is from the smallest pillar to the largest, i.e., from Al-Sughra to Al-Wusta to Al-'Aqabah.

Ninthly, the *Hajjis* leave Mina for Makkah before sunset on either the 12th or 13th of *Dhul-Hijjah*. The final act of *Hajj* is then to make the farewell *Tawaf* around the Ka'ba. Shortly after the farewell *Tawaf* has been completed, the *Hajjis* are to leave Makkah. The *Hajj* has now been completed.

G. SUMMARY

The five pillars of practice in Islam are *Shahadah* (the confession or testimonial of belief), *Salat* (the five daily prayers of worship), *Sawm* (fasting during *Ramadan*), *Zakat* (mandatory charity from one's economic surplus), and *Hajj* (the major pilgrimage to Makkah). These constitute the essential practices of Islam.

> ...My father 'Umar b. Khattab told me: "One day we were sitting in the company of the Messenger of Allah (may peace be upon him) when there appeared before us a man dressed in extremely white clothes, his hair extraordinary black. There were no signs of travel on him. None amongst us recognized him. At last he sat with the Apostle (peace be upon him). He knelt before him, placed his palms on his thighs, and said: 'Muhammad, inform me about Al-Islam.' The Messenger of Allah (peace be upon him) said: 'Al-Islam implies that you testify that there is no god but Allah and that Muhammad is the messenger of Allah, and you establish prayer, pay Zakat, observe the fast of Ramadan, and perform pilgrimage to the (House) if you are solvent enough (to bear the expense of) the journey.' He (the inquirer) said: 'You have told the truth.'...Then he (the inquirer) went on his way...He (the Holy Prophet) remarked: 'He was Gabriel (the angel). He came to you in order to instruct you in matters of religion.'" (*Muslim, Hadith # 1*; see parallels in *Al-Bukhari, Ahadith* 1: 47 and 6: 300, as well as in *Al-Nawawi, Hadith # 2*.)

However, it should be noted that at times Muslims also refer to *Jihad* as a "sixth pillar" of practice in Islam. Because of its importance within Islam, because *Jihad* has garnered so much attention in the wake of the heinous tragedy of September 11, 2001, and because the Western media so typically misrepresents and distorts both the meaning and the concept of Islamic *Jihad* in its broadcast and print coverage of current events, the Islamic meaning and concept of *Jihad* is summarized in the following chapters.

Notes

38. (A) *Abu Dawud, Ahadith* # 494-496. (B) *Fiqh Al-Sunnah,* volume 1, page 80.

39. (A) *Al-Bukhari, Ahadith* #1:301, 303, 317, 318. (B) *Fiqh Al-Sunnah,* volume 1, pages 71 and 80.

40. (A) *Qur'an* 4:101. (B) *Al-Bukhari, Ahadith* # 1:346; 4:101-103. (C) *Fiqh Al-Sunnah,* volume 2, pages 103, 104a, 105, 108, 112, 115, 118, and 119a.

41. (A) *Al-Bukhari, Ahadith* # 142, 159-162, 164-167, 186, 190-192, 196, 198, 201-205. (B) *Muslim, Ahadith* # 436-437. (C) *Abu Dawud, Ahadith* # 97, 106-165. (D) *Malik, Ahadith* # 31-38. (E) *Fiqh Al-Sunnah,* volume 1, pages 27-32.

42. "The father of Qasim." This is merely another way of referring to Prophet Muhammad, as Qasim was his firstborn son.

43. (A) Leon-Dufour X (1983). (B) *Numbers* 18:21.

Chapter 7

Jihad

But Allah doth call to the home of peace: He doth guide whom
He pleaseth to a way that is straight. (*Qur'an* 10: 25)

And the servants of (Allah) most gracious are those who
walk on the earth in humility, and when the ignorant address
them, they say, "Peace!"; (*Qur'an* 25: 63)

A. INTRODUCTION

The seeds of this and the following two chapters were planted
in September of 2000, in the wake of the Palestinian *Intifada*
(uprising; literally, a throwing off) against the occupation of
Palestinian land and the exploitation of the Palestinian people by
Israel. As reports of suicide bombings and of attacks against Israeli
civilians, including women and children, began to proliferate,
many Muslims became increasingly discomforted with what
appeared to be clear violations of Islam that allegedly were being
perpetrated in the name of Islam. This discomfort and distress
were greatly exacerbated in the spring of 2001, as reports begin to
circulate in the media about a group of tourists that was kidnapped
by a so-called Islamic resistance group known as *Abu Sayyaf,*
a group that was allegedly fighting for an independent Islamic
state in the southern portion of the Philippines. Discomfort and
distress turned to disgust as the news media reported that at least
one of the kidnapped hostages had been beheaded.

Devout Muslims were shocked and dismayed that a few self-
professed Muslims could so pervert the teachings of Islam as to
attempt to justify such hideous abominations as suicide bombings,
attacks against and the murder of civilian non-combatants, and
the killing of hostages. They were also appalled at the evident
"mission creep" that was beginning to surface in these acts of
terror. Stone throwing by Palestinian youth had given way to
suicide bombings and beheadings.

On September 11, 2001, four passenger planes were hijacked in the United States — two being crashed into the World Trade Center, one being crashed into the Pentagon, and one crashing in the Pennsylvania countryside. The "mission creep" of terrorism had now entered the phase of mass destruction, and the escalation of terrorism had journeyed from throwing rocks to crashing fuel-laden airplanes into skyscrapers. Bumps and bruises from thrown rocks had given way to the premeditated murder of approximately 3,000 individuals, almost all of them civilian non-combatants.

In the aftermath of that tragedy, Muslim voices began to be heard throughout the American media, each correctly claiming that Islam was a religion of peace and that Islam did not condone the sort of actions conducted by the hijackers. As this chorus of previously silent voices began to reach a crescendo, one could not help wondering how many non-Muslim Americans were becoming increasingly skeptical about the sentiments expressed in this litany. After all, where were these Muslim voices of rationality and restraint during the suicide bombings in Palestine? Where were they when Filipino guerrillas kidnapped and executed hostages? Why was it that they appeared to surface only in the wake of the World Trade Center massacre and its accompanying threat of a massive backlash against Muslims in America?

Given these musings, it seemed reasonable that non-Muslim Americans might be reassured by being presented with those specific fundamentals of Islam that prohibit all of the acts of terrorism previously noted. After all, it is much easier to dismiss a possibly self-serving chorus of voices chanting "peace" than it is to dismiss the actual scriptures and religious teachings that serve as the foundation for that chant.

Because the topic of *Jihad* is so often erroneously presented by the Western media and because *Jihad* is an issue of such grave concern to many Occidentals in the aftermath of September 11, 2001, the present chapter and the two subsequent chapters present *Jihad* in somewhat more detail than would otherwise have been done.

B. A DISCLAIMER

In the past, I have occasionally had the displeasure of watching a televised discussion on the Middle East, in which the conversation degenerated into an acrimonious exchange of who did what to whom, with each discussant attempting to use the indiscretions of the other side as a justification for the indiscretions of his own side. Quite frankly, this type of endeavor has all the edification of two young children arguing about who hit whom first, and of each attempting to use the other's prior punch as a reason to throw at least one more punch at the other. If it weren't for the fact that the actual Middle Eastern issues being discussed in these exchanges typically involve killing instead of roundhouse, childish swings of prepubescent fists, the discussants might be amusing. As amusement is far from the purpose of this discussion, this and the following two chapters avoid all such arguments and rationales.

Quite frankly, it is necessary to uncouple the issue of what is and what is not allowed within the Islamic concept of war from such issues as the Israeli-Palestinian conflict, American foreign policy in the Middle East, etc. As a Muslim who has visited Palestine on five different occasions in the last nine years, I am greatly distressed by the injustices perpetrated upon the Palestinian people by the Israeli occupation. As an American, I have grave objections to the history and pattern of American foreign policy in the Middle East. However, as deep as my distress and objections are, I realize that Israeli abuses and American foreign policy have absolutely no relevance to and bearing upon the Islamic limits of war, and are therefore not further addressed in this discussion. With regard to this point, others have previously noted that: "It is a well-established Qur'anic precept that the injustice of others does not excuse one's own injustice." [44]

Islam and the Islamic limits of war are defined first and foremost by the *Qur'an*, i.e., the verbatim revelation received by Prophet Muhammad from Allah via Jibril (Gabriel). In addition,

Islam and the Islamic limits of war are defined by the recorded teachings of Prophet Muhammad. These teachings are religiously authoritative and binding upon all Muslims. Therefore, it is solely to the *Qur'an* and to the *Ahadith* that one must turn in considering the issues of what is and what is not permissible behavior for Muslims during times of war.

C. THE CONCEPT OF *JIHAD*

Before turning to the proposed discussion of the Islamic limits of war, it is important to define the word *Jihad*. The Western media appears to delight in mistranslating *Jihad* as "Holy War", thus creating an almost automatic reflex of fear and disgust among non-Muslims whenever they hear the word *Jihad*. Such systematic mistranslation fosters hatred and intolerance of the Islamic religion. As such, the correct meaning of *Jihad* needs to be elucidated, and non-Muslim Occidentals need to understand what is actually meant by *Jihad* before entertaining a visceral reaction to the word.

The noun *Jihad* is from the verb *Jahada*, which means to strive or to exert. Thus, the correct translation of *Jihad* is striving, exertion, or effort. Within the Islamic context, *Jihad* means striving for the sake of Allah. Thus, any activity in which one strives for the sake of Allah is *Jihad*. In fact, the most prevalent form of *Jihad* is preaching or religious and moral exhortation, i.e., *Da'wah*. For example, this book and the author's previous books on Islam are expressions of *Jihad*, but are hardly examples of Holy War or of violence.

Jihad-as-exhortation may take many forms. The verbal invitation to non-Muslims to enter into the fold of Islam is *Jihad*–as-exhortation. Offering polite, verbal disapproval of the traditional worship of non-Muslims is *Jihad*-as exhortation. Verbal firmness in presenting the truth, especially as it relates to issues of religion, morality, and justice is *Jihad*-as exhortation. Educating others about the *Qur'an* and its message of divine revelation is *Jihad*-as-exhortation.

Furthermore, of the 36 times that *Jihad* and its derivatives occur in the *Qur'an*, not one instance refers to actual war. The following verses are representative of this fact.

> And strive (*Jihad*) in His cause as ye ought to strive, (with sincerity and under discipline)... (*Qur'an* 22:78)

> And if strive (*Jihad*) (with might and main), they do so for their own souls: for Allah is free of all needs from all creation. (*Qur'an* 29:6)

In practicing *Da'wah* as a means of *Jihad*, the Muslim *Dai'* (preacher or exhorter) has several responsibilities. He is to make people more aware of their true, spiritual identity. He is to inform them that they as individuals have a task to fulfill and that their task consists of: faith and belief in the *Tawheed* (Oneness) of Allah; the worship of Allah; and living their lives in an appropriate manner and with righteous conduct. He is then to leave them to make their decision free of any external compulsion — more on this in the following section. However, he may remind them of the divine rewards and punishments that will follow as a result of their decision.

It is this *Da'wah* or *Jihad*-as-exhortation that is enjoined upon Muslims in the following passages from the *Qur'an*.

> Let there arise out of you a band of people inviting to all that is good, enjoining what is right, and forbidding what is wrong: they are the ones to attain felicity. (*Qur'an* 3: 104)

> Invite (all) to the way of thy Lord with wisdom and beautiful preaching; and argue with them in ways that are best and most gracious: for thy Lord knoweth best, who have strayed from His path, and who receive guidance. (*Qur'an* 16: 125)

> Who is better in speech than one who calls (men) to Allah, works righteousness, and says, "I am of those who bow in Islam"? (*Qur'an* 4: 33)

Therefore listen not to the unbelievers, but strive (*Jihad*) against them with the utmost strenuousness with the (Qur'an). (*Qur'an 25: 52*)

How does one strive against someone with the *Qur'an*? Quite obviously, the *Qur'an* is not a sword or an implement of war, and one is not going to find an article on the *Qur'an* in *Jane's Defense Weekly* or in the *International Defense Review*. The *Qur'an* consists of words of revelation from Allah, and one strives against others with the *Qur'an* through the medium of preaching and verbal exhortation, whether in oral or written form. However, even in striving against others with the verbal message of *Da'wah*, the Muslim is directed to use "wisdom and beautiful preaching" and to argue "in ways that are best and most gracious."

As the above should illustrate, *Jihad*-as-exhortation is a far cry from holy war. Furthermore, it should be noted that Allah's words direct Muslims to strive in *Jihad*-as-exhortation "with the utmost strenuousness", suggesting that this type of *Jihad* is the greatest of all kinds of *Jihad*, a position taken by such famed Muslim scholars as Al-Nawawi, Ibn Rushed (Averroes), Imam Bahhouti, and Muhammad Al-Buti. This conclusion is echoed in the following *Hadith*, in which Prophet Muhammad emphasized the superiority of *Jihad*-as-exhortation.

> Abu Sa'id Al-Khudri reported the Apostle of Allah (may peace be upon him) as saying: "The best fighting (*Jihad*) in the path of Allah is (to speak) a word of justice to an oppressive ruler." (*Abu Dawud, Hadith # 4330*)

What should be the nature of that "word of justice to an oppressive ruler"? The instructions given to Prophet Moses and his brother, Prophet Aaron, serve as an example to all Muslims. One is to speak mildly, and not belligerently.

> Go, both of you, to Pharaoh, for he has indeed transgressed all bounds; but speak to him mildly; perchance he may take warning or fear (Allah). (*Qur'an 20: 43-44*)

In summary, *Jihad* means effort, striving, or exertion, and the highest form of *Jihad* is *Jihad*-as-exhortation. *Jihad* may also refer to an individual's struggle against his own base instincts or to any other effort engaged in for the sake of Allah, including marriage, parenting, being a good neighbor, etc. A man engages in *Jihad* when, for the sake of Allah, he strives to be a good husband to his wife and a good father to his children. A person practices *Jihad* when, for the sake of Allah, he attempts to benefit his neighbor and his fellow man. A person even practices *Jihad* when, for the sake of Allah, he expends the effort to smile at others. *Jihad* does not mean "Holy War", although it is possible that *Jihad* might include fighting for the sake of Allah. However, fighting or war is only one, small aspect of *Jihad*.

Ibn Rushed (Averroes) wrote in his *Muqaddimaat* that there were at least four primary types of *Jihad*: *Jihad* by the heart; *Jihad* by the tongue; *Jihad* by the hand; and *Jihad* by the sword. *Jihad* by the heart refers to struggling to make faith a spiritual force in one's own life. *Jihad* by the tongue is *Da'wah*, i.e., preaching the universal truth of Islam and exhorting oneself and one's listeners to live a life of righteous conduct. *Jihad* by the hand consists of doing good works and righteous deeds. Only *Jihad* by the sword constitutes *Jihad*-as-war, and, as noted above, Prophet Muhammad implied that *Jihad*-as-war is not the highest form of *Jihad*.

Nonetheless, the American media continues to insist on mistranslating *Jihad* as "Holy War", despite the fact that the Arabic equivalent of "Holy War" appears nowhere in the *Qur'an*, despite the fact that the term "Holy War" owes its popularity and conceptual foundation to its use by Christians in justifying the *Reconquista* (Christian conquest of Muslim Andalusia) and the Occidental barbarisms of the Christian Crusades, and despite the fact that Islam has no equivalent concept to the medieval Christian belief in *sacrum bellum* (Holy War).

D. *JIHAD*-AS-EXHORTATION AND FREEDOM FROM COMPULSION

Literally translated, Islam means submission or surrender, i.e., submission to Allah. However, as noted in chapter I, the three-letter, Arabic root word (*Slm* in the Roman alphabet) from which Islam is derived is the same three-letter root word from which the Arabic word for peace (*Salam*) is derived. Thus, one can see that the very name of Islam incorporates the concept of peace. Islam is a religion of peace, and advocates a peaceful co-existence among differing peoples and nations, regardless of ethnic or racial descent and regardless of religious orientation.

> O mankind! We created you from a single (pair) of a male and a female, and made you into nations and tribes, that ye may know each other (not that ye may despise each other). Verily the most honored of you in the sight of Allah is (he who is) the most righteous of you. And Allah has full knowledge and is well-acquainted (with all things). (*Qur'an* 49: 13)

> Narrated Abu Huraira: "The Prophet (peace be upon him) said: 'Allah, Most High, has removed from you the pride of the pre-Islamic period and its boasting in ancestors. One is only a pious believer or a miserable sinner. You are sons of Adam, and Adam came from dust. Let the people cease to boast about their ancestors. They are merely fuel in Jahannam (hell); or they will certainly be of less account with Allah than the beetle that rolls dung with its nose.'" (*Abu Dawud, Hadith # 5097*)

> Narrated Uqbah ibn 'Amir: "Allah's messenger (peace be upon him) said: 'These genealogies of yours are not a cause of reviling anyone. You are all sons of Adam, just as one sa' (a measure of volume) is near another when you have not filled it. No one has superiority over another except in religion and piety. It is enough reproach for a man to be foul, obscene, and niggardly.'" (*Al-Tirmidhi, Hadith # 4910*)

The Western media and academia have often presented Islam as being a religion that proselytizes by the sword and that forces conversion upon non-Muslims by the threat of death or armed conflict. In fact, nothing could be farther from the truth. Muslims are commanded by Allah to practice *Jihad*-as-exhortation, but this does not mean that Islam does not respect the rights of others to worship as they please. In fact, the *Qur'an* establishes freedom of religion as one of the fundamental rights of all people.

> Let there be no compulsion in religion: truth stands out clear from error: whoever rejects evil and believes in Allah hath grasped the most trustworthy handhold, that never breaks. And Allah heareth and knoweth all things. (*Qur'an* 2: 256)

As noted previously, it is a Muslim's duty to practice *Jihad*-as-exhortation by inviting non-Muslims into Islam, by warning others (and themselves) about false religious practice, by spreading the revelation contained within the *Qur'an* to others, and by speaking up for justice, for morality, and against tyranny. However, as the immediately above quoted passage from the *Qur'an* illustrates, such *Jihad*-as-exhortation does not and cannot take the form of compelling a non-Muslim to become a Muslim. Within the pages of the *Qur'an*, the words of Allah repeatedly make this very point by giving explicit instructions as to the non-coercive nature of *Jihad*-as-exhortation.

> If it had been the Lord's will, they would all have believed — all who are on earth! Wilt thou then compel mankind, against their will, to believe! (*Qur'an* 10: 99)

> Again and again will those who disbelieve wish that they had bowed (to Allah's will) in Islam. Leave them alone, to enjoy (the good things of this life) and to please themselves: let (false) hope amuse them: soon will knowledge (undeceive them). (*Qur'an* 15: 2-3)

Say, "The truth is from your Lord": let him who will, believe, and let him who will, reject (it): for the wrongdoers We have prepared a fire whose (smoke and flames), like the walls and roof of a tent, will hem them in: if they implore relief they will be granted water like melted brass that will scald their faces. How dreadful the drink! How uncomfortable a couch to recline on! (*Qur'an* 18: 29)

If then they turn away, We have not sent thee as a guard over them. Thy duty is but to convey (the message)... (*Qur'an* 42: 48a)

We know best what they say; and thou art not one to overawe them by force. So admonish with the Qur'an such as fear My warning! (*Qur'an* 50: 45)

It is not for Muslims, whether as individuals or as a collective unit, to force conversion to Islam upon non-Muslims. As in all things, the words of Allah are clear and binding: "Leave them (i.e., the unbelievers) alone, to enjoy (the good things of this life)... let him who will, believe, and let him who will, reject it... If then they turn away, We have not sent thee as a guard over them. Thy duty is but to convey (the message)...". Muslims are to exhort and to warn, but not to coerce or to compel. Punishment for those who reject the message is strictly the prerogative of Allah, and not the fief of individual Muslims.

Therefore do thou give admonition, for thou art one to admonish. Thou art not one to manage (men's) affairs. But if any turns away and rejects Allah — Allah will punish him with a mighty Punishment. For to Us will be their return; then it will be for Us to call them to account. (*Qur'an* 88: 21-26)

Then leave Me alone with such as reject this message: by degrees shall We punish them from directions they perceive not. A (long) respite will I grant them: truly powerful is My plan. (*Qur'an* 68: 44-45)

Whether We shall show thee (within thy lifetime) part of what
We promised them or take to Ourselves thy soul (before it
is all accomplished), thy duty is to make (the message) reach
them: it is Our part to call them to account. (*Qur'an* 13: 40)

By now, it should be apparent that *Jihad*-as-exhortation
is free from any kind of compulsion or enforcement. A Muslim's
Jihad-as-exhortation should be based on love, respect, kindness,
and wishing the very best for his fellow man.

Say: "O People of the Book! Come to common terms as
between us and you: that we worship none but Allah, that
we associate no partners with Him: that we erect not,
from among ourselves, lords and patrons other than Allah."
If then they turn back, say ye: "Bear witness that we (at least)
are Muslims (bowing to Allah's will)." (*Qur'an* 3: 64)

Invite (all) to the way of thy Lord with wisdom and beautiful
preaching: and argue with them in ways that are best and
most gracious: for thy Lord knoweth best, who have strayed
from His path, and who receive guidance. (*Qur'an* 16: 125)

And dispute ye not with the People of the Book, except with
means better (than mere disputation), unless it be with those
of them who inflict wrong (and injury); but say, "We believe
in the revelation which has come down to us and in that
which came down to you; our God and your God is one; and
it is to Him we bow (in Islam)." (*Qur'an* 29: 46)

Further, one notes the words of Prophet Muhammad in the
following *Ahadith*, where he refuses to curse the disbelievers,
and where he actively prays for the welfare and spiritual guidance
of those who had rejected his message.

Abu Huraira reported: "It was said to Allah's Messenger (may
peace be upon him): 'Invoke curses upon the polytheists,'

whereupon he said: 'I have not been sent as the invoker of curse, but I have been sent as mercy'." (*Muslim, Hadith #* 6284)

Narrated by Jabir ibn 'Abdullah: "When the people said, 'Messenger of Allah (peace be upon him), Thaqif's arrows have scorched us, so supplicate Allah to punish them', he said, 'O Allah, give guidance to Thaqif'." (*Al-Tirmidhi, Hadith* # 5986)

Narrated Abu Huraira: "At-Tufail bin 'Amr came to Allah's Apostle and said, 'O Allah's Apostle! The tribe of Daus has disobeyed (Allah and His Apostle), and refused (to embrace Islam), therefore, invoke Allah's wrath for them.' The people thought that the Prophet would invoke Allah's wrath for them, but he said, 'O Allah! Guide the tribe of Daus and let them come to us'." (*Al-Bukhari, Hadith* # 8: 406; see parallels in *Al-Bukhari, Ahadith* # 4: 188 and 5: 675)

Additional examples of Islam's guarantee of freedom of religious choice can be found in the conduct of 'Umar ibn Al-Khattab, the second Caliph of Islam after the death of Prophet Muhammad. For example, Ibn Abi Hatim quoted Asbaq, a page of 'Umar ibn Al-Khattab, as saying that 'Umar frequently used to invite Asbaq to Islam, but that Asbaq always refused this invitation, preferring to remain a Christian. 'Umar's only response to this refusal was to quote from *Qur'an* 2:256: "Let there be no compulsion in religion". Additionally, Zaid ibn Aslam narrated that 'Umar ibn Al-Khattab once addressed an old, non-Muslim woman, "O, you old woman, embrace Islam and you will be safe in the Hereafter, Allah sent Muhammad with the truth". The woman refused this invitation to Islam, and 'Umar merely asked Allah to bear witness that 'Umar had fulfilled his task of inviting the old woman to Islam, and then quoted again from *Qur'an* 2: 256.

E. SUMMARY

The routine translation of *Jihad* as "Holy War" is blatantly, if not intentionally, misleading. *Jihad* means effort or striving, and within an Islamic religious context *Jihad* refers to any striving or effortful behavior that is done for the sake of Allah. Of the various forms of *Jihad, Da'wah* or *Jihad*-as-exhortation was historically the first form of *Jihad*, and has always been considered the most important form of *Jihad*. In contrast, *Jihad*-as-war has always been a small component of the total concept of *Jihad*, and has always been considered a measure of last resort.

Note

44. Malik AA (2002), page 13

Chapter 8

Jihad-as-War and
the Teachings of Islam

But if the enemy incline towards peace, do thou (also) incline towards peace, and trust in Allah: for He is the One that heareth and knoweth (all things). (*Qur'an* 8: 61)

Therefore if they withdraw from you but fight you not, and (instead) send you (guarantees of) peace, then Allah hath opened no way for you (to war against them). (*Qur'an* 4: 90b)

A. PERMISSION TO FIGHT

While Islam is a religion of peace, it is not a religion of absolute pacifism, and that is an important distinction. In the *Qur'an*, Allah has granted permission for Muslims to fight and to conduct war in certain well defined and highly circumscribed situations.

To those against whom war is made, permission is given (to fight), because they are wronged — and verily, Allah is most powerful for their aid — (they are) those who have been expelled from their homes in defiance of right — (for no cause) except that they say, "Our Lord is Allah". Did not Allah check one set of people by means of another there would surely have been pulled down monasteries, churches, synagogues, and mosques in which the name of Allah is commemorated in abundant measure. Allah will certainly aid those who aid His (cause) — for verily Allah is full of strength, exalted in might, (able to enforce His will). (They are) those who, if We establish them in the land, establish regular prayer and give regular charity, enjoin the right and forbid wrong: with Allah rests the end (and decision) of (all) affairs. (*Qur'an* 22: 39-41)

The above statement of Allah, while giving permission for Muslims to fight in times of war, sets certain conditions that must be met for Muslims to wage war. Muslims may wage war if they are among "those against whom war is made". In other words, Muslims may fight a defensive war against those who have attacked them, provided that in being attacked the Muslims stand in the right —"permission is given (to fight), because they are wronged". This latter point needs to be emphasized. If, Allah forbid, Muslims were to be the party of wrong in a conflict, permission to fight back against an attack would not be present. Instead, it would be incumbent upon the Muslims to make amends for whatever wrong they had done. Specifically stated, when Muslims are directly attacked, and when they are wronged and made homeless for no other reason than that they are Muslims — "(for no cause) except that they say, 'Our Lord is Allah'", they are permitted to act in self-defense. Broadly stated, within the limits previously discussed, self-defense is one condition that justifies war. This concept of the permissibility of *Jihad*-as-war as an action of self-defense is reiterated in the following passages from the *Qur'an*.

> Fight in the cause of Allah those who fight you, but do not transgress limits; for Allah loveth not transgressors. (*Qur'an* 2: 190)

> Will ye not fight people who violated their oaths, plotted to expel the Messenger, and took the aggressive by being the first (to assault) you? Do ye fear them? Nay, it is Allah Whom ye should more justly fear, if ye believe! (*Qur'an* 9: 13)

> The number of months in the sight of Allah is twelve (in a year) — so ordained by Him the day He created the heavens and the earth; of them four are sacred: that is the straight usage. So wrong not yourselves therein, and fight the pagans all together as they fight you all together. But know that Allah is with those who restrain themselves. (*Qur'an* 9: 36)

It may be that Allah will grant love (and friendship) between you and those whom ye (now) hold as enemies. For Allah has power (over all things); and Allah is oft-forgiving, most merciful. Allah forbids you not, with regard to those who fight you not for (your) faith nor drive you out of your homes, from dealing kindly and justly with them: for Allah loveth those who are just. Allah only forbids you, with regard to those who fight you for (your) faith, and drive you out of your homes, and support (others) in driving you out, from turning to them (for friendship and protection). It is such as turn to them (in these circumstances), that do wrong. (*Qur'an* 60: 7-9)

In the first of the four passages quoted immediately above, permission is given to engage in *Jihad*-as-war against "those who fight you", which clearly implies the notion of self-defense. In addition, the passage establishes that there are limits beyond which one should not go in waging *Jihad*-as-war, an issue to which we will return in much greater detail later. In the second of the four passages, permission is given to fight "people who ... took the aggressive by being the first (to assault) you," which again implies fighting a defensive war. In the third passage, permission is granted to fight those "as they fight you", which limits *Jihad*-as-war to self-defense. However, even here, restraint is urged: "But know that Allah is with those who restrain themselves." In the fourth passage, Muslims are taught that today's enemy may be tomorrow's friend, that Muslims should treat "kindly and justly" those non-Muslims who do not wage war against them, and that *Jihad*-as-war is reserved for fighting against "those who fight you for (your) faith, and drive you out of your homes, and support (others) in driving you out."

Let those fight in the cause of Allah who sell the life of this world for the Hereafter. To him who fighteth in the cause of Allah — whether he is slain or gets victory — soon shall We give him a reward of great (value). And why should ye not fight in the cause of Allah and of those who, being weak, are ill-treated (and oppressed)?—men, women, and children, whose cry is: "Our Lord! Rescue us from this town, whose people are oppressors; and raise for us from Thee one who will protect; and raise for us from Thee one who will help!" Those who believe fight in the cause of Allah, and those who reject faith fight in the cause of evil: so fight ye against the friends of Satan: feeble indeed is the cunning of Satan. (*Qur'an* 4: 74-76)

The above statement of Allah offers additional permission for Muslims to wage war. However, once again, such permission is not absolute, but is severely conditional. One may fight for the sake of Allah, and one may fight for the relief of the suffering of innocent victims. Indeed, Muslims have a religious obligation to ease the suffering of the oppressed and to strive for social justice for "those who, being weak, are ill-treated (and oppressed)". Justice and the expectation of humane treatment are the rights of every individual, and it is the duty of Muslims to come to the defense of those who are denied these basic rights. In this respect, the permissible circumstances for *Jihad*-as-war parallel the Just War concept that developed within Christianity.

However, let it be noted that permission to wage war has not been granted for the acquisition of territory, for geopolitical advantage, for colonial exploitation, for ethnic pride, for political power, or for strictly nationalistic concerns. Let it be further noted that if one is fighting for the sake of one's own advantage or for the advantage of one's family, one's clan, one's tribe, one's ethnicity, or one's nationality, one is not fighting for the sake of Allah.

Let us briefly review the conditions so far enumerated, in which fighting is permitted to Muslims. (1) Muslims are permitted to fight in self-defense if they are the aggrieved party. (2) They may fight to alleviate and eradicate gross social injustice, if that is the only corrective open to them. (3) They may fight for the sake of Allah, but should be extremely careful not to confuse the sake of their own personal, familial, tribal, ethnic, nationalistic, and political goals with the sake of Allah. The following *Ahadith* are relevant with regard to this last point.

Narrated Abu Musa, may Allah accept him: "A man came to the Prophet (peace be upon him) and asked, 'A man fights for war booty, another fights for fame and a third fights for showing off; which of them fights in Allah's Cause?' The Prophet (peace be upon him) said, 'He who fights (with the sole objective) so that Allah's word (i.e., Islam) should be superior, fights in Allah's Cause.'" (*Al-Bukhari, Hadith* #4:65)

Abu Huraira reported: "A man said: 'Apostle of Allah, a man wishes to take part in Jihad in Allah's path desiring some worldly advantage?' The Prophet (may peace be upon him) said: 'He will have no reward.' The people thought it terrible, and they said to the man: 'Go back to the Apostle of Allah (may peace be upon him), for you might not have made him understand well.' He, therefore, (went and again) asked: 'Apostle of Allah, a man wishes to take part in Jihad in Allah's path desiring some worldly advantage?' He replied: 'There is no reward for him.' They again said to the man: 'Return to the Apostle of Allah.' He, therefore, said to him a third time. He replied: 'There is no reward for him.'" (*Abu Dawud, Hadith* # 2510; see also *Mishkat Al-Masabih*, page 816)

As the last quoted *Hadith* illustrates, there is no reward from Allah for the person who fights with a desire for "some worldly advantage", even when the cause in which he is fighting is "*Jihad* in Allah's path". In short, a pure and singular motive to serve Allah is a precondition for any heavenly reward to accrue to the Muslim soldier who is engaged in combat. If part of the motive is to reacquire confiscated land, there is no reward. If part of the motive is to establish a nation state, there is no reward.

Allah has given permission to His followers to wage war. Clearly, Islam is not a religion of absolute pacifism. However, as demonstrated previously, that permission for Muslims to wage war is highly conditional. If and only if those conditions are met, then it may even be that war becomes not only permissible for Muslims, but also mandatory.

Fighting is prescribed upon you, and ye dislike it. But it is possible that ye dislike a thing which is good for you, and that ye love a thing which is bad for you. But Allah knoweth, and ye know not. (*Qur'an* 2: 216)

Say to the unbelievers, if (now) they desist (from unbelief), their past would be forgiven them; but if they persist, the punishment of those before them is already (a matter of warning for them). And fight them on until there is no more tumult or oppression, and there prevails justice and faith in Allah altogether and everywhere; but if they cease, verily Allah doth see all that they do. (*Qur'an* 8: 38-39)

O ye who believe! Fight the unbelievers who gird you about, and let them find firmness in you: and know that Allah is with those who fear Him. (*Qur'an* 9: 123)

Truly Allah loves those who fight in His cause in battle array, as if they were a solid cemented structure. (*Qur'an* 61: 4)

However, it must be stressed that the above passages from the *Qur'an*, and others like them, are applicable only in the face of the conditions previously noted. They serve as no license to wage a war of conquest for the acquisition of territory, nor do they permit war to be a tool for enforced religious conversion. Furthermore, the *Qur'an* is quite explicit about the sanctity of human life and about the enormous cost for taking a human life without proper justification and sanction.

On that account: We ordained for the children of Israel that if anyone slew a person — unless it be for murder or for spreading mischief in the land — it would be as if he slew the whole people: and if anyone saved a life, it would be as if he saved the life of the whole people. Then although there came to them Our messengers with clear signs, yet, even after that, many of them continued to commit excesses in the land. (*Qur'an* 5: 32)

B. THE AUTHORITY TO CALL FOR *JIHAD*-AS-WAR

There is one issue that must be acknowledged as existing, even though an in-depth discussion of the issue would be too complex an undertaking within the confines of the present manuscript. This issue has to do with who has the actual authority to call the Muslim *Ummah* to *Jihad*-as-war.[45]

Without getting into a lengthy exegesis of various texts, it is here noted that there are two basic types of rules within Islamic jurisprudence: Rules of Conveyance or Communication; and Rules of Imamates. Rules of Conveyance are binding on all Muslims and include *Da'wah* or *Jihad*-as-exhortation. Every Muslim is to convey the message of Allah and Islam. In contrast, Rules of Imamates concern activities that must not be conducted unless authorized by a Muslim state, and this category of rules includes *Jihad*-as-war.[45]

In short, *Jihad*-as-war can only be declared by a legitimate Muslim government. This position has been firmly stated and elucidated by: Sheikh Saleh Al-Sheikh, Minister of Islamic Affairs, Kingdom of Saudi Arabia; the renown Islamic scholar Muhammad Al-Buti, Professor of Theology at Damascus University; the Canadian office of the Council on American Islamic Relations; Hamza Yusuf; and others.[46] As can thus be seen, calls for *Jihad*-as-war by individual Muslims who are not heads of state of a Muslim country have no religious authority and are better understood as vigilantism, rather than as Islam.

However, the above does not mean that individual Muslims have no right to exercise self-defense. An individual Muslim who is wrongfully attacked does have the right within Islam to defend himself. He may even ask the Muslim *Ummah* to come to his aid. However, he does not have the religious authority to issue a proclamation of *Jihad*-as-war. He may ask for a Muslim head of state to proclaim *Jihad*-as-war, but he has no religious authority to declare it himself.

C. "DO NOT TRANSGRESS LIMITS"

C1. INTRODUCTION

Having established that Muslims are permitted to wage *Jihad*-as-war only within certain set conditions, it must also be emphasized that strict limitations apply to the nature and conduct of any such warfare. The following passages from the *Qur'an* illustrate this point.

> Fight in the cause of Allah those who fight you, but do not transgress limits; for Allah loveth not transgressors. (*Qur'an* 2: 190)

> Nor take life — which Allah has made sacred — except for just cause. And if anyone is slain wrongfully, we have given his heir authority (to demand Qisas or to forgive): but let him not exceed bounds in the matter of taking life: for he is helped (by the law). (*Qur'an* 17: 33)

> On that account: We ordained for the children of Israel that if anyone slew a person — unless it be for murder or for spreading mischief in the land — it would be as if he slew the whole people: and if anyone saved a life it would be as if he saved the life of the whole people. Then although there came to them Our messengers with clear signs, yet, even after that, many of them continued to commit excesses in the land. (*Qur'an* 5: 32)

> The number of months in the sight of Allah is twelve (in a year) — so ordained by Him the day He created the heavens and the earth; of them four are sacred: that is the straight usage. So wrong not yourselves therein, and fight the pagans all together as they fight you all together. But know that Allah is with those who restrain themselves. (*Qur'an* 9: 36)

Allah informs us that there are "limits" and "bounds" to what is permitted in warfare and in the taking of human life, that one is to avoid "excesses in the land", and that "Allah is with those who restrain themselves." The religion of Islam does not permit Muslims to kill indiscriminately or excessively during times of war. To kill even one innocent person is to stand before Allah's judgment in the same position as if one had killed the whole of humanity. There are limits that must not be crossed. If those limits are exceeded, then the injured party has, or his heirs have, the right to demand *Qisas* (retribution or retaliation), and the offending party will eventually stand guilty before the bench of Allah's justice.

In the following passage from the *Qur'an*, Allah prohibits certain unseemly behavior and deportment by those engaged in war. Insolence and exhibitionism are to be avoided in one's personal conduct as a soldier of Allah. Such behavior is unsightly and unseemly and raises disturbing questions about a person's true motives. Insolence and exhibitionism are hardly consistent with soldiers fighting for purposes of self-defense, the alleviation of gross social injustice, or the sake of Allah. In addition, the following passage from the *Qur'an* directs Muslims to obey Allah and Prophet Muhammad when it comes to conduct in warfare.

> Oh ye who believe! When ye meet a force, be firm, and call Allah in remembrance much (and often); that ye may prosper: and obey Allah and His Messenger; and fall into no disputes, lest ye lose heart and your power depart; and be patient and persevering for Allah is with those who patiently persevere. And be not like those who started from their homes insolently and to be seen of men, and to hinder (men) from the path of Allah: for Allah compasseth round about all that they do. Remember Satan made their (sinful) acts seem alluring to them, and said: "No one among men can overcome you this day, while I am near to you": but when the two forces came in sight of each other, he turned on his heels, and said: "Lo! I am

clear of you: Lo! I see what ye see not; Lo! I fear Allah; for Allah is strict in punishment." (*Qur'an* 8: 45-48)

Muslims are to obey Prophet Muhammad with regard to the limits and bounds of warfare. Simply stated, this means that Muslims are to follow those injunctions regarding war that were commanded by Prophet Muhammad and that were preserved in the authentic *Ahadith*. An examination of these *Ahadith* quickly reveals that the limits and bounds of Islamic warfare are both strict and severe. In what follows, these limitations from the *Ahadith* on what Islam permits and forbids in the nature and conduct of war are grouped according to several relevant categories.

C2. LIMITS AND DESIRE

There are times when war becomes an awful necessity. However, as the following *Ahadith* demonstrate, no Muslim is to desire war.

It has been narrated on the authority of Abu Huraira that the Messenger of Allah (may peace be upon him) said: "Do not desire an encounter with the enemy; but when you encounter them, be firm." (*Muslim, Hadith* # 4313)

Narrated Salim Abu Al-Nadr, the freed slave of 'Umar ibn 'Ubaidullah: "I was 'Umar's clerk. Once 'Abdullah bin Abi Aufa wrote a letter to 'Umar when he proceeded to Al-Haruriya. I read in it that Allah's Apostle, in one of his military expeditions against the enemy, waited till the sun declined and then he got up amongst the people saying, 'O people! Do not wish to meet the enemy, and ask Allah for safety, but when you face the enemy, be patient, and remember that Paradise is under the shades of swords.' Then he said, 'O Allah, the revealer of the holy book, and the mover of the clouds and the defeater of the clans, defeat them, and grant us victory over them'." (*Al-Bukhari, Hadith* # 4: 266; see also *Muslim, Hadith* # 4314, and *Abu Dawud, Hadith* # 2625)

Prophet Muhammad instructed Muslims in warfare by saying, "Do not wish to meet the enemy..." and "Do not desire an encounter with the enemy...". *Jihad*-as-war is not something for which any Muslim should ever have any desire. *Jihad*-as-war is a means of last resort for correcting grievous wrongs and for conducting necessary and unavoidable self-defense. If someone actually desires war or wishes to meet the enemy in mortal combat, it would appear that his motives are subject to suspicion. If someone actually desires war, it is far more likely that personal hatreds and animosities are motivating his quest than it is that he is engaging in an act of war for the sake of Allah. Simply stated, his true motives are much more likely to be political or psychological, rather than spiritual. Thus, while Muslims are given permission to wage war in certain conditions, and may even be obligated to engage in war in certain conditions, this is not something that they should ever crave or desire.

To further buttress the point that Muslims are not to desire warfare, it is noted that Allah specifically instructed Muslims to accept offers of peace from their enemies, even when the Muslims strongly suspect that the peace offer is nothing more than deception or a stratagem of war. Rather than reject the peace offer on the basis of suspected deception, Muslims are to accept the proposed peace, and place their trust in Allah, Who "sufficeth thee".

> But if the enemy incline towards peace, do thou (also) incline towards peace, and trust in Allah: for He is the One that heareth and knoweth (all things). Should they intend to deceive thee — verily Allah sufficeth thee: He it is that hath strengthened thee with His aid and with (the company of) the believers... (*Qur'an* 8: 61-62)

> Therefore if they withdraw from you but fight you not, and (instead) send you (guarantees of) peace, then Allah hath opened no way for you (to war against them). (*Qur'an* 4: 90b)

C3. LIMITS AND SUICIDE

While some commentators on the *Qur'an* maintain that the *Qur'an* does not directly and unambiguously mention the issue of suicide, most Muslims take the following verse of the *Qur'an* as a clear prohibition against suicide.

> O ye who believe! Eat not up your property among yourselves in vanities; but let there be amongst you traffic and trade by mutual good will: nor kill (or destroy) yourselves: for verily Allah hath been to you most merciful. (*Qur'an* 4: 29)

However the preceding verse is interpreted, numerous *Ahadith* testify that suicide is a major violation of the teachings of Islam. Further, these *Ahadith* consistently state that the end result of suicide is hellfire. There can be little doubt about the authenticity of this set of teachings of Prophet Muhammad, as so many different *Sahabah* (companions of the Prophet) independently narrated *Ahadith* confirming this point. In just those *Ahadith* that are utilized in this section to demonstrate how adamantly the Prophet prohibited suicide, one finds five different *Sahabah* offering confirming narrations, including Abu Huraira, Thabit ibn Al-Dahhak, Jundab Al-Bajali, Sahl ibn Sa'd Al-Sa'idi, and Salama ibn Al-Akwa'. It is more than merely difficult to imagine how five different *Sahabah* independently misheard or inadvertently misrepresented the teachings of the Prophet. Obviously, Prophet Muhammad explicitly prohibited suicide, and warned that the end result of suicide was hellfire.

> It is narrated on the authority of Abu Huraira that the Messenger of Allah (may peace be upon him) observed: "He who killed himself with steel (weapon) would be the eternal denizen of the fire of hell and he would have that weapon in his hand and would be thrusting that in his stomach for ever and ever; he who drank poison and killed himself would sip that in the fire of hell where he is doomed for ever and ever; and he who killed himself by falling from (the top of)

340

a mountain would constantly fall in the fire of hell and would live there for ever and ever." (*Muslim, Hadith* # 199; parallel versions of this *Hadith* can be found in *Al-Bukhari, Ahadith* # 2: 446 and # 7: 670)

Narrated Thabit ibn Al-Dahhak: "The Prophet said, 'Whoever ... commits suicide with piece of iron will be punished with the same piece of iron in the hellfire'." Narrated Jundab: "The Prophet said, 'A man was inflicted with wounds and he committed suicide, and so Allah said: 'My slave has caused death on himself hurriedly, so I forbid Paradise for him'"'. (*Al-Bukhari, Hadith* # 2: 4 45; see also *Al-Bukhari, Ahadith* # 8: 73, 126, 647 and *Muslim, Ahadith* # 201-203)

The above two *Ahadith* are general indictments against suicide. The following *Hadith* concerns a specific person, event, and situation. In this narrative, we are presented with a seemingly valiant warrior, who appears to have been much respected by his peers and much famed for his fighting prowess. Nonetheless, Prophet Muhammad predicted that the warrior would be among the people of the hellfire. Disconcerted by the Prophet's statement, one man followed the warrior during the course of a battle, only to discover that the warrior committed suicide by impaling himself on his own sword, apparently in order to escape his wounds and his pain. The warrior's suicide was seen as confirmation, as though such confirmation were needed, of the Prophet's earlier statement regarding the warrior.

Narrated Sahl ibn Sa'd Al-Sa'idi: "Allah's Apostle (and his army) clashed with the pagans. Allah's Apostle (peace be upon him) returned to his army camps and the others (i.e., the enemy) returned to their army camps. Amongst the companions of the Prophet there was a man who could not help pursuing any single isolated pagan to strike him with his sword. Somebody said, 'None has benefited the Muslims today more than so-and-so'. On that Allah's Apostle said,

'He is from the people of the hellfire certainly'. A man amongst the people (i.e., Muslims) said, 'I will accompany him (to know the fact)'. So he went along with him, and whenever he stopped, he stopped with him, and whenever he hastened, he hastened with him. The (brave) man then got wounded severely, and seeking to die at once, he planted his sword into the ground and put its point against his chest in between his breasts, and then threw himself on it and committed suicide. On that the person (who was accompanying the deceased all the time) came to Allah's Apostle and said, 'I testify that you are the Apostle of Allah'. The Prophet said, 'Why is that (what makes you say so)?' He said, 'It is concerning the man whom you have already mentioned as one of the dwellers of the hellfire. The people were surprised by your statement, and I said to them, 'I will try to find out the truth about him for you'. So I went out after him and he was then inflicted with a severe wound, and because of that, he hurried to bring death upon himself by planting the handle of his sword into the ground and directing its tip towards his chest between his breasts, and then he threw himself over it and committed suicide'. Allah's Apostle then said, 'A man may do what seems to the people as the deeds of the dwellers of paradise but he is from the dwellers of the hellfire and another may do what seems to the people as the deeds of the dwellers of the hellfire, but he is from the dwellers of paradise'." (*Al-Bukhari, Hadith* # 5: 514; see also *Al-Bukhari, Ahadith* # 4: 147; 5: 518; 8: 500, 604, and *Muslim, Hadith* # 206)

With regard to what may have been a different situation or merely a different narration regarding the selfsame situation as that found immediately above, Abu Huraira reported the following.

Narrated Abu Huraira: "We witnessed (the battle of) Khaybar. Allah's Apostle said about one of those who were with him and who claimed to be a Muslim, 'This (man) is from the dwellers of the hellfire'. When the battle started, that fellow fought so violently and bravely that he received plenty of wounds. Some of the people were about to doubt (the Prophet's statement), but the man, feeling the pain of his wounds, put his hand into his quiver and took out of it some arrows with which he slaughtered himself (i.e., committed suicide). Then some men amongst the Muslims came hurriedly and said, 'O Allah's Apostle! Allah has made your statement true; so-and-so has committed suicide'. The Prophet said, 'O so-and-so! Get up and make an announcement that none but a believer will enter paradise and that Allah may support (this) religion with an unchaste (evil) wicked man'." (*Al-Bukhari, Hadith # 5: 515; see also Al-Bukhari, Ahadith # 4: 296-297; 8: 603; as well as Muslim, Hadith # 205*)

The extent to which the *Sahabah* honored the above injunctions against suicide can be seen by two *Ahadith* narrated by Salama ibn Al-Akwa' and recorded in *Muslim* (*Ahadith # 4440-4441*). According to these *Ahadith*, 'Amir ibn Al-Akwa', the brother of Salama, was one of the soldiers of Allah who fought under the Prophet's command at Khaybar. During the course of the battle, 'Amir struck at an opponent with a short sword. His opponent managed to deflect the blow, and 'Amir's blade recoiled backward and struck his own knee, resulting in a wound from which 'Amir died. As 'Amir had died from a wound from the sword of his own hand, the *Sahabah* were much distressed about his fate. Many of them thought that 'Amir's sacrifice had been in vain, and some were reluctant to invoke Allah's blessing on him. Needless to say, Prophet Muhammad clarified the situation by dismissing the suggestion that there was any suicide involved in this tragic death of 'Amir. He noted that 'Amir died "as God's devotee and warrior", and that 'Amir would receive "a double reward" for his sacrifice. A shorter version of these *Ahadith* was recorded in *Abu Dawud*, and is quoted below.

Salama ibn Al-Akwa' said: "On the day of the battle of Khaybar, my brother fought desperately. But his sword fell back on him and killed him. The Companions of the Apostle of Allah (may peace be upon him) talked about him and doubted it (his martyrdom) saying: 'A man who died with his own weapon'. The Apostle of Allah (may peace be upon him) said: 'He died as a warrior striving in the path of Allah'. Ibn Shihab said: 'I asked the son of Salama ibn Al-Akwa'. He narrated to me on the authority of his father similar to that, except that he said: 'The Apostle of Allah (may peace be upon him) said: 'They told a lie; he died as a warrior striving in the path of Allah. There is a double reward for him.'"'"
(*Abu Dawud, Hadith # 2532*)

Given that the death of 'Amir ibn Akwa' from the sword of his own hand was so clearly accidental, contemporary readers may wonder why the *Sahabah* were concerned that 'Amir's death had been in vain and why the *Sahabah* were reluctant to invoke Allah's blessing on him. Nonetheless, the *Ahadith* regarding this incident demonstrate just how literally the *Sahabah* understood the injunction against suicide, and just how loathe they were to consider any mitigating circumstances, even including clear evidence of accidental death.

Against this background, it appears absurd to maintain that those who take their own lives by blowing themselves up or by flying planes into buildings have not violated the prohibition against suicide. Who can seriously believe that the *Sahabah* would not have condemned all such suicidal behavior, when so many of them were concerned about the eternal fate of 'Amir ibn Akwa', whose death by his own hand was so clearly accidental and inadvertent? Far from being martyrs who have earned eternal bliss from their sacrifice, those who commit suicide as an act of war are, according to the unambiguous teachings of Islam, doomed to the hellfire. In that regard, it needs to be emphasized that such damnation is neither alleviated nor mitigated by the claimed justness of the cause for which these individuals are supposedly fighting. In the words of Prophet Muhammad:

"A man may do what seems to the people as the deeds of the dwellers of paradise but he is from the dwellers of the hellfire" (*Al-Bukhari, Hadith # 5: 514*).

C4. LIMITS AND COLLATERAL DAMAGE

It has only been within the last few years that the term collateral damage has entered the lexicon of the average English-speaking person. As typically used, collateral damage refers to the injury or death of civilians and noncombatants during times of war. The term is also occasionally used to refer to damage to or assault upon parts of the civilian infrastructure of an enemy. Contemporary military strategists sometimes speak in terms of acceptable and unacceptable levels of collateral damage in military strikes, implying a nicety of distinction that seeks implicitly to confirm the concept that some degree of collateral damage is simply part and parcel of the acceptable risk of conducting war.

In contrast to the secular attempt to define acceptable and unacceptable levels of collateral damage, the teachings of Islam are very clear and concise. Within Islam, the killing of women, children, and the aged is specifically and unequivocally prohibited. In short, it is a direct violation of Islam to kill civilian non-combatants, and there is no acceptable level of collateral damage.

In presenting the following *Ahadith*, it should again be emphasized that the very number of *Sahabah* who have independently narrated them prevents there being any serious question that the Prophet explicitly prohibited the killing of civilian non-combatants in times of war. Because of the great importance of proving beyond all reasonable doubt this aspect of the Prophet's teaching, a number of independently narrated *Ahadith* are presented below.

'Abd Allah (ibn Mas'ud) said: "A woman was found slain in one of the battles of the Apostle of Allah (may peace be upon him). The Apostle of Allah (may peace be upon him) forbade killing women and children." (*Abu Dawud, Hadith # 2662;* see parallel versions of this *Hadith* in *Al-Bukhari, Hadith # 4: 257* and in *Muslim, Hadith # 4319*)

Narrated Ibn 'Umar: "During some of the Ghazawat (raids, battles, or military expeditions) of Allah's Apostle, a woman was found killed, so Allah's Apostle forbade the killing of women and children." (*Al-Bukhari, Hadith* # 4: 258; also see parallel in *Muslim, Hadith* # 4320, and in *Mishkat Al-Masabih*, page 836.)

Nafi' reported that the Apostle of Allah (may peace be upon him) found women killed in some battles and he condemned such an act and prohibited the killing of women and children. (*Malik, Hadith* # 957)

Rabah ibn Rabi' said: "When we were with the Apostle of Allah (may peace be upon him) on an expedition, he saw some people collected together over something and sent a man and said: 'See, what are these people collected around?' He then came and said: 'They are round a woman who has been killed.' He said: 'This is not one with whom fighting should have taken place.' Khalid ibn Al-Walid was in charge of the van; so he sent a man and said: 'Tell Khalid not to kill a woman or a hired servant.'" (*Abu Dawud, Hadith* #2663;see also *Mishkat Al-Masabih*, page 838)

Anas ibn Malik reported the Apostle of Allah (may peace be upon him) as saying: "Go in Allah's name, trusting in Allah, and adhering to the religion of Allah's Apostle. Do not kill a decrepit old man, or a young infant, or a child, or a woman; do not be dishonest about booty, but collect your spoils, do right and act well, for Allah loves those who do well." (*Abu Dawud, Hadith* #2608; see also *Mishkat Al-Masabih*, page 838)

To briefly interrupt the flow of *Ahadith* proving that the killing of civilian non-combatants is prohibited within the teachings of Islam, it is noted that the following *Hadith* adds a prohibition against disfiguring or mutilating the dead — "do not cut ears and noses" — to the prohibition against killing women and children.

It reached Malik that 'Umar ibn 'Abd Al-'Aziz wrote to one of his administrators: "We have learnt that whenever the Apostle of Allah (may peace be upon him) sent out force, he used to command them: 'Fight taking the name of the Lord. You are fighting in the cause of the Lord with people who have disbelieved and rejected the Lord; do not commit theft, do not break vows; do not cut ears and noses, do not kill women and children.' Communicate this to your armies. If God wills, peace be on you." (*Malik, Hadith* # 959; also see *Abu Dawud, Hadith* # 2661)

The next *Hadith* to be quoted demonstrates just how stringently Prophet Muhammad's prohibition against killing civilian non-combatants is to be maintained. In the following example, a woman began to shout, warning the person about to be attacked, and giving away the position of the Muslim attackers. Yet even in these markedly extenuating circumstances, the absolute prohibition against killing female non-combatants was maintained.

'Abd Al-Rahman ibn Ka'b reported that the Apostle of Allah (may peace be upon him) prohibited those people who killed Ibn Abu Al-Huqaiq from killing women and children. One of them said: "The wife of Ibn Abu Al-Huqaiq shouted out and disclosed our presence and I raised my sword but, remembering the command of the Apostle of Allah (may peace be upon him), restrained myself. Had it not been so, we would have been rid of her also." (*Malik, Hadith* # 956)

The sum total of the foregoing *Ahadith* demonstrates the strict Islamic prohibition against killing civilian non-combatants during war. Specific examples of this include the prohibition against killing women (even those who are attempting to warn others of an impending attack by Muslim soldiers), the prohibition against killing children, and the prohibition against killing the aged. Of marked importance to the present discussion, these prohibitions were not merely temporary injunctions that were honored only during Prophet Muhammad's lifetime. These are prohibitions that know no temporal boundaries and that are unaffected by contemporary issues, events, and technology. To illustrate the permanent nature of these prohibitions, one need only turn to the instructions given by Abu Bakr, the first caliph of Islam, who ruled the Islamic *Ummah* after the death of Prophet Muhammad.

> Yahya ibn Sa'id reported that when Abu Bakr Siddiq sent an army to Syria, he went on foot with Yazid ibn Abu Sufyan who was the commander of a quarter of the forces. Yazid said to Abu Bakr: "Either you mount up or I shall dismount." Abu Bakr replied: "Neither you will dismount nor will I ride. I consider these steps to be a virtue in the path of the Lord. You will find some people who imagine they have devoted their lives to Allah (the hermits), leave them to their work; you will find some people who shave their heads in the middle (the Magi), strike them with your swords. I instruct you in ten matters: Do not kill women or children, nor the old and infirm; do not cut fruit-bearing trees; do not destroy any town; do not cut the gums of sheep or camels except for purposes of eating; do not burn date-trees nor submerge them; do not steal from booty and do not be cowardly."
> (*Malik, Hadith # 958*)

A parallel version of the above *Hadith* was recorded by Abu Ja'far Muhammad ibn Jarir Al-Tabari (Series I, Volume III, page 1850). According to this parallel of the above quoted *Hadith*, Abu Bakr instructed his army in regard to 10 explicit limitations on its behavior as soldiers of Allah. The army was forbidden to: (1) commit treachery; (2) deviate from the right path; (3) mutilate dead bodies; (4) kill a child; (5) kill a woman; (6) kill an aged man; (7) harm trees, especially those that are fruit-bearing; (8) burn trees, especially those that are fruit-bearing; (9) slaughter the enemy's livestock, except for reasonable food consumption; and (10) bother monastics and religious hermits.

There are several points that need to be made regarding

these latter two *Ahadith*. Firstly, as already noted, these *Ahadith* clearly demonstrate that Prophet Muhammad's prohibition against taking the life of civilian non-combatants was not confined to the Prophet's lifetime. As are the case with all of Prophet Muhammad's religious instructions and teachings, these prohibitions apply to all Muslims for all time. They are as binding on contemporary Muslims as they were on Muslims almost 1,400 years ago. Secondly, these two *Ahadith*, by extending the ban against killing the aged, women, and children, to a ban on killing or bothering monastics and religious hermits (the *Musnad* of Ahmad ibn Hanbal also lists a prohibition against killing people in places of worship), clearly demonstrate that Prophet Muhammad's injunction was a general prohibition against killing all civilian non-combatants. Thirdly, these *Ahadith* also elucidate a prohibition against attacking and disrupting the civilian infrastructure. In that regard, it is noted that Abu Bakr specifically instructed the Muslim army not to slaughter livestock (except for that which was needed to feed the army) and not to damage fruit-bearing trees. By extending the prohibition against killing non-combatant civilians to include a prohibition against destroying that part of the civilian infrastructure responsible for food production, Abu Bakr was not adding to Prophet Muhammad's teaching, but was merely merging into one statement the prohibitions of the already quoted *Ahadith* with the teachings of the *Qur'an*.

> There is the type of man whose speech about this world's life may dazzle thee, and he calls Allah to witness about what is in his heart; yet is he the most contentious of enemies. When he turns his back, his aim everywhere is to spread mischief though the earth and destroy crops and cattle. But Allah loveth not mischief. (*Qur'an* 2: 204-205)

Quite obviously, a military attack that slaughters livestock and lays waste to food producing plants is an attack against the civilian population. Such an attack exposes the civilian population to the risk of malnutrition and eventual starvation. Untold numbers of civilians might become seriously ill or even die, if such attacks against the civilian infrastructure were permitted. Within Islam, the solution is simple: it is forbidden to attack the civilian infrastructure in such a way as to risk the civilian population.

Finally, it is noted that Karen Armstrong, a former nun and best-selling author, has noted that when Prophet Muhammad sent Zaid as leader of a Muslim army, the Prophet gave explicit instructions that the army was prohibited from: (1) molesting in any way any priests, monks, nuns, and the weak and helpless who were unable to bear arms; (2) killing civilian non-combatants; (3) cutting down a single tree; and (4) pulling down any building.[47]

It is perhaps appropriate at this point to digress briefly. Within the framework of the so-called Mosaic law of the *Bible*, *Deuteronomy* 20:19-20 also specifically forbids the killing of a fruit-bearing tree. However, the context in which this prohibition is embedded is in shocking contrast to Islam's strict ban on killing civilian non-combatants. As seen in the following quotation, the Biblical ban on cutting down a fruit-bearing tree places the worth of the tree far above that of the lives of the civilian non-combatants that may be living in the towns being besieged. In stark contrast to the teachings of Islam, the following Biblical passage, while forbidding the cutting down of a fruit-bearing tree, permits, and even demands, the mass genocide of a civilian population.

> But as for the towns of these peoples that the Lord your God is giving you as an inheritance, you must not let anything that breathes remain alive. You shall annihilate them — the Hittites and the Amorites, the Canaanites and the Perizzites, the Hivites and the Jebusites — just as the Lord your God has commanded, so that they may not teach you to do all the abhorrent things that they do for their gods, and you thus sin against the Lord your God. If you besiege a town for a long time, making war against it in order to take it, you must not destroy its trees by wielding an ax against them. Although you may take food from them, you must not cut them down. Are trees in the field human beings that they should come

under siege from you? You may destroy only the trees that you know do not produce food; you may cut them down for use in building siegeworks against the town that makes war with you, until it falls. (*Deuteronomy* 20: 16-20)

Islam prohibits the killing of civilian non-combatants, and severely restricts attacks against the civilian infrastructure, forbidding any disruption of the civilian infrastructure that may lead to the inadvertent death of civilian non-combatants. These limits on collateral damage are severe and stringent. Many contemporary, secular military strategists would probably insist that such injunctions handcuff the military beyond all possibility of success. Having full faith in Allah, Muslims must reject all such issues of expediency and so-called practicality. Quite frankly, issues of expediency and practicality simply have no bearing when it comes to fulfilling the dictates of Allah and His prophet. Muslims must rely upon Allah, and not upon what is considered expedient or practical by the secular world.

C5. LIMITS AND TYPES OF WEAPONS

Not only does Islam limit who may be the target of a military attack, it also limits the types of weapons that can be employed. The following *Ahadith* illustrate one of these limits on weaponry.

Narrated Abu Huraira: "Allah's Apostle sent us in a mission (i.e., Sariya — a small army unit sent by the Prophet on Jihad, but without his being part of it) and said, 'If you find so-and-so and so-and-so, burn both of them with fire.' When we intended to depart, Allah's Apostle said, 'I have ordered you to burn so-and-so and so-and-so, and it is none but Allah Who punishes with fire, so, if you find them, kill them.'" (*Al-Bukhari, Hadith* # 4: 259; see parallel *Hadith* in *Abu Dawud, Hadith* # 2668)

Narrated 'Ikrima: "'Ali burnt some people and this news reached Ibn 'Abbas, who said, 'Had I been in his place I would not have burnt them, as the Prophet said, 'Don't punish (anybody) with Allah's punishment'." (*Al-Bukhari, Hadith* # 4: 260)

Abu Huraira and 'Ikrima were not the only *Sahabah* to testify that Prophet Muhammad prohibited the use of fire as a weapon of war. Hamzat Al-Aslami and 'Abd Allah ibn Mas'ud also narrated that Prophet Muhammad prohibited killing by burning with fire (*Abu Dawud, Ahadith* # 2667 & 2668). Given this prohibition, one can immediately see that such weapons of war as flame-throwers, napalm, and incendiary bombs are not permitted by Islam.

C6. LIMITS AND FIRST-THINGS-FIRST

While in certain circumstances war is incumbent upon Muslims, it has already been demonstrated that Muslims should not desire to meet the enemy in combat. Now, it can also be shown that, even in such cases where war is incumbent upon Muslims, war does not become the immediate priority. Other issues may well have precedence over war. In the following *Ahadith*, Prophet Muhammad elucidated some of those issues that may well supersede the individual Muslim's obligation to go to war. We begin with a *Hadith* narrated by 'Abd Allah ibn 'Abbas, the cousin of Prophet Muhammad. In this *Hadith*, Muslims are informed that certain family responsibilities take priority over the obligation to go to war, even when that war is justified and necessary.

> Narrated Ibn 'Abbas: "A man came to the Prophet and said, 'O Allah's Apostle! I have enlisted in the army for such and such Ghazwa (raid, battle, or military expedition), and my wife is leaving for Hajj.' Allah's Apostle said, 'Go back and perform Hajj with your wife'." (*Al-Bukhari, Hadith* # 4: 295; see also *Al-Bukhari, Hadith* # 4: 250).

In the above *Hadith*, a Muslim is informed that his higher responsibility is to serve as guardian and chaperone for his wife while she makes the *Hajj* pilgrimage to Makkah. This marital responsibility outweighs his responsibility to serve as a soldier in the Muslim army, even in times of a justifiable war that has been sanctioned by a legitimate authority. At least with regard to the specifics of the above case, Prophet Muhammad teaches that being a good husband is more important within Islam than being a good soldier. However, it is not just in the case of one's wife going on the *Hajj* pilgrimage that marital responsibilities take precedence over going to war. In the following *Hadith*, 'Abd Allah ibn 'Umar narrated that Prophet Muhammad also instructed Muslims to give precedence to caring for a sick spouse over fighting in *Jihad*-as-war.

> Narrated Ibn 'Umar: "'Uthman did not join the Badr battle because he was married to one of the daughters of Allah's Apostle and she was ill. So, the Prophet said to him, 'You will get a reward and a share (from the war booty) similar to the reward and the share of one who has taken part in the Badr battle'." (*Al-Bukhari, Hadith #* 4: 359)

Accompanying one's wife on the *Hajj* pilgrimage takes precedence over *Jihad*-as-war. Likewise, caring for a sick wife takes precedence over serving in a Muslim army during times of war. In addition, Jabir ibn 'Abdullah narrated a *Hadith* that indicates that the newly married husband is excused from serving with the army during war (*Al-Bukhari, Hadith #* 4: 211; see also *Al-Bukhari, Hadith #* 3: 589). Observant Christian and Jewish readers will note that the teaching of this last *Hadith* is consistent with the so-called Mosaic Law, which excuses a husband from serving with the army during the first year of his marriage.

> When a man is newly married, he shall not go out with the army or be charged with any related duty. He shall be free at home one year, to be happy with the wife whom he has married. (*Deuteronomy* 24: 5)

As seen above, marital responsibilities may well trump a Muslim's obligation to go to war. However, this is not the only family responsibility that takes precedence over the call to arms. In the following *Hadith*, Prophet Muhammad taught that filial duty to one's parents has a higher priority than the obligation to fight in a war.

> Narrated 'Abd Allah ibn Mas'ud: "I asked Allah's Apostle, 'O Allah's Apostle! What is the best deed?' He replied, 'To offer the prayers at their early stated fixed times.' I asked, 'What is next?' He replied, 'To be good and dutiful to your parents.' I further asked, 'What is next?' He replied, 'To participate in Jihad in Allah's Cause.' I did not ask Allah's Apostle anymore, and if I had asked him again, he would have told me more." (*Al-Bukhari, Hadith* #4: 41)

Lest anyone doubt that Prophet Muhammad explicitly ranked filial duty to one's parents as being a higher good than engaging in *Jihad*-as war, the following two *Ahadith* should end all such doubts. Of note, with the addition of these two *Ahadith*, there now becomes three different *Sahabah* who independently testified that the Prophet placed filial duty to one's parents above the responsibilities of serving in the army during times of war.

> Narrated 'Abd Allah ibn 'Amr: "A man came to the Prophet asking his permission to take part in Jihad. The Prophet asked him, 'Are your parents alive?' He replied in the affirmative. The Prophet said to him, 'Then exert yourself in their service'." (*Al-Bukhari, Hadith* # 4: 248; see parallels of this *Hadith* in *Abu Dawud, Hadith* # 2523, and in *Mishkat Al-Masabih*, page 811)

> Abu Sa'id Al-Khudri said: "A man emigrated to the Apostle of Allah (may peace be upon him) from the Yemen. He asked (him): 'Have you anyone (of your relatives) in the Yemen?' He replied: 'My parents.' He asked: 'Did they permit you?' He replied: 'No.' He said: 'Go back to them

and ask for their permission. If they permit you, then fight (in the path of Allah), otherwise be devoted to them.'" (*Abu Dawud, Hadith* # 2524)

C7. LIMITS AND SISTERS IN COMBAT

The summer of 2001 brought two new and disturbing events to the attention of the world. In the first instance, a Palestinian woman was arrested by Israeli authorities for allegedly attempting to carry explosives to a terrorist cell. In the second instance, occurring only a few weeks after the first, a Palestinian woman was arrested outside an Israeli police station, where she supposedly had been waiting with a knife, allegedly hoping to entice some Israeli policeman to come close enough to her to be stabbed. Whether these reported incidents, both from the *Jerusalem Post* and one from the *Jordan Times*, are accurate and truthful or false and misleading is outside the scope of the current discussion. However, these reports do raise the issue of Muslim women fighting as soldiers during *Jihad*-as-war, an issue that became even more prominent in 2002, as Palestinian women began acting as suicide bombers.

Muslims have it on no less of an authority than the wife of the Prophet Muhammad that the Prophet prohibited the use of women as combatants in war. According to the following *Ahadith*, 'Aisha narrated that the Prophet taught that women were to make the *Hajj* pilgrimage and that this was the manner in which they were to exert (*Jihad*) themselves for Allah. They were not to serve as combatants in the army.

> Narrated 'Aisha (that she said), "O Allah's Apostle! We consider Jihad as the best deed. Should we not fight in Allah's Cause?" He said, "The best Jihad (for women) is Hajj-Mabrur (i.e., Hajj which is done according to the Prophet's traditions and is accepted by Allah)." (*Al-Bukhari, Hadith* # 4: 43)

Narrated 'Aisha, the mother of the faithful believers:
"I requested the Prophet to permit me to participate in
Jihad, but he said, 'Your Jihad is the performance of Hajj'."
(*Al-Bukhari, Hadith* #4:127; see also *Al-Bukhari, Hadith*
#4: 128)

Aisha asked Allah's Messenger (peace be upon him)
whether Jihad was incumbent on women, and he replied,
"Yes, Jihad which does not include fighting is incumbent
on them. It is the *Hajj* and the *'Umrah* (the so-called minor
pilgrimage to Makkah)." (*Al-Tirmidhi, Hadith* # 2534)

While Muslim women are not to serve as actual combatants
in war, several *Ahadith* demonstrate that Muslim women are
permitted to give humanitarian and medical care to those men
who are fighting in *Jihad*-as-war or who have been injured in
Jihad-as-war. For example, the reader is referred to *Al-Bukhari*
(*Ahadith* # 4: 131-134), *Muslim* (*Ahadith* # 4453-4456), and *Abu
Dawud* (*Hadith* # 2525), where the following wartime activities
are permitted to Muslim women: giving water to combatants;
providing medical care to wounded combatants; and removing
slain and wounded combatants from the battlefield.

C8. LIMITS AND PRISONERS OF WAR

Islam also prescribes the humanitarian treatment of prisoners
of war. Approximately 1,300 years before the Geneva Conventions
were ratified, Prophet Muhammad prohibited the killing of captive
members of the enemy.

Ibn Ti'li said: "We fought along with 'Abd Al-Rahman ibn
Khalid ibn Al-Walid. Four infidels from the enemy were
brought to him. He commanded about them and they were
killed in confinement." Abu Dawud said: "The narrators other
than Sa'id reported from Ibn Wahb in this tradition: '(killed
him) with arrows in confinement.' When Abu Ayyub Al-Ansari
was informed about it, he said: 'I heard the Apostle of Allah

(may peace be upon him) prohibiting to kill in confinement. By Him in Whose hands my soul is, if there were a hen, I would not kill it in confinement.' 'Abd Al-Rahman ibn Khalid ibn Al-Walid was informed about it (the Prophet's prohibition). He set four slaves free." (*Abu Dawud, Hadith* #2681)

It should be noted that in the immediately preceding *Hadith*, 'Abd Al-Rahman ibn Khalid ibn Al-Walid freed four slaves as atonement for his excesses once those excesses were pointed out to him.

However, Islam goes beyond merely prohibiting the killing of prisoners of war. Islam also prescribes that prisoners of war be treated humanely and that their basic needs are met. This is illustrated by the following passage from the *Qur'an*, which enjoins proper care of captives, and by the following *Hadith*, in which the Prophet saw to the clothing needs of a prisoner of war, Al-'Abbas, who also happened to be the Prophet's uncle.

As for the righteous...they perform (their) vows, and they fear a day whose evil flies far and wide. And they feed, for the love of Allah, the indigent, the orphan, and the captive — (saying), "We feed you for the sake of Allah alone: no reward do we desire from you, nor thanks." (*Qur'an* 76: 5a, 7-9)

Narrated Jabir ibn 'Abdullah: "When it was the day (of the battle) of Badr, prisoners of war were brought including Al-'Abbas who was undressed. The Prophet looked for a shirt for him. It was found that the shirt of 'Abd Allah ibn Ubai would do, so the Prophet let him wear it. That was the reason why the Prophet took off and gave his own shirt to 'Abd Allah." (*Al-Bukhari, Hadith* # 4: 252)

D. THE SO-CALLED VERSE OF THE SWORD

In mid-October of 2001, a commentator on a nationally syndicated television show in the United States maintained that Islam was a religion of war, which preached that all Muslims were directed to kill all non-Muslims. (Of note, the same passage was reportedly quoted by Osama bin Laden in his so-called *Fatwa* of February 23, 1998, in which he urged the killing of all Americans, whether military or civilian, wherever they might be found.)

> But when the forbidden months are past, then fight and slay the pagans wherever ye find them, and seize them, beleaguer them, and lie in wait for them in every stratagem (of war)...
> (*Qur'an* 9:5a)

Unfortunately, the commentator had quoted a passage that had been ripped totally out of its context within the *Qur'an*. The appropriate context for the passage in question is established merely by quoting the four verses preceding this verse, the remainder of this verse, and the immediately subsequent verse.

> A (declaration) of immunity from Allah and His messenger, to those of the pagans with whom ye have contracted mutual alliances — go ye, then, for four months, backwards and forwards, (as ye will), throughout the land, but know ye that ye cannot frustrate Allah (by your falsehood) but that Allah will cover with shame those who reject Him. And an announcement from Allah and His messenger, to the people (assembled) on the day of the great pilgrimage — that Allah and His messenger dissolve (treaty) obligations with the pagans. If, then, ye repent, it were best for you; but if ye turn away, know ye that ye cannot frustrate Allah. And proclaim a grievous penalty to those who reject faith. (But the treaties are) not dissolved with those pagans with whom ye have entered into alliance and who have not subsequently failed you in aught, nor aided anyone against you. So fulfil your engagements with them to the end of their term: for Allah loveth the righteous. But when the forbidden months (in which fighting is prohibited) are past, then fight and slay the pagans wherever ye find them, and seize them, beleaguer them, and lie in wait for them in every stratagem (of war);

but if they repent, and establish regular prayers and practice regular charity, then open the way for them: for Allah is oft-forgiving, most merciful. If one amongst the pagans asks thee for asylum, grant it to him, so that he may hear the word of Allah; and then escort him to where he can be secure. That is because they are men without knowledge. (*Qur'an* 9: 1-6)

Read within its context, it is clear that the passage in question is not advocating the wholesale destruction of pagan people. Rather, *Jihad*-as-war is prescribed only against those pagans who are actually fighting against the Muslim *Ummah*. That this is the case is demonstrated by the injunctions to: honor prior treaties that have been upheld by the other side; accept any repentance and conversion to Islam that the pagans offer; and grant asylum and safe escort to a place of security for anyone who asks for it. Muslims are to grant asylum when asked for it by the person who was previously a combatant against them, and they should take that opportunity to practice *Jihad*-as exhortation, i.e., "so that he may hear the word of Allah." Whether or not the asylum-seeker accepts Islam, Muslims are then to "escort him to where he can be secure". Seen within this context, the Qur'anic passage quoted by the television commentator, and reportedly by Osama bin Laden, is anything but an injunction to kill all non-Muslims. Rather, the passage permits Muslims to wage *Jihad*-as-war against those who are actively fighting against them, but then directs Muslims to give asylum, religious exhortation, and safe conduct to anyone who lays down his arms. This is not religion by the sword, but a religion of mercy, for "Allah is oft-forgiving, most merciful".

It should be noted that Islam does not consider Christians and Jews to be pagans, but *Ahl Al-Kitab* (people of the book), i.e., people who have received a prior book of revelation from Allah. With this distinction in mind, the use of *Qur'an* 9:5 as some twisted justification to kill Christians and Jews, as reportedly in Osama bin Laden's Fatwa, becomes even more ludicrous.

E. SUMMARY AND CONCLUSIONS

By this time, three fundamental points about the Islamic teachings regarding *Jihad*-as-war should be abundantly clear. Firstly, permission to wage *Jihad*-as-war is highly conditional, and basically conforms to that of the Just War theory within mainline Christianity. Secondly, the authority to call for *Jihad*-as-war is markedly restricted. Thirdly, the permissible range of conduct of those Muslim soldiers who engage in *Jihad*-as-war is severely limited, even by traditional Western standards.

Notes

45. Al-Buti MSR (1995), pages 45-47.

46. (A) *Jordan Times* 10/19/2001;

    (B) Al-Buti MSR (1995);

    (C) *San Jose Mercury News* 9/16/2001.

47. Armstrong K (2001), page 36.

Chapter 9

Jihad-as-War and
the Lessons of History

A. INTRODUCTION

Lest any reader think that the previous chapter's discussion of the Islamic limits of *Jihad*-as-war was purely theoretical and that it has no counterparts in the real world, it is instructive to examine the historical record of the Islamic practice of *Jihad*-as-war. Unfortunately, the history of Islam is sometimes portrayed by the Western media as being a long series of religious conversions-by-the-sword and ceaseless battles and wars. However, as was shown in the previous chapter, permission to wage *Jihad*-as-war is severely conditional within Islam, and the rules regarding the conduct of *Jihad*-as-war are extremely limiting. Furthermore, as also previously demonstrated, Islam is a religion that guarantees freedom of religion.

In turning through the pages of history to document Islamic conduct in *Jihad*-as-war, two examples are particularly noteworthy. The first is taken from the life of Prophet Muhammad, and the second is drawn from Islamic conduct during the so-called Christian Crusades.

B. PROPHET MUHAMMAD AND *JIHAD*-AS-WAR

B1. SOME FACTS AND FIGURES

Islam is not a religion of the sword, and the actual historical record concerning the life of Prophet Muhammad clearly refutes any such erroneous presentation. As documented by Mansurpuri[48] and others, despite the seemingly unbearable persecution and assassination attempts documented in chapter III, Prophet Muhammad's entire life record reveals only 82 battles fought under his command or sanction. The duration of most of these battles was only a single day in length, and, if one were to add up all of these battles, they would occupy far less than one of the Prophet's approximately 62 years of life. Furthermore, throughout these 82 battles, only 1,018 people (259 Muslims and 759 non-Muslims) were actually killed. On the average, only 12.4 individuals lost their lives in each battle, demonstrating quite convincingly that killing was severely curtailed even in the midst of *Jihad*-as-war. Clearly, the Prophet's life serves as a superlative model of restraint in warfare.

> Ye have indeed in the messenger of Allah a beautiful pattern (of conduct) for any one whose hope is in Allah and the Final Day, and who engages much in the praise of Allah. (*Qur'an* 33: 31)

B2. SPECIFIC EXAMPLES

Two *Ahadith* regarding Prophet Muhammad's conduct in *Jihad*-as-war are highly enlightening. In the first *Hadith*, Prophet Muhammad refused even to curse an enemy army. In the second *Hadith*, after first demonstrating his absolute faith in and submission to Allah, Prophet Muhammad demonstrated amazing charity to one who had come to assassinate him.

> Narrated by Jabir ibn Abdullah: "When the people said, 'Messenger of Allah (peace be upon him), Thaqif's arrows have scorched us, so supplicate Allah to punish them', he said, 'O Allah, give guidance to Thaqif'." (*Al-Tirmidhi, Hadith* # 5986)

> Narrated Jabir bin 'Abdullah that he proceeded in the company of Allah's Apostle towards Najd to participate in a Ghazwa (military raid, in this case an instance of *Jihad*-as-war). When Allah's Apostle returned, he too returned with him. Midday came upon them while they were in a valley having many thorny trees. Allah's Apostle and the people dismounted and dispersed to rest in the shade of the trees. Allah's Apostle rested under a tree and hung his sword on it.

We all took a nap and suddenly we heard Allah's Apostle calling us. (We woke up) to see a Bedouin with him. The Prophet said, "This Bedouin took out my sword while I was sleeping and when I awoke, I found the unsheathed sword in his hand and he challenged me saying, 'Who will save you from me?' I said thrice, 'Allah'." The Prophet did not punish him but sat down." (*Al-Bukhari, Hadith* # 4: 158; see parallel in *Al-Bukhari, Hadith* # 5: 458 where the assassin is identified as having been Ghaurath ibn Al-Harith.)

Finally, as noted previously in section H13 of chapter III, Prophet Muhammad granted a general amnesty when Makkah fell to the Muslim army in 630 CE.

C. THE CRUSADES

C1. ATROCITIES

In late 1168, Bilgays fell to a conquering army. The entire population of the city was put to death after the city fell. Men, women, and children were all slaughtered, and numerous Coptic Christians were victims of that awful slaughter.

In 1194, approximately 3,000 civilian non-combatants (including women and children) and prisoners of war were summarily executed in Castle Acre. At the time of their execution, these individuals were completely defenseless. Approximately 2,700 of these victims were soldiers who had been taken captive and made prisoners of war, while almost 300 victims were women and children.

However, the atrocity perpetrated at Castle Acre was nothing compared to that at Jerusalem when the city fell to a conquering army on July 15, 1099. The atrocities committed over the next two days were almost beyond comprehension. (1) The victorious conquerors slaughtered between 40,000 and 70,000 people in Jerusalem, most of whom were civilian non-combatants, and many of whom were women and children. (2) In their desperation to escape the fearful slaughter, the Jews of the city had barricaded themselves inside a synagogue, hoping that the conquerors would respect their house of worship. However, the victorious soldiers promptly set the synagogue afire, and incinerated the Jewish population of Jerusalem. (3) The priests of the Basilica of the Holy Sepulchre were driven from their church, and many were tortured to get them to confess where they had hidden their religious relics. (4) In another house of worship within Jerusalem, the conquerors completely vandalized and desecrated the building, and stole everything of value.

One of the victorious combatants memorialized his participation in these atrocities at Jerusalem, and his comments are quoted immediately below.

> Wonderful sights were to be seen. Some of our men (and this was more merciful) cut off the heads of their enemies; others shot them with arrows, so that they fell from the towers; others tortured them longer by casting them into the flames. Piles of heads, hands and feet were to be seen in the streets of the city. It was necessary to pick one's way over the bodies of men and horses. But these were small matters compared to what happened at the Temple of Solomon, a place where religious services are normally chanted ... in the Temple and porch of Solomon, men rode in blood up to their knees and bridle reins."[49]

The barbarity of the above can hardly be imagined by any civilized man or woman. However, such barbarity paled beside the events following the fall of Ma'arra beginning on December 12, 1098. For three days, the victorious army slaughtered every man, woman, and child of the city. The death toll was enormous, and thousands upon thousands were put to the sword. However, the atrocities did not stop at that point. The conquerors practiced mass cannibalism upon the former inhabitants of Ma'arra. Two, independent eyewitness accounts from the ranks of the victors are worth noting.

In Ma'arra our troops boiled pagan adults in cooking pots; they impaled children on spits and devoured them grilled.[50]

Not only did our troops not shrink from eating dead Turks and Saracens; they also ate dogs![51]

Non-Muslim and Christian readers may well be appalled at the atrocities enumerated above, and may rather indignantly point out that these examples are a far cry from the conduct that the author has been maintaining are mandated by Islam during *Jihad*-as-war. To this charge, a Muslim can only agree. However, while agreeing with the charge, a Muslim can point out that all four examples cited previously were perpetrated by the so-called Christian Crusaders and not by Muslims.

(1) The slaughter of the defenseless inhabitants of Bilbays in 1168 was perpetrated by King Amalric of Jerusalem and his Crusaders. Of note, they made no distinction between Muslim and Coptic Christian in their fearful slaughter of the city's inhabitants. (2) The mass murder of civilian non-combatants and prisoners of war at Castle Acre in 1194 during the Third Crusade was specifically ordered by King Richard the Lionheart, King of England and Duke of Normandy. When burdened by prisoners of war, King Richard's solution was simply to have them executed. (3) The eyewitness account of the slaughter of between 40,000 and 70,000 inhabitants (both Muslims and Jews) of Jerusalem in 1099 during the First Crusade was penned by Raymond of Aguiles. It was the Christian Crusaders who incinerated the Jews of Jerusalem. It was the Christian Crusaders who, being Roman Catholics, expelled from the Basilica of the Holy Sepulcre and tortured the priests of the Orthodox Catholic rites. (A fact often not recounted by Western historians is that the Christians of the various Orthodox Catholic denominations frequently allied with the Muslims against their Christian co-religionists over the course of the Crusades. Given the above treatment of the priests of the Basilica of the Holy Sepulcre, such alliances are quite understandable, as these Orthodox Catholics knew that they would receive better treatment from the

Muslims than from their Roman Catholic counterparts in Christianity.) It was the Christian Crusaders who desecrated and looted the Dome of the Rock Mosque, the third holiest site in Islam. (4) The eyewitness accounts of the cannibalism practiced at Ma'arra in 1098 were recorded by Radulph of Caen and Albert of Aix.

No conscientious Christian would acknowledge the above behavior as being examples of Christian conduct in war, even though self-professed Christian Crusaders carried out such behavior. Therefore, intellectual consistency and basic fairness would insist that Christians understand and respect the fact that modern terrorism cannot be held to represent Islam, even when self-professed Muslims sometimes perpetrate acts of terrorism. However, rather than belabor this point, it is preferable to examine several examples of the behavior of the Muslim armies during the Crusades.

C2. MUSLIM CONDUCT IN THE SECOND CRUSADE

Odo de Diogilo, a monk of St. Denis, was the private chaplain to King Louis VII during the Second Crusade. In writing about his experiences, this Christian monk commented in some detail about the conduct of his Muslim opponents during this war, specifically noting the manner in which Muslim soldiers treated the surviving Crusaders of the Second Crusade. He noted that the Muslims were moved to pity at the sight of the Crusaders' misery, tended the sick, gave money to the poor, and fed the starving. De Diogilo contrasted that aid and comfort with the oppression these Crusaders had received from their Christian co-religionists of the Byzantium Empire. As a result of the Islamic conduct of the Muslims, de Diogilo reported that over 3,000 of the surviving Crusaders converted to Islam and joined the Muslim army.

It has been previously noted that adherents to the Orthodox Catholic denominations frequently allied with the Muslims against the Roman Catholic invaders from Europe, precisely because these Orthodox Catholic Christians received better treatment from the

Muslims than they did from their Roman Catholic counterparts. Given De Diogilo's account, it can now be seen that the Roman Catholic Crusaders frequently believed that they received better treatment from the Muslims than they did from their Orthodox Catholic counterparts, resulting in mass conversions to Islam from the ranks of the defeated Crusaders. This is not conversion-by-the-sword, but conversion by means of mercy, humane treatment, and love of fellow man!

C3. THE CONDUCT OF SALAH AL-DIN

An even more striking example of Islamic conduct during *Jihad*-as-war is exemplified in the pattern of conduct of Salah Al-Din, the military leader of the Muslims during the Third Crusade. The life of Salah Al-Din, who is better known in the West as Saladin, offers so many examples of virtuous conduct in *Jihad*-as-war that it is difficult to limit the number selected. Nonetheless, as this is not a biography of Salah Al-Din, the author has rather arbitrarily chosen a few specifics to recount.

During the course of the Third Crusade, King Richard I of England was stricken with a fever, and was ingloriously confined to his sickbed within a city besieged by the forces of Salah Al-Din. Hearing of the king's plight, Salah Al-Din kept daily runners scurrying to the besieged city with baskets of snow from the mountains to lower Richard's temperature and with baskets of fresh fruit to nourish his ravaged body. It is not too much to conclude that Salah Al-Din's generosity and mercy during *Jihad*-as-war was directly responsible for saving the life of Richard the Lionheart.

Once, after a battle at Beirut, 45 prisoners were taken by the army of Salah Al-Din. Among the 45 prisoners was an old man, who had trouble moving. Salah Al-Din saw the old man and inquired as to why he had come to the Holy Land from so far away. The old man replied that his home was several months' journey away and that he had merely come to make a pilgrimage to the Basilica of the Holy Sepulchre. Salah Al-Din immediately had the man released and supplied him with a horse so that he could continue his pilgrimage. At that time, some of Salah Al-Din's men then asked permission to kill the rest of the prisoners. Salah Al-Din refused, saying that his soldiers should not "become accustomed in their youth to the shedding of blood and laugh at it".

In 1187, Salah Al-Din defeated the Crusaders at the Battle of Hattin and took many prisoners, including King Guy and Reynald of Chatillon. While Reynald was executed for a pattern of particularly egregious and heinous war crimes, including the chronic breaking of truces, the torture and killing of civilian non-combatants, etc., King Guy and several other Crusaders were granted clemency and released.

On October 2, 1187, Salah Al-Din wrested Jerusalem away from the Crusaders. Given the fearful slaughter perpetrated by the Crusaders when they had taken Jerusalem 88 years previously, many must have anticipated that they would be slaughtered in fearful revenge. However, this was not the teaching of Islam, and thus it was not the practice of Salah Al-Din. The Christian Crusaders were merely expelled from Jerusalem, each being allowed to take his wealth and possessions with him. In fact, the very wealthy Crusaders were provided with armed escort to insure the safety of their possessions. The Orthodox Catholic Christians, who were not Crusaders, were allowed to continue living in Jerusalem in peace. Jews, who had been incinerated in their own synagogue by the Crusaders only 88 years previously, were once again allowed to live in Jerusalem. With regard to the latter point, the Jewish poet, Yuda Al-Harizi, memorialized Salah Al-Din's conquest of Jerusalem by noting that Salah Al-Din accepted back to Jerusalem all the children of Israel and that the Jews were now allowed to live in peace.

While it had been the habit of King Richard I of England to execute his prisoners of war rather than be burdened by their care, Salah Al-Din had a different strategy to avoid being bogged down by the care and policing of large numbers of prisoners of war. In short, his strategy was to release them upon their word that they would cease taking up arms against him.

D. CONCLUDING THOUGHTS

As has been demonstrated, the Muslim *Ummah*'s right to conduct *Jihad*-as-war is highly conditional. It may fight a defensive war against those who have attacked it, provided that the Muslim *Ummah* is an innocent victim of that attack, but then must grant asylum and safe conduct to anyone who lays down his arms. If the *Ummah* is not an innocent victim, if the *Ummah* or some part of it actually stands in the wrong, then it is incumbent upon the *Ummah* to make amends for the initial wrong committed by it or its members. The *Ummah* may also wage *Jihad*-as-war to correct grievous social injustice and wrongs that have been and are being perpetrated against otherwise defenseless individuals. In other words, as a last resort after having spoken "a word of justice to an oppressive ruler" (*Abu Dawud, Hadith # 4330*), Muslims may engage in war to alleviate the suffering of the oppressed. Finally, Muslims may engage in war for the sake of Allah, although they must be hyper-cautious to make sure they are not merely masking their own personal, ethnic, or nationalistic desires with the phrase "for the sake of Allah".

Even when the conditions have been met that allow Muslims to conduct *Jihad*-as-war, Islam prescribes severe and stringent limits on what sort of warfare is permissible. A Muslim must not desire war, and must not wish to engage the enemy. A Muslim is prohibited from committing suicide, whether as an act of war or otherwise. A Muslim may not kill or injure civilian non-combatants, and must not destroy the civilian infrastructure in such a way that eventually causes significant injury or death to civilians. A Muslim is prohibited from mutilating the dead. A Muslim is forbidden to use certain types of weapons, e.g., the use of flame-throwers, napalm, and incendiary bombs to burn others is strictly prohibited. A Muslim must realize and accept that he has certain familial obligations that outweigh his responsibilities to pick up arms, including specified marital and filial duties. A Muslim woman is not to be a combatant in any war, however permissible that war may be. Although, she may perform various non-combatant duties, such as caring for the wounded, removing bodies from the battlefield, giving food and drink to soldiers, etc. A Muslim must treat all prisoners of war in a humanitarian manner.

Notes

48. Mansurpuri S (---), pages 220-67.

49. Krey AC (1921), page 261.

50. Maalouf A (1984).

51. Maalouf A (1984).

Chapter 10
Summary and Conclusions

The sum total of the preceding introduction to Islam has necessarily been concise and quite abbreviated, even being rather superficial in places. Further, some areas have been handled in greater depth than others. *Insha'Allah* (God willing), the interested reader will expand his knowledge by turning to additional sources of information on Islam. Of these, the most important is a good English translation of the meaning of the *Qur'an*, and the author suggests that of 'Abdullah Yusuf 'Ali, that of Muhammad Taqi-ud Din Al-Hilali and Muhammad Musin Khan, or that put out by Saheeh International. Of these three, the typical American reader will probably be most comfortable with the translation of 'Abdullah Yusuf 'Ali, which is the most "user friendly" when it comes to the English language and vocabulary employed. Though not of the same caliber as the three translations mentioned above, Pickthall's translation is at least adequate. In contrast, the translations of AJ Arberry and of Rashid Khalifa should generally be avoided.

In addition to securing a good English translation of the meaning of the *Qur'an*, the reader is advised to consult a good and unbiased biography on Prophet Muhammad. Several such biographies are listed in the bibliography, and the reader is urged to begin his biographical reading with one of those listed there.

As an additional resource, the interested reader is advised to contact mosques in his local area. Many mosques maintain a speakers' bureau, while others offer informal classes explaining Islam to new converts and to non-Muslims interested in Islam. In almost any mosque, one will find Muslim brothers and sisters who are happy to take the time to talk about Islam to those who are interested in it or merely curious about it. If a mosque is not available to the reader, most large universities have a Muslim Student Association that can provide valuable resources for further study.

With regard to all that has preceded this closing, the author has made no intentional errors in presentation, and the author is currently aware of no mistakes in this introduction to Islam. Nonetheless, true and absolute knowledge rests only with Allah. May Allah guide the non-Muslim reader to the basic truth and beauty of Islam and to the true and acceptable worship of Allah. May He also guide the Muslim reader to a reaffirmation of his basic faith in and commitment to the religion of Allah.

Glossary of Arabic Terms

Abu Sayyaf = literally, father of the sword; an insurrectionist group in the Philippines.

Adhan = the call to prayer, which is made five times every day.

Ahadith = narratives concerning the teaching (both verbal and behavioral) of the Prophet Muhammad; singular = *Hadith*.

Ahl Al-Kitab = people of the book; a reference to Jews and Christians, and a recognition that books of revelation had been previously given to Jews and Christians

Ajza = portions; singular = *Juz*. The *Qur'an* is divided into 30 *Ajza* of approximately equal length.

Al-Kutub Al-Sittab = literally, the six books; the six standard compilations of *Ahadith*, i.e., those of Al-Bukhari, Muslim, Abu Dawud, Al-Tirmidhi, Al-Nasa'i, and ibn Majah.

Allah = literally, the One God; synonymous with the Hebrew *El*, *Elohim*, and *El-Elohim*, which words are typically translated as "God" in the Old Testament.

Allahu-Akbar = Allah is Greater; a recognition and statement that Allah is greater than this, that, or anything.

Al-'Isra = Prophet Muhammad's night journey from Makkah to Jerusalem and back.

Al-Mi'raj = Prophet Muhammad's ascent into heaven, where he received instruction in how many obligatory prayers were to be said each day.

Al-Muqatta'at = the abbreviated letters; the varied sequence of some letters found at the opening of 29 of the *Surat* of the *Qur'an*. See also *Fawatih*.

Al-Qa'ada = literally, "the base"; a loose organization constructed from Osama bin Laden's list of foreigners who entered Afghanistan to fight with the Afghanis against the Soviet occupation.

Al-Qadar = literally, measure, balance, or set amount; referring to the sixth article of faith of Islam.

Al-Salam 'Alaykum Wa Rahmatullah = peace and the mercies of Allah be upon you.

Amir = commander or prince.

Ansar = helpers; the inhabitants of Madinah who aided Prophet Muhammad.

Ansari = the helper or of the helpers.

Ayah = see *Ayat*.

Ayat = signs or verses; singular = *Ayah*. *Ayat* form the smallest divisional unit of the *Qur'an*.

Bismillah Al-Rahman Al-Rahim = in the name of Allah, most gracious, most merciful.

Dai' = preacher or exhorter.

Daif = a *Hadith* whose authenticity is considered to be weak. A *Daif Hadith* is not to be used as religious guidance by Muslims, nor is it to be used in matters of Islamic law and jurisprudence.

Dajjal = the Antichrist.

Da'wah = preaching or exhortation; inviting others to Islam.

Dua = a personal prayer of supplication, as contrasted with *Salat*.

Fatwa = a verdict regarding a point of Islamic law.

Fawatih = detached letters; the varied sequence of some letters found at the opening of 29 of the *Surat* of the *Qur'an*. See also *Al-Muqatta'at*.

Ghazawat = raids, battles, or military expeditions; singular = *Ghazwa*.

Ghazwa = raid, battle, or military expedition; plural = *Ghazawat*.

Hadith = a narrative concerning the teaching (both verbal and behavioral) of Prophet Muhammad (pbuh); plural = *Ahadith*.

Hafiz = someone who has successfully memorized the entire *Qur'an*.

Hajj = the religious pilgrimage that each adult Muslim should make at least once in a lifetime to Makkah, if physically and financially possible.

Hajj Al-Ifrad = the performance of *Hajj* without performing *'Umrah*.

Hajj Al-Qiran = the performance of *'Umrah* and *Hajj* as a joined act.

Hajj Al-Tamattu = the interrupted *Hajj*; the performance of *'Umrah*, followed by a brief interruption before beginning *Hajj*.

Hajj Mabrur = *Hajj* that is performed according to the traditions of Prophet Muhammad, and that is accepted by Allah.

Haram = forbidden or unlawful.

Hasan = a good *Hadith*, i.e., one that is judged by competent *Ahadith* scholars to be reliable, but not of the same, highest level of authenticity as the *Sahih Ahadith*.

Hijrah = migration; when used within an religious context, it refers to a migration made for the sake of Allah; there was a *Hijrah* from Makkah to Abyssinia in both 615 and 616 CE, but the *Hijrah* that begins the Islamic calendar was the *Hijrah* of Prophet Muhammad from Makkah to Madinah in 622 CE.

Hizbullah = literally, party of God; a militant group operating primarily in Lebanon and Palestine.

Ihram = the state of purity and the dress one dons when one begins either *'Umrah* or *Hajj*.

Insha'Allah = Allah willing or if Allah wills.

Intifada = uprising, literally a throwing off.

Islam = surrender or submission to Allah.

Isnad = the chain of transmitters of a *Hadith*; plural = *Asanid*.

Jahada = to strive, to exert, or to struggle.

Jahiliya = the time of ignorance; a reference to the times before the final revelation of Islam to Prophet Muhammad.

Jihad = striving, exertion, or effort; more specifically striving for the sake of Allah, one small part of which may include the concept of war.

Jumu'a = Friday, more specifically the congregational noon prayer each Friday.

Juz = see *Ajza*.

Ka'ba = the house of worship erected to Allah in Makkah by Prophets Abraham and Ismael, and which has subsequently been rebuilt upon occasion.

Khutba = sermon; the talk given before the congregational noon prayer on Fridays.

La Sharika = literally, no partners; a statement often used in reference to Allah, Who has no partners or associates impinging upon His Oneness and Unity.

Matn = the narrative portion of a *Hadith*.

Miqat = one of the designated places for entering into *Ihram* when beginning *'Umrah* or *Hajj*; plural = *Mawaqit*.

Mufti = judge; someone qualified to give a legal opinion or *Fatwa*.

Muhajir = emigrant; one of those early Muslims who emigrated from Makkah to Madinah to escape religious persecution.

Muhajirin = the emigrants; those early Muslims who emigrated from Makkah to Madinah to escape religious persecution.

Munafiqun = hypocrites.

Qadr = referring to the Night of Power, during which Prophet Muhammad received his first revelation.

Qisas = retribution or retaliation.

Raka = a unit of the prayer of worship (*Salat*); plural = *Rakat*.

Sadaqah = charity.

Sahabah = companions of Prophet Muhammad.

Sahih = sound and without defect; a type of *Hadith* that is judged by competent *Ahadith* scholars to be of the highest level of authenticity. A *Sahih Isnad* or a *Sahih* chain refers to a *Hadith* where the chain of transmitters of that *Hadith*, from Prophet Muhammad all the way to the recorder of the *Hadith*, is viable and beyond usual question, thus giving some assurance of the authenticity and genuineness of the *Hadith* in question.

Salam = peace.

Salat = the prayer of worship that comprises the second pillar of practice of Islam.

Sariya = a small army unit sent by Prophet Muhammad on *Jihad*, but without his being a member of it.

Sawm = fasting.

Shahadah = the testimony of faith of all Muslims, which comprises the first pillar of practice of Islam, and which means I testify that there is no god but Allah, and I testify that Muhammad is the messenger of Allah.

Sunnah = the customary religious practice of Prophet Muhammad, as determined by reference to the *Ahadith*.

Surah = step or chapter; the basic divisional unit of the *Qur'an*; the plural form is *Surat*.

Surat = see *Surah*.

Taliban= literally, students; the former ruling party in most of Afghanistan.

Tawheed = the Unity or Oneness of Allah.

Ummah = community or nation.

'Umrah = the so-called minor pilgrimage to Makkah.

Wudu = the ritual washing or ablution necessary before saying *Salat*.

Zakat = the obligatory charity encumbent upon all Muslims who have an economic surplus; one of the five pillars of Islamic practice.

Prominent Muslims
Named in the Text

Traditional Muslim names do not follow the Western convention of a given name, middle name, and surname. Typically,
a Muslim adult will have a *Kunya* (father of or *Abu* and then
the name of his firstborn son, or mother of or *Um* and then the
name of her firstborn son): a given name, a patronymic, and a
family, clan, tribal, or geographical place name. Complicating
things still further, Muslim rulers occasionally took regnal or
titular names in times past. In Islamic writings and *Ahadith*,
a given person might be identified by any or all of the above
names. In the list that follows, an attempt has been made to:
(1) record each individual under his or her most commonly
used designation; and (2) use alternative designations
to direct the reader to the designation containing the
information about that individual. The non-Muslim reader
is also cautioned that there are various alternative ways
of transliterating Arabic names, e.g., 'Abd Allah, 'Abdullah,
and Abdullah are all the same name, and may be translated
as servant or slave of Allah.

'Abd Allah ibn 'Amr ibn Al-'As = Al-'As (the disobedient) ibn
'Amr ibn Al-'As had his given name changed to 'Abd Allah (servant
or slave of Allah) when he embraced Islam. He narrated over 700
Ahadith and was one of the *Sahabah* who left a written record of
Ahadith.

'Abd Allah ibn Mas'ud = 'Abd Allah ibn Mas'ud was one of
the first people to embrace Islam. He was an expert on the *Qur'an*
and narrated 848 *Ahadith*. He died circa 652 CE.

'Abd Allah ibn 'Umar = 'Abd Allah ibn 'Umar (circa 613-692 CE) was the eldest son of the second caliph of Islam. He narrated some 2,630 *Ahadith*, being surpassed in number of *Ahadith* narrated only by Abu Huraira.

Abu Bakr ibn Abu Quhafah = Abu Bakr ibn Abu Quhafah of the Taym clan of the Quraysh (circa 573-634 CE) was one of the first converts to Islam. He was the father of 'Aisha, one of the wives of Prophet Muhammad. Following the death of the Prophet, he became the first caliph of Islam.

Abu Dawud = Abu Dawud Sulayman ibn Al-Ashath Al-Azdi Al-Sijistani (circa 818-889 CE) was a student of Ahmad ibn Hanbal Al-Shaybani. He authored *Kitab Al-Sunan*, which is one of the six standard collections of *Ahadith*, which includes about 4,800 *Ahadith*, and which is available in a three-volume English translation.

Abu Huraira = Abu Huraira 'Abd Al-Rahman ibn Sakhr Al-Dawsi was a companion of Prophet Muhammad. Abu Huraira was a nickname, reflecting its bearer's love of kittens. Abu Huraira narrated more *Ahadith* than did any other companion of Prophet Muhammad, with the total number of *Ahadith* credited to him equaling 5,374. He died in Madinah circa 677-680 CE at the age of 78 years.

Abu Musa = Abu Musa Al-Ashari (circa 602-665 CE) was originally from Yemen and converted to Islam in Makkah. He was later appointed governor of Yemen by Prophet Muhammad.

Abu Sa'id Al-Khudri = a companion of Prophet Muhammad and a member of the Khazraj tribe of Madinah. He was 13 years old at the Battle of Uhud, for which reason Prophet Muhammad refused to let him fight. He died circa 652 CE in Madinah. A total of 1,170 *Ahadith* have been attributed to him.

Ahmad = Ahmad ibn Hanbal Al-Shaybani (780-855 CE) established one of the four main schools of *Fiqh*, i.e., Islamic jurisprudence, which continue to exist. The founders of these four schools of *Fiqh* are sometimes referred to as the four *Imams*. His collection of *Ahadith* is known as the *Musnad*, and the *Ahadith* in it are not arranged by topic, but by the original narrator of the *Hadith*.

'Aisha bint Abu Bakr = 'Aisha was the only wife of Prophet Muhammad who was not widowed, divorced, or enslaved prior to her marriage to the Prophet. She was the daughter of the first caliph of Islam, was the first of the great female scholars of Islam, and narrated about 2,210 *Ahadith*. She was born circa 612-614 CE, finalized her marriage to the Prophet circa 623-625 CE, and died on July 15, 678 CE.

Al-Baihaqi = Abu Al-Fazli Al-Baihaqi (995-1077 CE) was a scholar at the Ghaznavid court. Among other works, he authored *Kilab Al-Hajj* and *Dala'il Al-Nubuwwat*.

Al-Bukhari = Abu 'Abd Allah Muhammad ibn Isma'il ibn Ibrahim Al-Bukhari Al-Ju'fi was born in 810 CE in Bukhara, in what is now Uzbekistan, and died in 870 CE. He was a student of Malik and was the author of *Kitab Al-Jami' Al-Sahih,* referenced within the text as *Al-Bukhari*, which is one of the six standard collections of *Ahadith*, and the one that probably has the largest acceptance and highest regard within the Muslim *Ummah*.

Al-Nasa'i = Abu 'Abd Al-Rahman Ahmad ibn Shu'ayb ibn 'Ali Al-Khursani Al-Nasa'i (circa 830-916 CE) was a student of Abu Dawud and authored *Al-Sunan Al-Mujtaba,* aka *Al-Sunan Al-Nasa'i*, which is one of the six standard collections of *Ahadith*.

Al-Nawawi = Muhi Al-Din Abu Zakariya Yahya ibn Sharaf Al-Hizami Al-Nawawi was born in 1233 in Nawa, which was a village just south of Damascus, Syria, and died in 1277 CE in the village of his birth. He was the author of *Riyad Al-Saliheen* and

The Forty Ahadith of Al-Nawawi, both of which are two very important collection of *Ahadith.*

Al-Tabari = Abu Jafar Muhammad ibn Jarir Al-Tabari (839-923 CE) wrote a major commentary on the *Qur'an, Jami Al-Bayan Fi Tawil Ayi Al-Qur'an,* as well as a classic, multi-volume history of the world, *Tarikh Al-Rusul Wa Al-Muluk,* the latter of which is in English translation under the title of *The History of Al-Tabari.*

Al-Tirmidhi = Abu 'Isa Muhammad ibn 'Isa ibn Sawrah ibn Shaddad Al-Tirmidhi (824-892 CE) was born in what is now Uzbekistan and was a student of Abu Dawud. He authored *Al-Jami' Al-Kabir,* aka *Al-Jami' Al-Sahih* and *Sunan Al-Tirmidhi,* referenced as *Al-Tirmidhi* within the text, which is one of the six standard collections of *Ahadith.* This work includes almost 4,000 *Ahadith.*

Al-Tabrizi = Wali Al-Din Muhammad ibn 'Abd Allah Al-Khatib Al-Tibrizi reworked Abu Muhammad Al-Husain ibn Mas'ud ibn Muhammad Al-Farra' Al-Baghawi's classic *Masibh Al-Sunnah* under the title of *Mishkat Al-Masabih,* and added 1,511 *Ahadith* to Al-Baghawi's 4,719 *Ahadith.*

'Ali ibn Abu Talib = one of the first converts to Islam and the paternal first cousin and ward of Prophet Muhammad. He was the fourth caliph of Islam and the husband of Prophet Muhammad's fourth daughter, Fatimah.

Anas ibn Malik = During his youth, Anas ibn Malik (circa 612-712 CE) was a servant to Prophet Muhammad. He was the father of Malik and was a reliable narrator of *Ahadith,* to whom over 2,000 *Ahadith* are credited in *Al-Bukhari* and *Muslim.*

Fatimah bint Muhammad = the fourth daughter of Prophet Muhammad and the wife of 'Ali ibn Abu Talib.

Hafsah bint 'Umar ibn Al-Khattab = Hafsah was one of the wives of Prophet Muhammad. She was a widow at the time of her marriage to the Prophet, narrated 62 *Ahadith*, and was the custodian of the only authorized *Qur'an* from the caliphate of Abu Bakr ibn Abu Quhafah through the caliphate of 'Uthman ibn 'Affan.

Hudayfah=Abu 'Abd Allah Hudayfah ibn Al-Yaman was a *Sahabah* and was known for his chivalry. He was appointed governor of Al-Madain by 'Umar ibn Al-Khattab, the second caliph of Islam. He died circa 656 CE.

Ibn 'Abbas = 'Abd Allah ibn 'Abbas was a paternal first cousin and companion of Prophet Muhammad. One of the early religious scholars within the Muslim *Ummah*, he narrated 1,660 *Ahadith*. 'Abd Allah ibn 'Abbas was the ancestor of the 'Abbasid caliphs of Baghdad.

Ibn Hanbal = see Ahmad.

Ibn Majah = Abu 'Abd Allah Muhammad Yazeed Al-Rabi Al-Qazwini, aka ibn Majah, was born in 824 CE and died in 886 CE. He was a student of Abu Dawud and authored one of the six standard collections of *Ahadith*. His collection includes 4,341 *Ahadith*, of which 3,002 may be found in one or another of the other five standard collections. However, his collection of *Ahadith* is frequently seen as not having used the same rigorous standards of verification as found in the other five "canonical" collections, and some scholars have concluded that as many as 613 of his *Ahadith* have *Daif Asanid*, and as many as 99 of his *Ahadith* were fabricated by unknown perpetrators. As such, his collection has the weakest following within the Muslim *Ummah*.

Ibn Um Makhtum = the blind man referred to in *Qur'an* 80: 1-12; he was sometimes left in charge of Madinah when the Prophet led a force of men on an expedition.

Ibn 'Umar = see 'Abd Allah.

'Ikrima = Abu 'Abd Allah 'Ikrima was a Berber slave of Ibn Abbas, who was freed upon the death of the latter. He was reputed to be a great scholar of the *Qur'an*.

Jabir ibn 'Abdullah Al-Ansari = a youthful companion of Prophet Muhammad and a member of the Khazraj tribe of Madinah. He narrated about 1,540 *Ahadith*.

Juwayriyah (Barrah) bint Harith ibn Abu Darir = Juwayriyah was of the Bani Mustaliq tribe. She was a widow at the time of her marriage to Prophet Muhammad in 627 CE. She died in 670 CE.

Khadijah bint Khuwaylid ibn Asad = the first wife of Prophet Muhammad and the first convert to Islam. She was born circa 556 CE and died in 619 CE. At the time of her marriage to the Prophet, she was a 40-year-old widow with three orphaned children.

Khalid ibn Al-Walid = the leader of the cavalry charge that defeated the Muslim *Ummah* at the Battle of Uhud, he later converted to Islam and became the greatest of all the Muslim generals during the so-called Islamic Conquest.

Malik = Malik ibn Anas ibn Malik ibn Abu 'Amr Al-Asbahi was born circa 712 CE and died circa 795 CE. He was the author of *Al-Muwatta*, an important collection of *Ahadith*, and was the founder of one of the four primary schools of *Fiqh*.

Maryam bint Shim'un = was a Christian slave sent to Prophet Muhammad by the patriarch of Alexandria. Prophet Muhammad manumitted her, she converted to Islam, and she married Prophet Muhammad circa 629-630 CE. Aside from Khadijah, she was the only wife of the Prophet to bear a child by him. However, their son, Ibrahim, died in infancy.

Maymunah bint Harith = Maymunah was a member of the Hawazin tribe of Bedouins. She had been previously divorced and widowed and was about 51 years old at the time of her marriage to Prophet Muhammad circa 629 CE. She died in 680 or 681 CE.

Muslim = Abu Al-Husain 'Asakir Al-Din Muslim ibn Al-Hajjaj Al-Qushayri Al-Naisabori was born circa 820 CE in Naisabor, in what is now Iran, and died in 875 CE. He began studying *Ahadith* at age 12 and journeyed widely throughout the Middle East in search of authentic *Ahadith*. He authored *Al-Jami' Al-Sahih*, referenced within the test as *Muslim*, which is one of the six standard collections of *Ahadith*, and which was arrived at after judiciously shifting through about 300,000 *Ahadith*. The collection of Muslim is typically held by the Muslim *Ummah* to be secondary in importance only to that of Al-Bukhari.

Nafi' = Nafi' was an ex-slave of 'Abd Allah ibn 'Umar ibn Al-Khattab and was a teacher to *Imam* Malik. He received many of his *Ahadith* from 'Abd Allah ibn 'Umar, but also reported *Ahadith* that he had received from 'Aisha bint Abu Bakr and Hafsah bint 'Umar ibn Al-Khattab.

Sahl ibn Sa'd Al-Sa'idi = Hazn (sadness or grief) ibn Sa'd Al-Sa'idi (circa 617-710 CE) was a member of the Khazraj tribe of Madinah. Upon accepting Islam, his given name was changed to Sahl (ease). He narrated 188 *Ahadith*.

Sawdah bint Zama'ah ibn Qays of the Bani 'Amir = the second wife of Prophet Muhammad. She was born circa 570 CE, married the Prophet circa 620 CE, and died in 643 CE. At the time of her marriage to the Prophet, she was a widow with an orphan son. Five *Ahadith* have been transmitted on her authority.

Um Al-Hakim Zaynab bint Jahsh = was a divorcee who married Prophet Muhammad circa 627 CE. She died in 641 CE.

Um Habibah bint Abu Sufyan = Um Habibah was an early convert to Islam who had migrated to Abyssinia with her husband. She was a widow with an orphan daughter at the time of her marriage to Prophet Muhammad circa 629 CE.

Um Salamah Hind bint Abu Umayyah ibn Al-Mughirah = Um Salamah had been left a widow with four orphan children when her husband died, secondary to wounds received in the Battle of Uhud. She married Prophet Muhammad in 626 CE and died in June or July of 683 CE.

'Umar ibn 'Abd Al-'Aziz = the eighth Umayyad caliph and 12th caliph over all. He ruled from 717-720 CE. He was famed as one of the most virtuous of all caliphs.

'Umar ibn Al-Khattab = the second caliph of Islam; the father of Prophet Muhammad's wife, Hafsah.

'Uthman ibn 'Affan = the third caliph of Islam; the husband of two of Prophet Muhammad's daughters.

Zayd ibn Harithah = Prophet Muhammad's former slave and adopted son.

Zaynab bint Khuzaymah ibn Harith = was known as Um Al-Masakin (mother of the poor) because of her longstanding generosity to the poor and those in need. Zaynab was widowed after the Battle of Badr and later married Prophet Muhammad in 625 CE. She died within eight months of her marriage to the Prophet.

Zaynab (Safiyyah) bint Huyayy ibn Akhtab = Zaynab was a member of the Jewish tribe of the Bani Nadir. She had been previously divorced and widowed at the time of her conversion to Islam and her marriage to Prophet Muhammad circa 629 CE. She died in September or October of 670 CE.

Bibliography

QUR'AN AND COMMENTARIES

'Ali 'AY: *The Meaning of The Holy Qur'an*. Brentwood, Amana Corporation, 1992.

Arberry AJ: *The Koran Interpreted*. New York, Macmillan Company, undated.

Hilali MT, Khan MM: *Interpretation of the Meanings of The Noble Qur'an: A Summarized Version of Al-Tabari, Al-Qurtubi, and Ibn Kathir with Comments from Sahih Al-Bukhari in English Language: Volumes 1-9*. Lahore, Kazi Publications, 1989.

Ibn Kathir IU: *Tafsir Ibn Kathir*: Volumes 1-10. Riyadh, Darussalam, 2000.

Pickthall MM: *The Meaning of the Glorious Koran*. New York, New American Library, undated.

Saheeh International: *The Qur'an: Arabic Text with Corresponding English Meanings*. Jeddah, Abul-Qasim Publishing House, 1997.

Usmani MSA: *Tafseer-'E-Usmani*. In Ahmad MA (trans.): *The Noble Qur'an: Tafseer-'E-Usmani: Volumes 1-3*. New Delhi, Idara Isha'at-E-Diniyat (P) Ltd., 1992.

AHADITH COLLECTIONS AND COMMENTARIES

Al-Asbahi MA (Malik): *Al-Muwatta*. In Rahimuddin M (trans.): *Muwatta Imam Malik*. Lahore, Sh. Muhammad Ashraf, 1985.

Al-Azdi SA (Abu Dawud): *Kitab Al-Sunan*. In Hasan A (trans.): *Sunan Abu Dawud*. New Delhi, Kitab Bhavan, 1990.

Al-Bukhari MI: *Kitab Al-Jami' Al-Sahih*. In Khan MM (trans): *The Translation of the Meanings of Sahih Al-Bukhari*. Madinah, ---, undated.

Al-Nawawi YBS: *Forty Hadith of Al-Nawawi*. In Zarabozo J: *Commentary on the Forty Hadith of Al-Nawawi*. Boulder, Al-Basheer Company for Publications and Translations, 1999.

Al-Nawawi YBS: *Riyad Al-Saliheen*. In Matraji M and Matraji FAZ (trans): *Riyad Us-Saliheen: The Paradise of the Pious*. Beyrouth, Dar El Aker, 1993.

Al-Qushayri MH (Muslim): *Al-Jami' Al-Sahih*. In Siddiqi 'AH (trans.): *Sahih Muslim*. ---, ---, 1971?

Al-Tibrizi WMA: *Mishkat Al-Masabih*. (A revision of the collection of *Ahadith* compiled by Abu Muhammad Al-Husain b. *Mas'ud* b. Muhammad Al-Farra Al-Baghawi.) In Robinson J (trans.): *Mishkat Al-Masabih: English Translation with Explanatory Notes*. Lahore, Sh. Muhammad Ashraf, 1963.

Al-Tirmidhi MI: *Al-Jami' Al-Sahih*. In --- (trans.): *Sahih Al-Tirmidhi*. In --- (eds.): *Alim Multimedia CD Rom*. ---, ISL Software Corporation, ---.

Sabiq S: *Fiqh Al-Sunnah*. In --- (eds.): *Alim Multimedia CD Rom*. ---, ISL Software Corporation, ---.

Zarabozo J: *Commentary on the Forty Hadith of Al-Nawawi: Volumes 1-3*. Boulder, Al-Basheer Company for Publications and Translations, 1999.

REFERENCES CONSULTED

---: *Jubilees*. In Charles RH (ed.): *The Apocrypha and Pseudepigrapha of the Old Testament in English: Volume II. Pseudepigrapha*. Oxford, Oxford University Press, 1969.

---: *A Guide to Hajj, Umrah and Visiting the Prophet's Mosque (In English)*. Saudi Arabia, The Ministry of Islamic Affairs, Endowments, Da'wah, and Guidance, 1416h.

Abbas AMA: *His Throne Was on Water*. Beltsville, Amana Publications, 1997.

'Abd Al-'Ati H: *Islam in Focus*. Beltsville, Amana Publications, 1998.

'Abd Al-Wahhab M: *Kitab Al-Tawhid*. In Al-Faruqi IR (trans.): *Kitab Al-Tawhid*. Malaysia, Polygraphic Press Sdn. Bhd., 1981.

Al-Buti MSR: *Jihad in Islam: How to Understand and Practice It*. In Absi MA (trans.): *Jihad in Islam: How to Understand and Practice It*. Damascus, Dar al Fikr, 1995.

Al-Mubarakpuri S: *Al-Raheeq Al-Maktum*. In --- (trans.): *The Sealed Nectar: Biography of the Noble Prophet*. Riyadh, Dar-us-Salam Publictions, 1996.

Al-Sadlaan SG: *Taysir Al-Fiqh*. In Zarabozo J (trans.): *Fiqh Made Easy: A Basic Textbook of Fiqh*. Boulder, Al-Basheer Company for Publications and Translations, 1999.

Al-Tabari MJ: *Ta'rikh al-Rusul wa'l-Muluk*. In Rosenthal F (trans.): *The History of al-Tabari: Volume I. General Introduction and From the Creation to the Flood*. Albany, State University of New York Press, 1989.

Al-Tabari MJ: *Ta'rikh al-Rusul wa'l-Muluk*. In Brinner WM (trans.): *The History of al-Tabari: Volume II. Prophets and Patriarchs*. Albany, State University of New York Press, 1987.

Al-Tabari MJ: *Ta'rikh al-Rusul wa'l-Muluk*. In Brinner WM (trans.): *The History of al-Tabari: Volume III. The Children of Israel*. Albany, State University of New York Press, 1991.

Al-Tabari MJ: *Ta'rikh al-Rusul wa'l-Muluk*. In Watt WM, McDonald MV (trans.): *The History of al-Tabari: Volume IV. Muhammad at Mecca*. Albany, State University of New York Press, 1988.

Armstrong K: *Holy War: The Crusades and their Impact on Today's World*. New York, Anchor Books, 2001.

Arnold T: *The Spread of Islam in the World: A History of Peaceful Preaching*. ---, Goodword Books, 2001.

Baird W: The gospel according to *Luke*. In Laymon CM (1971).

Baldwin MW: The Crusades. In --- (ed.): *Encyclopaedia Britannica CD 98*. ---, Encyclopaedia Britannica, 1998.

Beaven EL: *Ecclesiasticus*. In Laymon CM (1971).

Becker A: Urban II. In --- (ed.): *Encyclopaedia Britannica CD 98*. ---, Encyclopaedia Britannica, 1998.

Bewley A: *Glossary of Islamic Terms*. London, Ta-Ha Publishers, 1998.

Burch EW: The structure of the synoptic gospels.
In Eiselen FC, Lewis E, Downey DG (1929).

Caird GB: *Saint Luke*. Baltimore, Penguin Books, 1972.

Clapp N: *The Road to Ubar: Finding the Atlantis of the Sands*.
Boston, Houghton Mifflin Company, 1998.

Cragg AK, et al. : Muhammad and the religion of Islam:
The foundations of Islam: Islamic Scripture: Hadith, traditions
of the Prophet. In --- (eds.): *The Encyclopaedia CD 98.* ---,
Encyclopaedia Britannica, 1998.

Davies JN (1929a): *Mark*. In Eiselen FC, Lewis E,
Downey DG (1929).

Davies JN (1929b): *Matthew*. In Eiselen FC, Lewis E,
Downey DG (1929).

Dirks JF: *The Cross and the Crescent: An Interfaith Dialogue
between Christianity and Islam*. Beltsville,
Amana Publications, 2001.

Dirks JF: *Abraham: The Friend of God*. Beltsville,
Amana Publications, 2002.

Dirks JF, Dirks DL: *The Lineage of the Bedouin Horsebreeding
Tribes: Relationships to Biblical Tribes and Individuals and
to Key Individuals in Arabic and Islamic History*. Kiowa, Bani
Sham Association, 1998.

Duncan GB: Chronology. In Laymon CM (1971).

Ed-Din B: *The Life of Saladin*. Lahore,
Islamic Book Service, 1988.

Eiselen FC: *The Pentateuch*—Its origin and development.
In Eiselen FC, Lewis E, Downey DG (1929).

Eiselen FC, Lewis E, Downey DG (eds.): *The Abingdon Bible
Commentary*. New York, Abingdon-Cokesbury Press, 1929.

Fenton JC: *Saint Matthew*. Baltimore, Penguin Books, 1973.

Filson FV: The literary relations among the gospels.
In Laymon CM (1971).

Findlay JA: *Luke*. In Eiselen FC, Lewis E, Downey DG (1929).

Gabrieli F: *Arab Historians of the Crusades*. Berkeley & Los Angeles, U. of California Press, 1984.

Garvie AE: *John*. In Eiselen FC, Lewis E, Downey DG (1929).

Gottwald NK: The book of *Deuteronomy*. In Laymon CM (1971).

Hamilton W: *The Modern Reader's Guide to Matthew and Luke*. New York, Association Press, 1959.

Hardon JA: *Religions of the World: Volume I*. Garden City, Image Books, 1968.

Hathout M: *Jihad vs. Terrorism*. Los Angeles, Multimedia Vera International, 2002.

Haykal MK: *Hayat Muhammad*. In Al-Faruqi IR (trans.): *The Life of Muhammad*. Plainfield, American Trust Publications, 1976.

Hitti PK: *History of the Arabs: Tenth Edition*. New York, Macmillan, 1990.

Hoffman M: *Islam: The Alternative*. Beltsville, Amana Publications, 1999.

Hughes TP: *Dictionary of Islam*. Chicago, Kazi Publications, 1994.

Hussain F: *Wives of the Prophet*. Lahore, Sh. Muhammad Ashraf, 1984.

Ibn Abdullah M: *What Did Jesus Really Say?* Ann Arbor, Islamic Assembly of North America, 1996.

Josephus F: *Jewish Antiquities*. In Maier PL (trans.): *Josephus: The EssentialWritings: A Condensation of Jewish Antiquities and The Jewish War*. Grand Rapids, Kregel Publications, 1988.

Josephus F: *Jewish Antiquities*. In Whiston W (trans.): *The New Complete Works of Josephus*. Grand Rapids, Kregel Publications, 1999.

Hyatt JP: The compiling of Israel's story. In Laymon CM (1971).

Kee HC: The gospel according to *Matthew*. In Laymon CM (1971).

Kennedy H: *The Prophet and the Age of the Caliphates: The Islamic Near East from the Sixth to the Eleventh Century.* London, Longman, 1988.

Koester H: *Introduction to the New Testament:Volume II. History and Literature of Early Christianity.* New York, Walter DeGruyler, 1982.

Krey AC: *The First Crusade: The Accounts of Eye-Witnesses and Participants.* Princeton & London, 1921.

Laymon CM (ed.): *The Interpreter's One-Volume Commentary on the Bible.* Nashville, Abingdon Press, 1971.

Leiman SZ: Judaism: The Cycle of the Religious Year: Jewish Holidays: Pilgrim Festivals.
In *Encyclopaedia Britannica CD 98.* 1998.

Leon-Dufour X: *Dictionaire du Nouveau Testament.* In Prendergast T (trans.): *Dictionary of the New Testament.* San Francisco, Harper & Row, 1983.

Leslie EA: *Psalms* I-LXXII. In Eiselen FC, Lewis E, Downey DG (1929).

Lings M: *Muhammad: His Life Based on the Earliest Sources.* Rochester, Inner Traditions International, Ltd., 1983.

Maalouf A: *The Crusades through Arab Eyes.* New York, Schocken Books, 1984.

Mack BL: *Who Wrote the New Testament?: The Making of the Christian Myth.* San Francisco, Harper, 1996.

Malik AA: Forward. In Yahya H: *Islam Denounces Terrorism.* In Rossini C, Evans R (trans.): *Islam Denounces Terrorism.* Bristol, Amal Press, 2002.

Mansurpuri S: *Rahmat-ul-lil-'Alamin, Volume II.* As referenced in Siddiqi 'AH (trans.): *Sahih Muslim.* ---, ---, 1971?.

Marks JH: The book of *Genesis.* In Laymon CM (1971).

Marsh J: *Saint John.* Baltimore, Penguin Books, 1972.

Matthews AD: *A Guide for Hajj and 'Umra*. Lahore,
Kazi Publications, 1979.

Moffatt J: The formation of the *New Testament*.
In Eiselen FC, Lewis E, Downey DG (1929).

Nineham DE: *Saint Mark*. Baltimore, Penguin Books, 1973.

Noth M: *The History of Israel*. New York, Harper & Row, 1960.

Peritz IJ: The chronology of the *New Testament*.
In Eiselen FC, Lewis E, Downey DG (1929).

Pherigo LP: The gospel according to *Mark*. In Laymon CM (1971).

Platt RH, Brett JA (eds): *The Lost Books of the Bible and The
Forgotton Books of Eden*. New York, World Publishing Co., ---.

Rahman F, et al. : Muhammad and the religion of Islam:
The foundations of Islam: Islamic scripture: The *Qur'an*:
Doctrines of the *Qur'an*. In --- (ed.): *The Encyclopaedia
Britannica CD 98*. ---, Encyclopaedia Britannica, 1998.

Ringgren H, et al. : Muhammad and the religion of Islam: The
foundations of Islam:Islamic scripture: The Qur'an: Form. In ---
(ed.): *The Encyclopaedia Britannica CD 98*. ---, Encyclopaedia
Britannica, 1998.

Ringgren H, et al. : Muhammad and the religion of Islam:
The foundations of Islam: Islamic scripture: The *Qur'an*: Origins
and compilation of the *Qur'an*. In --- (ed.): *The Encyclopaedia
Britannica CD 98*. ---, Encyclopaedia Britannica, 1998.

Robertson AT: The transmission of the *New Testament*.
In Eiselen FC, Lewis E, Downey DG (1929).

Robinson JM, Koester H: *Trajectories through Early
Christianity*. Philadelphia, Fortress Press, 1971.

Robinson TH: *Genesis*. In Eiselen FC, Lewis E,
Downey DG (1929).

Rohl DM: *Pharaohs and Kings: A Biblical Quest*.
New York, Crown Publishers, 1995.

Schonfield JH: *Readers' A to Z Bible Companion.*
New York, New American Library, 1967.

Scott EF: The *New Testament* and criticism.
In Eiselen FC, Lewis E, Downey DG (1929).

Shabbir, M: *The Authority and Authenticity of Hadith.*
New Delhi, Kitab Bhavan, 1982.

Shelton WA: *Psalms* LXXIII-CL.
In Eiselen FC, Lewis E, Downey DG (1929).

Shepherd MH: The gospel according to *John.*
In Laymon CM (1971).

Siddiqui AH: *Life of Muhammad.* Des Plaines,
Library of Islam, 1991.

Stegemann H: *Die Essener, Qumran, Johannes der Taufer and
Jesus.* In --- (trans.): *The Library of Qumran: On the Essenes,
Qumran, John the Baptist, and Jesus.* Grand Rapids, William B.
Eerdmans Publishing Company, 1998.

Sundberg AC: The making of the *New Testament* canon.
In Laymon CM (1971).

Toombs LE: The *Psalms.* In Laymon CM (1971).

Werblowsky RJ: Judaism, or the religion of Israel.
In Zaehner RC (ed.): *The Concise Encyclopedia of Living Faiths.*
Boston, Beacon Press, 1967.

Wilson I: *Jesus: The Evidence.* London, Pan Books, 1985.

Wilson RM: The literary forms of the *New Testament.*
In Laymon CM (1971).

Yahya H: *Islam Denounces Terrorism.* In Rossini C, Evans R
(trans.): *Islam Denounces Terrorism.* Bristol, Amal Press, 2002.

Zaehner RC (ed): *The Concise Encyclopedia of Living Faiths.*
Boston, Beacon Press, 1967.

Zepp IG: *A Muslim Primer:Beginner's Guide to Islam.*
Westminster, Wakefield Editions, 1992.

---: Council of Clermont. In --- (ed.): *Encyclopaedia Britannica
CD 98.* ---, Encyclopaedia Britannica, 1998.